Law and Philosophy Library

Volume 123

The Law and Philosophy Library which has been in existence since 1985, aims to publish cutting edge works in the philosophy of law, and has a special history of publishing books that focus on legal reasoning and argumentation, including those that may involve somewhat formal methodologies. The series has published numerous important books on law and logic, law and artificial intelligence, law and language, and law and rhetoric. While continuing to stress these areas, the series has more recently expanded to include books on the intersection between law and the Continental philosophical tradition, consistent with the traditional openness of the series to books in the Continental jurisprudential tradition. The series is proud of the geographic diversity of its authors, and many have come from Latin America, Spain, Italy, the Netherlands, Germany, and Eastern Europe, as well, more obviously for an English-language series, from the United Kingdom, the United States, Australia, and Canada.

More information about this series at http://www.springer.com/series/6210

Åke Frändberg

The Legal Order

Studies in the Foundations of Juridical Thinking

Springer

Åke Frändberg
Uppsala University
Uppsala, Sweden

ISSN 1572-4395 ISSN 2215-0315 (electronic)
Law and Philosophy Library
ISBN 978-3-030-07665-8 ISBN 978-3-319-78858-6 (eBook)
https://doi.org/10.1007/978-3-319-78858-6

Softcover re-print of the Hardcover 1st edition 2018

Cover design: eStudio Calamar, Berlin/Figueres

Printed on acid-free paper

This Springer imprint is published by the registered company Springer International Publishing AG part of Springer Nature.
The registered company address is: Gewerbestrasse 11, 6330 Cham, Switzerland

Law is the soul of society.

To Ingmar

Acknowledgements

Several chapters in this book are substantially rewritten versions of work published earlier, mostly in Swedish, as follows:

Chapter 4: The legal philosophical addressee problem, *Logic, Law, Morality. Thirteen Essays in Honour of Lennart Åqvist* (K. Segerberg, R. Sliwinski, eds.), Uppsala Philosophical Studies 51, Uppsala University, Department of Philosophy, Uppsala, 2003, pp. 99–109.

Chapter 5: Om normativa modaliteter, *Tidsskrift for Rettsvitenskap*, Nr 3, 2012, pp. 281–293.

Chapters 8 and 9 are translations and revisions of chapters 3–5 in my *Om analog användning av rättsnormer*, 1973.

Chapters 10–12 and 16 are translations and revisions of chapters 3–6 in my *Rättsregel och rättsval*, 1984.

I would like to thank Lennart Åqvist, Anders Fogelklou, Patricia Mindus, and Torben Spaak for valuable comments on Chaps. 6 and 7. Thanks are also due to Robert Carroll for checking my English. Further, I would like to thank two anonymous reviewers from Springer for their painstaking examination of my manuscript and their valuable comments.

I also wish to thank the Royal Academy of Arts and Sciences of Uppsala for a generous grant that made the project possible.

Uppsala, Sweden
January 2018

Åke Frändberg

Contents

Chapter 1
Introduction

1.1 Law and Jurisprudence: *Ars Juridica*

It is vital to keep law and juridical thinking apart. Law is the content of legal rules and the systems of legal rules. Juridical thinking is the handling of the law by lawyers.

A wood-carver fashions things out of wood. Pieces of wood form the object of his work, the matter he works with. In order to perform this work, he needs tools: a saw, a chisel, sandpaper, etc. He also has in his mind certain ideas about what makes good wood-carving. For both the material tools and the standards of good wood-carving he has a certain terminology—the (technical and evaluative) language of his craft.

By analogy, the lawyer has his object, the matter he works with—the law. The difference between the wood-carver and the lawyer is that the latter's matter is ideas expressed in language. Like the wood-carver the lawyer, in addition to that, has a language of his craft, technical as well as evaluative. Logically, the language of the law and the language of juridical thinking are two different languages. But while the tools of the wood-carver are material things, the tools of the lawyer are ideas. For that reason the distinction between the law-language and the juridical language is often blurred. To a certain degree they may overlap one another extensionally, but the very distinction between them is clear.

The object of the lawyers' endeavours—the law—is indeed a highly abstract phenomenon. While lawyers tend to conceive of themselves as actors very close to reality, dealing with utterly concrete things like house purchases, fights, car accidents, marriages, deaths, strikes and cruelty to animals (as they no doubt do—the juridical activities are indeed almost as varied as life itself), they are more seldom aware of the fact that there are few intellectual activities—apart from the mathematical disciplines—that to such an extent as the lawyers' craft dwell in a world of abstractions. A man and a woman join together and enter into "a marriage", a number of people join together to form "a limited company", (whereby "a juridical person" comes into existence), someone has an "ownership" of something, another

Å. Frändberg, *The Legal Order*, Law and Philosophy Library 123,
https://doi.org/10.1007/978-3-319-78858-6_1

"a tenancy right", a third "a right of option". None of these phenomena can be observed by our senses or with the aid of instruments. The legal entities making up the law are abstractions, ideas of culture, created by human imagination in order to satisfy needs that emerge so long as human beings live together in societies. Biologists, for example, have a much more concrete object of study (dogs, ants, tulips, cells, genes, etc.) compared to lawyers.

Law without lawyers and juridical thinking is perfectly possible and is characteristic of earlier forms of legal orders. Through the rise of a certain law-handling caste—the lawyers—legal orders have, in a historical perspective, become more and more juridicalised. A legal order is juridicalised when its bodies are manned by professional functionaries, especially when these are academically educated and trained in law faculties, law schools and the like. The handling of Roman law was to a high degree juridicalised, but that was not the case with Athenian law. In ancient Greece the borderline between political, moral and juridical thinking was not yet marked out in a more precise way. The juridicalisation of the handling of legal orders in Europe has a break-through with the revival of the *Corpus Juris* and the scholarly study of it in the twelfth century and onwards.

The distinction made here is mirrored in some European languages—in German by the words *Recht* and *Jura*, in Norwegian by *rett* and *juss* and in Swedish by *rätt* and *juridik*. Italian has *diritto* for law and *giurisprudenza* for juridical thinking. But if we search in a Swedish-English dictionary, we find "law" for both *rätt* and *juridik*. The French word *juridique* is solely an adjective ("juridical"), not a noun (as opposed to, e.g., "logique", which is both an adjective and a noun).

The English word "jurisprudence" is highly ambiguous. It can mean the scholarly study of general and fundamental problems in connection with the law. Or it can mean legal science as a whole. It can also refer to a series of precedents. The Latin word *jurisprudentia* means prudence in dealing with the law ("juris-prudence"). Hence, "jurisprudence" might well be used as synonymous to what I have referred to as "juridical thinking". And just as terms such as "private law", "criminal law", "constitutional law", etc., are ambiguous in that they on the one hand refer to a part of the law and, on the other, to the science studying that part, the term "jurisprudence" could be taken to refer to, on the one hand, lawyers' ways of thinking and on the other the scholarly study of that thinking. In order to avoid confusion, however, I use the term "juridical thinking" for the ways in which lawyers think and "jurisprudence" for the scholarly study of this thinking.

During the Renaissance a number of *artes*—treatises or handbooks—were published in various fields of science and art, e.g., *ars anatomica*, *ars grammatica*, *ars historica*, *ars medica*, *ars mnemonica*, *ars rhetorica*, with classical works such as Horace's *Ars Poetica* and Ovid's *Ars Amatoria* as a model. The present work can be seen as a contribution to the study of the foundations of an *ars juridica*—the art of jurisprudence (or juridical thinking).

Now one might ask: When, in the Western cultural tradition, did (1) law, (2) juridical thinking (juridicalised law), and (3) jurisprudence come into existence? As for law, we find legal codes in cultures older than the culture reasonably referred to as "Western", namely in the so-called Fertile Crescent, including Mesopotamia and

Egypt. The oldest historically known one is the legal code of the ruler Urukagina (the actual text of which has not been found, but is known by later references to it) of the city-state Lagash in Mesopotamia (c. 2400 BCE). Somewhat later are the Laws of Eshunna (north of Ur on the Tigris River; c. 1930 BCE)—inscribed on two cuneiform tablets—and the laws of Hammurabi (c. 1800 BCE). Recorded Indian and Chinese purely legal texts are of a later date. In the European tradition we find the first law-codes in ancient Greece. Statutory law was highly revered there. Unfortunately, we just have fragments of them, engraved in stone or bronze. Only one is well-preserved: the Gortyn Code in Crete from c. 450 BCE (and, hence, roughly contemporaneous with the Twelve Tables of Roman Law).

When does juridical thinking and, which amounts to much the same thing, juridicalised law—which, in turn, is almost synonymous with secularised law—emerge?[1] Professional, secular juridical thinking is a European phenomenon. It was unknown to the Greeks, but is a heritage of Roman civilisation. The rise of juridical thinking in the Roman world is inextricably associated with the rise of Roman legal science. Quintus Mucius Scaevola (d. 82 BCE) is often mentioned as the founder of the study of law as a systematic scientific discipline. He wrote a treatise, no longer extant, on civil law. Part of a short legal handbook of his is incorporated in Justinian's *Pandectae.* Two phenomena, decisive for the future development of juridicalised law, emerge from the time of Emperor Augustus and onwards: the achievements of the classical jurists—from Labeo (d. 10 or 11 CE) to Modestinus (fl. c. 250 CE), with Julianus, Gaius, Papinianus, Paulus and Ulpianus in-between—and the establishment of special law schools. Between Modestinus and the compilation of the *Corpus Juris Civilis* in the sixth century there is a hiatus in the development of legal science. During that period the juridical culture is preserved by the teaching of the works of the classical jurists in law schools spread throughout the empire—the most famous of which were those in Rome, Berytus (Beirut), Alexandria, Athens, Carthage, Antioch, and Constantinople. Soon after the implementation of *Corpus Juris* a second, more disastrous, interval follows as a consequence of the fall of the Western part of the Roman Empire—the Dark Ages. If there are any law schools left, they are of little importance, and legal science is no longer a living intellectual enterprise. Justinian's *Digest* has fallen into oblivion. It would fall to the Bolognese glossators and commentators in the twelfth and thirteenth centuries to revive European legal science and professional legal education, and lay the foundations for what we build upon to this day. Despite the slight influence of the content of Roman law on English law, and the less scientific and more judge-dominated character of English legal life compared to that of the Continent, there can be no doubt whatsoever that the medieval English legal order, too, is a European-style juridicalised, professionalised, and secularised one.

---

[1] According to Roman tradition, a decisive step towards the secularisation of Roman law was taken in 304 BCE, when the monopoly of legal knowledge held by the guardians of the ancestral, religious tradition – the pontiffs – was broken up. Thereafter an increasing number of secular jurists (*jurisprudentes* or *jurisconsulti*), emanating from the Roman aristocracy, took over as masters of the law. Mousourakis (2015), p. 55 f.

The Roman jurists, the glossators, and the commentators made juridicalised law out of law by systematisation of the law and formation of legal concepts (concepts of law). But when does thinking about juridical thinking, i.e., thinking about the handling of law—jurisprudence—emerge? One could imagine that no such thing would appear until a more advanced juridical thinking had developed. But it is an expression of Greek genius to have been able to lay a foundation of jurisprudential thinking in spite of lacking a caste of specialised lawyers with a specialised way of thinking. Among the Greek contributions to jurisprudence in the stricter sense of a meta-juridical endeavour, we could mention above all the ascertainment, made by the sophists and Aristotle, that there is a "positive" law besides the universal natural law. The germ of an idea of legalism (the "rule of law") is visible in the writings of philosophers and historians as well as the idea of equality before the law (*isonomia*), and the idea of a fair trial in the sense that both parties in litigation shall have their say. Moreover, the Greeks were aware of the normative (deontic) character of the law. Also in Roman legal science we find traces of jurisprudential thinking in the sense of reflections on juridical thinking. For example, it took a stand on statutory interpretation ("*Scire leges non hoc est, verba earum tenere, sed vim ac potestatem*" (Celsus)—"Knowing the laws is not knowing their wording but their spirit"). The nature of legal rules is characterised by Modestinus, as cited in the *Digest*, as follows: "The effect of a statute is to command, to prohibit, to permit, or to punish".[2] Methodological issues were eagerly discussed in the medieval law-schools. As for legal philosophy in general during the Middle Ages and up to the nineteenth century, a widening gulf between the lawyers' philosophy of law (jurisprudence) and the philosophers' philosophy of law is clearly ascertainable. As for the latter, this field has more often than not been regarded not as a distinct branch of philosophy but one included in, or supplementing, a certain general philosophical doctrine. The focus has been on the nature of law in very general terms. First at the end of the eighteenth and in the nineteenth century did a breakthrough of a lawyers' philosophy of law take place. The pioneer among philosophers when it comes to the investigation of basic *juridical* concepts is Bentham, followed by Austin and in the twentieth century by Hohfeld and Kelsen, among others.

Juridical thinking can be studied from many different points of view—from the perspective of, e.g., history, the history of ideas, legal sociology, doctrines of legal sources and interpretation, comparative law and legal dogmatics. Not least it offers fruitful problems for philosophers. Each of these perspectives is necessary in order to understand the multifarious phenomenon of juridical thinking in a comprehensive way, and none of them alone is sufficient for that purpose.

This book contains studies in philosophical jurisprudence. It especially concerns *the lawyer's philosophy of law. Its subject is basic ideas of juridical thinking.* My task is to shed light on juridical thinking by investigating some of its basic ideas (concepts). I prefer the term "philosophical jurisprudence" to the otherwise common "analytical jurisprudence". As I see it, an important aim of philosophical

[2] *De legibus* 1.12.33. Quoted from Kelly (1992), p. 69.

investigations of an area of thinking is to *clarify* the concepts forming the basis of that thinking. This goes beyond pure analysis of the existing use of language (the value of which is disputable).[3]

The craft of the lawyer takes different shapes. Juridical thinking (as thought-content, not as thinking as a psychological process) manifests itself in the different law-handling roles. The differences between these roles are considerable but the similarities greater. The following five tasks for lawyers to fulfil form the core of their endeavours.

1.1.1 The Lawyer as Law-Applier

The relationship between valid law and application of law can be characterised in the following way. Application in general means that something is applied to something else. Application of law is an intellectual procedure that, taking its starting point in a general normative idea belonging to valid law (a valid legal rule), assigns a normative character to an individual, factual situation, in that way creating a normative legal position corresponding adequately to the general normative idea. (Application of law will be investigated in Chap. 13.)

Application of law is a social function "between" the legislator and the executive authorities. The legislator creates general rules. The executive authorities operate on the individual level (although these operations themselves are governed by general rules). The law-applier "confronts" the general with the individual. He is "individualising" the law. If the law-applying level did not exist, what would be missing? Answering this question is very much the same as answering the question "Which public interests are satisfied by the application of law?" The following are central: (i) That the legislator's teleological intention (the purpose, the operative goal) of the general rule is realised in the individual situation. (ii) That the operative goal is realised without violating certain important background goals, such as legal equality or certainty (see further Chap. 15). (iii) That the legal judgment is based on proven facts. (iv) That the legally relevant facts correspond adequately to the prerequisites of the general rule (legality, i.e., taking the wording seriously, which amounts to taking the legislator seriously). (v) That the parties involved can make their voices heard (*Audiatur et altera pars*). (vi) That the individual sanction is adequate and reasonable. (vii) That law is created by the law-applier (according to the prohibition of denial of justice) in the spirit of existing law when the valid law is obscure or non-existent. (viii) That the parties are allowed to play a more decisive role in optional areas of the law (where the law-applying function is a kind of service function). To these eight interests can be added the following four, which concern the controlling function of the law-applying authorities vis-à-vis other public authorities: (ix) That the legislator has not exceeded his competence. (x) That the

[3] More about my view on clarification in Frändberg (2014), pp. 25–30.

prosecutor's claims are adequate and reasonable. (xi) That defects in the laws are brought to light. (xii) That the limits of competence (the division of power) between legislator, law-applying authorities and executive authorities are not violated.

The application of law, the legal process and the court of law are phenomena closely tied together. The application of law is an intellectual activity within the framework of the process, usually resulting in a decision (a judgment). The process is a formal ("ritual"), step-by-step progressing activity, within the institutional framework of the court. The legal process is the hub of the legal order. It is, no doubt, one of the most ingenious social inventions ever made. The court of law provides the legal process with an institutional framework. The court is the right place to house the process. The process is the right framework for the application of law.

1.1.2 The Lawyer as Legal Strategist

The role of the lawyer as a legal strategist (notably the advocate) differs in many respects from that of the lawyer as law-applier (notably the judge). The difference lies in their dissimilar attitudes towards the valid law. The strategist shall not apply the law. His task is to build strategies on the law—he shall help his client to preserve or achieve an advantageous legal position. His relationship to the valid law is twofold. On the one hand, the law is a resource, a challenge for the legal imagination of the strategist. In his dealing with the law it can, e.g., sometimes be to his client's advantage to try to problematise an apparently obvious statutory interpretation. On the other hand, law is a limitation; the strategist's legal imagination must not result in a transgression of the law. His strategy might be defensive—aiming at protecting given legal positions, at conflict avoidance (*ex ante*) and even at tactical withdrawal (e.g., accepting a less favourable position in order to preserve a family relation or a long-standing business relation). But his strategy might also be offensive—aiming at placing his client in a more favourable position than his actual one by means of, e.g., contracts or litigation. As for the advocate, his focus of attention shall be the interests of his client and nothing else. His client must be able to rely on him, and his sole task is to help his client. The advocates serve the public welfare by restricting their support exclusively to individuals, be it human beings or legal persons.

In a certain sense, however, the advocate, too, "applies" the law. In order to predict a certain outcome, he would be wise to put himself in the judge's shoes and act the part of the judge, trying to argue the way the judge would have argued. In this way, the advocate plays a role (the judge) in a play within the play where he has the role of the advocate—just as Francis Flute, the bellows-mender, acts the part of Thisbe in the play within *A Midsummer Night's Dream.*

1.1.3 The Lawyer as Draftsman

Among the roles played by lawyers, the part of the draftsman has a venerable age in Western juridical culture. The importance of this juridical branch is immense. Specialised lawyers played a crucial role in the development of Roman law, and in medieval times they assisted emperors, kings, popes and bishops in their legislative endeavours. And it was owing to this kind of lawyers that the great codifications in modern times were accomplished. Two famous draftsmen in European juridical history should be mentioned: Tribonianus (*Corpus Iuris Civilis*) and Portalis (*Code Civil*). This notwithstanding, the role of the draftsman is still a rather unexplored field of research and it is my impression that, in most countries, it is rather neglected in the legal education as well.

Generally speaking, the task of the draftsman, or legislative technician, is to "realise" the ideas and intentions of the legislating politicians. The draftsman shall transform these ideas and intentions into statutes that fulfil certain quality criteria of what statutes shall look like. These criteria have a technical as well as a moral character. The role of the draftsman is not restricted to that of a writer and an editor. The draftsman also has a controlling function.

An important task for the draftsman is to see to it that the new statute is brought into harmony with the existing legal system and that the provisions of the statute are mutually in harmony. Another important task is to see to it that the law becomes possible for the addressees to comply with and for the law-appliers to apply.

While the law-applier handles law *ex post*, i.e., after the law has acquired legal force, the draftsman handles it *ex ante*. From their different positions in relation to the law, though, they do very much the same thing. The draftsman shall facilitate for the law-applier to fulfil his tasks, some of which were mentioned above under Sect. 1.1.1—in the first place functions (i), (ii), (vi), (vii), (ix), (xi) and (xii). (All of these "background goals" will be dealt with in Chap. 15.)

In fact, especially in earlier times, the borderlines between the legislator and the draftsman were indefinite. Today it is possible to differentiate between draftsmen in the stricter sense of writers and controllers and in a wider sense verging on the role of the investigator, to be presented in the following.

1.1.4 The Lawyer as Investigator

Not infrequently, lawyers are used as investigators, alone or as members of *ad hoc* committees (commissions of inquiry), when something extraordinary has happened, such as air or ship disasters, natural disasters, corruption or political scandals (in the more bigoted of our nations even of the type sex scandals). The reasons for this are probably the lawyers' knowledge of the law and their training as lawyers, which promote a capacity to look at things objectively, to evaluate evidence and to distinguish between what is relevant and not relevant from some given point of view. The role of the investigator has strong similarities with the role of the judge (the law-applier).

The relationship between the role of the investigator and the valid law is not altogether clear. One could say that it is a more indirect one than the relationships between the valid law and the law-applier, the legal strategist and the draftsman. The investigator examines factual states of affairs from the viewpoint of a possible future legal judgment of them, thereby paving the way for legal actions on the part of the ordinary legal authorities. The investigator is an extraordinary resource for extraordinary circumstances.

Several legal professions represent a kind of intermediary form between the law-handling roles just mentioned. For instance, the prosecutor is a legal strategist, to a certain degree an investigator, and a law-applier. The arbitrator is something of a legal strategist, looking for the optimal outcome by taking the interest of both parties into consideration, and a law-applier. The parliamentary *ombudsman* is a mixture of investigator and, to a certain degree, a legal strategist and a law-applier.

1.1.5 The Lawyer as Jurist (Legal Scholar)

Within the realm of legal science we can make a distinction between dogmatic (systematic, juridical, internal) legal sciences and non-dogmatic (meta-legal, external) ones. The object of the former is some part of the valid law. The latter stand in a more pronounced meta-relation (external relation) to the law. Usually they study law from the viewpoint of some non-legal science. This distinction is mirrored in our languages. The names of the dogmatic legal sciences end with "... law" (e.g., "civil law", "criminal law", "constitutional law") while the names of the non-dogmatic ones are formulated as "legal ...", "... of law" or "law and ..." (e.g., "legal history", "legal philosophy", "legal sociology", "history of law", "philosophy of law", "sociology of law", "law and economics", "law and logic"; cf. "*Zivilrecht*", "*Rechtsgeschichte*"; "*droit pénal*", "*sociologie du droit*").

When I talk about jurists here, what I have in mind are representatives of the dogmatic legal sciences exclusively, not representatives of the meta-legal ones. Lawyers belonging to the former category not only study the law, they also handle it in ways similar to law-appliers and draftsmen. Like the law-applier, the jurist's perspective of law is traditionally *ex post.*

What is the relationship between the role of the jurist and valid law? The aim of the jurist, as I see it, is to produce *a better version* of some part of the valid law—better, that is, than the official version as it appears in statutes and precedents. What, then, characterises such a better version? On the one hand, it is not a better version if it only reproduces the official one. On the other hand, it is no version at all if it suggests a completely new alternative to the valid law. That would be policy, not science. It is a version which in some respects is better than the official one but at the same time preserves it with respect to its content. It could be said that a version, *L**, of a piece of valid law (i.e., law in the official version), *L*, is a better version of *L* if

(a) L^* offers an intellectually better rendering of L, (b) L^* includes a critical scrutiny of L, and (c) L^* inserts L into a wider context. This, it seems to me, is what legal dogmatists usually aim at. Valid law is the natural point of departure of dogmatic legal science, not its final product (see further Chap. 13).

Version L^* is intellectually better than L if it is (i) clearer, more explicit and articulated by means of more precise concepts than L, (ii) rendered within the framework of a more elaborate systematics than L, and (iii) making L more precise by supplying L with interpretations of rules in L on crucial (maybe hypothetical) generic cases. Further, L^* is a better version of L if (iv) L^* critically scrutinises L from the viewpoint of legislative technique (not least with respect to possible built-in inconsistences in L, where L^* can recommend solutions) and (v) from the viewpoint of *L's* capability to fulfil its purpose (operative goal) and to do so without violating other goals (e.g., legal certainty). Finally, L^* is a better version of L if (vi) L^* investigates L in the light of a larger part of the legal system of which L is a part, and (vii) examines L from a comparative[4] as well as (viii) a historical perspective.

Only by offering better versions of parts of the law can legal dogmatics be of value to legislators, law-appliers and other lawyers as well as, and not least, to the legal education.

The various tasks of the lawyers presented above differ from each other in that, in their accomplishment, valid law is handled in different ways. But all lawyers have a common ground in a shared structure of thinking, a shared *juridical culture*, a shared juridical cultural heritage. This culture, in turn, has as its basis certain intellectual and evaluative ideas (concepts), which will be briefly introduced in the following section.

1.2 L-Concepts and J-Concepts: J-Concepts Systemised

Let us, in keeping with the fundamental distinction between law and juridical thinking (jurisprudence), make a distinction between concepts with a law-stating function (law-concepts, concepts of law; *L-concepts* for short) and concepts with a juridical-operative function (concepts about law, juridical, or jurisprudential, concepts; *J-concepts* for short).[5] As was pointed out in Sect. 1.1, the craft of lawyers, like all other crafts, demands a professional, technical vocabulary, or language, of its own. This language is not the same language as "the law-language", i.e., the

[4] "It may indeed be that the mere interpretation of positive rules of law in the way traditionally practised by lawyers does not deserve to be called a science at all, whether intellectual or social. Perhaps legal studies only become truly scientific when they rise above the actual rules of any national system, as happens in legal philosophy, legal history, the sociology of law and comparative law". Zweigert and Kötz (1987), p. 4.

[5] This distinction is more thoroughly elaborated in Frändberg (2009), pp. 1–16.

language of statutes, legal decisions, etc. J-concepts are members of the juridical, or jurisprudential, language. My concern in this book is J-concepts.

Within the class of J-concepts we shall distinguish between two main groups: *technical-juridical concepts* and *ideological-juridical* (or *evaluative-juridical*) *concepts*. The former are concerned with the purely intellectual handling of the law, and do not comprise any other value than that of intellectual stringency (e.g., "legal source", "legal rule", "normative modality", "application of the law", "analogy"). The latter, on the other hand, contain as their most important ingredient a valuating attitude towards the juridical handling of the law (e.g., "legality", "legal certainty", "equality before the law"). This distinction mirrors the basic and important fact that juridical thinking is an inextricable amalgamation of technical devices and evaluative ideas.

1.2.1 Technical-Juridical Concepts

Suppose that a system of technical-juridical concepts—the lawyers' intellectual armoury—would be constructed from scratch. One reasonable way to proceed would then be to form, initially, some idea of the need of such concepts. It seems to me that at least the following four types of such concepts are essential.

1. We need a set of concepts that would help us to *structure* the law in a logical and functional respect.
2. We need a set of concepts that would help us to indicate the phenomena to which the law is applicable, and also to separate from each other the *areas of application* for different legal systems—concepts that indicate the "topology" of the law.
3. We need a set of concepts that would help us to speak clearly and articulately about *the relations between law and action*—be it lawful or unlawful actions.
4. We need a set of concepts that would help us to describe in a precise manner *the methods of the professional-juridical handling of the law* (in the first place application of law and legislation).

For each of these there is a corresponding family of J-concepts, the members of which will meet the need in question, so that:

- for 1. there is a corresponding set of *morphological J-concepts.*
- for 2. there is a corresponding set of *topological J-concepts*
- for 3. there is a corresponding set of *praxeological J-concepts*
- for 4. there is a corresponding set of *methodological J-concepts.*

My concern in this book is such technical-juridical concepts.

1.2.1.1 Morphological J-Concepts

There is an important branch of philosophical jurisprudence that could be termed *legal morphology* (the accidence and syntax, or "grammar", of the law). This branch is concerned with the investigation of the purely formal way in which the law is structured: the form, as abstracted from the law content, of legal rules and systems of legal rules. Concepts used for that purpose we call "morphological J-concepts". Concepts such as "legal rule", "(pre)requisite"—"legal consequence", "right", "duty", "competence (or power-conferring) rule", "primary" and "secondary rule" all belong to this category.

"Morphology" is a term that is used in a number of disciplines—for example zoology and linguistics—simply to denote the study of purely structural and technical-functional characteristics of different phenomena. But whereas the objects studied in zoological morphology are physical entities (wings, gills, etc.), the objects studied in juridical morphology are abstract entities, products of human culture and thought processes. This is why logical analysis occupies a central position in juridical morphology and is inseparably linked with a technical-functional analysis.

By taking as a starting point the concept "legal rule", it is possible within legal morphology to differentiate between two different levels—one *micro-morphological* and one *macro-morphological*. At the former level it is the component parts of particular legal rules that are studied and here we encounter concepts such as "(pre) requisite—legal consequence", the various concepts of rights and duties (legal positions, jural relations), the various normative modalities "shall", "ought", "may", "must not" (obligation, permission, prohibition), and so on. Here legal morphology comes into very close contact with deontic logic. The aim of micro-morphological investigations, one could say, is to lay bare the internal structure of legal rules of various kinds. In the process an attempt can be made to reproduce rules of a certain kind to *a standard form* for rules of this type. Micro-morphological investigations are performed in Chaps. 2, 4 and 5 of this book.

At the macro-morphological level the phenomena studied are the legal rules as units, incorporated in *systems* of legal rules (legal systems). Macro-morphology differentiates and examines legal rules of different kinds and various kinds of relations that can prevail between legal rules in a legal system. In fact, it is the existence of such relations that makes it possible at all for a mass of rules to be apprehended as a system. The aim of macro-morphology is ultimately to arrive at a theory concerning the structure of legal systems taken as wholes. Macro-morphological investigations are performed in Chap. 2 of this book.

1.2.1.2 Topological J-Concepts

The morphological aspect of a legal rule is obviously only one aspect among many others from which such rules can be studied. After all, a legal rule also stands in many and complicated relations to phenomena external to it. Indeed, one important characteristic is that in certain circumstances it is *applied* to some factual situation (case) belonging to a certain set of such situations. Let us call such a set *the sphere of operative facts* of a legal rule. One important aspect of the legal rule is consequently the one that concerns the relation between the legal rule and its corresponding sphere of operative facts.

But there are many other important relations between legal rules and legal cases. Let *r* be a legal rule and *C* the set of cases such that *r* is in some way or another of interest with respect to its application or non-application to cases in *C*. Such a wide set of cases we call *the sphere of operation* of *r*. A topological conceptual framework can then be required to express concepts that indicate different kinds of juridically relevant subsets of *C* other than the sphere of operative facts—or, in other words, concepts that indicate various relations between *r* and members of *C*. In Chaps. 7, 8, 9, 10, 11 and 12 I attempt to develop such a conceptual framework.

The most basic topological concepts are presented in Chap. 7. In Sect. 7.2 I define the concepts "legal case", "operative fact" and "potential operative fact". Operative facts can be individual or (more or less) generic. In Sect. 7.3 I analyse the logical structure of legal cases a bit further. After that I shift focus to the ontology of legal cases (Sect. 7.4). I find that they usually are "ontologically mixed". An individual case can be composed of brute facts, legal positions and acts-in-the-law. My next step is to make a distinction between single-system and multi-system topology, which is done in Sect. 7.5. Single-system topology concerns the relation between legal case and legal rule when the legal system itself is held constant—all rules involved belong to the same system—, while with respect to multi-system topology the rules involved belong to two (or more) separate legal systems. A special concern of the former is two important types of conflicts between legal rules, viz. collision and competition (investigated in Chap. 10). The latter deals in the first place with some other important kinds of conflicts between legal rules, viz. spatial conflicts (conflicts between different national legal systems, which is the business of international private law)—investigated in Chap. 11—and temporal conflicts (conflicts between earlier and later legal rules materially applicable to the same case, which is the business of transitional (inter-temporal) law)—investigated in Chap. 12. The temporal conflicts are regarded there as conflicts between rules belonging to different (short-lived) legal systems within one and the same inter-temporal legal system.

There are topological relationships not only between requisites and cases but also between legal consequences and factual states of affairs. Take the rule "If the seller due to delay on the part of the buyer has had costs for the proper care of the goods, the buyer shall pay damages to the seller for those costs". The legal consequence "The buyer shall pay damages to the seller for those costs" is a normative sentence, containing a normative modality ("shall"), and this modality operates on a factual state of affairs, "the buyer pays damages to the seller for the costs". Such states of affairs I call "normativised facts". They will be investigated in Sect. 7.7.

I conclude the introduction to juridical topology (Sect. 7.8) by distinguishing between different "topological spheres" (relative to a legal rule), all indispensable for a deeper understanding of what lawyers do with legal rules: "the linguistic sphere of cases, *L*", "the sphere of operative facts, *OF*" (the set of cases to which a rule is actually applied), "the sphere of influence, *I*" (the set of potential operative facts) and "the sphere of operation, *O*", which is the union of *OF* and *I*.

1.2.1.3 Praxeological J-Concepts

There is a close relation between norm and action.[6] For good reasons, it could even be called a logical one, since the phenomena that are obligatory, prohibited or permitted are acts (individual or generic). Following von Wright I call concepts concerned with man as an agent "praxeological concepts."[7] Such concepts are, e.g., "act", "action", "activity", "agent", "behaviour" and concepts logically related to them.

It is often required to speak of the observance (following, complying with) and breach of legal rules. But what is meant by this? The praxeological concepts "to observe" or "comply with", and "to break a legal rule" are not unambiguous.[8] They are logically dependent on the normative modality of the legal rule. A breach of an obligation is not the same as a breach of a prohibition and a genuine permission cannot be broken at all (it is always followed). In order to understand, e.g., the nature of the competence norm or the statutory definition, we must have a clear idea about what it means to break such rules. Some legal rules regulate action (You shall, must not do . . .") others qualify actions as legal actions ("Actions *A* are theft", "Actions *B* are making a will"). Basic juridical praxeological concepts are investigated in Chap. 13.

Some praxeological concepts describe a relation between legal systems and social reality. Such a concept is "the teleological basis for a rule" (or simply "legal basis"; Germ. *Rechtsgrund*), signifying what justifies the rule teleologically (to be investigated in Sect. 9.3.4). This concept is logically connected to action concepts.

Another important group of praxeological concepts are concepts signifying typical professional-juridical activities such as "application (of law)", "qualification" and "evaluation of evidence" (to be investigated in Sect. 13.3), and "interpretation" (Chap. 14).

A highly disputed concept in the philosophy of law is "validity". In Sect. 13.4 I argue in favour of a praxeological concept of "validity".

1.2.1.4 Methodological J-Concepts

The methodological J-concepts can be divided into two different categories, sources of law concepts and programmatic concepts.

---

[6]The modern classic in the field is von Wright (1963a).

[7]See von Wright (1968), p. 12 f.

[8]Cf. Frändberg (2014), Subsection 4.2.

(1) We need a set of concepts about the factual basis of legal rules, i.e., texts, utterances, usages, etc., from which, according to more or less elaborated methods, lawyers in general derive legal rules—which are usually referred to as "sources of law". We can call such concepts *sources-of-law concepts* and among them we find concepts such as "statutory law", "case law", "precedent", "custom", "practice", "*travaux préparatoires*"—and, not least, the concept "source of law" itself.
(2) Programmatic concepts are methodological in a more genuine sense, representing, as they do, the principles guiding legal reasoning, and especially interpretative reasoning.

The doctrine of juridical method, as it is presented in textbooks on jurisprudence, can be seen as a collection of programmes indicating how lawyers in general, within the framework of their respective professional roles and the institutional forms of their activities, should proceed when they derive general legal rules from sources of law and individual legal norms from general legal rules. The names of such programmes (varying somewhat from country to country, although the concepts corresponding to them are very much the same) express *programmatic concepts,* and some examples are "literal", "linguistic", "logical-grammatical", "systemic", "objective", "subjective", "intentional", "teleological", "pragmatic" and "consequentialist interpretation". The never-ending debate on methodological matters among lawyers would no doubt gain much from a clarification and systematisation of the concepts belonging to this family. An attempt in that direction is made in Sect. 14.3.

But the programmes for the technique of legislative drafting belong as well to the doctrine of juridical method. While administration of law is endowed with a lot of accompanying programmes, the reverse is the case where the drafting of statutes is concerned. This is due to the fact that legal science—mainly in the German-speaking countries—has just recently started to develop a theory and methodology of legislation in a more sustained way. Some aspects of legislative argumentation are given in Chap. 15.

1.2.2 Ideological-Juridical Concepts

I have devoted a whole book to concepts belonging to this category and I am not going to repeat myself in this one.[9] Let me only—in order to get some balance between the presentations of the two main groups of juridical concepts in this introductory chapter—say a few words also about the ideological-juridical concepts.

Lawyers do not only need concepts with the aid of which they can handle law technically. They also examine law and its handling from an evaluative point of view—and, indeed, should do so. It is a matter of comparing actual law and

[9]Frändberg (2014).

law-handling to certain standards of *good* law and law-handling. For that purpose certain instruments are needed. Such instruments consist of fruitful and precise concepts. Let us call them "ideological-juridical" (or "evaluative-juridical") concepts as opposed to the technical-juridical ones. Among them we find concepts like "legality", "*Rechtsstaat*" ("law-state"), "the Rule of Law", "legal certainty", "legal equality (before and in the law)", "legal security" and "legal accessibility"—all of which are fundamental to our juridical culture.

It may appear strange to regard such concepts as operative-juridical, i.e., as concepts about the legal handling of the law. My reason for doing so is due to the following circumstance. In creating and applying law, technique and ideology are closely interwoven. The ideal of legal certainty, for instance, has undoubtedly had a profound effect on the shaping of both legislative technique and principles of statutory interpretation. The term "ideological-juridical concepts" has been chosen simply because these concepts constitute the components of something that can be said to be the special ideology of lawyers in general in modern law-states, and this ideology is to no small degree about the way the legal technique should be constructed. For that reason the technical as well as the ideological concepts have been assigned to the same category, J-concepts.

The ideological-juridical concepts are, most of them at least, normative entities of the kind called "principles". These ideological-juridical principles are primarily not concerned with the social conditions of individuals but with the very handling of the law, and in this respect they differ from other so-called legal principles such as, e.g., the general fault liability rule. They are, considered logically, principles about the law, or law-handling (J-principles), not principles in the law (L-principles)—although they can become L-principles as well, i.e., when the legislator chooses to regulate the law-handling itself in some respect.

Juridical thinking is an inextricable fusion of value ideas and technique. In my book just mentioned, *From* Rechtsstaat *to Universal Law-State*, I have investigated what I regard as the most important of the former—the humanistic law-state values. The present work is about the latter—the instruments of the juridical craftsmanship. For some, this juridical technique might seem a bit too artificial. However, although always standing a risk of being perverted, it has proved to be a fruitful device in the service of the perennial aim of legal orders, namely, that of preserving peace in human societies, and doing so by peaceful means. (The main task of a legal order is, indeed, to settle social tensions by means of intelligence and reason, not by superiority or violence—even if this noble task often falls short due to the deplorable fact that an insufficient amount of intelligence and good sense is put into the project.) Assuredly, organising society by means of legal orders is itself a technique—a normative technique. But this technique is sustained and reinforced by the juridical technique developed by those professionally in charge of the legal order. (Lawyers are, after all, the principal guardians of the legal orders. If they fail, we are, no doubt, all in trouble.)

1.2.3 JL-Terms

There is nothing to prevent a certain term from being ambiguous in the respect that it expresses both an L-concept and a J-concept. Such terms—JL-terms—have a certain capacity for bringing about confusion in juridical thinking, and the reason for this will be touched upon by means of one or two examples.

The concept "analogy" is a J-concept that plays an important role in juridical thought. The analogy can be understood as a certain type of relation between legal rules, based on a certain kind of resemblance between them (rule r as applied to case c is analogous to rule r' as applied to case c'; analogical use of legal norms is dealt with in Chap. 9). Now it may well happen that the legislator is interested in regulating, in some particular area of the law, the construction of rules performed by courts by means of analogy. He may, e.g., wish to counteract the creation of rules detrimental to the accused by means of analogy where criminal law is concerned. If a prohibition to that effect is issued in the law, the concept of analogy thereby becomes an element in a rule, i.e., an L-concept.

But as soon as a concept becomes an L-concept, it starts to have a life of its own. After a while the courts perhaps discover that the analogy ban cannot be upheld to the letter. Hence they begin redefining the concept "analogy" by stating that certain analogies are not analogies at all but "extensions" that are not covered by the ban. Such redefinitions can be explained by the teleological justification of the rule in question and can be completely justified, when the analogy concept is an L-concept.

On the other hand, it would lead to absurd consequences if this analogy concept would be used in general discussions about analogies or in presentations of the concept in textbooks in jurisprudence, i.e., if the analogy concept as a J-concept would be identified with the analogy concept as an L-concept. The circumstances that influence the forming of the L-concept are special for the particular area of law to which it belongs, and circumstances relevant there are often of no interest at all when a technical J-concept with the same name is defined. Such a concept must be defined on purely intellectual grounds and one must be on one's guard against (crypto) normative influences when defining the concept.

"Retroactivity" is another example of a JL-term. Also here is the case that interpretation in legal practice of a legislative ban on retroactivity can assign to the retroactivity concept, as an L-concept, a content that is quite impossible as a content of a general retroactivity concept of the J-type.

A certain vigilance is therefore justified when dealing with terms that have a dual function of this kind.

1.3 Juridical Modes of Thinking

Basic J-concepts are basic not least because they provide the cornerstones of certain *juridical modes of thinking*. Let me mention some of the most important of them—all of which are closely tied to each other but also capable of coming into conflict with one another, and often subject as well to modifications and exceptions. They have been developed in European juridical thinking over centuries and form a central part of Western culture. We find corresponding ideas in other cultures as well.

One such mode of thinking is *the rule thinking*—the well-established habit of lawyers to think in terms of rules (to be treated in Chap. 3). Included in the rule thinking is the idea that legal rules shall be *general*. They shall be about classes of persons and states of affairs, not individual human beings and unique events. Closely connected to this mode of thinking is *the legality thinking* (legalism), i.e., the idea that the law-appliers shall respect the existing legal rules by complying with them as they stand and not applying them outside their linguistic sphere of application or making exceptions to them.[10] A third juridical mode of thinking is *the systems thinking*, i.e., lawyers' efforts to classify rules into different branches of law, institutions, types of contracts, etc. The systems thinking had its most magnificent manifestation in the great European codifications of the eighteenth and nineteenth centuries.

A most important component of juridical thinking is *the rights thinking*—lawyers' inclination to order social life by ranging individuals and human organisations in mutual legal relationships, and in networks of complicated legal positions consisting of a variety of different rights and duties. The rights thinking is firmly established in Western juridical thinking, although alternative ways of rendering the law exist in the form of types of action, such as the Roman *Actio* and the English *Writ*. The more abstract, "intellectualised", rights thinking is probably a necessary condition for a more comprehensive codification of the law.

A most powerful mode of juridical thinking is *the similarity thinking*: like cases shall be treated alike and even similar cases shall be so treated (*the analogy thinking*—to be investigated in Chap. 9); things exchanged in contractual relations shall be equivalent (the equivalence principle); damages shall be equivalent to the loss, in the law of torts; a crime shall be met with a punishment in due proportion to the crime; equality before the law shall prevail, etc. The close connection between the similarity thinking and the rule thinking is obvious.

A fifth mode of juridical thinking is *the continuity thinking*: law shall be changed slowly and carefully, solutions of new problems in society shall preferably be attained by the use of established, well-known categories (new creations are often met with great resistance) and interference in existing legal relations shall be avoided (the continuity thinking is investigated in Chap. 16).

[10] Frändberg (2014), Chapter 4.

1.4 Legal Doctrines and Juridical Systematisation

The influence of lawyers on law is, however, much greater than what the foregoing survey might suggest. Without bringing into the picture the role of *legal doctrines* as important elements of legal systems of the Western type, an understanding of the relationship between the handling of legal orders by lawyers and the law content will be defective.

What is, then, a legal doctrine? It is difficult to draw a clear dividing line between legal doctrines and the rest of the law content—and trying to construct such a line would, no doubt, be a futile effort. For example, we might talk about the doctrine of *mens rea* as well as about *mens rea* (*simpliciter*). My intention here, however, is only to draw attention to the fact that legal doctrines are often constructed by lawyers outside the legislature, notably judges (especially in the common law domain) and by legal scholars (especially in the continental European domain). They can adequately be characterised as an expression of "learned law".

A legal doctrine can roughly be characterised as (i) a normative solution (ii) to a problem of principle (iii) expressed in a special conceptual framework and (iv) incorporated in a legal system. Often this conceptual framework has the shape of a distinction. Some examples of legal doctrines, among many others, include: "the doctrine of underlying assumptions of the contract", "the doctrine of burden of proof", "the doctrine of *res judicata*", "the doctrine of *rebus sic stantibus*", the doctrine of "*actio in rem* and *actio in personam*" in Roman Law, "the doctrine of *titulus* and *modus acquirendi*" in German *usus modernus*, "*la doctrine classique*" and "*la doctrine personnaliste*" in nineteenth century French civil law, "the doctrine of due process", "the doctrine of *ratio decidendi*", "the doctrine of *stare decisis*" and "the doctrine of *caveat emptor*" in English law. An outstanding example of a legal doctrine, which we owe the Commentators, is the idea of *the legal person* (*persona ficta*). Since the revivification of Europe in the High Middle Ages, in order to meet the demands of the new economic development, the need of legal devices for organising the co-operation of a large population became urgent. The legal person fulfilled such a function. In fact, the invention of the legal person is one important factor behind the rise of modern capitalism and, later, the industrial revolution in Europe.

When a new legal doctrine is introduced and established, an innovation has come about within the legal system in question. This innovation usually is of both a normative and a conceptual character. But it may also be the case that it is of a purely conceptual character. If this is the case, the law content remains the same but the way of conceiving it has changed. A new way of thinking has been established. Of course it may sometimes be difficult to ascertain whether both a normative and a conceptual, or only a conceptual change, has come about.

Let me illustrate this by an example (which is also an example of a tradition of successive legal doctrines). It concerns the handling of third-party conflicts in the law of property.[11] The doctrines developed in order to tackle the problems that such conflicts give rise to have their roots in the Roman distinction between *actio in rem* and *actio in personam*, which was a distinction of a procedural character. Where we today think of rights, e.g., ownership, the Romans imagined persons to have a metaphysical power, by which they dominated over things or other persons. This power was exercised by *actio in rem* with respect to things and *actio in personam* with respect to other persons. This procedural doctrine was transformed by the Glossators and the Commentators into a material one. Their idea was that every *actio* had a *causa,* i.e., a material basis. The *causa* of *actio in rem* was *ius in re* and the *causa* of *actio in personam* was *obligatio.* In the natural law teaching of the seventeenth and eighteenth centuries the Roman idea of a metaphysical power is superseded by the modern concept of right. The procedural aspect disappears. The German doctrine makes a corresponding material distinction between *ius ad rem* (what today is known as *Sachenrecht*) and *obligatio* (*obligatorisches Recht*). For the natural law scholars the criterion of *ius ad rem* was the legal protection against a third party. (Henceforth, I use the terms *Sachenrecht* and *obligatorisches Recht.*) In the beginning of the nineteenth century a shift in the view of the distinction between *Sachenrecht* and *obligatorisches Recht* takes place. The historical school then dominant teaches that *Sachenrecht* is a legal relation between a person and a thing, while *obligatorisches Recht* is a legal relation between persons. This idea, however, is heavily criticised in the latter part of the nineteenth century. Instead, a "personalistic" view is developed: legal relations can only exist between persons—an idea taken up somewhat later by Hohfeld. To a given *Sachenrecht* corresponds a duty of all other persons to respect that right. In France this idea is called *la doctrine personnaliste.* In the Scandinavian civil law doctrine of the twentieth century the distinction is articulated in yet another way and the very terms *Sachenrecht* and *obligatorisches Recht* are abandoned by some authors. Ross makes a distinction between dynamic and static protection against a third party.[12] A person has, according to Ross, dynamic protection in situations where the right comes about or where a change has taken place with respect to the subject, i.e., when the right is transferred. A person has static protection in positions where she is "situated in" the right in question, i.e., when there is no question of the creation, cessation or transfer of the right (the right being "in a state of rest"). Hessler makes a distinction between strong and weak rights, fully realising that third-party protection is a matter of degree.[13] Strong rights are rights that enjoy complete or partial third-party protection, e.g., ownership. Weak rights enjoy only protection against rights of a similar type, e.g., usufruct with respect to movables. (I shall not here bring up the difficulty

[11]For this short survey I have profited from Forssell (1976), Chapter 3. Unfortunately this work is only available in Swedish.

[12]Ross (1934) and Ross (1935), both only available in Danish.

[13]Hessler (1973), only available in Swedish. However, an illuminating summary of it is found in Hessler (1974), pp. 5–32. See also Åqvist (1981), pp. 3–27.

of distinguishing between a certain right and other rights protecting the former, see however Sects. 2.7 and 2.8 below.)

When investigating doctrines of the kind mentioned above it is strikingly difficult to ascertain whether they are both normative and conceptual innovations or only conceptual ones (what Åqvist calls "pure theories"). The latter is obviously the case with Ross and Hessler. But with respect to older doctrines the question is not easily answered.

Another important juridical interference with the law (i.e., the law-content) is the systematisation of it. This kind of law-handling is mainly a task for the dogmatic legal sciences (civil law, criminal law, etc.). The fulfilling of this task is not only a purely intellectual project, facilitating for legal practitioners to find their way through the jungle of law in its original shape and to "diagnose" legal problems. It is not least of great value in legal education. In addition to that, the systematisation of law often has a significant impact on the interpretation of law with respect to individual cases.

What is systemised are legal rules from the point of view of, e.g., the legally relevant character of the persons involved or the specific area of social life concerned (e.g., family life and working life). A common general systematisation, often taken to be exhaustive within the legal system as a whole, is the one distinguishing between civil law, concerning the relationships between private subjects of law (be it natural or juristic persons), and public law, concerning the relationships between public and private, or between different public subjects of law.

Just as is the case with legal doctrines, dogmatic systematisations of law are not always neutral, and at times interfere with the law, but also sometimes change it.

How shall we characterise the concepts used in juridical-dogmatic systematisations? They could be conceived of as a special kind of J-concepts. After all, they belong to the juridical handling of the law. But that conception would not do justice to the fact that they have a much more intimate contact with the norm-content that expresses L-concepts than with the J-concepts. For that reason I prefer to look upon them as special kinds of L-concepts.

Let us make two distinctions between types of L-concepts: (i) one between official and dogmatic L-concepts, and (ii) one between rule constituents and systematising L-concepts.

Official L-concepts we find in the legal sources. Dogmatic L-concepts are found in legal-dogmatic works. Examples of the latter are "causality", "proximate cause", "right *in rem*" and so on. They are many.

Dogmatic L-concepts can, but need not, have equivalents among the official L-concepts. Legal dogmatists can quite well create their own concepts when they consider the official battery of concepts to be insufficient and, as we know, this happens now and then. Such concepts can later be incorporated in the law. Historically speaking, there are a number of concepts which, as products of academic treatment of the law, are to be found in the law or are implicitly contained within it.

Further, a term that expresses an official L-concept need not have the same meaning that it has when it expresses a dogmatic L-concept. (This seems, e.g., to be the case with the Swedish terms "negligence" and "possession".) That such divergences can arise between a concept that appears in the law and one that appears in legal dogmatic writings—even though both are clothed in the same terminology—comes as no surprise when the terms in question are used by two different categories of persons—legislators and legal dogmatists—, who are occupied with the same material but from different viewpoints.

When one states law, one makes use of two different types of L-concepts, rule constituents and systematising L-concepts. The former are concepts that are included in separate legal rules, either as components in the description of operative facts (the prerequisites) or in the formulation of legal consequences. Systematising L-concepts are included in the systematics of legal rules and the systematics is also an element in the stating of law, whether it is a systematics in the official law itself or one constructed by legal dogmatics. Systematising L-concepts are expressed by the names of different types of contract or other legal institutions ("purchase", "gift", "larceny", "marriage", etc.) but also by terms belonging to the more fundamental systematics (e.g., "public law—civil law", "the law of third-party conflicts—the law of contracts and torts").

With respect to the systematising L-concepts, the difference between official and dogmatic concepts often becomes quite apparent. The classical systematisation of the law of property in legal dogmatics (the division into the law of third-party conflicts and the law of contracts and torts, etc.) is, e.g., not reflected in any effective way in Swedish legislation in this field of law, whose classification is constructed according to more "down to earth" criteria.

1.5 Philosophical Jurisprudence

The philosophy of law has something important to learn from the way legal doctrines are constructed by lawyers. Whether normative and conceptual innovations, or exclusively conceptual ones, they form an essential part of a continual effort to *improve* the conceptual apparatus, i.e., to make it more appropriate (adequate) for its purpose—e.g., to present problems and solutions with respect to third-party conflicts as clearly as possible. The important thing is *an adequate concept formation.* This might involve making concepts more precise, excluding ambiguity, substituting concepts for others or augmenting the conceptual resources.

The same can be said about science on the whole. Hempel argues that "concept formation and theory formation in science are so closely interrelated as to constitute virtually two different aspects of the same procedure".[14] Knowledge and the conceptual ordering of knowledge are, indeed, inseparable.

What urges representatives of different sciences and philosophers to improve their conceptual apparatus is, of course, that this apparatus is felt to be in some way or another inadequate or insufficient. As von Wright excellently puts it, "[t]he

[14]Hempel (1952), pp. 1 f.

concept still remains to be *moulded* and therewith its logical connexions with other concepts to be *established.* The words and expressions ... are so to speak *in search of a meaning*". The conceptual apparatus is not yet completed.[15] This also explains why concepts like "water", "circle", or "metre" are philosophically uninteresting. They are already "completed".

For the philosopher thinking about a certain kind of thinking (e.g., juridical thinking) the task is the same: to improve that thinking intellectually. In my book *From* Rechtsstaat *to Universal Law-State* I have referred to this philosophical activity, which I am there and here occupied with, as "clarification".[16] *Clarification is, indeed, concept formation.* The value of this kind of philosophical activity is that it, well performed, can make us more conscious about the ways we think in spheres of human thinking where that is important. Using Arne Naess's brilliant term, it is a matter of widening our depth of intended meaning.[17] "With practice we can become better at distinguishing between an articulate and a superficial grasp of what an expression means. Such a skill enables us to appreciate the richness and subtlety of intelligent remarks, just as it equips us also to see through the shallow glare of catch phrases and propaganda."[18]

In this book I make a modest use of formal logic. As I see it, formalisation is not a special kind of analysis but an instrument for the purpose of clarification. A short formula can express just as much as an abundance of words.

1.6 The Law and the Juridical Handling of the Law: "Legal Order" as the Fundamental Juridical Concept

The great legal project—to obtain and maintain peace, order and conditions for human co-operation with respect to support, etc.—consists in the final analysis of human activities; some people make laws, others apply these laws authoritatively, others again plead causes before a court of law, there are police officers preventing and investigating crimes and there are executive authorities enforcing judgments. Legal life, the effectively working legal order, is essentially *human activity.*

But not just any human activity. It is all about *idea-guided activities.* All the activities just mentioned are caused and guided by ideas of various kinds, notably *normative ideas.* Without knowledge of these ideas legal activities remain utterly inconceivable. That a person shall be punished for theft, if the prerequisites of theft are complied with is a trivial example of a normative idea. That equality before the law shall be respected is another normative idea. That capital punishment is forbidden in a legal system is a third normative idea.

[15]See von Wright (1963b), pp. 4–6.

[16]Frändberg (2014), Subsection 3.2.1.

[17]Naess (1966), pp. 34 ff.

[18]Naess (1966), p. 53.

Within jurisprudence and legal philosophy theories have been presented where the role of ideas, especially the role of normative ideas, are more or less played down or even reduced completely (naturalism). Such attempts characterise the realistic movements influential during the first half of the twentieth century—American and Scandinavian realism. Today it is satisfactorily obvious that attempts to that effect have been failures. The more such a reduction takes place—e.g., in a behaviouristic direction—the more *the genuinely legal in law* evaporates. Without whole-heartedly adopting Kelsen's pure theory of law, there are strong reasons to give him support in his resistance to such realistic reductions. Rather, in a somewhat incisive wording, we have every reason to reduce the importance of pure action in legal life—not because it does not exist but because it is rather uninteresting from a theoretical point of view. What is interesting with respect to law—what makes law law—are ideas. And ideas are not easily conceived of as natural things.

The—normative—system of ideas that we call "law" is handled by juridical thinking—which also, as regards its basic structure, is a system of ideas. Both law and juridical thinking (juris-prudence) are cultural creations, which in fact make legal science a humanistic science. The most fundamental concepts of juridical thinking, such as "law", "legal order", "legal system", "legal rule", "right" "application (of law)"—and also value-laden ones such as "law-state" ("*Rechtsstaat*", "the Rule of Law"), and "legality"—all belong to a highly complicated conglomeration of ideas, some of which will be investigated in this book. It must be strongly emphasised that what I am investigating are those concepts conceived of as *juridical* concepts (not as, e.g., sociological ones).

In order to bring about some kind of structure within the conglomeration of basic juridical ideas (concepts), I have chosen the strategy of selecting one certain concept as fundamental and then trying to relate the other juridical concepts to this fundamental one. The strategy, then, will be to (1) present this fundamental concept and establish its significance, (2) investigate some other juridical concepts and (3) describe the relationship between them and the fundamental concept. This is, to be sure, easier said than done.

I have come to the conclusion that this Archimedian point is the concept *legal order*. Hence the title of this book. The reason for this standpoint will be accounted for in due course.

Let us conceive of a very general idea transcendental to juridical thinking—let us call it *the Fundamental Idea of Law* (*FIL*). *FIL* is the notion that by the use of a legal order peace and order shall be maintained in society: social order through legal order. This idea is not trivial, since other ways of organising society are possible and have also existed in the course of history, e.g., interpersonal control in very small societies, religious social orders, or military regimes. As we see, the concept "legal order" is contained in *FIL*. And, as we also see, according to *FIL* legal orders are the means, the instruments, for achieving certain social states of affairs, not goals in themselves. *FIL* expresses a teleological view of legal orders.

A basic juridical idea of an evaluative character is *the Law-State Idea.*[19] It is an extra-legal standard evaluating the quality of the law and its handling from certain viewpoints. It can be formulated: "The individual shall have protection, given by the state, against the state's misuse of law by violating the individual's legal certainty, legal equality, legal safety and legal accessibility, which are all based on legality and justified by the humanistic idea of a life in human dignity".

There is a logical (conceptually necessary) connection between the concepts "legal order" and "law-state". The latter implies the former—but, alas, the former does not imply the latter. To all law-states belongs necessarily a legal order but not every state having a legal order is a law-state.

Hence, we can formulate a time-honoured idea that combines *FIL* and the Law-State Idea, say *the Advanced Idea of Law*, i.e., the idea that being governed by a legal order and holding the law-state values in respect when handling it is a necessary condition for a society to be a good society. This combined idea is, in my opinion, one of the most valuable civilising ideas human culture has ever created.

But let us take one step further and formulate a third, even more advanced, idea of law—let us call it *the Humanistic Idea of Law.* In *From* Rechtsstaat *to Universal Law-State*[20] I argued that the law-state values could be justified only by the humanistic value of the individual's life of human dignity and that this value idea can appear in two forms—as a moral principle belonging to our private morality, and as a social value, forming a humanistic value basis of society. Components of this value basis, I argued, were (i) the liberal idea of the individual's freedom to live as she wishes as long as she does not harm others unduly, (ii) the democratic idea of the individual's right to have a say in matters of concern to herself, and (iii) the individual's law-state protection. The idea of law-state protection, having a necessary relation to the legal order, I included in the Advanced Idea of Law. Let us now, in addition to that, formulate a broader idea—the Humanistic Idea of Law—combining the Advanced Idea of Law with an idea of protection and guarantee of individual freedom and democracy *by legal means*—thereby making these two ideas *legal* ideas, which, together with the idea of law-state protection, correspond to the humanistic value basis of society. The Humanistic Idea of Law asserts individual freedom through law as well as democracy through law. The humanistic idea of law claims inclusion in the law of liberal rights and duties, democratic rights and duties, and law-state rights and duties—all of them rights and duties in the law and protected by the law.

A society where the three ideas now described are realised we can call *a community of law* (in an ideal-typical form). It goes without saying that societies can be more or less communities of law in different respects and to varying degrees. A rather primitive one is the society where only the Fundamental Idea of Law is (more or less) realised but not the Advanced Idea of Law. On a higher level a society where the Advanced Idea of Law is (more or less) realised (and, hence, being a

[19]Investigated in my book Frändberg (2014).

[20]Frändberg (2014), pp. 161 f.

Law-State) but not the Humanistic Idea of Law is a community of law. On the highest level the Humanistic Idea of Law is (more or less) realised.

To summarise. The fundamental task of the legal order in civilised societies is to preserve internal peace, individual freedom, and democracy. And this shall be accomplished by observing the claims of the law-state idea on the handling of the legal order.

By "law" I refer to the norm-content which manifests itself in legal rules (norms). As I shall argue in the following chapters, rights (and legal positions in general) are related to legal rules in such a way that they too have a normative character. Legal systems are sets of legal rules and legal orders contain, in my conception, both sets of legal rules and sets of certain legal positions. That gives legal systems and legal orders a purely normative character as well. The legal order is, in my opinion, a structure consisting exclusively of normative ideas.

Law in its original shape appears to us somewhat higgledy-piggledy, unsorted and elliptic, and derived from highly different so-called sources of law. Law in its original shape is systemised with respect to its content and structured with respect to its form by juridical thinking performed by lawyers, thereby intellectualising the legal order—or even creating a legal order out of the legal sources by means of intellectual processes.

The juridical handling of the law is the lawyers' handling of the instrument legal order. This handling, e.g., its application to clear individual cases, usually leaves the legal order itself intact. But now and then lawyers interfere with the law and change it, e.g., by creating precedents in hard cases or introducing new legal doctrines (see Sect. 1.4 above).

So there is a fundamental relation, let us call it *the basis of juridical thinking*, between law (the legal order) itself and the juridical handling of it. The aim of this book is to clarify (parts of) this relation.

In this endeavour J-concepts of all the types presented in Sect. 1.2 are mobilised. In keeping with my idea that "legal order" is the fundamental concept in juridical thinking, I argue that every J-concept stands in a certain necessary conceptual relationship to "legal order". They all imply the concept "legal order".

Let me finally, by way of introduction, mention four main types of juridical handling of the law, of which the first two can be seen as a kind of paving the way for the latter two.

(1) *Systematising the law.* This type of juridical law-handling has been briefly presented in Sect. 1.4 above. I shall not dwell further upon the systematisation of law in the present work.
(2) *Structuring the law.* While systematising the law has to do with the law-content, structuring the law has to do with the form of the law.[21] Like the former, the

[21]Somló distinguishes between the content of the law and its form, and makes corresponding distinctions between *Rechtsinhaltswissenschaften* (= mainly legal dogmatics) and *die Wissenschaft von der Rechtsform* (= *die Juristische Grundlehre*), and between *Rechtsinhaltsbegriffe* and *Juristische Grundbegriffe.* Concerning the latter he says, referring to Austin and Bierling, that

latter has obvious intellectual functions, and is mainly performed by legal theorists. But it also serves the purpose of ordering the juridical thinking within the administration of law. Its most important practical function is performed in connection with the drafting of statutes. In structuring the law it is of course the morphological J-concepts that are called into play. Structuring the law will be dealt with in Chap. 2.

(3) *Interpreting the law*. The term "interpretation" as it is commonly used in juridical thinking is highly ambiguous. In a narrow sense it designates (i) the act of attributing a certain meaning to a legal rule, *r*, when it is doubtful whether *r* is applicable to a certain individual case, *c*, or not (*c* being a hard case). More generally it can mean (ii) the ascertaining of the meaning of *r* with respect to an individual case, whether clear or hard. Even more generally it can be taken to mean (iii) the same thing as (i) and (ii) but *in abstracto* with respect to some generic case, i.e., to ascertain "the general meaning" of *r*. Interpretation of legal rules will be investigated in Chap. 14.

A very special, but important, use of the term "interpretation" is the Kelsenian one. What interpretation in this sense amounts to is not the interpretation of particular legal rules but (iv) the derivation of legal rules from legal sources. Interpretation in this sense will be discussed in Sect. 2.4.

With respect to interpretation the topological, methodological and ideological J-concepts come to the fore first of all.

(4) *Applying the law*. Application of law to some case—the most important of all juridical tasks—amounts to assigning a normative character to some state of affairs as a result of an intellectual procedure having its starting point in a legal rule derived from a legal source. Application thus conceived consists of several different moments, among which interpretation is central. The application of law will be investigated in Sect. 13.3.

"Systemising", "structuring", "interpreting" and "applying the law" are praxeological concepts. Among the J-concepts the praxeological concepts designate the very activities involved in the juridical law-handling, while the morphological, topological, methodological and ideological J-concepts designate ideas associated with these activities.

Those were the preliminaries. Let us now go into details. In Chaps. 2, 3, 4, 5, and 6 we shall investigate the juridical morphology and the ontology of normative phenomena, in Chaps. 7, 8, 9, 10, 11, and 12 the juridical topology and in Chaps. 13, 14, and 15 the juridical praxeology and methodology. Introductory chapters to each of these three parts are Chaps. 2, 7 and 13.

The legal order is the backbone of civilised society. The lawyers are the principal guardians of the legal order and the law-state, i.e., of an accomplished community of

---

they are "*jene, deren sich jedermann zum Ausdruck einer Rechtsnorm notwendigerweise bedienen muss oder die er dabei notwendigerweise voraussetzt*". I, for my part, do not assume such a necessity with respect to J-concepts. Somló (1917).

law. For this purpose a special way of thinking has evolved among lawyers in the course of many centuries, juridical thinking (or jurisprudence). Juridical thinking is in the service of the legal order and the law-state. The legal culture is a wider phenomenon than the juridical culture, but the latter is the hub of the former. In my book *From* Rechtsstaat *to Universal Law-State* I took on the task to investigate *the value basis* of juridical thinking. In the present work my task is to investigate *its intellectual basis* (including the juridical technique). If one is devoted to the legal order and the law-state values, and wants to preserve, defend and improve them, it cannot be without value to try to formulate a well-thought-out notion of what it is that one wants to preserve, defend and improve—or, in other words, to clarify what lawyers are in the service of.

References

Åqvist L (1981) On the pure theory of third party conflicts in dynamic property law. Rev Int Philos:3–27
Forssell H (1976) Tredjemansskyddets gränser (The limits of third party protection). Norstedt, Stockholm
Frändberg Å (2009) An essay on legal concept formation. In: Hage JC, von der Pfordten D (eds) Concepts in law. Springer, Berlin, pp 1–16
Frändberg Å (2014) From Rechtsstaat to universal law-state. An essay in philosophical jurisprudence. Springer, Berlin
Hempel CG (1952) Fundamentals of concept formation in empirical sciences. University of Chicago Press, Chicago
Hessler H (1973) Allmän sakrätt (General principles of third party protection in the law of property). Norstedt, Stockholm
Hessler H (1974) Property and third party protection. In: Annales Academiae Regiae Scientiarum Upsaliensis. Almqvist & Wiksell, Stockholm, pp 5–32
Kelly JM (1992) A short history of western legal theory. Clarendon Press, Wotton-under-Edge
Mousourakis G (2015) Roman law and the origins of the civil law tradition. Springer, Berlin
Naess A (1966) Communication and argument. Allen & Unwin, Crows Nest
Ross A (1934) Virkelighed og Gyldighed i Retslaeren (Reality and validity in legal theory). Levin & Munksgaard, Copenhagen
Ross A (1935) Ejendomsret og Ejendomsovergang (Property and transfer of property). Levin & Munksgaard, Copenhagen
Somló F (1917) Juristische Grundlehre. Meiner, Hamburg
von Wright GH (1963a) Norm and action. A logical enquiry. Routledge and Kegan Paul, London
von Wright GH (1963b) The varieties of goodness. Humanities Press, London
von Wright GH (1968) An essay in deontic logic and the general theory of action. North-Holland Pub. Co, Amsterdam
Zweigert K, Kötz H (1987) An introduction to comparative law, vol I, 2nd edn. Clarendon Press, Wotton-under-Edge

Chapter 2
The Legal Order: Morphological Levels

2.1 The Legal Alternative

When lawyers, as sometimes happens, are seized with a desire to acquire a general and comprehensive view of the legal phenomena, they often resort to comparative law for help. And, no doubt, this discipline can provide a kind of overall view by comparison and systematisation of legal orders as far as *the content* of various legal systems is concerned.

But there is an even more fundamental aspect of law, which is lost in a comparison between legal orders exclusively, and with respect to their content only.

Suppose—as is now and then done in general jurisprudence for pedagogic reasons—that we are given the task of organising the social life of a group of people on a given territory—that is, to create a society. As a matter of principle, the first thing to do then is not to choose the basic legal principles, or the structure of the legal organisation, for that society, but to decide upon the even more fundamental question of what kind of *social order* we shall choose for the organisation of our society.

Every legal order is a social order, but there are social orders that are not legal orders (legal orders being a proper subset of social orders). As examples of non-legal social orders can be mentioned interpersonal control in very small societies, "mandarin justice", social order through negotiations, religious orders, military regimes or sheer terror. In fact, modern legal orders have emerged out of, or borrowed a great deal from some of them and there are, of course, intermediate forms too. From this point of view, the legal order is an alternative to the others—the legal alternative.

In order to establish the differences between legal orders and other social orders, a study of the content of legal systems only is inadequate. More fundamental structures must be brought into daylight. By doing so, we can, I think, learn much about "the nature of law".

Å. Frändberg, *The Legal Order*, Law and Philosophy Library 123,
https://doi.org/10.1007/978-3-319-78858-6_2

2.2 Elements of the Legal Order (LO-Elements): Morphological Levels

A legal order is, in very general terms, a social phenomenon in the respect that it is a technique, or an instrument, for organising societies. A legal order is a cultural phenomenon in the respect that it is an abstract entity, created by men. Like Kelsen and many others, I am fully convinced that legal orders in all their aspects can be studied in a purely scientific manner without any ethical or other evaluative commitments on the part of the jurisprudent.

From the viewpoint of form we suppose that a legal order is some kind of *structure* consisting of *LO-elements.* One way of clarifying the concept "legal order" would then be (i) to discern these elements, and (ii) to establish the relationships between them. This approach to the general study of legal orders I would like to call *morphological.* In this chapter I present an outline of a *morphological theory of the legal order* based upon these two suggestions.

That a concept is fundamental with respect to some structure may mean (1) that it denotes "the lowest common denominators" of that structure—for instance in the way Hohfeld regarded his eight conceptions, denoting the particles on which rights are built as "the lowest common denominators of the law". But a concept may also be fundamental, or basic, in the sense (2) that all other concepts pertaining to the structure in question are definable in terms of that concept. A certain concept may be fundamental in sense (1) but not in sense (2), and *vice versa.*

It is sometimes supposed that the concept *legal norm,* or *legal rule,* is the fundamental concept of law. In my opinion, it is fundamental neither in sense (1) nor in sense (2). It is not fundamental in sense (1) since there are "smaller" law elements by which legal rules are constructed: prerequisites, legal consequences (normative modalities and their themes)—and, for that matter, also Hohfeld's eight basic concepts. It is not fundamental in sense (2), because, as will be argued in Sect. 13.4, in order to avoid circularity, *(valid) legal rule* must be defined in relation to a whole structure to which it belongs, viz., *(valid) legal order. Legal order* is a more basic concept than *legal rule.*

LO-elements can be structured on different *morphological levels* with respect to their "fundamentality" in sense (1). The lowest level, then, would be that of "the lowest common denominators" among the law elements. The highest level would be *a general morphological conception of the legal order.* Between these two levels we find intermediate levels of increasing complexity.

Here I find it appropriate to emphasise that I do not equate such a general morphological conception of the legal order with a general theory of law (whatever that would be). By a general morphological conception of the legal order I mean a well-organised system of interrelated, well-defined concepts, denoting various LO-elements—i.e., an intellectually satisfying panorama picture of the legal landscape from a formal viewpoint. (A general theory of law, it seems to me, must be something much more pretentious: a kind of synthesis including conceptual, comparative-dogmatic, sociological, economical, psychological and ethical elements.) Since legal morphological levels logically speaking are relations between different entities, they will be presented here as sets of ordered couples, triples, etc.

2.3 A First Step Towards a General Morphological Conception of the Legal Order: The "Nucleus" of Legal Orders

Let us start with some preliminaries.

There is a close relationship between legal orders and power. This relationship is twofold. On the one hand, the legal order is a means to uphold peace and order by setting bounds to human rampage, i.e., by limiting, controlling and channelling human power. On the other hand, in order to organise society legally, legal orders themselves must be richly equipped with power. Law-state thinking demands furthermore that also rampage exercised by functionaries of legal orders is limited, controlled and channelled—by law. In a somewhat incisive wording: law transforms power into authority. Self-assumed power shall be replaced by power given by law, i.e., authority. Authority restricts certain kinds of power and, on the other hand, reinforces certain other kinds of power.

In my opinion, it is a truism to state that legal orders are creations of man. In the legal enterprise man mobilises different mental faculties: his passions (hopefully mostly what Hume called the "calm passions" of man—"either certain instincts originally implanted in our natures, such as benevolence and resentment, the love of life, and a kindness to children; or the general appetite to good, and aversion to evil, consider'd merely as such" –, which passions, according to Hume, are often mistaken for reason[1]) as well as his reason and his will. (Legal realism has overestimated the emotions (passions), natural law theory reason, and classical positivism the will.) Every general conception of legal orders must be built on a view that has man at the centre.

By means of legal orders power is controlled by transforming it into authority. In broad outline, this task is performed in three different respects, the first being *with respect to legal sources,* the second *with respect to human beings* and the third *with respect to human actions.*

(1) By objectification of the sources of power man can limit power. Certain ascertainable factual phenomena—such as certain texts (statutes, preparatory materials to statutes, court decisions, contracts, etc.), customs or practices, that is, what we usually call "legal sources"—are "endowed" by man with an authority of their own. Objectification usually means limitation of power, since henceforth no other phenomena than the legal sources—whether it be men, things or

[1] Hume (1984), p. 464 f.

habits—have authority as a legal source in the field of life regulated by law (unless given such authority for some certain case in virtue of the legal sources).

(2) By conferring competences on human beings—officials and private persons—law warrants, or reinforces, person *P's* power to do action *a* by giving *P* a competence[2] to do *a*, since, in this way, law gives *P's doing a* a legal protection. On the other hand, acting outside one's competence is to act *ultra vires* and such acting is legally invalid. In our present context, officials—legal functionaries—having legal competence are of a special interest.

(3) Just as human beings and certain other empirically observable phenomena—legal sources—can be endowed with authority, also particular human actions, it seems to me, can meaningfully be said to be authoritative or not. Suppose that *P* has a general competence to do something, e.g., to marry people, and, further, that two people are not properly married unless they are pronounced man and wife by the person officiating at the wedding. That action can then be said to be an authoritative legal action. If *P* omits that action, a marriage has not taken place, although *P* has a competence to marry. In our present context, also authoritative legal actions performed by legal functionaries are of a special interest.

Thus, from the viewpoint of power and authority, *legal functionaries, legal activities* (performed by legal functionaries) and *legal sources* (in different ways a basis for, or otherwise related to, legal activities performed by legal functionaries) are in focus. Hence, let us say that *the nucleus of a legal order* is a set of ordered triples, {<*LF, LA, LS*>}, where *LF* is a set of legal functionaries, *LA* a set of legal activities and *LS* a set of legal sources, such that:

(i) the legal status of members of *LF* is defined by (the content of) *LS*
(ii) the legal character of members of *LA* is defined by (the content of) *LS*
(iii) *LS* is created by members of *LF* by means of actions which are members of *LA*.

The nucleus of the legal order is a comparatively "concrete" model of such orders. Some realists (Scandinavian as well as American) have made the (in my opinion impossible) endeavour to reduce the legal phenomena to "brute facts" (legal naturalism). Kelsen (and, after him, Ross, Searle, and MacCormick and Weinberger) has taught us that legal phenomena have an irreducible quality of law, a quality which, according to Kelsen, is bestowed upon brute facts by interpretation of legal norms; the norm functions as "a scheme of interpretation", as Kelsen puts it.[3] Also Ross, following Kelsen, talks about schemata of interpretation.[4] Searle talks about institutional facts, based on institutions which are systems of constitutive rules.[5] In the same vein, MacCormick and Weinberger present their theory as an institutional

[2]See the close analysis of this concept in Spaak (1994).

[3]Kelsen (1992), p. 10 f.

[4]Ross (1959), pp. 29 and 35.

[5]Searle (1969), p. 50 ff. See also Searle (1995).

one.[6] The underlying idea for all of them seems to me to be very much the same (in spite of obvious differences in terminology).

Perhaps there are legal phenomena that are completely abstract, conceptual, "one hundred percent legal". After all, in certain contexts we can talk about *rights, duties, legal rules* or *norms, legal orders,* etc. in what seems to be a purely abstract manner. But maybe we are then expressing ourselves in an elliptic kind of way, where variables over objects (including human beings), actions and events—i.e., phenomena in the physical world—are understood. However that may be, the elements of the ordered triples, which are elements of the set (relation) *the nucleus of legal orders,* all have a pretty solid component of brute facts: human beings, engravings on paper, sound waves, bodily movements (including such movements that are necessary for writing, talking, reading and listening).

Let us regard the nucleus of legal orders as the starting point of our reconstruction of "law" in terms of morphological levels. I see a point in being as realistic as possible with respect to our *explicandum*—taking "realism" to mean here "reduction to ascertainable phenomena in the physical world". What is left, as it were, after such a reduction is what I have called above the irreducible quality of law. It is important to take one's point of departure in rather concrete matters, since a general conception of legal orders, with the ambition to give a morphological panorama picture over the whole of the legal landscape, must of necessity be a highly abstract conceptual construct. (To be sure, "abstract" is certainly not the same as "impractical", nor is "concrete" the same as "practical".)

Admittedly, by taking our point of departure in the nucleus of legal orders, we begin already from a rather abstract model of LO-elements. In constructing the nucleus, the reconstruction of a general morphological conception of legal orders is already far on the way. However, we have to start somewhere, and my starting point consists of those phenomena which, no doubt, most obviously meet the eye in connection with "law": certain human beings acting "in the name of law"—judges, advocates, legislators, policemen –, certain typical activities performed by such human beings, and the libraries filled with statute books, law reports, doctrine, *travaux préparatoires*—in short, the bulk of legal sources.

2.4 Some Remarks on Legal Sources and Legal Rules

A common, and reasonable, conception of the legal order is that it is a—highly abstract—phenomenon emanating from sources of law. The legal sources form the basis of the legal order. A legal order is a kind of intellectualisation of legal sources. From legal sources legal rules are extracted and, with the addition of statements about certain operative facts, also legal positions, which have a normative character as well. A distinctive feature of the *juridical* interpretation of legal sources is that it

[6]MacCormick and Weinberger (1986).

shall result in a legal rule (norm). As a comparison, a historian interpreting a medieval historical document or a literary historian interpreting a poem have, indeed, aims totally different from that of laying down norms.

What, then, can we reasonably mean by the concept "legal source"? There are scholars who claim that any factor whatsoever influencing judges in their formulation of legal rules is a legal source.[7] This amounts to the standpoint that any final legal decision whatsoever is entirely determined by legal sources. Such a concept of "legal source" does not seem to me to be particularly fruitful. After all, judges can be influenced by anything. It is better then, as is also usually done, to conceive of a legal source as *a special category* of influencing factors, viz., such factors that are regarded as relevant by judges in general and also, typically seen, form the basis for decisions in particular cases—such as statutes (and their preparatory material), certain cases (which, when used as legal sources, are called precedents), customs, contracts, etc. Regarded in this way, it is not at all necessary that every final court decision is entirely determined by some legal source. The ideas prevailing in law-applying circles in a society concerning what legal sources there are and their mutual order of preference are usually called "the doctrine of the sources of law" of that society. One cannot be too careful in stressing that existing doctrines of the sources of law are without exception incomplete and vague—attempts now and then occurring in the juridical literature to present them as would-be well-worked-out systems of rules, even regarded by some as a part of the legal system itself,[8] are, in my opinion, either a false intellectualisation of them or a normative proposal for how they should be drawn up. The history of law gives us examples of how legislators now and then have tried to determine some doctrine of the sources of law. Such attempts have more often than not been failures.

The concept "legal source" that we use must be dependent upon what we want to use the concept for. The need for an umbrella term covering everything under the sun that can influence judges in their decision-making does not seem particularly urgent. On the other hand, it seems important to have a term for factors on which the most "certain" of rules are generally based—rules, of which can be said with good reason that they are applied if they come to the fore (which is the same thing as saying that they are valid). If we conceive of "legal source" in this way, it comes natural to look upon the legal sources as the basis of the legal order.

It might be fruitful to make a distinction between legal *authority sources* and *argument sources*.[9] Authority sources are such sources that are considered having authority regardless of their content (i.e., whether or not their content has value as positive arguments), while argument sources are precisely those sources where judges regularly look for good arguments. The most obvious authority source is no doubt legislation. I am fully aware of the fact that it is often difficult, with respect to some doctrine of the sources of law, to ascertain whether some source is an

[7]See, e.g., Ross (1959), p. 77.

[8]Ross (1959), p. 77.

[9]Cf. MacCormick and Summers (1991), p. 475 f.

authority source or an argument source. Furthermore, the distinction is not absolute; something can be an authority source to a greater or lesser degree. The thought presents itself immediately, though, that in order to get a well-defined concept of "legal source" we had better identify it with "legal authority source".

The doctrines of the sources of law in Western juridical culture are, with respect to their essential features, rather similar, but differ, sometimes substantially, as regards the weight of the different types of sources. Legislation is everywhere the most important legal source, and the other ones often have a secondary position in so far as they come to the fore only as a means of interpreting statutory provisions. In a historical perspective we find that all established legal sources, legislation included, have had their heyday as well as their periods of decline.

As is evident from the definition of the nucleus of legal orders, legal norms—and legal rules, if they are taken to be something different from legal norms, which I do not need to assume at this stage—are not elements of the nucleus; only legal sources are.

The concept *legal rule* is more abstract than the concept *legal source.* A legal norm is not something which naturally meets the eye when we are confronted with some legal source.

The juridical interpretation (in the above-mentioned, very broad, Kelsenian meaning) varies depending on which type of legal source we are dealing with. Statutory provisions are norms—the object of interpretation and the result of interpretation are both norms. But not even with respect to what Ross refers to as the completely objectified type of sources, viz., legislation, does a ready-made rule exist. (According to Ross, a legal source is objectified in the same degree as it offers the judge a ready-formulated legal rule.[10]) Because in order to make a judgment based on statutory law with respect to a certain case, the conventional entities—the legal provisions—are more often than not of a fragmentary character and must be connected to each other in order to form a ready-formulated rule with respect to the case at trial.

As for authoritative court decisions—precedents—we are not confronted with any rule at all (not even in a fragmentary shape) but with an often very comprehensive text from which the judge shall, as it were, distil an applicable rule. When we claim that a rule with a certain content "is embedded in" such a text we have to present arguments for that claim, and the criteria of adequacy for that kind of argumentation are notoriously vague.

Interpretation of statutory provisions (and the preparatory material connected with them), precedents and contracts is a matter of interpreting linguistic phenomena, usually in written form. But with respect to interpretation of custom as a legal source, what shall be interpreted are certain regularities of human behaviour.

[10]Ross (1959), p. 78.

So when we talk about legal systems as sets of legal rules, we move in fact on a very high level of abstraction: the legal rules are thought of as extracted from their sources, objectified and put into some kind of systematic order.

It is not unreasonable to argue that statutory provisions, fragmentary as well as "complete", provide us with the formal, or morphological, models of legal rules in general. By that is meant that any legal rule extracted from other legal sources than statutory law can be formulated as a statutory provision—albeit often as a statutory principle or a general clause.

The concept *legal rule* is not more fundamental than the concept of *legal position* in sense (1) above, since legal positions are "smaller" entities than the former. But *legal rule* is more fundamental than *legal position* in sense (2), since the latter is defined in terms of the former.

I have placed the concept "legal source" among the methodological J-concepts. This might seem a bit strange. However, "legal source" is a juridical concept exclusively and it is exclusively used by lawyers in their handling of the law. A legal source is an interpretative basis from which lawyers derive legal rules. The way they do that can reasonably be characterised as a matter of methodology.

From this it does not, of course, follow that legal sources are completely at the lawyers' disposal and that lawyers are in a position to freely choose their legal sources. The most important of legal sources, legislation, is not at all at the lawyers' free disposal. But other legal sources can be more or less so, e.g., *travaux préparatoires*. Some legal sources are outside the scope of lawyers' free disposal, others they can more or less pick and choose. The latter can perhaps be better regarded as argument sources rather than authority sources, and hence as no legal sources at all—or legal sources in no more than a rather weak sense.

It could be argued that the way we have understood the concept "legal source" would amount to a circularity by claiming: (i) Legal sources tell us what is the law, and (ii) the law tells us which the legal sources are.

I do not find that objection particularly devastating. (i) expresses a necessary conceptual relation—legal rules are interpretations of legal sources—while (ii) expresses an empirical, contingent one. Some legal orders contain rules indicating one or many factors as legal sources, others do not. (See also Sect. 2.13.)

But is not the circularity objection more profound than this? For the dilemma could be reformulated in the following way. On the one hand legal sources are interpretative bases from which judges derive legal rules. But, on the other hand, rules derived in this way decide who is a judge.

I do not regard the legal sources themselves as belonging to the legal order (cf. Sect. 2.13). But the rules derived from them belong, of course, to the legal order.

My solution of the circularity objection—on which, in fact, my conception of a legal order is based—is presented in Sect. 13.4.2 below.

2.5 The Morphology of Legal Orders: Juridical Accidence and Juridical Syntax

I shall—in analogy, to some extent, with linguistics—differentiate between *the accidence* (Ger. *Formenlehre*) and *the syntax* of legal orders and refer to them together as *the juridical morphology* (or "grammar"). Just as the accidence of a language consists of boxes containing nouns, verbs, adjectives, etc., juridical accidence is a series of boxes, each containing some kind of LO-elements. And in the same way as the syntax of a language consists of rules combining elements of the accidence into meaningful units, there is a juridical syntax combining elements of the juridical accidence into juridically useful units.

In the following I shall present a morphological theory of legal orders based on the idea that legal orders, morphologically, consist of different morphological levels. Each morphological level except the lowest (I) and the highest (V) includes both accidence and syntax. A syntax *s on* a given level is the syntax *for* the accidence on all lower levels. The units constructed by *s* constitute the accidence of the syntax on all higher levels. The lowest level is pure accidence. The highest level is pure syntax.

My exposition in the following sections of the morphological structure of legal orders is a modest attempt to exhibit how ingeniously complex a construction these instruments in the service of civilisation are.

2.6 Pre-legal Basic Normative Units (Normative Nuclei)

Even the most elementary legal components—its lowest common denominators (Sect. 2.7 below)—are non-monolithic, compound entities. Although the lowest common denominators as *legal entities*, they are not so as *normative entities simpliciter*. They are compounds of two basic pre-legal components, one normative, the other non-normative.

The normative component is a normative modality—"shall", "may not", "may". These components are no specific legal phenomena; they cover a wider normative field (not least the field of morality). The non-normative component is a proposition stating some state of affairs—usually an act-description stating some action (e.g., "You smoke in the library"). Such a proposition is logically connected to the modality in that the modality governs the normative status of the proposition (e.g., "Forbidden: You smoke in the library").

A normative modality together with a factual proposition connected to it we call *a normative nucleus*. Normative nuclei are the pre-legal basic components of which the lowest common denominators of legal orders consist.

To govern human behaviour by normative means is to control peoples' alternatives of action. The normative modalities are regulators for that purpose. (More on normative modalities in Chap. 5.)

2.7 Morphological Level I: The Level of Basic Legal Positions (Micropositions)

The lowest common denominators of legal orders are what I shall call *basic* (indivisible) *legal positions.*[11] Legal positions in general are logical conclusions from (perhaps unstated) legal rules. In order to function as a premise in a logical derivation of a legal position, the legal rule must often be a compound norm, i.e., a norm which connects two or more fragmentary rules. From complete norm sentences in conjunction with sentences expressing certain operative facts we can derive sentences expressing legal positions. For example:

(1) Anyone who rents a house has an obligation to pay rent on the day of maturity.
(2) *A* rents a house from *B* and the day of maturity has arrived.
(3) *A* has an obligation to pay rent to *B*.

(3) expresses a legal position. Another example:

(1') Any judge who finds the defendant guilty of theft shall sentence him to imprisonment
(2') Judge *C* finds defendant *D* guilty of theft
(3') Judge *C* shall sentence *D* to imprisonment.

(3') expresses that judge *C* stands in the normative relation (is in the legal position) towards *D* such that *C* shall sentence *D* to imprisonment.

Legal positions of the types exemplified are legal positions which are compounds (macropositions; Sect. 2.8 below) of basic positions (micropositions). Famous examples of types of basic legal positions are Hohfeld's classic eight fundamental jural relations (right (or claim), duty; no-right, privilege; power, liability; disability and immunity) and Kanger's eight simple types of rights (claim, freedom, power, immunity, counter-claim, counter-freedom, counter-power and counter-immunity).[12]

A macroposition is ultimately a conglomeration of micropositions. Hohfeld's classification of the latter (although he does not use the term "microposition" but "jural relation") is one of the most beautiful results of jurisprudence ever.[13] His eight basic positions are the following.

(1) *Claim.* That person X has a claim against person Y as to A (some legal act) means that Y shall perform A. Example: X has a claim of damages of 50,000 Swedish kronor against Y. Y shall pay that sum to X.
(2) If X has a claim against Y, then Y has a *duty* against X.
(3) *Privilege.* That X has a privilege against Y as to A means that X does not have a duty against Y not to do A. Example: If in some society there is a legal right of

---

[11] See the close analysis of the concept "position" in Lindahl (1977).

[12] Kanger and Kanger (1966), pp. 85–115.

[13] Hohfeld (1917).

access to private land (open country) and this right is a privilege, then X does not have a duty not to pass over Y:s premises.

(4) If X has a privilege against Y as to A, then Y has a *no-right* against X as to A. Privilege is a weak position. If a right of access to private land is a privilege, the landowner does not violate that position if he for instance hampers people's access by means of fencing.

Well-developed legal systems are also equipped with a kind of "second-order" basic positions, viz., positions that enable their possessors to change their own or others' legal positions. Hohfeld takes into account four micropositions of this type.

(5) *Power* (I for my part, prefer the term "competence"). That X has a power to place Y in the legal position LP by performing A means that X, by performing A, actually places Y in LP. Example: X has the power to transfer the ownership of a piece of land to Y by selling it to Y.

(6) If X has a power against Y, Y has a *liability* against X. (This example also shows that powers and liabilities in contractual relations are mutual—Y has certain other powers against X and X certain other liabilities against Y.)

(7) *Immunity*. That X has an immunity against Y as to Y, by performing A, places X in LP means that Y has no power to place X in LP by performing A. Example: Landowner X has an immunity against his neighbour Y leasing an easement on X:s land.

(8) If X has an immunity against Y, Y has a *disability* against X.

2.8 Morphological Level II: The Level of Compound Legal Positions (Macropositions)

The basic positions belong to morphological level I and the combinations of them to level II. Level II is the syntax of level I. An example of a compound legal position is my ownership of my car, which consists, among other fundamental positions, in a Hohfeldian right (or claim) that other people abstain from using my car without my permission, a privilege to use it myself, a power to sell it and an immunity as against some other person's selling it without my permission. The atomic type of right (in Kanger's terminology) "X has versus the Swedish state a right that a manuscript written by X is published in Sweden" is a combination of a power, an immunity, a counter-power and a counter-immunity.[14] Often such compounds are so common that they have names of their own (ownership, tenancy right, easement, option, freedom of opinion and expression, etc.).

An important (in my terms syntactical) contribution to the investigation of compound legal positions has been provided by Wellman (who talks simply about rights, not of compound positions). If we articulate compound legal positions in

[14]Kanger and Kanger (1966), p. 91.

terms of Hohfeld elements, compound legal positions are, he says, "no mere random aggregate of legal claims, liberties, powers, immunities and duties, however; it is a unified and structured system of Hohfeld elements".[15] A compound position consists of a core element to which some associated elements are attached. The core element "defines" the whole position. For instance, the compound position of a creditor's right to repayment has, according to Wellman, as its core element the creditor's "legal claim against the debtor that the debtor repay him the agreed sum at the agreed time". Around this core element revolves a set of associated Hohfeld elements, e.g., that the creditor has a competence (legal power) of waiving repayment and a legal liberty to exercise or refrain from exercising this competence.

2.9 Morphological Level III: The Level of Legal Rules

2.9.1 Introduction

Level III is the syntax for the units (LO-elements) of levels I and II.

Legal rules are, as it were, a kind of superstructure added to legal positions. Take, e.g., the rule

(r_1) If a driver exceeds the speed limit, he shall be sentenced to fines.

The legal consequence of r_1 is a legal position. The driver stands in the position to a law-applier that the latter shall sentence him to fines. A norm (or, more precisely, the legal consequence component of a norm) and its "corresponding" position are in fact the same thing, seen from two different perspectives. A normative nucleus can be conceived of as a norm as well as a normative position due to perspective, just as the famous duck-hare. "The law-applier shall sentence the driver to fines" is a norm when read "Shall: The law-applier sentences the driver to fines" and a position when read: "The law-applier stands in the legal relation to the driver that he shall sentence the latter to fines".

But also operative facts defined by the prerequisites of a rule can be, and often are, legal positions. Take the rule

(r_2) If somebody owns real estate on the territory of the state, he shall pay tax on it.

Ownership (property) is a compound legal position. The operative fact "Smith owns Blackacre" is an individual compound legal position.

How shall we regard legal positions as operative facts? Now if "ownership" is defined in terms of its legal consequences, r_2 is an analytic statement. The duty to pay tax is a legal consequence of being an owner. But if the normative position "ownership" is defined in terms of the conditions for its coming about and still

[15] Wellman (1978), p. 218 f.

existing, r_2 is non-trivial. When legal positions appear as operative facts it comes natural to look upon them as defined in the latter way.

If a legal rule is taken as a superstructure added to normative nuclei, we find that this superstructure contains non-normative components, e.g., "the driver exceeds the speed limit". Many operative facts are, of course, factual states of affairs, not normative positions. The conditional connective "if. . .so" is non-normative as well.

2.9.2 Standard Forms for Ordinary Regulatory Rules

Since there are different types of legal rules, there are also different types of relations between the LO-elements constituting them. A task for the morphological study of legal orders is to reconstruct these relations. One way of doing that is to present a *standard form* (or canonical form) for each type of legal rule.[16]

In Sect. 2.9.3 I shall present a taxonomy of different types of legal rules. However, in order to give the reader some idea of what such a standard form can look like, I begin with a closer analysis of the most important kind of legal rules, viz., ordinary regulative rules (obligations and prohibitions).

The rule

(*n*) If the seller due to delay on the part of the buyer has had costs for the proper care of the goods, the buyer shall pay damages for those costs

can be divided into different elements such as:

(1) *the (pre)requisite(s)*: "due to delay on the part of the buyer the seller has had costs for the proper care of the goods"
(2) *the legal consequence*: "the buyer shall pay damages for those costs"

and the legal consequence in turn into

(3) *the normative modality*: "shall"
(4) *the norm-theme* (NT): "the buyer pays damages for those costs".

I prefer the term "prerequisite" to the terms "condition" or "ground" usually used in the Anglo-Saxon jurisprudential literature. The reason for that is that I find the term "prerequisite" (henceforth shortened to "requisite") more precise for my purposes than the other more general and ambiguous terms.

n is a rule addressed to citizens (sellers and buyers). The standard form for citizen addressed, ordinary regulative rules of action have the following structure (*a* being the addressee):

[16]Cf. the excellent work of Atienza and Ruiz Manero (1998), where we find a similar approach to the study of legal rules (they prefer, though, the term "legal sentence"). In contrast to this writer they regard legal sentences as "the most elementary units of law" (p. xi).

(SFC) If . . ., then *a* shall (must not, may) . . .

But if a buyer does not fulfil his obligation, the seller might bring the matter before a court of law. If the judge sustains the claim of the seller in virtue of *n,* what he does in fact is to apply a judge-addressed norm *n',* which is a kind of unwritten counterpart to *n* (a phenomenon developed in more detail in Chap. 4).

A complicated element of legal norms is the conditional relation ("if ... then") between (pre)requisite(s) and legal consequence.

2.9.3 A Taxonomy of Legal Rules

Of course, legal rules can be classified from many different points of view. In legal dogmatics, classifications based on the content of rules are, for obvious reasons, prevalent. However, from a morphological viewpoint such classifications are of no interest. What matters there are the structural and technical properties of the rules. Well-known systematisations of this kind are, e.g., Merkl-Kelsen's *Stufenbau* theory and Hart's distinction between primary and secondary rules, and—within the latter category—between rules of recognition, change and adjudication.

Rules based on statutory provisions can be more or less "substantial", i.e., more or less directly aimed at achieving the social goals that are intended by the legislator. Some rules are immediately aimed at achieving these goals, others are so in a more indirect way. Some provisions have mainly an editorial function in that they express rules that are designed to facilitate the very reading of the statutory texts. Some rules even have a purely cosmetic function. Let me present a simple classification of legal rules based on their (more or less) substantial qualities.

Statute books provide us with a rich supply of basic data for classifications, and that is why statutory provisions can be taken as models of legal norms in general. Even a rather cursory study of statutes shows that some rules are more substantial than others. We make a distinction between *traditional legal regulation* and *goal-regulation*, and within each of these categories from the viewpoint of substantiality, between *elementary* and *supplementary rules* with sub-distinctions:

I. TRADITIONAL LEGAL REGULATION

A. *Elementary rules (ordinary regulative rules)*

1. Ordinary legal obligations (and "should-rules")
2. Ordinary legal prohibitions

B. *Supplementary rules*

1. Validity rules

   a. Competence rules
   b. Form-prescribing rules

2. Statutory manifestos
3. Editorial rules

   a. Permissions
   b. Qualificatory rules (statutory definitions)
   c. Statutory guidelines.

II. GOAL-REGULATION

A. *Elementary rules (goal-directives)*
B. *Supplementary rules*

I regard all types of legal rules as *norms*—as do classic writers such as Bentham, Austin, Kelsen and Hart. Also von Wright takes this view.[17] This idea has, however, been disputed. What is especially problematic is the status of permissions, competence rules and qualificatory rules. That some laws (legal rules) are not norms is argued by Raz (what he calls "permission-granting laws" are not norms),[18] Alchourrón and Bulygin (legal definitions, political declarations, expressions of purpose and conceptual rules are not norms but fragments of norms),[19] and Atienza and Ruiz Manero (power-conferring rules are not "deontic" norms).[20]

Here I shall try to clarify the logical structure of the most important rule-types by expressing them in *a standard form* for each such type. In my opinion, it comes natural to express them by means of the standard forms suggested here. I argue that (1) all legal rules are (deontic) norms (the standard form SFC formulated in Sect. 2.9.2 above as well as those formulated below are best expressed as models of *norms*), (2) all legal rules are *different kinds of* mandatory (duty-imposing) norms and (3) all "primitive" legal rules are fragmentary. What I mean by (3) will be explained in connection with our dealing with the syntactical aspects (Sect. 2.11 below).

Traditional Legal Regulation

By "traditional legal regulation" I mean the kind of regulation we are used to finding in our codes and statutes for centuries—obligations, prohibitions, permissions, competence rules, etc.—having an instrumental character in that they are, alone or

---

[17]See von Wright (1963), p. 6 f.

[18]Raz (1980), p. 172 ff. In Raz (1975, reprinted 1990), p. 89, however, he regards also permission-granting laws as norms.

[19]Alchourrón and Bulygin (1971), p. 58 f.

[20]Atienza and Ruiz Manero (1998), p. 45.

in combinations, the *means* of achieving certain aims, though these aims are usually not formulated explicitly in the statutory provisions themselves.

However, in recent times a new kind of legal rules has emerged, let us call them "goal-directives" (I am not particularly happy with this term but let us use it *faute de mieux*).[21] Goal-directives are rules formulating some (general, abstract or more specific) *goals,* but leaving the choice of the means of achieving them to the norm-addressee. The most conspicuous examples of such goal-regulation are the directives of the European Union Law, but this legislative technique is used in many national legal systems as well. The means can be formulated as more specific goal-directives, as ordinary regulative rules or, perhaps, not formulated at all. Goal-regulation will be examined under point II below.

There is a kind of rules such that (i) a legal system cannot exist without containing at least some rule belonging to that kind, and (ii) it is logically possible that a legal system consists exclusively of such rules. Let us call them "elementary rules". Elementary rules are rules directly aimed at actions the performance or omission of which are intended to result in, or maintain, certain social states of affairs, and they do so by enjoining or forbidding such actions under certain circumstances. Supplementary rules are neither necessary nor sufficient in this way—although they can be more or less substantial.

Ordinary obligations and prohibitions can in fact be regarded as one simple category of elementary rules—*ordinary mandatory rules*—since they are inter-definable. If it is obligatory for a person to do some action, then it is forbidden for her not to do it, and vice versa.

The category *"should-rule"* needs, no doubt, some kind of explanation. These rules are "weaker" than obligations but "stronger" than permissions, e.g., a rule to the effect that "Prisoners should be given opportunity to practice sport". The "should-rules"—at least some of them—can be conceived as elliptic obligatory norms, either with an understood complementary requisite or an understood complementary norm-theme. For instance, the rule just mentioned can be explicated as "Prisoners shall be given opportunity to practice sport if there are safe and appropriate premises available for it". Such rules may be used by the legislator when he is unable to guarantee that the necessary conditions for the realisation of the rule exist, e.g., that there are in fact premises available in prisons, or because he for political reasons promises more than he can keep. But it can also be elliptic in that there is an understood complementary norm-theme: "Prison authorities shall give prisoners opportunity to practice sport and see to it that this is possible".

Although it might be logically possible to construct a legal system without *validity rules,* such rules are in practice unavoidable. Let us start with *competence rules.* Competence is a right giving its holder a possibility to change legal relations (positions), and competence rules are rules giving competence to persons or authorities, or

[21]See further Westerman (2010), pp. 211–226. Westerman does not use the term "goal-directive", she talks in a more general way about "goal-regulation" (which term I have borrowed here).

depriving them of competence.[22] Acting according to one's competence is a necessary condition for *the validity* of that acting. Acting without competence makes the action performed *invalid*. Competence rules are more substantial than other supplementary rules in that they play a far more important social role than the others. The legal order is fundamentally a peace order, and in order to support it, unhampered human rampancy must be checked in many respects. In this connection power is essential. Power is, of course, not the same as competence—one can have power without competence and competence without power. Power is a factual state of affairs, competence is a right. But the relation between them is that giving competence in legal forms is a means of regulating, allocating and controlling power. One basic idea of law-state thinking is the idea of division of power between state organs that mutually control each other for the purpose of protecting individuals from abuse of power. And division of power means a strict allocation of competences.

However, is a legal system really possible which (i) does not contain any competence rules, or (ii) consists exclusively of competence rules? As for (i): I think it is. Such a system would, indeed, be a most primitive one and also a heavily overloaded one. For what can be contained in a competence rule would in such a system be split up into an immense lot of ordinary mandatory rules. But such a system is still possible. As for (ii): I think not. The complying with the competence rules would with respect to such a system only amount to producing other competence rules. But the legal positions created by competence rules must in the end contain some normative relations to the effect that persons shall, may not, or may do some actions which are not creating competences. In this respect ordinary mandatory rules are more fundamental than competence rules.

Let me give a few examples of what might reasonably be called competence rules:

(1) A minor may dispose of what he has earned by his own work after he has reached his sixteenth birthday (Swedish Code of Parenthood, Ch. 9, Article 3).
(2) A person under 18 years (a minor) . . . may not on his own dispose of his property or make undertakings [unless . . .] (Swedish Code of Parenthood, Ch. 9, Article 1).
(3) The *Riksdag* passes statutes (Swedish Instrument of Government, Ch. 1, Article 4).
(4) Decision to detain someone is rendered by the court (Swedish Code of Judicial Procedure, Ch. 24, Article 5).

Which is the normative status and logical structure common to rules (1)–(4)?

Some authors claim that they are permissions, e.g., Bentham,[23] von Wright,[24] Alchourrón and Bulygin,[25] and Kanger.[26] Against this claim Spaak has convincingly

[22]See Spaak (1994).

[23]Bentham (1970), pp. 17 and 22.

[24]See von Wright (1963), p. 192.

[25]Alchourrón and Bulygin (1971), p. 151 f.

[26]Kanger (1972), p. 125 f.

argued, by reference to actual legal cases, that it is possible to have competence to achieve some legal position by some action, even though that action is forbidden.[27] Furthermore, as will be argued below, the idea that competence rules are permissions does not capture the way such rules actually function when legal systems are used.

Another way of conceiving competence rules is to hold that they are duty-imposing rules addressed to persons other than the persons who have the competence. Thus, e.g., Swedes have a duty to (shall) follow statutes issued by the *Riksdag* (the Swedish Parliament), and if a minor allegedly is selling his estate, this transaction shall be regarded as invalid by all others. For that reason, according to Ross, competence rules are indirectly expressed mandatory norms.[28] Such rules of course exist, but, as far as I can see, they are not competence rules in any reasonable sense of the word, as they do not focus on the competence itself, i.e., who has the competence and in what the competence consists.

Thirdly, competence rules can also be looked upon as a kind of qualificatory rules (legal definitions), i.e., rules that qualify (or classify) persons, things, relations, etc. by conferring upon them a certain legal quality. That quality would, with respect to competence rules, be competence. Competence rules are regarded as defining legal positions of the type "*x* has competence to achieve the legal position *LP*". According to Strömberg, a competence rule can always be transformed to a qualificatory rule. He gives the example that a certain rule gives a person a competence to marry people. This rule can be conceived of as (a part of) a qualificatory rule defining the concept "spouse".[29] But, as Eckhoff and Sundby have pointed out, in this manner also ordinary duty-imposing rules can be regarded as qualificatory rules, defining "*x* shall count as being under a duty to . . .".[30] This would reduce the whole legal system to a set of qualificatory rules, which does not seem to be a particularly fruitful way of conceiving it. Furthermore, as will be argued below, conceiving competence rules as qualificatory rules leaves out an important behaviour-guiding component included in competence rules.

Fourthly, competence rules can be interpreted as *constitutive rules* in Searle's sense.[31] Constitutive rules are rules constituting an activity "the existence of which is logically dependent on the rules" and often has the form "*X* counts as *Y* in context *C*". Constitutive rules "constitute" the very game, be it chess, football or legal order. Constitutive rules are pretty close to qualificatory rules and my objections against conceiving competence rules as qualificatory rules hold for constitutive rules as well.

Fifthly, competence rules can also be regarded as technical norms in von Wright's sense.[32] Such norms pertain to the relation between means and end. "If you want to avoid being wet, you shall bring your umbrella" is an example of a technical norm.

[27]Spaak (1994), p. 80-87.

[28]Ross (1959), p. 32.

[29]Strömberg (1988), p. 57.

[30]Eckhoff and Sundby (1991), p. 100 f.

[31]Searle (1969), pp. 33–36.

[32]See von Wright (1963), p. 9 ff.

Typical technical norms are directions for use. Atienza and Ruiz Manero suggest that competence rules belong to this type of norms.[33] According to them, the competence rule—or, as they say, power-conferring rule—has the canonical form (standard form) "If state of affairs *X* obtains and *Z* performs action *Y*, then institutional result (or normative change) *R* is produced".[34] Also Spaak seems to be of that opinion.[35] A rule giving some persons a competence to make wills would on this analysis, as Hart argues, have the form "If you wish to make a will, you shall proceed in manner *m*".[36] Competence rules "provide individuals with *facilities* for realizing their wishes".[37] I do not find this idea satisfying. In the first place, it is incomplete in that it does not indicate *who* has the competence. Secondly, as will be argued below, it does not give an altogether correct description of the function competence rules have when legal systems are used.

In my opinion, competence rules are a special kind of *mandatory*, duty-imposing norms, addressed to the persons who have the competence. Their standard form is

(SF Comp) If *LP* is to be brought about in *LP*′, then persons belonging to *X* shall do *A*

where *LP* and *LP*′ are legal positions, *X* a set of persons and *A* an action-type.

In order to rule out what the Germans call "*Deliktsfähigkeit*", i.e., the "competence" of a criminal to change his legal position by committing a crime, I follow Raz[38] and Spaak[39] in laying a restriction upon *A* to the effect that competence is restricted to actions which the legislator *aims to* qualify as the exclusive means of changing legal positions. That is obviously not the case with committing crimes or being negligent.

As we see, SF Comp is "the reverse" of Atienza's and Ruiz Manero's standard form. The "object" of the competence ("the what") is presented in the antecedent, and "the who" and "the how" (the action enjoined) in the consequent. Thus the normative character of the competence rule is brought about in a distinct way. Hence, the structure of the rules in examples (1)–(4) above can be rendered:

(1′) If *LP* is to be brought about in *LP*′, then persons over 16 years shall do *A*
(2′) If *LP* is to be brought about in *LP*′, then persons over 18 years shall do *A*
(3′) If *LP* is to be brought about in *LP*′, then the *Riksdag* shall do *A*
(4′) If a decision to detain someone is to be valid in *LP*′, then the court shall do *A*.

[33] Atienza and Ruiz Manero (1998), p. 61 f.
[34] Atienza and Ruiz Manero (1998), p. 59.
[35] Spaak (1994), p. 178.
[36] Hart (1994), p. 28.
[37] Hart (1994), p. 27.
[38] Raz (1998), p. 452 f.
[39] Spaak (1994), p. 17 ff.

(2) is what we may call "a negatively formulated" competence rule ("may not").

Is it necessary that *LP* and *LP′* are non-identical? No, I do not think so. Suppose that a creditor has a competence to suspend the time for barring by limitations by means of notifying the debtor of his claim. Then he must do a certain action in a legal position in order to maintain this same legal position.

Let me make some remarks on SF Comp. First it could be said that, if competence rules cannot be permissions since the action by which a legal position is brought about can be forbidden, this objection must (*a fortiori*) apply to competence rules interpreted as duty-imposing rules. But, as I have constructed SF Comp, it escapes this objection, since the duty here concerns exclusively the successful bringing about of a legal position by some action. If some other rule in the system forbids this action it is another matter.

Secondly, if we regard competence rules as permissions, something important concerning the function of competence rules is left out. The legislator certainly demands observance of competence rules. Such rules are no "empty" rules of the game. They usually have an important social function. Assigning competence to a certain kind of persons (and no others), and working out the kind of actions (and no others) these persons have to perform, is no random matter but usually based on weighty social reasons.

Thirdly, looking upon competence rules as technical rules does not, for the same reason, fully capture the social function of competence rules. That they provide individuals with facilities for realising their own wishes, as Hart argues, is certainly true. But it is not the whole truth. From the viewpoint of "the player", i.e., the person who exercises her competence, it may come natural to conceive of competence rules that way. But from the viewpoint of the legislator the social function of the competence rules is what matters and that is why he demands observance of them. The legislator wants something more from the competence rules than only providing facilities. *LP* is not good enough unless it is produced by a member of *X* (and no others) by means of a member of *A* (and no others). Of course, if the competence rules are optional (as could be the case in contract law) the facility aspect is more prominent.

Another kind of validity rules are *form-prescribing rules*. (I do not think that there are any other kinds of validity rules than these two). Form-prescribing rules (e.g., a rule requiring written form for purchase of real estate) stipulate, for the same reason as competence rules, necessary conditions for actions being valid or invalid.

Validity rules, then, are norms in that those subject to the legal system in question shall "play the game", i.e., adapt their actions to what validity and invalidity demand in that respect. The addressee shall use the rule correctly. A validity rule is broken if this is not the case, i.e., when a person acts *ultra vires* or does not bother about prescribed forms—or, in other words, if he uses the rule incorrectly.

A *statutory manifesto* is a statutory provision expressing the purpose (in a wide sense) of the statute it belongs to. Typical statutory manifestos are, e.g., the so-called preambles of the European Union Law. Their function is to serve the teleologically inclined European Court of Law in its interpretative work. They are normative at least in that the Court shall take them into consideration and broken if the Court does not do so.

Substantially related to statutory manifestos—although expressed as ordinary legal obligations—are certain moral appeals now and then appearing in statutory texts. Technically they have a more or less cosmetic role. In the Swedish Marriage Code (Chapter 1, Article 2) we find the provision "Spouses shall show each other fidelity and consideration. They shall together take care of home and children and in consultation with each other devote themselves to the good of the family" [my trans.]. This wise and beautiful provision could be removed from the code without any change of the Swedish law of marriage whatsoever resulting from it.

I assign *permissions* to the category editorial rules. The reason is the following. Permissions might seem an odd sort of legal rules, since a genuine permission can never be broken. However, when permissions, this notwithstanding, occur in statutes, they have a function which can be called "editorial". Sometimes they are redundant in that they are intended to emphasise that some action is optional, although that follows from the legal system anyway. More often, I think, they are complementary to other rules in that they state exceptions from these rules in accordance with the pattern principal rule-exception, i.e., from prohibitions or, with negated norm-theme, from obligations. Permissions have the same standard form as ordinary regulative rules.

Qualificatory rules[40] (statutory definitions) play a more mediate role in the legal system than validity rules and permissions. Their function is to qualify (or, perhaps better, classify) *non-legal phenomena* such as human beings, actions, states of affairs, things, etc., and relations between them, by making *legally relevant distinctions* between them. Such distinctions are made by means of legal rules, i.e., qualificatory rules, in which the distinguishing criteria are formulated. Just as is the case with validity rules, qualificatory rules are normative in that they shall be used by persons subject to ("playing the game of") the legal order in question—and broken if such persons do not do that. They belong to the rules of the game. Some people are Swedish citizens, others are not, some actions are acts-in-the-law or criminal acts, others not, some chattels are fixtures to real estate, others not, some human relations are marriages or limited liability companies, others not.

Qualificatory rules have a defining function. If one wants to state the necessary as well as jointly sufficient conditions for a concept, one usually does so in the form of an explicit definition. Also legislators do so, viz. by means of statutory definitions. But definitions can also be implicit. In a great many provisions the fact that somebody is married is a requisite among others. If we would explicitly formulate a statutory definition of the term "marriage" ("X is married to Y") implicit in, e.g., Swedish legal rules, we must mobilise a huge amount of provisions about the entering into and dissolving of a marriage (X is married to Y if he has entered into a marriage with Y and that marriage is not dissolved), which provisions contain among other things competence rules and ordinary rules of action addressed to

[40]The term coined by Prof. Tore Strömberg, Lund.

people officiating at weddings, judges etc. A law-applier breaks a qualificatory rule if he does not use the definiens for the definiendum, when the definiendum is a requisite in a legal rule. I suggest the following standard form for qualificatory rules:

(SF Qual) If term t appears in the provision p, then the addressee of p shall substitute t' for t when making use of p.

Rules with a defining function of a weaker character than qualificatory rules are *statutory guidelines* (or principles), as I shall call them. They are normative in that they indicate factors that the law-applier shall take into consideration when deciding whether a provision is applicable to some state of affairs or not. Let me give an example. In the Swedish Criminal Code, Ch. 3, Article 6, paragraph 1, the crime gross assault is defined (by means of a qualificatory rule in the preceding article). Then it is added: "When judging whether the crime is gross shall particularly be taken into consideration if the act was fatal or if the offender has inflicted severe bodily injury or serious illness or otherwise shown particular ruthlessness or brutality" [my trans.]. Guidelines are arguments fixed in the form of statutory provisions. The law-applier breaks a guideline when he omits taking into consideration the factors enumerated. But he does not necessarily break the guideline if any of the factors mentioned is present, but he nevertheless does not sentence the offender for gross assault but for assault *simpliciter*. For he may have weighed such a factor against other factors pointing in the opposite direction and attached greater importance to the latter.

Statutory guidelines have a (weaker) defining function in that they contribute to the clarification of some requisite in another provision. Paragraph 2 in our example contributes to making the concept "gross assault" more precise. The reason why the circumstances mentioned there are not included in the definition in paragraph 1 is that they can be "overruled" by other circumstances. The standard form of the statutory guideline can be formulated:

(SF Guide) If a law-applier shall decide whether a certain state of affairs is to be qualified as *LP*, then he shall take into consideration factors $f_1, \ldots f_n$.

Goal-Regulation

As mentioned above *goal-directives* are rules formulating some (general, abstract or more specific) goals but leaving the choice of the means of achieving them to the norm-addressee. As reasons for goal-regulation it has been argued that it may reduce overregulation and, perhaps more important, that it makes it possible for expert knowledge and the shop-floor to have the main influence on the shaping of the means. Both these arguments, however, have been called in question.[41]

A normative system entirely built on goal-regulation consisting exclusively of goal-directives (i.e., without any supplementary rules), is not only logically but also empirically possible. There are three necessary components in a goal-directive, the existence of which makes goal-directives elementary in the same sense of

[41]Valuable contributions to the investigation of goal-regulation have been presented by Westerman (2010) which contains further references.

"elementary" as with respect to traditional legal regulation: (i) an explicit formulation of a goal, (ii) an explicit or implicit indication of an addressee (that can be a public or a private organ), and (iii) a normative component making it obligatory for the addressee (a) to create means of achieving the goal and (b) to further the achievement of the goal with the aid of these means.

Hence, as a standard form for goal-directives could be suggested

(SG-D) *a* shall further *g* by creating and using a means within the limits of the legal system for the purpose of realising *g*

where *a* is a norm-addressee and *g* some goal.

The main difference between goal-regulation and traditional legal regulation is that in the former the goal of the regulation is explicitly stated, while in the latter it must be found out with the aid of interpretation of the statutory provisions.[42]

Such normative systems would, no doubt, be a rather primitive kind of social systems, and they are not likely to appear in the real world. In reality they are usually parts of systems built mainly on traditional legal regulation and, moreover, completed by a set of supplementary rules. While ordinary regulative rules are elementary in a legal system based on traditional legal regulation, such rules are supplementary in a legal system based on goal-regulation. Of course, the more ordinary regulative rules are part of a system based on goal-regulation, the less is the difference between goal-regulation and traditional legal regulation.

When is a goal-directive broken by its addressee? Obviously, it is not necessarily broken if the addressee does not attain the goal. In that respect goal-directives are kindred with statutory guidelines (it is sufficient to "further" and to "take into consideration" respectively). There is also a certain similarity between goal-directives and should-rules—"shall further" has very much the same meaning as "should bring about". A goal-directive is broken (i) when the addressee is not creating and using some device which he in all honesty believes will attain the goal or (ii) when the device is against the law. He is, e.g., breaking the goal-directive if he deliberately creates a device which he knows is counterproductive for the purpose of attaining the goal, either because he is against that goal or out of sheer laziness. He is also breaking the goal-directive if he uses a means, however effective, which is against the law. The legal system as a whole delimits the range of operation for the norm-addressee.

When is goal-regulation appropriate? In the following situations at least, it seems to me: (a) When things are better done at the shop-floor level, (b) when what is important to achieve is some result the importance of which lies in the future—the prospective aspect is the important thing –, e.g., with respect to custody of children, health care and environmental interests, (c) when different, equally good means may exist, and (d) when the legislator is uncertain about appropriate means.

[42]Westerman (2010), p. 216.

When is goal-regulation not appropriate? Generally speaking, when there are strong claims on the qualities of the very means. This is above all the case when people's legal certainty is especially important, e.g., with respect to the use of criminal law, procedural coercive measures, tax law and compulsory commitment for mental health services. However, it could be argued that, within criminal law, while the definition and qualification of what is a crime is not a task for goal-regulation, the choice of sanction could be such a task, since what matters here is to a large extent whether the sanction is appropriate as a means of achieving some good in the future. Here the conflict between legal certainty, legal security and legal equality, on the one hand, and the demands of criminal policy in individual cases, on the other, brings matters to a head.

Let us think of a normative system consisting exclusively of goal-directives (which, as has been argued above, is logically as well as empirically possible). How shall we characterise such a system? Can it reasonably be called a legal system? Perhaps it should rather be called "a policy system". However that may be, it is clear, though, that such a system must be parasitic on a legal organisation provided by a legal order (see Sect. 2.12 below). The goal-directives themselves must be issued by a legislator who cannot be any other than the legislator of the legal order of the state in question. Disputes concerning the interpretation of goal-directives, notably in the form of complaints from "clients", must, as a last resource, be decided by a court of law. And, not least, the control of the addressees of the goal-directives and the sanctions against them must be in the hands of the legal order of the state, which has a monopoly on coercive measures. Generally speaking, the legal order of the state decides the scope of goal-regulation.

Let me in this connection call attention to an important phenomenon appearing in the international legal history of recent decades—we may call it *the grand delegation*. Goal-regulation is an example of this phenomenon. The grand delegation is, roughly speaking, the general tendency in our day to transfer norm-creating competence to bodies outside the national legislatures—be it state authorities or private organisations—or accept norms developed in such organs. The most striking example is the so-called *transnational law*, operating mainly in international commercial life and generally regarded as one of the main manifestations of globalisation. Transnational law embraces very powerful and important private "legal orders". All the same, these private "legal orders" are incomplete and lacking in independence as being parasitic upon national legal orders. They are incomplete in that they are exclusively concerned with special areas of social life. They are parasitic on national legal orders in that in the end they must rely on the resources of the latter. Although private "legal orders" instead of courts of law may have dispute-resolution mechanisms of their own, e.g., arbitration and executive devices built on agreement, national legal orders still claim jurisdiction in these respects. Private awards may conflict with national mandatory rules concerning, e.g., the validity of contracts and even with national criminal law, and when it comes to execution the national legal orders retain their monopoly of force and violent means as well as their competence to interfere in transnational law. We are not, as is often suggested, witnessing the emergence of completely independent legal orders besides the national and public international ones. The grand delegation to private transnational law is in fact an enormous quantitative expansion of the use of the optional, non-mandatory field of legal systems—mainly within the law of contract and property—not an emergence of a completely new kind of legal orders. Transnational law is a cuckoo in the nest of state legal orders.

I shall not go into the causes of the development of phenomena like private transnational law and goal-regulation here. They are not at all completely new, though; we are all familiar with so-called standards—legal rules referring to extra-legal norms, e.g. "sound business practice". Let me only point out the fact that this development is to a large extent welcomed and urged on by the official legislatures. From the viewpoint of sociology and political science the grand delegation is of much interest. From a jurisprudential viewpoint it raises important problems concerning the protection of law-state values such as legal certainty, legal accessibility and legal equality when these new normative orders are handled. On the other hand, the jurisprudential description of these orders is not problematic—the established conceptual apparatus (part of which is investigated in this chapter) has more than enough resources for performing that job.

There are, though, as could be expected, some developments contrary to the grand delegation. Let me give just one example. In the European Union Law we have in later years witnessed a tendency in many areas to substitute more detailed decrees for more open directives.

2.10 "Soft Law"

Our discussion of goal-directives and transnational law prompts us to take a stand on the question of where the line of demarcation is to be drawn between what could properly be called "law" on the one hand and other social norms on the other. A key concept in this connection is "soft law", a concept that in recent times has gained a certain amount of popularity among lawyers. It is usually contrasted with "hard law". What does it mean? Does it have a useful function as a juridical concept? Soft law is often referred to as having no legally binding force. To my mind, the concept "soft law" is both intellectually misleading as a concept depicting legal realities and highly dubitable morally since it blurs certain borderlines which should not be indistinct. We can do better without it.

The concept has emerged from international law. There soft law includes phenomena such as resolutions and declarations (e.g., the UN Universal Declaration of Human Rights), statements, principles, and codes of practice drawn up by international organisations. Ironically enough, the decisive line between hard and soft law is especially difficult to draw in international law, since it could be argued that all international law is soft law. At the present stage of human civilisation the only kind of institution that can claim a general, supreme and heteronomous competence to create social norms binding for people is the state. And from a moral point of view, this argument gets even stronger force with respect to democratic states. It could be claimed that the weaker the connection is between state and norm-creation, the less the norms created are law. The international community is no state. So the only part of international law that can reasonably be designated "hard law" are rules established by treaties between states and decisions of the International Court of Justice, established as it is by states, with respect to the particular parties of the case. The rest of "international law" is better seen as a kind of extra-legal standard to be used for the evaluation of international law in this narrower sense and for providing arguments in law-making and decision-giving. "Soft law" is not a good term for denoting these phenomena, since they are better conceived of as being no law at all but rather a kind of ideal for the law to live up to. That private organisations such as NGOs do not have, nor should have, a heteronomous law-giving competence over people seems to me obvious. Hence, what they produce in the form of social norms is not soft law but no law at all, however excellent the norms might be. According to Article 71 of the UN Charter their status is consultative, which fits with my view of them as a kind of extra-legal standards. My view of "soft law" in international law applies *mutatis mutandis* also to "soft law" in the law of the European Union.

The concept "soft law" has forced its way into the juridical characterisation of domestic law as well. There it is used for denoting many, rather different phenomena. As examples could be mentioned directives and recommendations issued by semi-official and private organisations such as committees of review, (councils on business practices or press fair practices), boards for consumer complaints, trade associations for, e.g., the insurance or banking business, arbitration boards, trade unions, and employers' associations. This use of the concept with respect to national law is even more disastrous than with respect to international law.

For two reasons the term "soft law" is infelicitous for the proper characterisation of the phenomena denoted by it—one empirical and one evaluative. From an empirical point of view "soft law" does not properly mirror legal realities. There is at least one decisive difference between law as we encounter it in statutes and precedents on the one hand, and in directives and recommendations of various kinds produced by semi-official or private organs on the other. The difference is simply that these organs do not have a general heteronomous legal competence to issue *legal* rules at all, binding for members of society at large. Norms given by them are from a legal point of view only recommendations or contractual obligations.

And this is exactly how it should be. The law shall come about in a democratic way. It is not for powerful industrial companies, banks, insurance companies, trade unions, law-firms, etc. to legislate for us. To call this "soft law" is to blur this important distinction and in a way to legitimise "soft law" as law. "Soft law" is pseudo-law (from Greek "ψευδής", "false", "untrue").

A more adequate way of conceptualising the phenomenon "soft law" is, in my opinion, the following. "Soft law" denotes *extra-legal, legally accepted, socially important norms*, ELNs, (I do not want to use the word "system" since these norms are usually too few and too scattered to be conceived of as a system). ELNs are not law but accepted, and sometimes even presupposed, by the law (which rules out possible mafia-created norms playing a socially important role in some unhappy society or another) and they are an important factor in social life. There are two main types of ELNs: *alternative* and *supplementary norms*, i.e., alternative and supplementary to legal rules. (It is a misconception to say that norms created by means of legal rules are necessarily themselves legal rules or even legal norms.)

Alternative ELNs are norms that are created by private persons, and which norms are allowed by legal rules to regulate issues of a legal character *instead of* legal rules covering the same issues. Alternative ELNs are law-substitutes. An example would be so-called standard contracts used by, e.g., insurance companies, associations of landlords and car dealers. Also "transnational law" belongs to this category.

Supplementary ELNs (law-supplements) are norms that are allowed by legal rules to supplement legal rules. The legal rules that allow them are often goal-directives or so-called standards, i.e., rules containing requisites of the type "fair commercial practices" and "generally accepted accounting principles". The filling in of such standards is performed by law-supplements and it is presupposed by the legislators that this will be the case.

The legal order always trumps the ELNs. The legislator can at any time make them illegal by means of legislation. By the way, it is striking to what extent legal orders exert a heavy influence on extra-legal practices and organisations. Legal orders are frequently imitated in many respects, not least with respect to courts of law and the judicial procedure. Private boards, tribunals, etc. often use judicial decision-making as a model.

My view of "soft law" as a non-legal phenomenon does not at all imply that I regard it as uninteresting from the point of view of legal science. The close connection between ELNs and legal orders makes the socially important ELNs a legitimate and suitable object of study for legal science.

2.11 Morphological Level IV: The Level of Legal Systems

What makes a legal system a system? First of all, what is a legal system a system of? The view taken here is that it is a system of legal norms exclusively. Secondly, which connections between the norms of the system make this mass of norms a system? The following four, at least it seems to me. (a) They are connected by having the same genesis, i.e., they all stem from the same set of legal sources. (b) They are connected by virtue of their content, i.e., social matters such as family, work, trade, crime and welfare. (c) They are connected by being handled by legal functionaries belonging to a unique legal organisation which, together with the legal system, constitutes a legal order (on the concept "legal order" see Sect. 2.12 below). (d) They are connected syntactically—in order to apply norms belonging to the system to factual states of affairs and to establish compound legal positions, norms must be coupled together in different ways. (a)–(d) taken together are, I think, sufficient for claiming that sets of norms of this kind are legal systems. Here the syntactical connections are our main concern.

The syntactical (morphological) relations between legal norms (rules) within a given legal system are not the only ones. The relations between legal norms (*legal norm-relations*; henceforth *n-relations*) are many and varied. I shall present a classification of n-relations below. I make a distinction between (i) *system-inherent n-relations*, (ii) *genetic* (*system-transcending*) *n-relations* and (iii) *choice of law-relations*. Within the first group I differentiate between (i.a) *syntactical n-relations* and (i.b) *application-guiding n-relations*. The meaning of these terms will be explained in due course.

But let me first mention two other types of n-relations outside the scope of my classification. The first is of a more general kind, viz. *logical n-relations*. Among these the following two are of special interest from a juridical viewpoint.

(i) The interdefinability of deontic modalities. If we take permission, *Pp* ("it is permitted that *p*"), as the primitive (undefined) concept we can define "it is forbidden that *p*" by means of *Pp* and the negation ("~") as ~*Pp* and "it is obligatory that *p*" as ~*P*~*p*. (ii) Normative collision between norms, e.g., between "it is forbidden that *p* in circumstances *C*" and "it is permitted that *p* in circumstances *C* (or in circumstances C', where C' is a proper subset of *C*). For the lawyer, collision is no doubt looked upon as an accident at work, an accident, however, which now and then actually occurs. But collision can sometimes be used as a legislative device, viz., if the permission is an exception from a prohibition with the status of a principal rule (or the other way round).

The second n-relation outside the scope of my classification is the one between a general legal rule, *gr*, and an individual norm that is the result of an application of *gr* to some case. (That legal rules can be more or less general, or general in different senses, will be shown in Chap. 3.) *I do not regard individual norms, created by means of general norms belonging to a legal system, S, as members of S* (unless an individual norm is raised to the rank of precedent; but, if so, it has become a general rule). My reason for this stance is that the general rules are permanent over longer periods of time and have much more relevance for the citizens in general than the more ephemeral individual norms. The latter are products of the legal system rather than members of it. (The closer relationship between general rules and individual norms will be investigated in Sect. 13.3.2.)

2.11.1 System-Inherent N-Relations

2.11.1.1 Syntactical N-Relations

The juridical syntax is necessitated by the fact that legal systems are elliptical (incomplete). They contain implicit rules which we gather from explicit ones in the system. If each explicit rule in the system was ready-made (complete) for application to each relevant case, no syntax, taken as a type of n-relations, would be needed. The implicit rules are gathered from the explicit ones in a more or less mechanical manner.

Let us divide the syntactical n-relations into four groups: (a) Many–one relations (*supplementing n-relations*), (b) one–many relations (*specifying n-relations*) and

(c) one–one relations (*transforming n-relations*)—where the norms to the left of the hyphen are explicit in the system and the norms to the right are implicit. In a certain sense we can also talk about (d) many–many relations (*connecting n-relations*).

With respect to the lists below I do not claim completeness – there might just as well be other n-relations.

Supplementing N-Relations

(1) A qualificatory (defining) rule supplements another rule in the system. Example: In a Swedish statutory provision (r_1) the word "bus" is defined as "a car mainly constructed for conveyance of passengers and equipped with more than eight seats besides the driver's seat". Another statutory provision (r_2) tells us that "... a bus with a total weight of at the most 3.5 tons ... shall when travelling on a road [defined by another qualificatory rule] be equipped with snow tyres ... 1 December–31 March where there is a winter state of the road". By substituting r_1 for "bus" in r_2 we get the implicit rule r_3 "a car mainly constructed ... the driver's seat with a total weight ... winter state of the road". r_1 is supplementary to r_2 and coupled together they state r_3. Between on the one hand r_1 and r_2, and r_3 on the other, there is a many–one relation.

(2) A mandatory judge-addressed rule supplements a mandatory citizen- addressed rule where both are explicitly stated in statutory provisions. Example: A Swedish rule says. "A road-user shall obey a policeman's instructions as to the traffic" (r_1). In another provision, r_2, we find: "A driver of a motor driven vehicle who intentionally or by carelessness violates what is prescribed in provisions...[r_1] ...shall be sentenced to money fines". r_1 and r_2 imply r_3: "A road-user not obeying a policeman's instructions shall be sentenced ...".

(3) A competence rule and a mandatory obligation to the effect that there is a duty to use the competence in a certain situation supplement each other. Example: A clergyman has a competence to marry people. Supplementing this rule there is another rule to the effect that he has a duty to marry people when at least one of the spouses-to-be is a member of his congregation. If we add together these two rules we get a more complete, implicit rule.

(4) A permission supplements a prohibition, and a permission with a negated norm-theme supplements an obligation, when the prohibition and the obligation are principal rules and the permissions are exceptions. This can be formulated in one single rule.

(5) A supplementary rule supplements a goal-directive by laying restrictions on the way the goal-directive may be implemented. This too can be formulated in one single implicit rule.

(6) "Material" rules and corresponding procedural ones usually appear separately, often in different statutes. Example: Divorce is regulated in one place and the rule of jurisdiction concerning divorce proceedings in another. Coupled together they constitute an implicit rule in the system.

(7) In many continental European legal systems a division is made between "a general part" and "a special part" of some field of law, appearing apart from each other, e.g., in criminal or civil law. Example: The rule of criminal intent is formulated in the general part and shall be used together with the description of

the different crimes described in the special part. Coupled together they too constitute an implicit rule in the system.

Specifying N-Relations

(8) These are one–many *n*-relations. An explicitly expressed rule is a carrier of two (or more) implied rules. There are legal rules, in practice statutory provisions, which are logically unspecified in that they in fact consist of two (or more) distinct legal rules—and this can be revealed by a purely logical analysis of the former. Example: In the Swedish Code of Parents and Children, Ch. 9, Art. 2a, we find the following formulation: "A minor with a household of his own may for daily housekeeping perform such legal transactions as are customarily performed for these purposes". In fact, in this rule two different ones are pupated, a competence rule and a permission. Transactions performed in accordance with the provision are valid (the minor has competence to make valid transactions) and the minor is also permitted to perform them.

Transforming N-Relations

These are one–one *n*-relations. One explicitly formulated rule is transformed into another, implied rule.

(9) The relation between a not explicitly stated judge-addressed norm and a corresponding explicitly stated citizen-addressed norm, where the former is constructed by means of the latter (to be investigated in Chap. 4).

(10) The relation between a not explicitly stated citizen-addressed norm and a corresponding explicitly stated judge-addressed norm, where the former is constructed by means of the latter (also to be investigated in Chap. 4).

Connecting N-Relations

(11) These are many–many *n*-relations. What I have in mind here are connections between legal rules of the kind that was analysed and vividly discussed in the so-called Scandinavian debate on rights in the 1940s and 1950s.[43] What we connect are two or more rules establishing the existence of a compound legal position and two or more rules stating the legal consequences (the significance) of being in that legal position. (By contrast with the supplementing, specifying and transforming *n*-relations, rules on both sides of the " – " can be implicit in the system.) The coupling is made by means of so-called intermediate concepts. Between the first group of rules and the intermediate concept there is a many–one relation and between the intermediate concept and the latter group of rules there is a one–many relation. Let us take "ownership" as an example of such an intermediate concept. Suppose that we have the following alternative rules establishing ownership:

(i) If someone has bought a thing and . . ., he owns it
(ii) If someone has been given a thing and . . ., he owns it

[43]For a survey, see Sundby (1968), p. 72-107.

(iii) If someone has inherited a thing and. . ., he owns it.

In order to make these rules complete we have to fill in the space "..." with requisites like "has not subsequently sold the thing or given it away or . . .".

Suppose further that we have the following conjunction of legal consequences of ownership:

(a) If someone owns a thing and . . ., he may use it
(b) If someone owns a thing and . . ., he has a competence to sell it
(c) If someone owns a thing and . . ., he may destroy it.
(d) If someone owns a thing and . . ., he has a duty to pay tax.

In order to make these rules complete we have to fill in the space "..." with further restricting requisites.

The rules (i)–(iii) on the one hand and (a–d) on the other are in a many-many relation to each other.

The function of the use of intermediate concepts is "economic". By means of "ownership", the relevant rules can be expressed in seven ones by addition: ((i)–(iii) + (a)–(d)). Take away the intermediate concept, and the same set of rules must be expressed in 12 rules by multiplication (3 × 4): ((i) + (a)) + ((i) + (b)), + . . ., + ((iii) + (d)).

Notice that the term "own" in rules (i)–(iii) has another meaning than it has in rules (a)–(d). In the first case it is an abbreviation of a conjunction of legal consequences, in the latter it is an abbreviation of a disjunction of operative facts. Rules of these kinds are in fact qualificatory rules (statutory definitions).When the term appears in (i)–(iii) it is the *definiendum* of "ownership" in terms of its legal significance (consequences), indicated in (a)–(d) as the *definiens*. When it appears in (a)–(d) it is the *definiendum* of "ownership" in terms of its origin and extinction, indicated in (i)–(iii) as the *definiens*.

2.11.1.2 Application Guiding N-Relations

These relations hold between some rule(s), *r*, in the system and some other rule, *g*, in the system, where *g* is giving guidance as to the application of *r*.

(1) *g* gives guidance with respect to the interpretation of *r*. This can be done by means of statutory guidelines pertaining to particular rules or in a more general way where *g* attaches to many rules. Example: The Swedish Freedom of the Press Act, Ch. 1, Art. 4 reads: "Anyone entrusted with the task of judging concerning abuse of the freedom of press or otherwise of seeing to the observance of this Act ought always to keep in mind that the freedom of press is a foundation of a free type of society, and always pay attention to contrariety to the law more with respect to the topic and the thought rather than with respect to

the expression, more with respect to the purpose than to the style, and when unsure give the author the benefit of the doubt".

(2) *g* gives guidance with respect to the evaluation of evidence concerning some legal fact corresponding to a requisite in *r*. The French Code Civil, Art. 1315, reads: "Celui qui réclame l'exécution d'une obligation doit la prouver. Réciproquement, celui qui se pretend libéré, doit justifier le paiement ou le fait qui a produit l'extinction de son obligation". ["Anyone claiming execution of an obligation shall prove it. Correspondingly, anyone asserting to have been released from an obligation shall confirm the payment or the fact that has produced the extinction of his obligation".] This rule guides the evaluation of evidence with respect to legal facts pertaining to requisites in several other "material" rules in the Code Civil.

2.11.2 Genetic (System-Transcending) N-Relations

The relations pertaining to juridical genetics are about the creation of *new* rules—not rules which are implicit in the legal system—by means of existing and explicitly stated rules, and the new rules are *detached* from the rules by which they are created. Juridical genetics deals with the production of legal rules. Let me mention two important genetic norm-relations.

(1) The relation between a competence rule, *cr*, and the rule(s) created by means of *cr*.
(2) The relation between explicitly stated legal rules and rules created on the basis of them by means of analogical, extensive, reductive, restrictive or *e contrario* use of the former. Not least with respect to this kind of genetic relations, the topological aspects are crucial and, indeed, inescapable. Analogy, for instance, amounts to creating a rule, r', for application to a case, c', with the help of an existing rule, *r*, as applied to a case *c*. For this reason I call these norm-relations *genetic-topological norm relations*. (They will be investigated in Chap. 8.)

2.11.3 Choice-of-Law Relations

Members of this kind of *n*-relations can be either system-inherent or system-transcending, but I assign them to a category of their own due to their special function in the juridical use of legal systems, viz. to—by means of a certain set of rules (*choice-of-law rules*)—make a choice between two (or more) rules applicable to a given case. A choice-of-law relation is a relation between at least three different norms. The general structure of a choice-of-law relation is

(CLR) According to r_1, r_2 shall be preferred to r_3 with respect to application to case *c*.

Let me mention four types of choice-of-law relations (and, accordingly, four types of choice-of-law rules).

(1) The relation between *coherence rules*—choice-of-law rules solving problems which arise when a legal system is inconsistent or incoherent, i.e., when rules within the system either collide logically or compete in different respects—and the corresponding colliding or competing rules. As for this type of choice-of-law relations, all norms so related belong to the same legal system—they are system-inherent. (Coherence rules are investigated in Chap. 10.)
(2) The relation between *international choice-of-law rules* (studied in private international law (conflict of laws)) and the rules in the competing national legal systems. This is, of course, a system-transcending relationship. (The crucial concept in this relation, "connecting factor", is investigated in Chap. 11.)
(3) The relation between *transitional rules* and rules in two different competing momentary legal systems within the same intertemporal legal system. Example: In the law of some country the rules are changed as regards the relation between spouses in matters of property. A transitional provision is issued to the effect that, concerning marriages entered into before the new regulation has come into force, the older law, in force when the marriage was entered into, shall be applied, not the new one. (Intertemporal problems will be dealt with in Chap. 12.)
(4) The relation between *extra-national choice-of-law rules*, a rule in a national (state) legal system and a rule in a "non-national legal system". Such "non-national legal systems" are mainly rules created by private persons by means of contracts or commercial, or local, customs, when rules of a national legal system give them preference to the system's own rules. Such preference rules are extra-national choice-of-law rules, e.g., a statutory provision making some statute optional (cf. p. 52 f. above about "the grand delegation"). An example of such a provision, The Swedish Sale of Goods Act, Art. 3, reads: "The provisions of this statute are not applicable to the extent that something else follows from the contract, from practice established between the parties or from commercial customs or some other custom which must be considered binding on the parties".

2.12 Morphological Level V: The Level of Legal Orders

We have now reached the highest morphological level – the legal order itself. This level is the syntax of all lower levels.

A (well-developed, ideal-typical) legal order, *LO*, is a relation between a set of norms, *N*, and an organisation *O*,—i.e., a set of ordered couples {<*N*, *O*>}—such that

(i) norms in *N* constitute *O*
(ii) the function of *O* is (mainly) to handle norms of *N* (i.e., the task of the functionaries of *O* is to handle norms of *N*)

(iii) the function of *N,* in its totality, is to regulate social life in its fundamental parts and in a comprehensive way
(iv) some part of *O* has the function to settle disputes among persons in accordance with norms in *N* and to take a stand on alleged non-compliance with obligations or prohibitions of *N* (i.e., courts of law)
(v) some part of *O* has the function to impose and execute sanctions (punishment, damages, etc.) on persons under certain conditions, stated by *N*, as the ultimate resource for obtaining the goals of the norms of *N*.[44]

- *A legal system* is any such set, *N*, of norms.
- *A legal rule* is any member of a legal system.
- *A legal position* is a normative relation, deduced from legal rules.
- *A legal organisation* is a special set of legal positions.

The concept "legal organisation" must be a bit more thoroughly explained. Let me offer a preliminary definition of the concept (to be qualified in two important respects below) in the following way:

(*Lorg*) A legal organisation is the set of all organisations (sets of positions) that (i) are deduced from rules in the legal system and (ii) are obligatory according to that system.

A particular organisation belonging to a legal organisation we call *an authority*.

In exactly the same manner as the relationship between a husband and wife, or a seller and a buyer, constitutes sets of legal positions, created deductively from legal norms in the way described above (p. 38), the authorities of the legal organisation are clusters of legal positions constituted by deduction from legal rules. An authority is a set of legal positions. Such positions are relations that exist between persons and it is rules in the legal system that regulate how they come into existence and how they cease to exist as well as what their functions are and how these functions shall be performed. (I have dealt elsewhere with legal orders where the main focus is on the legal system, and where it is on the legal organisation, respectively.[45]) I regard norms as a kind of abstract entities (ideas, thought-contents). Legal positions, including authorities, have the same ontological quality as norms, deductively derived, as they are, from legal norms.

The difference between the members of the legal organisation and other products of the legal system, such as limited companies and marriages, is that the former are *obligatory* according to the legal system. Hence clause (ii) in *Lorg*. There are rules in the system stating, or at least presupposing, that certain bodies shall exist—e.g., the Stockholm Court of Appeal, The Swedish Government, Uppsala University and the Swedish Bar Association, according to the Swedish legal system—while, on the other hand, this is not the case with respect to marriages and limited companies. The legal system does not state, or even presuppose, that such entities *shall* in fact exist.

[44]Cf. Frändberg (2014), Chs. 2 and 9.

[45]Frändberg (2014) pp. 177 f.

It only states that if persons want to create them, this must be done according to rules in the legal system.

The system of relations forming an authority has, among others, the following important features.[46]

(1) These relations are *normative relations.* Certain persons have competence to (or shall, may, or may not) perform certain actions. Such relations can have this or that deontic status, but a characteristic of authorities is that, among these relations, there is always a core of power relations (competence): to persons in authority are assigned powers over the citizens and the former are in a relation of superiority to the latter.

(2) Authorities are usually *institutions.* The legal system defines a number of "places" (positions) such that if a person fulfils certain qualifications, also usually indicated by the legal system, and certain other circumstances are at hand, then this person has assumed a position in some authority, she has become a person in authority. And as long as she holds this position, her relations—to the public and to other authorities—are connected to the place in question (according to the legal system).

An institution in an ideal-typical form, as I use the term "institution" here, is an organisation such that a person p_1 can be replaced by another person p_2 in any place in the organisation with the consequence that p_2 in the exchange takes over exactly the same relations within the organisation as those p_1 held at the time. In this sense an authority or a joint stock company is an institution (although not in the ideal-typical form). Hence, if the director-general in the former or the managing director in the latter are replaced, no new authority or joint stock company has come into existence. But if a husband divorces his wife and marries another woman, the same marriage does not continue with another place-holder; rather a new marriage has come about. Marriage is not an institution. The institutional form is necessary for achieving permanence in the legal relations tied to more extensive organisations.

(3) The relation-system that structures an authority can be split up in three functionally different subsystems. (a) An authority has an internal structure of relations, which structure solely concerns the relations between the different positions within that authority. An authority is usually hierarchically constructed with a head person at the top. (b) When an authority is part of a legal organisation, it takes on certain relations to other organs within that organisation. An authority can be superior or subordinate to another authority, it can have a controlling function with respect to another authority, it can be linked to other authorities in different forms of co-operations, etc. (c) Thirdly, and most importantly, authorities are related in a great many (external) ways to private persons, the public. In this connection it is a matter of complicated control and service functions.

[46]Cf. Frändberg (2014) Section 9.2. In order to save my readers the trouble to turn to that book I repeat myself a little here.

Our first qualification of *Lorg* is the following. *Lorg* can be said to define "legal organisation" *in a wide sense* of the term. The legal organisation is a system of authorities. But for jurisprudential purposes it can also be justified to define *Lorg in a strict sense.* This is based on the insight that courts of law play a fundamental role in a proper *legal* organisation. In this sense the legal organisation is seen as including the courts and the organs that are more intimately (although not necessarily) connected to the courts. In the strict sense, a legal organisation is a court-centered organisation.

Such organs that are closely connected to the courts comprise (i) legislative organs, producing the rules that the courts shall apply, (ii) police and prosecution authorities, providing the courts with criminal cases, (iii) executive authorities, executing the judgments of the courts, and (iv) authorities having a controlling function over courts or organs of types (ii)–(iii), or control the administrative authorities with trial at a court as the last resource.

Beyond the legal organisation in the strict sense but belonging to the legal organisation in the wide sense, then, there are such authorities as, e.g., the Swedish Board of Education, the National Board of Fisheries and the Uppsala Public Cleansing Division according to Swedish law.

However—and now we come to the second qualification of *Lorg*—there is one crucial legal function, intimately connected to the judicial function and performed by a certain body in a well-developed legal order, which is conspicuously missing in both definitions: the function of the advocate, the body of the bar association. It differs from the organs (i)–(iv) in the respect that it usually is a private body. Hence, to the legal order in the strict sense we incorporate the body of advocates.

So, in a legal organisation we find the following, typical functions: (1) The law-creating function (performed by legislative assemblies and courts whose decisions have precedential force), (2) the conflict-solving function (performed by courts in civil cases), (3) the breach-of-rule handling function (performed by police and prosecution authorities and criminal courts in a functional co-operation), (4) the executive function (performed by executive authorities and the correctional system), (5) the controlling function (performed by ordinary courts having the competence of judicial review, constitutional courts, international courts of the type the European Court of Human Rights, *Ombudsmen*, etc, and (6) the party-assisting function (performed *par préférence* by members of private bar associations).

To sum up, a legal order consists of a legal system (a system of legal rules) and a legal organisation (obligatory, general legal positions, derived from rules in the system). All these phenomena have a normative character. So, when we say that norms of *N* constitute *O*, we mean that the legal positions which together form *O* are deduced from norms in *N*. On the other hand, position-holders in *O*—people of flesh and blood—create, remove, change, interpret and administer rules in *N*, or give advice to persons how to act given the existence of *N*—in short, they all *handle norms of N* (in that way *maintaining the legal order*). In more developed legal orders we can discern different kinds of position-holders, with corresponding separate professional roles.

The clauses (iii)–(v) in our clarification of the concept "legal order" are justified by the following considerations.

Clause (iii), which states that legal systems have, as it were, general social ambitions—their norms, taken together, regulate social life as a whole and constitute a kind of framework for it—has the function of excluding from the class of legal orders, on the one hand moral systems, and on the other social orders such as trade unions, religious communions (churches) or the Mafia.

Clause (iv) makes the existence of courts of law (or bodies with essentially the same functions) a necessary component of legal orders. For a social order to be a genuine *legal* order, some kind of institution trying disputes and alleged non-compliance with the social norms, which institution is distinct from, and independent of, other, purely administrative authorities, must be a necessary ingredient of a legal order. On the other hand, clause (iv) cannot be a sufficient condition for a social order to be a legal order; also the Mafia may have its special "courts of law".

A social order lacking a mechanism of sanctions (clause (v)) is little more than institutionalised morality. As a last resource legal orders resort to force and violence, and that is a characteristic feature of them. It also seems strange to imagine the existence of courts of law without a mechanism of sanctions attached to them.

Conceived in this way, legal orders are abstract objects: intersubjective systems of ideas, structured normative thought-contents (or meaning-contents) and as such artefacts, products of human culture, usually constructed and amended by a collective effort often ranging over a very long period of time.

By way of excursion, let me say a few words about the relationship between the legal order and the state. The state is a special kind of organisation and, hence, it could seem natural to compare it with the legal organisation in the wider sense. If we do so, the following observations seem to be apt.

Since a legal organisation in the wider sense includes the authorities of the legal order in the stricter sense—as I have defined them—then, if a state is a legal organisation in the wider sense, the state must contain the authorities in the stricter sense. But is it the case that a state is a legal organisation in the wider sense and does a state necessarily include the authorities of a legal organisation in the stricter sense?

(1) A legal order can exist without being a state, and a legal organisation in the wider sense can exist without being a state. Examples include modern supranational organisations such as the European Union. (2) A legal organisation in the stricter sense can exist without a state. States have in fact emerged from rudimentary legal organisations, too embryonic to be called "states". (3) A state can exist without being a legal organisation in the wider sense. We can imagine states organised by means of normative orders other than legal orders, e.g., states ruled in military or religious forms by military or religious organs. Such "non-legal states" can very well be subjected to international law. (4) A state can exist without having a legal organisation in the stricter sense. For examples of such states we must turn to very primitive tyrannies such as that of Idi Amin in Uganda and Pol Pot in Cambodia. The upshot of my observations is that, from a conceptual point of view, states are legal creations in a rather weak sense. There is no such close relation between "legal order" and "state"

as is taught by Kelsen. However, although the necessary, conceptual relation is weak, there is nevertheless a strong empirical connection between the two phenomena. But this strong connection might, seen in a broader historical perspective, turn out to be a merely historical coincidence.

2.13 Legal Phenomena Outside the Legal Order

There are "legal phenomena" outside the legal order. The legal order, however, is at the centre of the realm of legal phenomena, and those outside the legal order are in some way or another necessarily (conceptually) related to legal orders. But the reverse does not hold. While the concepts expressing these phenomena necessarily imply the concept "legal order", the latter does not necessarily imply the former.

The ambition of constructing a general conception of legal phenomena—an ambition I certainly do not have in this book—would be to embrace all conceivable such phenomena within it. But which are those phenomena? Let me here only mention a few of them. Legal phenomena outside the legal order can be (i) actions, (ii) states of affairs other than actions, (iii) human beings, (iv) things and (v) ideas (including normative ideas). Some of them can be called "products" of the legal order. Let us try to bring some order among them by grouping them into five categories.

I. *The factual basis of law* (the legal sources), i.e., certain texts and habits (see Sect. 2.4 above).

II. *Topological phenomena necessary for the application of legal rules.* A necessary condition for a legal rule, *r*, to be applied is that there are phenomena to which *r* can be applied. There must be states of affairs corresponding adequately to the requisites of *r* (*operative facts*), e.g. actions like entering into a contract or committing a murder, states of affairs other than actions like a natural death or a natural disaster, or an individual legal position, i.e., a normative idea such as "X owns the property Y", (see further Chap. 7). Also things can acquire a legal tinge by being referred to in legal rules or presupposed by them, such as courthouses, refrigerators (as appurtenances to real estate), traffic lights and electric chairs.

   Furthermore, there must be persons corresponding adequately to the addressee of *r*, e.g., a seller, a judge or a person liable to pay damages. If there are no such persons a rule in force may become obsolete. There must also be actions corresponding adequately to the norm-theme of *r*, i.e., that which shall, must not or may be done, such as paying the purchase money, exceeding a speed limit or sentencing a murderer to prison.

   In a more mediate relation to the legal order stand *evidentiary facts* in that they are immediately related only to legal states of affairs outside the legal order, viz. operative facts. An evidentiary fact is a state of affairs aimed at proving an operative fact or another evidentiary fact in a chain of such facts ultimately proving an operative fact. Example: A driver is accused of having exceeded a speed limit of 80 km an hour (the operative fact). As a proof the prosecutor refers to the fact that a surveillance camera has recorded 140 km an hour (an evidentiary fact).

III. *Products of the legal order.* There are certain phenomena which can rightly be called products of legal orders, since the very function of legal orders is to produce such phenomena. It is important to separate between products of legal orders and the legal orders themselves. Two groups of such products are of special importance.

   (1) Individual legal norms as well as judgments and other legal decisions such as "A is sentenced for arbitrary conduct to a fine of 5,000 kronor" or "B is the lawful owner of Blackacre".
   (2) Individual, "concretised" legal positions, such as the marriage between A and B, the purchase relation between C and D, the duty of judge E to sentence F to imprisonment for theft, or the set of relations constituting the limited company Volvo.

   Legal micropositions and macropositions are LO-elements. But they are not only LO-elements. They are also elements of products of legal orders such as individual judgments and individualised legal positions—be they micro- or macropositions. That the child is made up of the same kinds of cells as its parents is of course not to be wondered at. But that is no reason for including such positions in the legal order.

IV. *Justificatory bases of legal rules.* By this I refer to arguments aimed at justifying legal rules. Such arguments (in German called *Rechtsgründe*, "legal bases") usually rest upon an instrumental view of legal orders. (The character of justificatory bases will be investigated in Sect. 9.3.4.)

V. *Juridical ideas.* Such ideas—not in the law but about the law—constitute together the juridical world of ideas, technical as well as evaluative (normative), roughly presented in Chap. 1—morphological concepts, principles of statutory interpretation, the law-state values, etc. Ideas of this kind are what this book is actually about.

2.14 Concluding Remark

What this chapter has dealt with is legal orders "immediately" created, applied and otherwise handled by human beings. However, we envisage a future where all these things might be performed by "virtual", or "artificial", agents (robots), which perhaps can even be placed in legal positions. The consequences of this for the shaping of legal orders and their handling in the future remain to be seen.

References

Alchourrón CE, Bulygin E (1971) Normative systems. Springer, Berlin
Atienza M, Ruiz Manero J (1998) A theory of legal sentences. Springer, Berlin
Bentham J (1970) Of laws in general (The collected works of Jeremy Bentham: principles of legislation). Athlone Press, London
Eckhoff T, Sundby NK (1991) Rettssystemer (Legal systems), 2nd edn
Frändberg Å (2014) From Rechtsstaat to universal law-state. Springer, Berlin
Hart HLA (1994) The concept of law, 2nd edn. Clarendon Press, Wotton-under-Edge
Hohfeld WN (1917) Fundamental legal conceptions as applied in judicial reasoning. Yale Law J 26:710 ff
Hume D (1984) In: Mossner EC (ed) A treatise of human nature (1739–40). Clarendon Press, Wotton-under-Edge
Kanger S, Kanger H (1966) Rights and parliamentarism. Theoria 32:85–115
Kanger S (1972) Law and logic. Theoria 38:105–132
Kelsen H (1992) Introduction to the problems of legal theory, translated from German by B. Litschewski Paulson and S. L. Paulson
Lindahl L (1977) Position and change, a study in law and logic. Springer, Berlin
MacCormick N, Weinberger O (1986) An institutional theory of law. New approaches to legal positivism. Springer, Berlin
MacCormick DN, Summers RS (1991) Interpreting statutes. A comparative study. Routledge, Abingdon
Raz J (1975, reprinted 1990) Practical reason and norms, Princeton University Press, Princeton
Raz J (1980) The concept of a legal system, 2nd edn. Clarendon Press, Wotton-under-Edge
Raz J (1998) Voluntary obligations and normative powers. In: Paulson SL, Litschewski Paulson B (eds) Normativity and norms. Critical perspectives on kelsenian themes. Oxford University Press, Oxford, p 452 f
Ross A (1959) On law and justice. The Lawbook Exchange, Ltd, Clark
Searle J (1969) Speech acts. Cambridge University Press, Cambridge
Searle J (1995) The construction of social reality. Free Press, Florence
Spaak T (1994) The concept of legal competence. Dartmouth Pub Co, London
Strömberg T (1988) Rättsordningens byggstenar (the building stones of the legal order). Studentlitteratur, Lund
Sundby NK (1968) Legal right in Scandinavian analyses. Nat Law Forum 13:72–107
von Wright GH (1963) Norm and action. Springer, Berlin
Wellman C (1978) Legal rights, in Uppsalaskolan - och efteråt (The Uppsala School of Legal Philosophy – and afterwards), Acta Universitatis Upsaliensis. In: Symposia Universitatis Upsaliensis Annum Quingentesimum Celebrantis, vol 6. pp 213–221
Westerman P (2010) Arguing about goals: the diminishing scope of legal reasoning. Argumentation 24:211–226

Chapter 3
The Juridical Rule Thinking

3.1 Introduction

In Sect. 1.3 above I presented some "juridical modes of thinking". One of these I termed "the rule thinking". In the present chapter I shall consider this mode of thinking in some of its aspects. In Sect. 3.2 I will elaborate on the function of legal rules in juridical thinking. In Sect. 3.3 I present some reflections on what kind of entities legal rules, as well as the other LO-elements, are, i.e., on the ontological status of these phenomena. Finally, I elaborate on the fact that legal rules can differ with respect to their generality (Sect. 3.4) as well as to their "strength" (Sect. 3.5).

3.2 The Function of Legal Rules in Juridical Thinking

What to a large extent characterises the jurisprudence and legal philosophy of the late nineteenth and the twentieth centuries is what has been called "rule scepticism".[1] Historically, it can to some extent be seen as a reaction to what we could call "the idea of completeness" in nineteenth century positivism, having its most spectacular expression in French juridical thinking after the passing of the *Code Civil*, and still informing the way French judges write their judgments. The idea of completeness has it that the law, notably the statutes, are complete in the sense that any case whatsoever can be decided by means of already existing rules. The legal system is complete.

A variant of rule scepticism *in extremis* is, of course, the claim of Scandinavian realists that there are no legal rules at all. But apart from that we find from the late nineteenth century and onwards a strong negative reaction against what has been

[1] We find that term in Frank (1949a), p. 73; and Hart (1961), p. 132. A far-reaching rule scepticism is expressed by Frank (1949b), section 46.

Å. Frändberg, *The Legal Order*, Law and Philosophy Library 123,
https://doi.org/10.1007/978-3-319-78858-6_3

characterised as "rule absolutism", meaning in the first place the idea of completeness and the idea of extreme legalism, or formalism. The critique, although appearing in the most varying shapes, still has a common tendency: to clear away the whole arsenal of false fronts and sundry junk in the shape of strained definitions of legal phenomena and methodological conjuring tricks which were regarded as characteristic especially of continental positivism. Ihering's "jurisprudence of interests", Gény's "libre recherche scientifique", the German free law movement (the *Freirechtslehre*), American and Scandinavian legal realism and also Kelsen's pure theory of law, to mention a few, can all be regarded as an expression of sobering down, of connection with reality and, at least as for the realists and Kelsen, of a more scientific attitude. Against the *Paragraphenrecht* of the older school, the free law movement pleads for a *freie Rechtsfindung*, where (a sense of) justice should be the guiding-star of the judge's decision-making. Although normativity is central to Kelsen's theory, he has a realist's view on the application of law. When judging, the judge does not just perform a deduction with a general rule and a description of the case as premises and an individual norm as a conclusion, but is in fact creating law. The traditional methods of interpretation are only false fronts, behind which the lawyers hide their law-making activities. The idea that it is the courts that are the real law-makers is also basic in the legal theory of one of the "founding fathers" of American legal realism, Gray. "The courts put life into the dead words of the statute", he exclaims expressively.[2] Ross, to conclude this list of examples of different kinds of rule scepticism, argues that the juridical technique of argumentation is not a decision-making technique but a technique of legitimation. By means of the juridical technique of argumentation the judge erects a façade—the traditional principles of statutory interpretation are mere tools for legitimising the decision. They do not determine the result—it is the result that determines them.[3]

The main objections to the juridical rule thinking can be summarised as follows. Statutory provisions are more often than not vague and ambiguous. It is notoriously difficult to extract a legal rule out of a precedent. Sometimes it is even possible to decide with impunity *contra legem*. Application of law is no simple deduction, it necessarily comprises an evaluation. The formalistic view contributes to alienate legal science and legal education from society. All this is public property from the jurisprudence of the nineteenth and twentieth centuries, and it is hard to exaggerate the value of the more realistic view of administration of law provided by the rule sceptics as contrasted with earlier, to a large extent ideologically determined, misconceptions of it.

However, sometimes one gets the impression that this criticism moves along two different and even contradictory lines. On the one hand it, more or less, attacks legalism, or legal formalism, which is conceived of as an illusion, not to say a sham. What is criticised then is that judges feel obligated to be *more* bound to statutes and precedents than they should be. On the other hand, critics argue that judges actually

---

[2]Gray (1921), p. 125.

[3]Ross (1959), p. 151 ff.

deliberately take into consideration other factors than statutes and precedents but that they *conceal* this by means of a false technique of legitimation. In the first case what is considered wrong is legal formalism, in the second a kind of betrayal. What most rule sceptics want is, of course, less formalism and, to use a vogue word of today, more transparency.

I find it useful to distinguish two positions of rule scepticism, let us call them moderate and radical rule scepticism. Moderate rule scepticism takes the standpoint that reference to applicable rules extracted from ordinary sources of law, in the first place statutes and precedents, comprises the most important but not the only arguments involved in the administration of law. Also, e.g., consequentialist arguments, arguments built on justice and other moral considerations, and a common sense of justice influence the outcome—although arguments of the latter kind are often not explicitly spelled out. Nowadays moderate rule scepticism probably appears to most of us as pretty trivial.

Radical rule scepticism is something much stranger. It is the standpoint that the judge is never—perhaps with the exception of utterly clear cases—guided by the standard sources of law. What—consciously or unconsciously[4]—actually determines the outcome are factors of the kind just mentioned. Reference to statutes and other standard sources of law are only devices in the service of the façade legitimation. We find advocates of this view in the German free law movement and in American realism.

Here something must be utterly wrong. In Sweden, to take an example, thousands of pages of statutory texts are produced each year. The parliament and other state organs producing these texts are obviously doing this with a view to the texts being loyally followed by their addresses, thereby resulting in the social state of affairs that these organs consider desirable. But if judges and other law-applying functionaries were guided by other, entirely different matters than the law, and the law were only a façade, we would be confronted with a huge social swindle, or a self-deception of almost unrivalled proportions. Either this is the case, or otherwise much that has been written in jurisprudence over the last hundred years or so is highly exaggerated or, in fact, totally wrong. For my part I am inclined to espouse the latter standpoint.

Anyone with the slightest familiarity with actual juridical reasoning knows that moderate rule scepticism is nearest to the truth. In clear cases the judge probably applies the law more or less automatically. In hard cases he seeks first of all, where statutory interpretation is involved, guidance in precedents and perhaps *travaux préparatoires*, and when rules are lacking he uses rules in the system analogically. But moderate rule scepticism does not at all deny that other considerations also play a role. However, in Western "judge ideology" such considerations are conceived of as secondary and complementary, and this is no doubt a "living" ideology. Radical rule scepticism is in fact not realistic. Later in the present work we shall have a thing or two to say about application of law and statutory interpretation.

---

[4]See Frank (1949b), Law and the Modern Mind, where we find a psychoanalytic variant of American realism.

However, it would be a great mistake to conclude that, by rejecting rule absolutism—extreme legalism and façade legitimation—the juridical rule thinking is also thereby rejected. This is not the case. We can without inconsistency adhere to moderate, and even radical, rule scepticism and still consider it valuable for lawyers to "think in rules". For an important distinction must in this connection be made. It is one thing to claim or reject formalism as a fact or as an ideal, quite another is the more general matter of how to make up one's mind on how to most fittingly construct the basic categories of juridical thinking. The former concerns the relation between a normative idea and its application to a case. The latter has a wider scope in juridical thinking. Whatever stand we take with respect to formalism there is nothing to prevent us from regarding the legal rule as a useful tool for, and a basic category in, juridical thinking in general.

Let me elaborate on this idea a little further. The juridical rule thinking is valuable in at least the following four, partly overlapping, respects.

(1) It is a most useful *"unit of information"*. Suppose that a foreigner comes to your country, totally ignorant of the law of your land. If you want to assist him in legal matters in your country, which way of doing so would be clearer and more intelligible than formulating your information according to the scheme:

In circumstances . . ., you shall (may not, may) do . . .?

Perhaps our foreigner wants to get answers to questions such as:

(i) I am in circumstances *C*. In what legal position am I (i.e., what may I, may not or shall do)?
(ii) I want to do action *a*. In what circumstances may I do *a*?
(iii) I am in *C* and contemplate doing *a*. Is *a* permitted, forbidden or perhaps even obligatory?

In all these cases the questioner can be given a clarifying answer (if there is one) by filling in information in the blanks of the scheme. The usefulness of the rule scheme is also evident in the legal education.

In addition to this, incidentally, legal rules can in a more implicit way be carriers of information in many other respects. In fact, legal rules such as statutory provisions are often highly pregnant with information about a good deal; they can be looked upon as a concentration of relevant knowledge. For this reason the formulation of the rule may give an intimation of the arguments which prompted the issuing of the rule, and we can often understand which social states of affairs the legislator has found desirable—a putting together of a bunch of legal rules may convey the picture of his ideal society. Not least in a historical perspective the formulation of legal rules can give an illuminating picture of the problems confronting people in the society in question at a certain period of time in the past. Closely connected with legal rules being regarded as information units is the fact that legal rules can be conceived of as a kind of elliptical arguments—a judge sentencing a thief to imprisonment with reference to a statutory provision in the criminal code can in a sense be said to base his judgment on the arguments that inspired the legislator to issue that provision.

(2) The legal rule scheme provides us with an effective *mould* for structuring our normative ideas. In the case of legislation this is too obvious to waste words on. But it can also prove helpful to judges and others interpreting precedents. For expressing the basic idea of a precedent (its *ratio decidendi*) the scheme is highly appropriate (not least to the interpreter himself). Perhaps even more important, interpretations of statutory provisions are themselves best looked upon as legal rules. Also when alternatives to valid legal rules are proposed, e.g., in connection with a critique of such rules (in discussions *de lege* or *de sententia ferenda*), the discussions have much to gain by the use of the scheme, with the aid of which *alternative rules* can be formulated.

(3) Legal rules as units are excellent *building stones*, which I take the liberty to claim that I have shown in a satisfactory way in Sect. 2.11 above. In addition to what has been said there it seems to me that legal rule-units are the natural objects of the systematisation of the law (see Sect. 1.4 above). Legal rules are highly portable, as it were,—they can, without change, be connected to other rules for different purposes and they can unchanged be transported from one kind of dogmatic systematisation to another.

(4) The concept "legal rule" is extremely important as *a basic concept* in many different respects (although I regard "legal order" as even more basic). Remove "legal rule" from the system of basic juridical concepts and it would drag a considerable amount of other essential juridical concepts, more or less bound together and in different ways conceptually tied to "legal rule" with it, viz., the morphological ones (e.g., "requisite", "legal consequence", "claim", "duty", "competence rule", "legal system", "legal order"), the topological ones (e.g., "operative fact", "analogous application", "retroactivity"), at least some praxeological ones (e.g., "application" "validity") and at least some methodological ones (e.g., "literal", "intentional" and "consequentialist statutory interpretation").

In order to mould a concept "legal rule" suitable as a category of juridical thinking some claims on its formation must be made. At least the following six seem to me to be indispensable.

(C1) The concept formation shall capture the specifically juridical use of the concept "legal rule", not the use the term may have in, e.g., sociology or the psychology of law.

(C2) Our concept "legal rule" shall, on the other hand, be extensive enough to be of use for all requirements legal practice as well as legal science can have for it.

A reason for a highly extensive concept is that it gives us the possibility to make important distinctions within this category. For instance, lawyers make use of a concept "valid legal rule", where the set of valid legal rules is regarded as a proper subset of the set of legal rules. If this distinction is not to be totally pointless, there is no reason to define "valid legal rule" so widely that it becomes more or less identical to "legal rule" *simpliciter*, as is now and then the case, e.g., among American realists. Or, put in another way, if the distinction shall have some meaning, we must be able to distinguish an interesting category of non-valid rules. (On the concept "validity" see Sect. 13.4.)

In Sect. 2.12 I defined "legal rule" as a norm belonging to a legal system. And that is, no doubt, the central meaning of the term. Let us refer to such rules as "legal rules in a stricter sense". However, in their work lawyers often handle different types of norms that are not legal rules in the stricter sense, but have a great structural and functional similarity to such legal rules. There are good reasons to characterise also such norms as legal rules—let us call them "legal rules in a wider sense". They are rules that could be legal rules in the stricter sense with respect exclusively to their morphological structure and function. When talking about legal rules in a wider sense what I have in mind is, e.g., rules that once were (valid) legal rules but are no more (e.g., Roman Law), rules appearing in a proposed bill that can become (valid) legal rules in the future, private norms created by the consent of statutory provisions (contracts), rules created by courts of law by analogy from valid legal rules, rules proposed *de lege ferenda* by some legal scientist, etc. Since we also have the category "valid legal rule" at our disposal we can, I think, allow ourselves to be a little more generous in our use of the term "legal rule". Often when lawyers talk about legal rules, this is an elliptical way of referring to valid legal rules, being by far the most important subcategory of legal rules. With this in mind, it might be easier to accept my wide denotation of the concept "legal rule".

(C3) In the concept "legal rule" no more than what is necessary shall be inserted for the concept to function in juridical thinking.

While C2 concerns the denotation of the concept, C3 concerns its connotation. C3 is an application of Occam's razor, which has my sympathies. As we see, C1 and C3 are closely connected to each other. From C3 follows that many qualities attachable to legal rules are best left outside the connotation of the concept, e.g., that they actually are applied by legal authorities when actualised, that they are efficient with respect to their capacity of attaining the social goals they are designed for attaining, that they are in accordance with the sense of justice common in society, that they comply with morality or whatever. Of course this does not mean that such qualities are unimportant. But they are not necessary components of the concept "legal rule".

(C4) The concept legal rule must be formed in a way that makes it possible to conceive of legal rules as *units*.

This is best done by constructing standard forms for different types of legal rules (see Sect. 2.9 above). Raz refers to the construction of suitable units as "individuation of rules", and he formulates some claims on how this shall be done.[5]

(C5) The concept "legal rule" shall allow for the shaping of fruitful syntactical relations between the rules, by means of which legal systems can be constructed (see Sect. 2.11 above).

[5]Raz (1980), pp. 140–147.

(C6) The concept "legal rule" shall allow for its capacity as a basic concept to attach fruitful accessory concepts to it. Let me list some examples of such accessory concepts among many others (*r* and *r*′ are rules, *c* is a case):

(i) *r* is *complied with* (*broken*)
(ii) *r* is *applied to c*
(iii) *r* is *efficient* for its purpose
(iv) *r* is *valid*
(v) *r* is *in force*
(vi) *r* is *obsolete*
(vii) *r* is *a consequentialist interpretation* of *r*′
(viii) *r* is *analogous to r*′
(ix) *r* is *applied retroactively* to *c*
(x) *r* guarantees a high degree of *legal certainty* to its addressees.

(Concepts (i)–(ix) will be dealt with later in this work. As for (x) I refer to my book *The Law-State*, Chapter 6.)

3.3 The Ontology of Legal Rules (LO-Elements)

What kind of entity are legal rules—and LO-elements on the whole? What is their ontological status?

This question obviously exceeds the philosophy of law. LO-elements are normative phenomena and must ontologically be lumped together with other normative phenomena, e.g., moral or conventional. And these normative phenomena must in turn ontologically be lumped together with human ideas other than normative ones. So the fundamental question is: What kind of entity are human ideas? Although not particularly a legal philosophical question, it is no doubt of value for lawyers to have some reasonable idea about the nature of the matter they deal with and handle.

By saying this I have already dismissed the view of ontological naturalism that legal rules are behavioural entities (actions). It seems to me that by taking that naturalistic position the normative quality of legal phenomena evaporates altogether. Hägerström and other realists found, correctly, that the "conventional" conception of legal rules did not fit in with naturalism. Legal rules thus conceived do not have real existence. Therefore they redefined the concept. In my view, (i) there are legal rules and (ii) they do not fit in with a behaviouristic naturalistic ontology. What, then, is their ontological status?

I also reject the great importance Kelsen attaches to the distinction between "the world of is" and "the world of ought" as ontologically fundamental. The fundamental distinction is, in my view, not this one but the one between natural (brute) entities on the one hand and human ideas, evaluative/normative or not, on the other. Hence, by the way, legal and juridical ideas both belong to the same ontological category (more on normativity in Chap. 5).

The task of ontology is not to invent (or abolish) "realities". It is to categorise phenomena we already know exist and to try to ascertain in what way they exist (i.e., what it means that they exist). As Bertrand Russell once put it, philosophy can no more than zoology assume the existence of centaurs—and, as G. E. Moore could have put it, philosophy can no more than zoology deny the existence of horses.

From the viewpoint of ontology two questions are in this connection fundamental:

(Q1) What ontological categories ("realities") are there?
(Q2) To which "reality" belong human ideas?

Some things exist independently of the existence of human beings, others do not. To the latter category belong (trivially) human ideas. In that respect these are subjective, i.e., necessarily tied to human beings—no human beings and there are neither human languages nor legal orders. But how are they tied? This question is fundamental to the humanistic sciences.

At this point Popper's three world ontology comes to the fore.[6] Against a monist (or even dualist) conception of "the universe" he proposes a pluralist view. World 1 consists of "physical bodies: of stones and of stars; of plants and of animals; but also of radiation, and of other forms of physical energy". World 2 is "the mental or psychological world, the world of our feelings of pain and of pleasure, of our thoughts, of our decisions, of our perceptions and our observations". World 3 is "the world of the products of the human mind, such as languages; tales and stories and religious myths; scientific conjectures or theories, and mathematical constructions; songs and symphonies; paintings and sculptures". It is the world of "thought contents". Michelangelo's sculpture *The Dying Slave* "is both a block of marble, belonging to the world 1 of physical objects, and a creation of Michelangelo's mind, and as such belonging to world 3".[7]

In order to justify the theory of world 3, Popper gives us two arguments. The first I shall call "the continuity argument".[8] The continuity argument has it that a thought content, e.g., Einstein's theory of relativity, the play *Hamlet* or, why not, the content of my thought process an hour ago and now forgotten by me "It is probably raining in London", (also the utterly trivial or most obscene thoughts must reasonably have the same ontological status as the most lofty and sublime ones) *exists* at time *t* even if no "corresponding" thought process exists at *t*. Thought contents are ontologically independent of thought processes (although causal relations may exist between them in both directions). The second argument, let me call it "the argument of logic", has it that logical relations can hold only between thought contents, not between mental, or psychological, processes.[9]

[6]First presented in Popper (1972). We find an informative, more concentrated presentation in Popper (1980), pp. 142–167, from which I quote.

[7]Popper (1980), p. 143 f.

[8]This argument is logically implied in Popper's reasoning.

[9]Popper (1980), p. 158.

Popper's ontology is, no doubt, a valuable contribution to philosophical thinking in this notoriously difficult field. However, in certain important respects it seems dubious to me. That there is a world 1 cannot reasonably be denied, but what I find questionable is both the ontological separation of worlds 1 and 2 and the distinction between thought (as thought processes) and thought content, i.e., the ontological separation of worlds 2 and 3.

As for the separation of world 1 (the world of physical bodies) and world 2 (the world of mental states and processes), it is doubtful whether such purely mental processes (world 2 thought processes) exist at all. Could it not be that these processes are in fact brain processes belonging to world 1, although not yet scientifically observed as natural processes? At the present state of knowledge we know very little about what is going on in our brains when we think, i.e., what thought processes actually are. It is a *terra incognita.* What we have is, on the one hand, perceivable cerebral processes studied by neurophysiologists, and on the other, perceivable expressions of thought in speech or writing. But what there is "in-between" for the most part escapes us so far. In the present situation ontology had better postpone its categorisation until more empirical evidence is available.

As for the separation between thought (processes) and thought content—worlds 2 and 3—the reasons for my doubts are the following two.

(1) First, to my mind the continuity argument is mistaken. There is no reason to assume thought contents as an independent ontological category in order to explain the continuity of thoughts. They can be taken as independent mental processes or as brain processes and still exist continuously. This is so, because they can be conceived of as hypothetical facts. Take the natural law "Metals expand when heated" (I have been told that this in fact does not apply to all metals, but that does not invalidate my argument). This is true even if at some time no heating of a metal has taken place or even if there never was any heating of any metal. It is still a fact. But it is a hypothetical fact: *If* some metal is heated, then it will expand. In reality hypothetical facts are extremely frequent. With respect to human beings, we often talk about hypothetical facts in terms of dispositions. To say that a person has a disposition to be violent when drinking alcohol is the same as saying that if she drinks alcohol, she becomes violent.

Now it could be said that thoughts—as world 1 or world 2 phenomena—are hypothetical facts. Einstein's theory of relativity, Descartes' *Cogito ergo sum* or some utterly lascivious thought of mine yesterday exist in that, if some trigger works, then somebody thinks of Einstein's theory, etc. Of course, this does not imply that this person's thought must be identical to what, e.g., Einstein thought at a certain moment or to the whole of his theory. It is enough that she at some moment has Einstein's theory in mind. By regarding thoughts as hypothetical facts I repudiate Popper's idea that (at least some) thought contents (as world 3 objects) are a kind of idealised, objective phenomena, a view that, by the way, in fact makes him a value objectivist. World 3, he says, contains "*objectively* great" literary works, theories and symphonies.[10] Thoughts are better conceived of as subjective and intersubjective phenomena, not extra-subjective (objective) ones.

A more realistic view, which I can endorse, that also gives an explanation to the phenomenon of human communication of thoughts, is that this communication consists in one person's thought causing (by "triggering") a corresponding (though not necessarily identical) thought in another person's brain. In fact, our languages, legal orders, science, philosophy, art, religions and other cultural phenomena are quantitatively and qualitatively extremely complicated sets of communicated thoughts—as hypothetical facts—between people most distant in time and space. This makes human culture utterly diffuse and fragile, but also astonishingly strong and resistant—like a spider's web or a wasp's nest. Although the communication between us is far from perfect, we are neither completely prisoners in our own bell-jars, nor are our thoughts totally exposed to others (thank God!). This being so is a part of the human predicament.

(2) My second reason for doubting the separation of world 2 thought processes and world 3 thought contents has to do with Popper's claim that logical relations can hold only between thought contents, not between mental processes. This is the standard conception of the difference between logic and psychology. Now it is important to bear in mind that, in Popper's view, real numbers belong to world 3 and that logical relations (logical necessity and contradiction) and the ideas of truth and falsity "apply" only to thought contents. But if truth/falsity is an idea, it must, in Popper's view, belong to world 3, and if logical relations "apply" to thought contents in the same sense as truth-values, logical relations, too, seem to be human ideas. But if we reject the ontological category "world 3" and place things Popper claims to belong to world 3 in world 2 or 1, what about real numbers, logical relations, and truth-values?

Let me suggest an answer to that question. There is something that could be called *the general state* (or *character*) *of the universe*, *GSU*, (i.e., the universe consisting of all things belonging to worlds 1 and 2). This is *not* an ontological category but a characterisation of how the whole of the universe happens to be constructed in some of its most fundamental respects.[11]

(i) Real numbers are part of *GSU*. Suppose, for instance, that a tyrannosaur lies resting in a glade some 70 millions of years ago. Suddenly another tyrannosaur enters the glade. Then the reality is that—it is a fact that—there are

[10]Popper (1980), p. 149 ff.

[11]Ideas somewhat similar to mine are found in Hage (2015), pp. 3–48. Hage says: "Logic may well be interpreted as a theory of the (logically) necessary relations between facts in the world" (p. 3). He talks about "the interpretation of logic as specification of the structure of the world" (p. 4) and argues: "Moreover, since the truth of sentences depends on the facts described by the sentences, logic is also a study of the necessary relations between facts. – Deductive logic is as much the study of such necessary relations between facts as a study of the validity of arguments" (p. 5).

two tyrannosaurs in the glade. "Two-ness" is a component of reality, built into it, not a human idea.

(ii) Let *p* stand for "There are two tyrannosaurs in the glade". In fact, there are two tyrannosaurs in the glade. Hence *p* is true and ~*p* false. ("~" stands for "not", "*v*" below for "or".) This is an example of the relation between reality and truth-values. This relation is a part of *GSU*, not a human idea.

(iii) If *p* is true, then, e.g., ~ ~*p*, *p v q* and (if also *q* is true) *p & q* are true and ~*p & q* is false. This is an example of the relation between truth-value and logical necessity (and contradiction)—and, hence, between reality and logic. Also this relation is a part of *GSU* and no human idea.

In other words, real numbers, truth-values and logical relations belong neither to world 1, world 2 nor world 3. They are built into and structure the reality to which these worlds belong. They are no separate entities, but, for practical reasons, we hypostatise them.

When I talk about logical necessity, what I have in mind is deductive models such as *modus ponens* and *modus tollens*. (This kind of logical necessity not even the gods can change.) However, we also talk about logical necessity in the sense of conceptual necessity (conceptual implication). For instance, the concept "legal rule" is "necessarily" conceptually tied to the concept "legal order". The existence of a legal order is a necessary condition for the existence of a legal rule—"legal rule" implies "legal order". This kind of logical relationship is a product of human thinking, not a component of *GSU*. It can disappear in a moment by means of redefining the concepts concerned.

Human beings are able to think about what they think. It is when we think about our thinking—a second order thinking of sorts—that we might discern the logical relations between our thoughts. These relations, however, are not invented by human minds, but are discovered by them. This "second order thinking" is informed by an intellectual ordering of our "first order thinking" by reducing the relations inherent in it to their logical form as abstracted from their content. This process of discovery is itself a hypothetical thought process. But what we discover is a component of *GSU*.

Let me sum up. Our capacity to think of concepts and other human ideas in isolation, disregarding (abstracting from), e.g., their originators, does not in itself move these ideas into another ontological world. Legal and juridical ideas, being human ideas, can ontologically be understood as thought contents, not in the sense of entities belonging to a Popperian world 3, but in the sense of hypothetical thought processes. (This will be further developed in Sect. 6.1 below.)

3.4 The Generality of Legal Rules

To study legal rules with respect to their generality is a time-honoured custom in the philosophy of law. Aristotle did it, and Thomas Aquinas followed suit.[12] Bentham devotes a chapter in *Of Laws in General* for this purpose.[13] His distinctions there are in the first place based upon the extent of the power (competence) of the issuer of the rules.

Obviously, legal rules can be general in different ways and in different degrees.[14] By means of two distinctions I shall try to construct a typology depicting various ways in which legal rules can be general. The distinctions concern legal *norms*, since also individual legal norms are included among them.

I. A distinction between individually and generally addressed legal norms. *An individually addressed legal norm* is a legal norm whose addressee is a unique individual or a unique collective of unique individuals. Example: "If Andersson (or the limited company Sun and Springtime) has borrowed one million Swedish kronor from Karlsson, he (it) shall pay back that sum on the day of maturity". *A generally addressed legal norm* is a legal norm that is not individually addressed. Example: "If anyone negligently damages some other person's property, he shall pay damages for it".

   The addressee designation in generally addressed legal norms does not designate unique persons but a set of such persons. However, the generally addressed legal norms are of two kinds: (i) such norms where the set of persons at any given point of time contains many persons and (ii) such norms where the set of persons contains only one unique person at any given point of time, although during a certain space of time it contains many different persons. Let us call a legal norm of the first kind *a simultaneously and generally addressed legal norm* and a norm of the second kind *a successively and generally addressed legal norm.* A norm of the former kind can be complied with by many people at the same time (the majority of drivers on Swedish roads at a given point of time no doubt follow the traffic regulations). A norm of the latter kind can only be obeyed by one single individual at a certain point of time. Example: Provisions in a state's constitution addressed to the head of the state. The provisions to that effect, say, in the Swedish constitution are not addressed to the present king Carl XVI Gustaf but to the member of the unit set {the head of the state}, whose only member he is just now. If he is succeeded by another person, the constitution needs no change because of that.

II. A distinction between momentary and iterative legal norms. *A momentary legal norm* is a norm that each unique individual or each unique collective of unique individuals can follow only once. Example: (1) "Every person who for the first

---

[12]Thomas Aquinas, Summa Theologica. Treatise on Law, Question 96, First Article.

[13]Bentham (1970), chapter IX.

[14]As observed already by Bentham (1970), p. 76.

time is employed in the State service shall undergo a medical examination", (which is a simultaneously and generally addressed as well as a momentary norm). (2) "Every new head of state taking office shall take the oath of allegiance to the nation when inaugurated" (which is a successively and generally addressed as well as a momentary norm).

An iterative legal norm is a norm that is not momentary. Example: "Everyone exceeding a speed limit shall be sentenced to fines". The iterative legal norms, however, are of two kinds. (i) Such a rule is *continuously iterative* if and only if it can be complied with at any point of time whatsoever as long as it is valid. Example: "If anyone negligently damages another person's property, he shall pay damages for it". (ii) Such a rule is *periodically iterative* if and only if it can be complied with only during certain periods of time during the space of time when it is valid, but not during other such periods. Example: The Swedish Game Act contains a provision (Art. 23) which reads: "During periods prescribed by the government persons without shooting rights who live on a farm or have a garden there may kill or catch and keep the following animals entering the farm or the garden: wild boar, fox, raccoon dog, badger, etc.".

By combining my distinctions (and their subdivisions) we get the following nine combinations. Combination (1) is a purely individual legal norm (and, hence, not a legal rule). Combinations (2)–(3) are a mixture of individuality and generality. Combinations (2)–(9) are in a certain sense (general) legal rules. It could also be said that the series (1), (2), . . ., (9) indicates a scale of generality, where (9) is the most and (1) the least general norm.

The combinations are the following (A and B are unique individual persons).

(1) Individually addressed, momentary legal norms.
Example: "If A has borrowed one million Swedish kronor from B, then A shall pay B back that sum at the day of maturity."
(2) Individually addressed, periodically iterative legal norms.
Example: "If A owns a car, he shall once a year have it undergo inspection".
(3) Individually addressed, continuously iterative legal norms.
Example: "If A negligently damages another person's property, he shall pay damages for it".
(4) Successively and generally addressed, momentary legal norms.
Example: "Every new head of state taking office, shall take the oath of allegiance to the nation when inaugurated".
(5) Successively and generally addressed, periodically iterative legal norms.
Example: "The king shall every year declare the parliamentary session opened".
(6) Successively and generally addressed, continuously iterative legal norms.
Example: "If the government resigns, the speaker of the *Riksdag* shall nominate a new head of government".
(7) Simultaneously and generally addressed, momentary legal norms.
Example: "Every person who for the first time is employed in the State service shall undergo a medical examination".

(8) Simultaneously and generally addressed, periodically iterative legal norms.
Example: "Every person employed in the State service shall undergo a medical examination every third year".
(9) Simultaneously and generally addressed, continuously iterative legal norms.
Example: "If anyone negligently damages another person's property, he shall pay damages for it".

Let us call a legal norm "fulfilled" when it, solely by having been complied with, no longer can be complied with. Legal norms of type (1) are completely fulfilled by being followed only once. If A, in the example of (1), has paid his debt to B, the norm has served its purpose and can, so to speak, be discarded. This is of course not the case with norms of type (2)–(9).

We can also talk about the generality of legal rules in a more "quantitative" way simply by relating it to the extent of the persons' (including the addressees'), actions and other states of affairs designated by the rules. In this respect the rule:

(1) "Creditors have a claim against debtors that the debtors fulfil their duties to the creditors"
is more general than the rule
(2) "Sellers have a claim against buyers that the buyers make payment for the merchandise"

since sellers are a proper subset of creditors (as well as they also are a proper subset of debtors with respect to delivering the goods), buyers a proper subset of debtors (as well as of creditors with respect to the sellers' delivering the goods)) and the legal acts of making payment for the merchandise is a proper subset of the legal acts of fulfilling one's contractual duties. This conception of generality, however, is of less interest as a basic idea in juridical thinking.

3.5 The Strength of Legal Rules

Legal rules can be more or less strong (and, hence, less or more weak) and they can be so in different respects.[15] A rule can be more or less strong with respect to its requisites, its addressees, its normative modality and its norm-theme.

Let us conceive of the strongest possible category of legal rules, *R**. This conception is an ideal-typical one. We will never meet such a rule in real life—and considering the appalling rigidity of a rule of that kind this is no doubt a good thing. The ideal-type is four-dimensional: every legal rule, *r**, in *R** is perfectly self-

[15]I owe the distinction between strong and weak rules to Malt (1986), pp. 167–191 (this illuminating article is unfortunately only available in Norwegian). However, Malt applies his distinction to a much wider scope of legal phenomena than I do. My concern is weakness with respect to the formulation of legal rules only. In Malt (1985), he investigates one type of weak norms, viz., what he calls "probabilistic norms".

contained, clear, determined and non-alternative. That it is perfectly self-contained means that one can decide if it is applicable or not to any case whatsoever without mobilisation of any supplementary norms. That it is perfectly clear means that there is no doubt whatsoever as to its meaning. That it is determined means that its normative modality leaves no room for choice on the part of the addressee. That it is non-alternative means that the action type that the rule determines normatively is one and one only.

In *r** the requisites are perfectly self-contained and clear. With respect to its addressee-designation there is no doubt at all as to which persons are its addressees. It is self-contained and clear. With respect to its modality we realise at once what it means to follow or break the rule. The modality is determined in the sense that it is either an obligation ("shall") or a prohibition ("may not"). *r** can never be a permission. With respect to its norm-theme it is completely obvious what shall, may not or may be done. There is no room for choice, *r** is non-alternative. Compared to *r** the "real" rules which we find in statutes and elsewhere are all more or less weak. (*R** may be the legislator's dream, but realised it would no doubt put hundreds of thousands of lawyers all over the world out of a job.)

With respect to requisites, they can be made weak unconsciously or consciously. Obvious examples of weak requisites are those that are vague, obscure or ambiguous. In many situations legislators prefer, for some reason or another, weak rules. As for weakness as a legislative technique there are, among others, two well-established devices. (1) The so-called *general clauses* (which had their breakthrough in the German *Bürgerliches Gesetzbuch* of 1900). They are statutory provisions characterised by having a requisite that is (i) highly general and (ii) evaluative. Typical examples of such requisites are "undue", "unreasonable" and "contrary to faith and honour". (2) *Blank provisions*, which appear in two forms which we can call internal and external blank provisions respectively. Common to both is that they have a requisite the meaning of which must be ascertained by norms outside the provision itself or the statute in which it appears. Internal blank provisions depend on legal rules inside the legal system itself. Example: According to the Swedish Narcotic Drugs Act persons who without permission transfer drugs are committing a crime. But this act does not tell us what counts as drugs. In order to find that out we must go to another statute where we find a list of what counts as drugs with respect to the Narcotic Drugs Act. External blank provisions, on the other hand, often referred to as standards, depend on norms outside the legal system itself, indicated in the provisions by means of requisites such as "fair commercial practice", "generally accepted accounting principles" and "good advocate mores". Standards are usually general clauses as well. From the viewpoint of legislative technique the advantage of blank provisions, both internal and external, is that, even if the supplementary norms are changing, e.g., as for what counts as drugs, the blank provisions themselves can remain unaltered. They are apparatuses capable of being reprogrammed without changes in the apparatus itself.

With respect to the addressee-designation, weakness can mean that the legal rule is not self-contained; you have to look elsewhere to find out who its addressee is—or, in the worst of cases, there is no addressee to find at all, neither in the rule nor in the legal system, in which case the rule might never have been intended to be used at all, but only to serve as a façade. Or it can be formulated as an alternative, e. g., addressed to two different authorities, in which case the observance of the rule might fall between two stools. The addressee-designation can also be vague in the sense that it is unclear who is a proper addressee. For example, to whom does the designation "person officiating at weddings" refer if the law is silent on this point: must it be some kind of priest or some kind of official, or can it be a relative or a friend?

With respect to modalities, obligations and prohibitions are determined. Should-rules are of a weaker kind—it is not altogether clear what it means that you should do something, i.e., when you follow the rule and when you break it. Even weaker than should-rules are independent permissions, i.e., permissions which are not exceptions to rules with a determined modality. To be sure, it could be said that permissions are not weak at all, on the contrary they are very strong in the sense that whatever you do, you do it in compliance with the permission. You can never break it. But permissions are weak in the sense that they give no guidance as to how to act.

With respect to norm-themes, legal rules can be weak in that the norm-theme is either vague or formulated as an alternative. Also weakness with respect to norm-themes can be used as a legislative technique. As for alternative norm-themes, e.g., ["...shall] be imposed a fine or sentenced to imprisonment for at the most six months", the weakness consists in the uncertainty that may arise when choosing between them. As for vagueness, in criminal law the norm-theme is often formulated as a latitude, e.g., ["shall] be sentenced to imprisonment for at least 6 months and at the most 6 years"—a technique that became generally accepted through the French *Code Pénal* of 1810.

References

Bentham J (1970) Of laws in general (The collected works of Jeremy Bentham: principles of legislation). Athlone Press, London

Frank J (1949a) Courts on trial. Princeton University Press, Princeton

Frank J (1949b) Law and the modern mind. Coward-McCann, New York

Gray JC (1921) The nature and sources of the law, 2nd edn. Columbia University Press, New York

Hage J (2015) The (onto)logical structure of law: a conceptual toolkit for legislators. In: Araszkiewicz M, Pleszka K (eds) Logic in the theory and practice of lawmaking. Springer, Berlin, pp 3–48

Hart HLA (1961) The concept of law. Oxford University Press, Oxford

Malt GF (1985) Deontic probability. In: Bulygin E et al (eds) Man, law and modern forms of life. Springer, Berlin, pp 233–240

Malt GF (1986) Svake normer (Weak norms). Tidsskrift for Rettsvitenskap:167–191

Popper K (1972) Objective knowledge: an evolutionary approach. Oxford University Press, Oxford

Popper K (1980) Three worlds. In: Sterling MM (ed) The Tanner lectures on human values. University of Utah Press, Salt Lake City

Raz J (1980) The concept of a legal system, 2nd edn. Oxford University Press, Oxford

Ross A (1959) On law and justice. University of California Press, Berkeley

Chapter 4
The Addressee Problem

4.1 Introduction

In his most important work from the viewpoint of analytical jurisprudence, *Of Laws in General,*[1] Jeremy Bentham discerns different ways in which a person can be affected by the law.[2] There are, Bentham tells us, three different ways in which a party may be concerned in or affected by a law (a legal rule): (1) by being *bound* or coerced by it, (2) by being exposed to *suffer* by it, and (3) by being *favoured* or intended to be favoured by it.

In every law there must be one or more persons concerned in each of these ways. And one and the same person can be affected by a law in more than one of these ways. For example, a judge is bound by a criminal statutory provision to pass a judgment, a criminal is a party made to suffer by means of punishment—as Bentham puts it, "[t]o make a law is to do evil that good may come"—and the party favoured can be the victim of a crime, or society at large. People may also be affected by laws in more remote ways—which might be known but not intended by the legislator, or not even known by him. Bentham gives the following example: "Everybody knows for example into what a multitude of remote and sometimes imperceptible branches the mischief produced by a tax will oftentimes divide itself". Another example could be the wife and children of a person sentenced to imprisonment; they are, no doubt, in a tragic way exposed to suffering by the law—or, more accurately, by the application of the law.

Now one might ask: Of those affected by a law, who is *the addressee* of that law? This is the basic one among the questions which together may be labelled *the jurisprudential addressee problem.*

A law, or legal rule, is a norm. It seems to me natural to use the term "addressee" for that individual or collective of individuals, the action of which the normative

[1]Bentham (1970).

[2]Bentham (1970), chapter VI: "Of the parties which may be affected by the law".

Å. Frändberg, *The Legal Order*, Law and Philosophy Library 123,
https://doi.org/10.1007/978-3-319-78858-6_4

modality of the norm operates on. We call an action governed by a normative modality *the theme* of the norm. A theme may be obligatory, prohibited or permitted. The addressee of the norm is bound in Bentham's sense of the word.

The function of a norm is to influence behaviour. Hence, only human beings and, possibly, other more advanced animals can be under obligations, prohibitions and permissions to do things. A legislator laying obligations on houses or prohibitions on stones would no doubt be regarded as somewhat eccentric. When nevertheless things like that actually happen, such a norm is of an elliptical character, being in fact a fragment of a more complete norm with a human being as its addressee.

4.2 The Problem

The jurisprudential addressee problem emerges from the following peculiarity concerning legal systems.

Take, e.g., a rule in a Sales of Goods Act

(r) If the seller due to delay on the part of the buyer has had costs for the proper care of the goods, the buyer shall pay damages for those costs.

The requisite might be fulfilled when the buyer does not take possession of the goods at the time agreed upon and the goods are stored at the expense of the seller.

The addressee of *r* is the buyer. He is the one who shall pay damages. But suppose that the buyer does not fulfil this obligation and that the seller brings the matter before a court of law. Can the judge do anything at all by virtue of *r*? He is, as a matter of fact, not even mentioned in it. *r* says nothing whatsoever about the behaviour of the judge.

Or we might ask another question. On what grounds can we say that, e.g., Swedish law forbids you and me to steal or murder? We look in vain for provisions to that effect in the Swedish criminal code. What we actually find are provisions to the effect that, *if* someone has stolen or murdered, the judge shall behave in a certain manner.

In the first example, what meets the eye in the statute book is a rule addressed to buyers, in the other a rule addressed to judges. How then can a judge have a duty to do certain things according to *r*—things that differ from what buyers are obligated to do according to *r*? And how can a citizen have a duty to refrain from certain things, which differ from what judges are obligated to do according to the criminal code?

The Swedish philosopher Ingemar Hedenius formulates the addressee problem in the following way [my transl.]: "The task is to explain in what way genuine legal sentences [= normative legal sentences] can have both authorities and ordinary citizens as their addressees and, when that happens, at the same time impose on or permit these two categories of people totally different things. The explanation must be a hypothesis about which semantic status these two-way directed norms have".[3]

Two other questions pertaining to the addressee problem might be added. (1) Why does the legislator sometimes formulate rules as addressed to citizens while the corresponding judge-addressed rules are understood, sometimes in the reverse manner, and sometimes formulate explicitly both a citizen-addressed and a corresponding judge-addressed rule? (2) In what way can an investigation of the addressee problem contribute to the general theory of legal systems? Can we learn something important about legal systems by examining the addressee problem? I think we can.

4.3 The Legal System in a Spelled-Out Version

As I see it, the addressee problem is not, from an analytical point of view, a particularly interesting problem *per se.* It is interesting in a more indirect way in that it indicates an important duplicity in the idea of a legal system.

As we have seen, the legal system in its explicit formulation is incomplete. In order to formulate the complete legal system ("completeness" of course is not used here in its logical sense), which is, as it were, *inherent in* the explicit formulation, we must, for one thing, add the understood corresponding rules to the system. We can make a distinction between *the legal system in a concentrated version*, consisting of the explicitly formulated rules (hereafter called "provisions"), and *the* (wider) *legal system in a spelled-out version*, the latter including the former. The legal system in a spelled-out version *is intended by* the legislator; it is not a creation of dogmatic legal science or jurisprudence.

However, in addition to the adding of corresponding, unwritten, rules to the provisions, we must, in order to formulate a legal system in a spelled-out version, also take into consideration another variation of concentrated legal rules, which we can call "provisions" as well. It is sometimes the case that one and the same provision is "a carrier" of two different rules, belonging to different types of legal rules, and that, in order to formulate these different rules, we are not required to formulate another, corresponding rule by *adding or removing* components of the provision but rather *to make a distinction by way of interpretation of* the provision itself. The components of the two rules formulated in such a manner are *contained in* the very same provision—we do not need to add or remove anything from it according to some "legal syntactical" meta-rules. It is a matter of specifying a one-many norm relation. I refer to the example given in Sect. 2.11 (under the heading Specifying n-relations) above—a provision in the Swedish Code on Parents and Children containing the normative modality "may", which can be interpreted

[3]Hedenius (1978), p. 48.

either as "has a competence to", making the provision a competence rule, or as "is allowed to" making it a permission.

Hence, there are two ways of transforming rules of a legal system in a concentrated version into one in a spelled-out version: either by *change* (adding or removing rule components) or by *distinction.* In the first case the provision is *unambiguous* in the respect that it contains one and only one rule of a certain type (but, of course, the rule may be ambiguous in the sense that it is doubtful whether it is applicable to a certain case or not). The provision we take as *a basis for constructing* a corresponding legal rule by adding or removing components of it. In the latter case the provision is *ambiguous* in that it contains two (or more) different legal rules, belonging to different types of such rules.

From the viewpoint of the addressee problem, spelling out a system by change comes to the fore. For the corresponding rule, which is added to a provision by change, usually has *another addressee* than that of the provision, while the addressees are identical in rules spelled out by distinction. In the example mentioned above, the addressee of the competence rule is identical with that of the permission.

By examining the relationship between a provision and a corresponding implicit rule, interesting features of the morphology of legal systems are revealed. Let us in the following first analyse the relationship between a citizen- addressed rule and a corresponding implied, unwritten, judge-addressed rule (Sect. 4.4) and, after that, the opposite relationship, where the citizen- addressed rule is implied (Sect. 4.5).

4.4 Transformation of Legal Rules

As was pointed out in Chap. 2, any legal rule can be represented by *a standard form* for the type of legal rule to which the rule belongs.

The standard form for citizen-addressed, ordinary obligatory rules of action we represented by this structure:

(SFOC) If . . . , then *a* shall do . . .

We divided SFOC into different components, viz. the requisite(s) and the legal consequence, and the latter into its normative modality ("shall", "may not", "may") and its norm-theme, i.e., that which the normative modality operates on—or, in other words, that which is obligatory, prohibited or permitted. The requisites and the legal consequence are connected by "if, . . . then", indicating the hypothetical (conditional) character of the rule. As an example of a rule, *r*, conforming to SFOC we used (Sect. 4.2 above):

(*r*) If the seller due to delay on the part of the buyer has had costs for the proper care of the goods, the buyer shall pay damages for those costs.

To transform a citizen-addressed rule conforming to the standard form SFOC into a corresponding judge-addressed rule is to reconstruct it in such a way that it conforms to another standard form, viz., the standard form for judge-addressed rules, SFOJ. The test of the adequacy of such a transformation is that the reconstructed rule fits in with the latter standard form. We continue to use *r* as an example.

Let us now construct the standard form for the corresponding judge-addressed rule, SFOJ, discern its different components and examine the relation between SFOC and SFOJ.

(SFOJ) If . . . & ~NT & PA, then shall$_1$, (may not$_1$, may$_1$): *j* decides: *a* shall$_2$, (may not$_2$, may$_2$) . . .

where "~" = "not", "NT" the norm-theme – in *r* "the buyer pays damages for the costs"—"*j*" indicates the judge in question and "PA" certain appropriate actions of a procedural character.

The judge-addressed rule, *r*′, corresponding to *r* could be spelled out in the following manner. *r*′ is the rule actually applied by the judge.

(*r*′) If (i) the seller due to delay on the part of the buyer has had costs for the proper care of the goods *and* (ii) the buyer does not pay damages for those costs *and* (iii) the seller performs *pa* [= certain specified appropriate procedural actions, e.g., to commence an action at a court of law], then the judge shall$_1$ decide that the buyer shall$_2$ pay damages for those costs.

r′ consists of the following components:

(1) *The requisites:* "(i) due to delay on the part of the buyer the seller has had costs for the proper care of the goods and (ii) the buyer does not pay damages for those costs and (iii) the seller performs *pa*"

Notice the following relations between *r* and *r*′. The requisite (i) in *r*′ is identical with the requisite of *r*. Requisite (ii) in *r*′ is the negation of the norm-theme of *r*. Requisite (iii) in *r*′ is an additional requisite of a procedural character, not included in *r*. Requisites of type (ii) and (iii) are necessary components of a judge-addressed rule corresponding to a citizen-addressed one. If the buyer voluntarily pays damages, the judge, of course, shall not judge in favour of the seller, who has already got his due. And if the seller does not commence an action at the jurisdiction in question, or does not do so in a proper way, the judge is under no obligation whatsoever with respect to deciding the case.

(2) *The external legal consequence*: "the judge shall$_1$ decide that the buyer shall$_2$ pay damages for the costs".

The external legal consequence can be divided into the following components:

(3) *The external normative modality*: "shall$_1$"

(4) *The external norm-theme*: "the judge decides that the buyer shall$_2$ pay damages for those costs".

The external norm-theme consists of

(5) *The legal performative component*: "the judge decides that"

(6) *The internal legal consequence* (= what the judge decides): "the buyer $shall_2$ pay damages for those costs".

The legal performative component is called so because when a judge, by means of some written or oral utterance, decides that a person is in a certain legal position, e.g., the one described by (6), that legal position is *thereby* created.

The legal consequence of *r* is identical with the internal legal consequence of *r*′. The legal consequence of *r* is part of the external legal consequence of *r*′.

Here we are faced with something very similar to a dilemma. How can we reconcile the idea that a new legal position has been created performatively with the observation that the legal consequence of *r* is identical with the internal consequence of *r*′? If those two are identical, the positions described by them, or so it seems, must be identical too. But then no new legal position has emerged. What the judge has done is simply ascertained an already existing legal position. But that, on the other hand, is an unrealistic description of what making judicial judgments is really about.

A plausible solution of this "dilemma" is the following—and here I draw on an idea formulated by Carl Wellman.[4] If we articulate legal positions in terms of Hohfeld elements, a compound legal position is a cluster of such elements. A compound legal position can be conceived of as attaching certain associated elements to a defining core (a core element). For instance, the compound legal position of a creditor's right to repayment has, according to Wellman, as its core element the creditor's "legal claim against the debtor that the debtor repays him the agreed sum at the agreed time". Around this core element revolves a set of associated Hohfeld elements, e.g., that the creditor has a legal power (competence) of waiving repayment and a legal liberty to exercise or refrain from exercising this power.

Let me, in order to solve "the dilemma" mentioned, use Wellman's idea in the following way. There is a compound legal position, the core element of which is the position described by the legal consequence of *r*—and, hence, by the internal legal consequence of *r*′. *r* and *r*′ have the same core element. But, in fact, by the pronouncing of the judgment, to this core element some associated elements are tied, the function of which is to contribute to *the realisation of* the core element. A mere assertion of the core element cannot achieve that purpose.

A legal position has its own "life". It is created at a certain time and it expires at another, either through realisation (by voluntary action or by the help of forceful means used by authorities), or through extinction (either by just ceasing to exist, e.g., by cancelling or by limitation). Before it has expired, the legal position is usually in a state of latency. This state of latency, however, can be transformed into a state of mobilisation, e.g., when an obligation is contested or, without being contested, simply not fulfilled. A legal position is in a state of mobilisation when a court of law, performatively through a judgment, has made the position exigible. The court has created a more comprehensive and reinforced legal position, including the

[4]Wellman (1978), p. 218 f.

original one (the core element); it has provided the latter position with a trigger. In this we find a central component in the legal organisation of society. (The core element in our sense, the position described by the legal consequence of *r*, may itself be a complex position with associated elements.)

What kind of associated elements are we talking about here? They are elements functioning as a means of realising the core element. By realising the core element I mean the performance of some act-in-the-law that conforms to the theme of the position. For example, the position "Buyer B shall pay damages for the costs C to seller S" has the theme "B pays damages for C to S" and this theme is realised by B's paying damages for C to S, or by some executive authority seeing to it that B's personal property is used for paying damages for C to S.

Suppose that the seller/plantiff wins his case. Then at least the following elements are added by the judgment. As for the seller, what is added is a competence to deprive the buyer, by means of executive authorities, of (certain) personal property and a freedom (privilege in Hohfeld's terminology) to use that competence by initiating executive measures. And if he actually uses that competence—i.e., pulls the trigger—he has a claim upon these authorities that they take the appropriate measures. As for the buyer, what is added is a liability (loss of immunity) with respect to his ownership of personal property. As for the executive authorities, what is added is a duty to perform executive actions.

The internal legal consequence, finally, consists of

(7) *the internal normative modality*: "shall$_2$"
(8) *the internal norm-theme*: "the buyer pays damages for the costs".

(And if he does, justice is done. Otherwise, further legal steps must be taken, in the last resort by the use of force. But that is not the judge's business.)

The requisites and the external legal consequence are connected by the "if, ... then ..." clause.

Let us now take a further step. Suppose that the citizen-addressed rule is not an obligatory norm but a prohibition. How shall we then describe the relation between the citizen-addressed rule and the adequately corresponding judge- addressed rule?

In this case a mere transformation of the citizen-addressed rule is not sufficient. It must also be supplemented in a certain way. This is due to the trivial fact that an action performed in violation of a prohibition never, whether by legal or other means, can be made undone—while, with respect to an omission to comply with an obligation, it is usually (but not always) possible to perform the omitted action later or realise it by coercive measures. Hence, if the citizen-addressed prohibition has the following standard form

(SFPC) If *x*, then *a* may not (do) *y*

(for example, "If *a* drives his car on a road where there is a speed limit, *a* may not exceed that limit"), we cannot construct a judge-addressed rule corresponding to the prohibition in the same way as is possible with respect to obligations, viz., by letting the legal consequence in the judge-addressed rule enforce the performance of what is omitted in violation of the citizen-addressed rule. Unless the citizen-addressed prohibition shall remain a pure *lex imperfecta*, it must *be combined with* a (secondary) judge-addressed rule, the legal consequence of which *contains something more* than can be gathered from the citizen-addressed prohibition, viz., in general terms, a kind of substitute for the performed forbidden action. The standard form of such a rule is

($SFOJ_{pc}$) If x & y, then $shall_1$: j decides: $shall_2$: w

(for example, "If *a* drives his car on a road where there is a speed limit (x) and the speed limit is exceeded (y), the judge shall sentence the driver to fines" (i.e., "that the driver shall pay fines"). "w" is this "more" that is added ("the driver pays fines").

The norm-theme w can be characterised as *a legal substitute*, something that "compensates for" the action that cannot be undone, a "next best" of sorts, aiming at minimising or compensating for the injurious effects of an action performed in violation of a prohibition. Usually this legal substitute is a sanction. When constructing this sanction the legislator generally draws on some kind of relation between w and y, e.g., the relation that, if w is performed (the driver pays fines), then he will not do y (exceeding speed limits) in the future (individual prevention) and others will avoid doing so as well (general prevention), or a relation of equivalence between damage made (y) and damages awarded in compensation for it (w).

Hence, we have shown an incongruity between the obligation and the prohibition. The obligation is transformed and some requisites of a procedural character are added. The prohibition must not only be transformed and some procedural requisites added, but also supplemented with a substitute (notably a sanction). To be sure, also with respect to obligations, later fulfilment can now and then be impossible, e.g., when a seller is prevented from delivering the goods due to the fact that goods of this kind are no longer available. If this is the case, what has been said about prohibition applies *mutatis mutandis* also to obligation.

In fact, we can distinguish a third category of legal rules besides citizen- and judge-addressed ones, viz., what can be called executive rules. Here the addressee is the executive authorities (the executor). To the judge-addressed rule r' corresponds the executor-addressed rule:

(r'') If the judge has sentenced the buyer to pay damages to the seller according to r' *and* the buyer, this notwithstanding, does not do so *and* the seller claims execution, then the executor shall execute the judgment.

Let "z" represent the rule component in SFOJ "j decides: a $shall_2$ ...", and "*EX* (y)" represent some executive gambit concerning y (y is, e.g., that buyer a pays purchase money to seller b and *EX*(y) that the seller claims execution). Then the standard form for executive rules of type r'' can be rendered

(SFEX) If z & $\sim y$ & *EX*(y), then shall: the executor sees to it that y.

If this relation between SFOJ and SFEX holds with respect to two rules of type r' and r'', r'' then adequately corresponds to r'.

It is important to notice that the original operative fact, x, itself (e.g., that the seller due to delay on the part of the buyer has had costs for the proper care of the goods) is not a requisite in SFEX but *z* instead of *x*. *z* can be the case although *x* is not the case (due, e.g., to error on the part of the judge). This mirrors on the morphological level the fact that exercising executive authority is not on the same level as exercising judicial authority. It is not for the executor to retry the case. The executor shall take the court's judgment for granted. This is an important part of the division of power in a law-state.[5]

4.5 Reversed Transformation

Let us now examine the relation between a judge-addressed provision and a corresponding unwritten citizen-addressed rule.

Let us as an example take Chapter 3 Article 1 in the Swedish Penal Code from 1962 (my translation)

(*p*) Whoever deprives another person of his life is sentenced for *murder* to imprisonment for a definite time, at least ten and at the most 18 years, or for life.

After a meaning-preserving transformation into a norm in a hypothetical form we get

(*p**) If anyone deprives another person of his life, then the judge shall sentence him for *murder* to imprisonment for a definite time, at least ten and at the most 18 years, or for life.

It is not difficult for the law-abiding citizen to derive from this provision a rule addressed to himself to the following effect:

(*c*) It is forbidden for anyone to deprive another person of his life.

How shall we describe the relation between the judge-addressed obligation *p** and the citizen-addressed prohibition *c*? To my mind, two features are of importance.

(1) The requisites of *p** are the norm-theme of *c*. This relation, however, cannot be generalised to every judge-addressed provision and its citizen-addressed counterpart. There might be requisites in the former which are not part of the norm-theme of the latter, e.g., the occurrence of certain (probable) future events being consequences of the criminal act. But even then it is possible to formulate the adequately corresponding citizen-addressed rule.
(2) The norm-theme of *p** (the sentencing to imprisonment) is used some way or another for ascertaining the normative status—obligation or prohibition—of *c*.

In this respect, our cautious and law-abiding citizen can, for good reasons, be supposed to use two rough, precautionary guidelines:

[5]See Frändberg (2014), p. 181.

(PG1) An action legally resulting in a criminal sanction is forbidden.
(PG2) An action the omission of which legally results in a criminal sanction is obligatory. (If you do not pay a tax in due time, you are fined. Hence, it is obligatory to pay the tax in due time.)

4.6 Whom Shall the Legislator Address?

Why do certain legal rules have citizens as addressees?

One reason is that, within the sphere of optional rules in civil law, no intervention by authorities is needed. A seller who has sold a car with some hidden defect might, for example, voluntarily provide the buyer with another, faultless car. And a person who has caused damages on another person's property can voluntarily compensate for it.

Another reason lies in the instrumental character of legal orders. After all, the task of legal orders is ultimately to direct the behaviour of the public, and this goal might best be achieved if its rules, when possible, are addressed to the public. The public is in that way explicitly told what to do and not to do without any more or less disturbing transformations needed.

Why do certain legal rules have authorities as their addressees?

First, there are certain legal consequences that citizens themselves cannot perform. You cannot appear in front of the prison gate one early morning, begging: "Yesterday I killed my aunt. Now I severely repent it. I want to be imprisoned for life. That's what I deserve. Please let me in!" You cannot legally sentence yourself. That must be done by a court of law.

Secondly, the legislator expects from citizens to have sense enough to derive the corresponding prohibitions or obligations pertaining to them by the help of the rather self-evident guidelines PG1 and PG2.

Thirdly, the effect of the regulation might be stronger from a socio-psychological viewpoint if criminal provisions are formulated in terms of sanctions, handled by judges, making the sanction stand out in a more striking way than a threat or a warning. Most people in a society governed by law would not imagine stealing or murdering anyway, so a provision to the effect that these things are forbidden would be somewhat superfluous. Nor would some people be more reluctant to steal or murder if such a provision existed.

Fourthly, in a well-developed legal order there must, of course, be rules of a constitutional, administrative and procedural kind, regulating the activities of official functionaries, which rules can not at all be formulated as citizen- addressed.

Sometimes the legislator combines a citizen-addressed obligation or prohibition with a judge-addressed sanction rule. This is often the case in more specialised areas of criminal law. We find many examples in the Swedish legislation concerning traffic offences. One reason for this combination is of a legislative technical, or editorial, character—the same sanction is tied to several different offences. Another reason is that it is important to formulate clearly what is obligated or prohibited and under which circumstances this is the case, especially with respect to more complicated regulations—something that is facilitated by a formulation in a provision separated from the corresponding sanction rule and addressed directly to the citizens.

4.7 Conclusion

The so-called jurisprudential addressee problem is not, as Hedenius formulated it, a question of explaining the phenomenon of a single, semantically two-way directed norm. It is, in my opinion, a question of exploring relationships between two separate rules, where one is contained in an explicit provision and the other is an unwritten rule, constructed in accordance with certain morphological (syntactical) rules working on the provision and not identical with it.

References

Bentham J (1970) Of laws in general (the collected works of Jeremy Bentham: principles of legislation). Athlone Press, Edinburgh

Frändberg Å (2014) From Rechtsstaat to universal law-state. Springer, Berlin

Hedenius I (1978) Om den rättsfilosofiska domstolsrealismen (On the legal philosophical court realism). In: Uppsalaskolan – och efteråt (The Uppsala School – and afterwards). Acta Universitatis Upsaliensis, Symposia Universitatis Upsaliensis Annum Quingentesimum Celebrantis, vol 6. pp 41–49

Wellman C (1978) Legal rights. In: Uppsalaskolan – och efteråt (The Uppsala School – and afterwards). Acta Universitatis Upsaliensis, Symposia Universitatis Upsaliensis Annum Quingentesimum Celebrantis, vol 6, pp 213–221

Chapter 5
Normative Modalities

5.1 Introduction

We have many times already presented the structure of ordinary legal rules of action in terms of requisites and legal consequences in this way:

- If . . ., then person *a shall (may not, may)* . . . .

(Examples: "If a person is found guilty of murder, the judge shall sentence him to imprisonment for life", "If the seller considerably delays delivery of the goods, the buyer may rescind the contract", "If a car is driven on a public road where a speed limit is indicated, he may not exceed that limit".)

In this chapter we shall investigate the normative modalities ("*shall*", "*may not*", "*may*") of norms, notably conditional legal rules, where the modalities occur in the legal consequence. Our fundamental question is: Do these words *mean* anything? And if they do, what? Do normative modalities—and modalities at all—have any semantic function? For the Scandinavian realists the answer to that question was in the negative. For them the normative modalities are merely a kind of in themselves meaningless, psychologically operating means of bringing pressure on people, or, in other words, signals, just like traffic signals. In this chapter it will on the contrary be argued that they—and modalities on the whole—have a semantic meaning.

Let me first investigate modalities on the whole. In this connection I take the term "modality" to denote a much wider scope of words as is usually the case. In Sect. 5.2 I discuss modalities generally and in Sect. 5.3 normative modalities exclusively. The basic idea is that the semantic function of modalities is to presuppose all possible alternatives and block or accept some of those alternatives. In the concluding Sect. 5.3.4 I have a few words to say about normativity.

Å. Frändberg, *The Legal Order*, Law and Philosophy Library 123,
https://doi.org/10.1007/978-3-319-78858-6_5

5.2 On Modalities Generally

5.2.1 Modalities in a Very Wide Sense

Logicians have taken great interest in so-called alethic modalities ("possible", "necessary", "impossible"; like in sentences such as "It is possible that it rains in Uppsala today"), deontic modalities ("permitted", "obligatory", "prohibited") as well as epistemic ("know") and doxastic ("believe") modalities. In linguistics, modalities are everything that can be expressed by so-called modal auxiliaries, followed by a verb in the infinitive or a that-clause (e.g., "It will snow", "I know that it snows") or with different grammatical moods, for instance subjunctive, or modal adverbs, like "perhaps". In my very wide sphere of modalities I also include verbs like "hope" and "fear" (e.g., "I fear that she comes") and, in addition to that, what logicians call sentential connectives ("not", "and", "or", "if ... then", "if and only if"). Finally I include temporal ("sometimes", "always", "never") and spatial ("somewhere", "everywhere", "nowhere") adverbs. Common to all these modalities is their close connection to the verb. (Also the so-called quantifiers, the pronouns "some", "all", "none", could be regarded as a kind of modalities, although they are closer to nouns than to verbs.)

Modalities are phenomena in natural languages. In formal languages operators that appear are something (partly) different. Thus, the modal auxiliary "shall" corresponds (but perhaps not wholly adequately) to the deontic operator "*O*".

5.2.2 Modalities as Semantic Phenomena. Their Structuring Function: To Presuppose All and Block Certain Alternatives

The function of presenting and blocking alternatives is not a purely syntactical matter. It has a semantic character as well. Modalities have (semantic) meaning. They have a semantic function although they lack semantic reference contrary to, e.g., "car" or "number". Their function is to structure, together with the other sentence components, a meaningful sentence. Without modalities certain sentences cannot provide the information they were meant to provide. They split meaningfully up the universe of discourse by *presupposing all alternatives* and "*blocking*" some of these alternatives (but not all). In this way, the modalities *moderate an initial position where all possible alternatives are available.*

Let me in what follows illustrate what I have in mind when I talk about presupposing and blocking alternatives by means of examples. For the sake of brevity I use some standard logical symbols, viz., the following.

(i) "*p*" ("*q*", "*r*") for some sentence, e.g., "It is raining in Uppsala today".
(ii) "~" for negation ("not"). ~*p* can, e.g., stand for, "It is not raining in Uppsala today".
(iii) "*M*" for possibility ("it is possible that"). *Mp* can, e.g., stand for "It is possible that it is raining in Uppsala today".
(iv) "*N*" for necessity ("it is necessary that"). ~*Np* can, e.g., stand for "It is not necessary that it will rain in Uppsala today".
(v) "*P*" for permission ("it is permitted that"). *Pp* can, e.g., stand for "Smoking is permitted in this area".
(vi) "$K_a p$" for knowledge ("*a* knows that *p*"). $K_a p$ can, e.g., stand for "Anderson knows that it is raining in Uppsala today".
(vii) "$H_a\, p$" for hope ("*a* hopes that *p*"). $H_a\, p$ can, e.g., stand for "Anderson hopes that it rains in Uppsala today".
(viii) "*p v q*" for disjunction ("*p* or *q*"). *p v q* can, e.g., stand for "It is raining or snowing in Uppsala today".
(ix) "*p & q*" for conjunction ("*p* and *q*"). *p & q* can, e.g., stand for "It is raining and it is windy in Uppsala today".

5.2.3 Presupposing Alternatives. Formulation of Initial Positions

Every discussion has a more or less well-defined universe of discourse—that which the discussion is about. One way of making a universe of discourse more precise is to think of *the "potential" alternatives* within this universe—without asserting them and without them being the case. If the discussion is about the state of affairs that it is raining in Uppsala today, these alternatives are reasonably (i) "It is raining in Uppsala today" (*p*) and (ii) "It is not raining in Uppsala today" (~*p*).

Let us moreover assume that it is possible, with respect to these alternatives, to lay down *an initial position* for the discussion. By that I mean a position *where all alternatives are possible.* We can characterise the initial position as *the maximally open* initial position for the discussion. The initial position is *Mp & M~p.* This position obliges to nothing. In formulating the initial position the modality has an "extending" function (blocking, on the other hand, has a "restricting" function).

The initial position is formulated by means of the modality *M*. The alternatives are fixed by logic. The initial position consists of all alternatives which are logically possible. This gives *M* a unique position. Contrary to the other modalities (with a certain exception for *P*), *M* has in addition to a blocking function also an extending, completing function with respect to the potential alternatives.

5.2.4 Blocking Alternatives

Let me explain what I mean by "blocking alternatives" by means of an example. An alternative, we say, is "available" when not blocked. The potential alternatives are: *p*, *~p*. The initial position is: *Mp* & *M~p*.

(1) Negation. *~p* is the case. Then *p* is blocked by ~, while *~p* is available.
(2) Necessity. *Np* is the case. Then *Mp* remains available but *M~p* is blocked by *N*.
(3) Knowledge. $K_a\,p$ is the case. Then *K* blocks $K_a\,{\sim}p$ and ${\sim}K_a\,p$, while $K_a\,p$ and ${\sim}K_a\,{\sim}p$ remain available.
(4) Hope. $H_a\,p$ is the case. Then *H* blocks $H_a{\sim}p$ and ${\sim}H_a\,p$, while $H_a\,p$ and ${\sim}H_a\,{\sim}p$ remain available.
(5) Disjunction. *p v q* is the case. Then *p* & *~q*, *~p* & *q* and *p* & *q* are available, only *~p* & *~q* is blocked by *v*.
(6) Conjunction. *p* & *q* is the case (and then, of course, available). *p* & *~q*, *~p* & *q* and *~p* & *~q* are all blocked by &.

Alternatives are blocked by (i) logic, (ii) nature, or (iii) mankind. Alternatives are blocked by logic when all alternatives in the initial position are logically possible but one or more alternatives become logically impossible (contradictory) when a modality is introduced. Example: Initial position: *Mp* & *M~p*. *Np* is introduced. Then alternative *~p* is blocked.

Alternatives are blocked by nature when all alternatives in the initial position are logically possible but one or more alternatives become physically impossible—although still logically possible—when *~Mp* is introduced. Then alternative *p* is blocked, e.g., "Anderson can jump twenty meters in a high jump".

Alternatives are blocked by human beings when all alternatives in the initial position are logically possible but one or more alternatives become "culturally" impossible, due to emotional, ethical, legal, conventional or other circumstances related to mankind—although still logically possible. Let us as an example take H_a *p*. Both in the initial position and after the modality *H* is introduced, *Mp* and *M~p* is the case. But *H* blocks *~p*—by hoping that *p*, *~p* becomes a non-alternative "in the perspective of hope". That an alternative *~p* is blocked by *a* in the perspective of hope means roughly that *a* has a strong wish that *p* combined with a certain amount of credence that *p* will be the case. This shows, by the way, that blocking can be more or less strong.

What is blocked by logic is the logically impossible. What is blocked by nature is the physically impossible. What is blocked by human beings ("culture") is the (in some person's eyes) undesirable.

Blocking by means of modalities brings order in chaos by eliminating certain alternatives. The function of modalities is not only the syntactic one of creating a grammatically correct sentence; its function is semantic in that each of them has its special meaning. *p* & *q* means something other than *p v q*, *Np* means something other than *Mp*.

All alternatives cannot be blocked by means of modalities without contradiction. *~Mp & ~M~p* is an absurd use of the modality *M*. The function of a modality is to make at least one alternative available and at least one alternative blocked. By means of modalities an "absolute" initial position is made relative without a new "absolute" position coming about. The function of a modality is, as the word *"modus"* suggests, modulating.

In the following we shall focus on the normative modalities.

5.3 On Normative Modalities Exclusively

5.3.1 Presupposing Alternatives

A normative sentence is a sentence with a normative modality. Such a sentence expresses a norm. Necessary components of a normative sentence (norm) are (i) a modality, (ii) a norm-theme (that which shall, may not or may be the case) and (iii) an addressee. As for *Pp*, *p* is the norm-theme, for *P~p*, *~p* is the norm-theme. Modality and norm-theme must, I think, always be stated explicitly in the normative sentence, while the addressee can be implicitly indicated—it can be self-evident who the addressee is.

The initial position for normative modalities incorporates the initial position for modalities generally. But in order to achieve an initial position for normative modalities, everything that is possible in the initial position must also be permitted. To the general initial position *Mp & M~p* must, with respect to the normative realm, be added *Pp & P~p*.(Of course, this does not mean that I think that *Pp & P~p* follows from *Mp & M~p*.) Normative modalities modulate an initial position where all potential alternatives are permitted.

5.3.2 Accepting Alternatives. A Permission Is an Expressed Acceptance

Let us make a distinction between *natural norms* and *norm artefacts*. Natural norms are norms that develop "spontaneously" in a society, such as moral and, more usually, conventional norms. Natural norms lack specified norm-givers and often the circle of addressees is indeterminate. Norm artefacts, on the other hand, are created by means of conscious thought processes and within institutional frameworks. Legal rules, with the exception of customary rules, are norm artefacts. In the following I focus on norm artefacts. In conclusion I shall say a few things about moral norms.

What, then does it mean to block alternatives within the normative realm with respect to norm artefacts? As for normative modalities exclusively, the available (non-blocked) alternatives are the alternatives that are *accepted* by the norm-giver. Blocked alternatives are the alternatives that are *not accepted* by the norm-giver. By means of normative modalities the norm-giver announces which alternatives he accepts (and hence does not want to block but, perhaps, even wants to encourage) and not accepts (and hence wants to block). These announcements on the part of the norm-giver are *the meaning of* the normative modalities he uses. Normative modalities have meaning in this way.

What do I mean by acceptance and non-acceptance? The interesting term is non-acceptance. By introducing a modality everything within the universe of discourse is no longer permitted. The non-acceptance is manifested by the blocking of alternatives.

Non-acceptance of p is not the same as willing that $\sim p$, or the same as just evaluating $\sim p$ positively, nor the same as wishing that $\sim p$. It includes all three (with modifications which I shall come back to) but it is necessary to add one further component to them. Non-accepting is to burst the rampart between evaluation and norm-making. A tolerance limit has been transgressed; p is so contrary to my evaluations that an inner driving force induces me to try to influence people's behaviour in the direction of $\sim p$. "I do not accept this any longer, I have to do something about it", an inner voice tells me. The norm is a "propositional attitude" of sorts.

Norm-making, for its part, consists of two components: (1) Non-acceptance and (2) announcement of the non-acceptance. The latter is done by issuing a sentence containing a normative modality (and, hence, a norm) or by some behaviour which can be translated to such an issuance. The issued sentence's character of a norm is in no way lost even if the contemplated addressees neglect it and do not care in the least about it. Also an inoperative norm is a norm. To express one's non-acceptance in the form of a norm can be an effective intervention by a strong power or just a noble attempt or even a desperate move.

A permission can be conceived of as an expressed acceptance. Also an acceptance is a modality ("norm-giver n accepts that p"; $A_n p$). A_n behaves logically in the same way as P:

(i) $Pp \rightarrow A_n p$
(ii) $\sim Pp \rightarrow \sim A_n p$
(iii) $P\sim p \rightarrow A_n \sim p$
(iv) $\sim P\sim p \rightarrow \sim A_n \sim p$.

And now to the modifications! Let us make three, in this connection inevitable, distinctions.

Between (i) Proper Norms and (ii) Supplementary Norms

Proper norms (rules) are norms created because the evaluations of the norm-giver force him to block some behaviour by means of a norm. Supplementary norms (rules) are norms created for the purpose of facilitating the application and realisation of the proper norms (e.g., statutory definitions). Supplementary norms have a legislative-technical character.

Between (i) Instigators (Initiating Legislators, Norm-Givers Sensu Stricto) and (ii) Non-Instigators

The distinction is mainly applicable within institutionalised legislation (i.e., within legislative assemblies). Instigators are those legislators who, urged by their evaluations and "the normative driving force", have brought about the issuance of the rules by the legislative assembly. Non-instigators are the rest, i.e., those who have voted for the rules in a routine fashion or even voted against them but *ex post facto* accepted a majority resolution, and also later members of the assembly maintaining the rules.

Between (i) the Acceptance of Some Behaviour (Primary Acceptance) and (ii) the Acceptance of a Norm Regulating This Behaviour (Secondary Acceptance)

The *behaviour* that is accepted by the norm-giver in his own proper norms is accepted *primarily* by him. *Secondary* acceptance of a *norm* refers to (a) the instigators, (b) the non-instigators or (c) the norm addressees. The instigators probably accept the supplementary norms chiefly in the secondary sense. The non-instigating legislators probably usually accept both the proper and the supplementary norms in the secondary sense (so long as they join in the game) but do not necessarily accept the proper norms in the primary sense.

Of course it might also be the case that a person accepts a certain kind of behaviour (primarily) but does not accept the norm aimed at promoting that behaviour (secondarily). This person can be of the opinion that the norm does not promote this kind of behaviour.

Axel Hägerström and other Scandinavian realists made great play of the indisputable fact that an ignorant, oppositional or later legislative assembly cannot reasonable be said to "will" the rules issued. For that reason, the classical will-theory cannot be upheld, and I am sure they would say the same about acceptance in my sense. I do not find this objection convincing. To be sure, such legislators perhaps not at all "will" (accept) the norm in the sense that they "will" (accept) that the behaviour disapproved by the initiators is blocked. But it is reasonable to say that they "will" (accept) that *the norm issued* itself is valid law until abrogated. If this is the case, Hägerström's argument loses much of its sting.

Also the norm addressees, if they are loyal to the legal order, accept the issued norms in the secondary sense, but not necessarily in the primary sense. They can, e.g., deeply disapprove of the fact that a certain kind of behaviour is forbidden. But just as is the case with the non-instigators it is sufficient that they, for some reason or another, accept *the norm*. As for the addressees it is enough that they accept the norm by complying with it. Obviously the instigators want the addressees to embrace the underlying evaluation (for instance by relying on the so-called moral-formative function of punishment). However, we know indeed little about how such a moral-formative function works in real life—and, for that matter, about what induces people to comply with the law on the whole. (In Sect. 5.3.4 we shall say a few things about "normativity" and "binding force"—concepts that are closely related to questions about norm-complying.)

Let us incidentally say something about acceptance of natural (moral) norms belonging to the so-called positive morality. Also with respect to them the distinction between acceptance or non-acceptance of behaviour (valuation) and of norms seems to me to be relevant. If you embrace such a morality, you probably often wish that other people do so in the primary sense as well, and not only in the secondary sense. But in real life we often must be satisfied with secondary acceptance only.

5.3.3 *Blocking Alternatives*

(1) *The initial position* (*Pp* & *P~p*). The norm-giver (legislator) accepts everything with respect to *p*. The more the norm-giver accepts positions like *Pp* & *P~p*, *Pq* & *P~q*, *Pr* & *P~r* etc., the more freedom prevails within his sphere of competence. A state of affairs where *total freedom prevails* in this way can be called *anarchy*.

In the initial position one has no attitude at all with respect to *p*. Everything is accepted, the norm-giver is indifferent. *Pp* & *P~p* brings about nothing normative. For this reason it can be called into question whether *Pp* & *P~p* is a normative position at all. I shall not take up a definite position on this question here. On the other hand, the norm-giver can appreciate the freedom of choice itself. But that is not a normative position but an evaluation.

Now the norm-giver performs blockings with respect to the initial position.

(2) *Prohibition* (*~Pp*). *p* is not accepted and hence blocked. *~p* is accepted. Deontically:

(i) alternative *Pp* is blocked
(ii) alternative *~Pp* is accepted (and, indeed, asserted)
(iii) alternative *P~p* is accepted
(iv) alternative *~P~p* is blocked.

(3) *Obligation* (*~P~p*). *p* is accepted and *~p* is blocked. Deontically:

(i) alternative *Pp* is accepted
(ii) alternative *~Pp* is blocked
(iii) alternative *P~p* is blocked
(iv) alternative *~P~p* is accepted (and asserted).

(4) Let us imagine *the total lack of freedom*: *~Pp* & *~P~p*, *~Pq* & *~P~q*, *~Pr* & *~P~r* etc. Nothing is accepted, everything is blocked. It is true that *~P~p* is an obligation and for that reason could be regarded as an acceptance of *p*. But *~P~p* in conjunction with *~Pp* blocks everything. Whatever you do, you are violating a norm. This situation is contradictory (not to say perverse). A society where the total lack of freedom prevails is *a totalitarian society*—the citizens are completely subject to the pure arbitrariness of those in power.

A norm-giver can also revoke blockings by returning to the initial position. From the prohibition *~Pp* or the obligation *~P~p* he returns to *Pp & P~p* thereby deregulating normatively certain possible situations.

5.3.4 Norm Components Apart from Modality and Norm-Theme: Demystifying the Normative Modality (and Normativity)

A norm must contain its modality, its norm-theme and its addressee (although the latter can be implicit). But legal rules often contain more than this.

Common components of legal rules are the following: (i) requisite(s), (ii) explicit indication of the addressee, (iii) certain limitations with respect to persons, geographical location and time ((ii) and (iii) can also be seen as requisites), (iv) secondary legal consequence (i.e., the legal consequence the norm addressee is subjected to if he does not comply with the primary legal consequence of the rule addressed to him; usually, however, we find the secondary legal consequence in a rule of its own with its own requisites or else the primary rule is understood, as is usually the case in criminal law), (v) statutory definitions (unless expressed in rules of their own), (vi) interpretative directions, (vii) justification of the rule (although often expressed separately in preambles, particularly in international conventions) and, sometimes, (viii) indication of the lawgiver.

Now we may ask ourselves: What information, apart from what is given by (i)–(viii), gives us the modality itself? The answer is, I think, already given. The modality tells us which alternatives that are blocked within a set of alternatives. This is their semantic function. The normative modalities are not only the means of bringing pressure to bear on people, which has been claimed above all by Karl Olivecrona. If they were: How could we differentiate between permissions, obligations and prohibitions? Modalities are not meaningless.

Normative modalities can occur in norms as well as in normative propositions, the latter taken as descriptive propositions with truth value, claiming that a certain norm belongs to some set of norms, e.g., that the legal rule *r* belongs to the set of valid Swedish legal rules. For a normative proposition to be an adequate rendering of the corresponding norm, terms occurring in the latter must have the same meaning as they have when occurring in the former. Otherwise the proposition is no adequate rendering of the corresponding norm. This applies also to the modalities. Just as the term "adoptive parent" means the same thing in the norm and in its corresponding normative proposition, also, e.g., the term "has a duty to" must mean the same thing in both kinds of normative sentences. In my conception of the semantic function of normative modalities they do.

But what became of "the normative loading"? Of normativity? Of the "binding force" of the law? These phenomena are closely linked to the normative modalities. It seems to me that the normative modalities are shrouded in mystery, in a veil that

Hägerström and the other Scandinavian realists made a point of uncovering—only to find that under the veil were concealed highly complicated mental courses of events, which perhaps did not make the normative modalities less mysterious. Hans Kelsen speaks solemnly of "the world of ought" as ontologically totally separated from "the world of is". Normativity has been mystified, which has perhaps been detrimental to the analysis of it.

The significance of the modality for explaining "normativity" must not be exaggerated. I take it for granted that "normativity" is not taken to refer to something within the norm itself, indicating why the norm *shall* be complied with. For that would amount to no more than repeating the modality itself. So either normativity means that the norm shall or shall not be followed according to another system of norms than that to which the norm belongs or to some moral principle. Or else the term refers to factors that in fact urge the addressees to follow the norm. If so, the normative loading does not only, or even in the first place, relate to the modality. The modality has more informative value than normative force. The normative loading, urging the addressees to comply with the norm, emanates no doubt mainly from things like threats of sanctions when rules have been violated, respect for the authority of the legislator and the sanctity of the legal order, common moral and conventional opinions in the population and the like.

If there is any such thing as normativity or binding force at all, it cannot be anything but an emotional attitude in the direction of complying with the norm, which attitude is caused by phenomena of the kind just mentioned. ("Normativity" refers, as I see it, to phenomena outside the legal order and, hence, my view of it does not conflict with my ontological view of norms (Sects. 3.3 and 6.1).) Factors causing such attitudes can be indicated by the norm itself (e.g., the threat of sanctions) or they are factors not so indicated (e.g., a widely spread moral opinion), which the law-maker falls back on. The norm-giver does not bring about normativity by using a modality. At the most he might be able to trigger the activation of factors of the kind mentioned. Just as beauty lies in the eye of the beholder, normativity lies in the mentality of the addressees. The study of the psychology of obedience, or norm-compliance, is in the first place an empirical, not a philosophical, task (although the investigation of the concept "norm-compliance" itself has a philosophical character). Here, of course, both negative acceptance factors (sanctions) and positive ones (approval) are at work. But if complete consensus existed between norm-givers and addressees, norms would be needed for no other purpose than to give information, including the information given by the modalities. However, a law-maker can never count on such a consensus. The matter being so, he tries as a first step, before resorting to forceful means, to influence addressees he has in mind by means of words only, i.e., by issuing norms. (Indeed, norms are usually not issued for the purpose of giving the powers that be the opportunity to punish people—with the exception, though, of regimes like Hitler's and Stalin's.)

Chapter 6
The Place of the Normative in the Ontological Universe

6.1 Shapes of Reality

In Sect. 3.3, where I investigated the ontology of legal norms (and LO-elements on the whole), I argued that such phenomena are best understood as hypothetical facts (or objects). I suggested that thought contents are no ontological category of their own (belonging to a Popperian world 3) but belong either to world 2 or world 1 in Popper's sense. I left open the answer to the question whether world 2 is reducible to world 1 or not.

Thought contents are no independent ontological category. They are thoughts belonging to world 2 (or 1) whatever "the content" may be. We can think about a certain tree or about Winston Churchill—which both belong to natural reality—as well as about the relativity theory or the concept "legal validity"—which belong to artificial reality (a concept that will be explained in what immediately follows). The separation between thought contents referring to natural objects (brute things) and thought contents containing objects (concepts, ideas) created by the human mind (the relativity theory, the concept "legal validity") is a subdivision within the realm of human thinking. Only in this sense can world 3 phenomena be conceived of as a special ontological category. It is the special kind of thought phenomena—themselves world 2 (or 1) phenomena—which are (1) components of thought processes (actual or hypothetical) and (2) created by human thought processes that I assign to the category artificial reality. The members of that category are "second order" thoughts generated by thoughts (and, hence, they too belong to world 2 (or 1)).

Let us, on the basis of this conception, draw a kind of map over the different shapes of reality within the ontological universe.

I. *Actual reality* (the universe of actual reality).

1. Natural actual reality (the (sub)universe of natural actual reality).
2. Artificial actual reality (the (sub)universe of artificial actual reality).

Å. Frändberg, *The Legal Order*, Law and Philosophy Library 123,
https://doi.org/10.1007/978-3-319-78858-6_6

II. *Hypothetical reality* (the universe of hypothetical reality).

1. Natural hypothetical reality (the (sub)universe of natural hypothetical reality; in the following referred to as "the universe of mere possibilities").
2. Artificial hypothetical reality (the (sub)universe of artificial hypothetical reality).

The universe of actual reality consists of things and their interrelations (facts) that fill a part of the spatial-temporal space (or, in the case of mental occurrences perhaps only existing in the temporal dimension; in any case they are at least confined spatially to the brain). Object *o* exists in the sense of having actual reality at time *t* if and only if *o* fills a part of the spatial-temporal space at *t*. The universe of natural actual reality has as its members phenomena located outside human thought contents. They exist independently of human thinking. The universe of artificial actual reality has as its members realised, i.e., actualised, human thought contents, i.e., thought contents starting out as hypothetical and then, by triggering, taking on actual reality.

Members of the universe of hypothetical reality are those phenomena (including thought contents) that could logically belong to the universe of actual reality but do not do so, and that get actual reality if they are actualised (or realised)—however unlikely that may be –, i.e., triggered by some phenomenon belonging to the universe of actual reality, for instance, my reading Proust's *À la recherche du temps perdu* at *t* when in fact at *t* I am sitting in front of my computer writing what you just now read. Assuredly, this universe is, indeed, immense. Hypothetical reality is timeless, eternal reality.[1]

The universe of mere possibilities is the part of the universe of hypothetical reality that exists independently of human thinking—although what triggers the realisation of a member of this universe can be the content of a human thought. The fact that, if a piece of metal is heated and, hence, expands, is no human thought content; neither is the fact that, if person X drinks alcoholic beverages, she gets violent. When realised, they belong to the universe of natural actual reality. Moreover, I expand this ontological universe as far as to include also states of affairs that have occurred in the universe of actual reality at different points in the past but no longer do so, e.g., the killing of Julius Caesar.

The universe of artificial hypothetical reality is the part of the universe of hypothetical reality which has its place in human thought contents. For instance, the concept "legal validity" belongs to the universe of hypothetical reality when it does not form an integral part of a piece of thinking of mine but exists only as a disposition of mine to that effect. When realised, thought contents belong to the universe of artificial actual reality. So we see that an idea can simultaneously belong to actual reality at time *t* and to hypothetical reality at *t*. This is the case when, e. g., the idea is actualised in the mind of person A at *t* but not in the minds of persons B, C and D at *t*. Human ideas being subjective phenomena, this is not to be wondered at.

[1]The close similarity between this idea and David Lewis' conception of the ontology of possible worlds is obvious. Lewis (1987).

In the following I shall use this map in order to illuminate the function of norms, notably legal rules. I shall do so by examining the relations between norms as thought contents (human ideas) and phenomena in the other shapes of reality (and also to a certain extent the relation between norms and other human ideas, notably evaluations). I pay special attention to the relation between norms as members of artificial reality and human actions as members of natural reality.

Legal and juridical ideas are not, as has been suggested, fictional in the same sense as are creations of art (literature, the visual arts and even, but to a lesser degree, the more abstract art of music). What I have in mind here could be called "describing art" (e.g., the description in James Joyce's *Ulysses* of a day in Leopold Bloom's life, Botticelli's description (portrait) of *The Birth of Venus* or the tale told in Prokofiev's tone poem for children *Peter and the Wolf*).

It seems to me that the ontology of aesthetical objects is an ontology in two different shapes.

In order to explain what I have in mind, I must expand my conception of ontology. So far I have taken reality to be the concern of ontology. But let us, to the benefit of aesthetics, make a distinction between existence and reality. Let us assume that existence is a wider concept than reality and that reality is only a part of existence. We could even expand the term "ontology" as far as to say that ontology is the investigation of how the verb "to be" operates. (After all, the term "ontology" is derived from the present participle in the neuter *on* of the Greek verb *eimí*, "I am".) So let us within the universe of existence separate between the universe of reality and the universe of fictional existence.

To be sure, aesthetical ideas belong to the universe of reality as being hypothetical artificial thought contents. But with respect to the describing arts it seems a bit out of place to conceive of, e.g., Raskolnikov's killing of the old woman in Dostoyevsky's *Crime and Punishment* as a state of affairs capable of being actualised in the real world—even if this is logically and even empirically possible. This aspect is somehow beside the point. Better then to conceive of the universe of fictional existence as a make-believe ontology, a kind of reflection imitating or, rather, taking over the universe of reality. For instance, within the universe of fictional existence, in which Dorothy L. Sayers's *Gaudy Night* is one realm, there exists a college named Shrewsbury College on the spot where, in the universe of reality, we find the cricket-ground of Balliol College. In the universe of fictional existence it is true that Shrewsbury College is situated on the spot and false that the cricket-ground does. In the universe of reality it is the other way round. In the universe of fictional existence it is false that Harriet Wane is a married woman with five children—that state of affairs being only a hypothetical natural fact there—(just as it is false that Sherlock Holmes lived at 221A Baker Street) and it is a pseudo-actual (fictional) hypothetical natural fact that Miss Hillyard has a disposition to lose her temper when family life crops up in discussions. The ontology of the universe of fictional existence is in a way detached from the ontology of the universe of reality and its members live a life of their own. The fictional world is something we enter, like Alice entered Wonderland. We talk about Raskolnikov and Madame Bovary as if they existed in the universe of reality and we might even ask ourselves: "What happened to Orestes in Aeschylus'*Oresteia* after his being acquitted?" or "Was Hercule Poirot gay?", although the literary works where these persons appear do not tell us anything at all about these things. In the case of Poirot we can say that, what concerns his sexual preferences, Agatha Christie leaves us with a lacuna. In fact, an important difference between the universe of reality and the universe of fictional existence is that the latter but not the former can contain such ontological lacunae and must in practice necessarily do so. Moreover, the Julius Caesar in Shakespeare's play is not the Julius Caesar who died in the real world in 44 BCE and the person depicted in a so-called drama documentary (biopic) is always another person than the person appearing in it, however "realistic" the biopic is. The former person belongs to the universe of reality, the latter to the universe of fictional existence. The ontology of the universe of fictional existence becomes even more sophisticated when we find a work of art within a work of art, such as, e.g., the play in the play *A Midsummer Night's Dream.*

Legal and juridical ideas are something totally different from such a make-believe ontological universe, imitating the universe of reality. They belong to a kind of more "direct", non-fictional abstract creation of the human mind.

How does the ontology outlined in Sect. 3.3 and in this section square with the classical ontological distinction between realism and antirealism?

As Michael Moore puts it, philosophical realists "emphasize the world's independence from our concepts and language"—or, in more general terms, from our human consciousness—and antirealists "deny that the 'furniture of the universe' exists in any way independent of us".[2] Now it is, as Moore wisely reminds us, important to realise that a philosopher might be a realist with respect to some entities and an antirealist with respect to others: "One might be a realist about natural science and psychology, for example, but a conventionalist [conventionalism is a kind of antirealism] about mathematics, morality, and law.[3]

What is in focus here is actual reality.

Is my ontological position a realistic or an antirealistic one? With respect to brute things (facts) I am no doubt a realist—stones, planets, and human beings exist independently of our human consciousness. Likewise, I am in a certain sense a realist with respect to real numbers, logical and mathematical relations, and truth-value. These phenomena are "built into" nature as belonging to what I have called "the general state (or character) of the universe" (*GSU*; see Sect. 3.3). Real numbers etc. are, I argue, fundamental and necessary properties of nature, they structure reality.

But what about human ideas, including legal and juridical ones (phenomena belonging to what I call "artificial reality"): languages, legal orders, science, art, religions, and concepts such as "ownership" "legal competence (power)" "democracy", "cubism", "wisdom", and "anti-Semitism"—and universals on the whole?

[2]Moore (1988–89), p. 872.
[3]Moore (1988–89), p. 881.

It would be tempting to take an antirealistic stand with respect to such phenomena. After all, they do not exist independently of human consciousness. On the contrary, they are rather creations of it. This speaks for antirealism. On the other hand, human minds as such are natural things and so are thought processes as well. This speaks for realism.

The human mind (human consciousness) itself is not any more than stones a product of the human mind but a product of evolutionary biology. For this reason I prefer a realistic view also of products of our thoughts. An antirealistic stand amounts, it seems to me, to little more than the triviality that thoughts can create thoughts.

So I suggest a modified realism that allows us to include "artificial reality" ("thought contents") in the universe of reality. Such a modified realism could be formulated in the following way:

(1) Natural things (brute things and facts) exist (belong to reality) independently of human consciousness.
(2) The human mind is a natural thing.
(3) Phenomena necessarily tied to the human mind belong to reality in the realistic sense.

Phenomena belonging to artificial reality—thought contents of the kind exemplified above—are necessarily tied to the human mind.

It follows from this that I am definitely not an ontological legal realist in the sense defined by Moore.[4] I do not accept the notion that legal ideas exist "in a way not dependent on what we or anyone else think about them".

6.2 The Logic of Change

In the analysis of the relation between norms and other shapes of reality, the concept of change, i.e., changes in the universe of reality, is crucial.

By his logic of change, von Wright has constructed a fruitful tool for the analysis of the concept of change. I shall profit from it here.

von Wright introduces a symbol . . .T. . . . The blanks are filled by expressions describing states of affairs.[5] pTq is a transformation from p to q; p "changes into" q. p is an initial state and q an end-state. To use one of von Wright's own examples, let p mean that a certain window is open ("~" symbolises negation).

(i) ~pTp means that the window is being opened; first it was closed, then it is open.
(ii) pT~p means that the window is being closed; first it was open, then it is closed.

[4]Moore (1988–89), p. 882.

[5]See von Wright (1963), p. 28 ff.

(iii) pTp means that no change takes place; the window remains open. First it was open and then it is open.
(iv) ~pT~p means in a similar manner that the window remains closed.

If the states of affairs described by p and ~p on each side of T in (i)–(iv) belong to the universe of actual reality, then, in relation to every p, ~p belongs to the universe of mere possibilities, and, in relation to ~p, p (= ~ ~p) belongs to the universe of mere possibilities. If the initial state and the end-state are not identical, the end-state belongs to the universe of mere possibilities ex ante, i.e., before the transformation is actually performed. And ex post, i.e., when the transformation is performed, the initial state belongs to the universe of mere possibilities.

The end-state in an event, described by a formula of type ...T..., can be a desirable state of affairs, and it may be regarded as a good thing if the initial state is transformed into the end-state.

The idea that transformation can be a transfer of an event from the universe of mere possibilities to the universe of actual reality, and that the end-state can be a desirable state of affairs—the qualification of an event as desirable being an idea belonging to the universe of human ideas—can, I think, shed some light upon the relationship between the norm and other shapes of reality. ...T... can in this respect be conceived of as *a normative mechanism*, operating on all of our ontological universes.

6.3 Transformational Mechanisms

Norm-giving (legislation) is to decide that some state of affairs shall be removed from the universe of actual reality (and incorporated in the universe of mere possibilities), and other states of affairs incorporated in the universe of actual reality (and removed from the universe of mere possibilities)—all in accordance with, and under the guidance of, values belonging to the universe of human ideas and *by means of norms* (also contained in the universe of human ideas) *and their enforcement* (in the universe of actual reality). This is a description *in nuce* of the normative mechanism.[6]

Let us regard von Wright's symbol ...T... as a variable over a set of *transformational mechanisms*, of which the normative mechanism is one. Other such mechanisms could be, for example, non-intentional occurrences in nature (e.g., the wind slams the window shut), or an intentional, non-normative act performed by a human being (e.g., if a person in a room shuts the window in order not to be cold). If

[6] Hage (2015) talks about "interfacing the world of law and the outside world" and argues: "The world of law is not a goal in itself; it is meant to have impact on the 'outside world', the world that consists of facts which are not the result of the operation of legal rules" (p. 36). See also what he says about "bridges" from the world of law to the outside world (p. 45).

that person, on the other hand, takes it as a duty to shut the window as soon as the temperature of the room falls below 20° C the normative mechanism is at work.

In the first example, the transformational mechanism itself (i.e., the wind slamming the window shut) belongs entirely to the universe of actual natural reality. In the second and the third examples, the transformational mechanism involves elements of which some belong to the universe of actual reality and some belong to the universe of human thought (i.e., the universe of artificial reality). In the third example but not in the second, normative ideas belong to the transformational mechanism.

Let us now regard the normative transformational mechanism a little closer. As was suggested above, this mechanism consists of the following components: (i) a legislator (in a wide sense of the word) who (ii) decides upon (the striving for) a transfer of some state of affairs from the universe of actual natural reality to the universe of mere possibilities, or vice versa, and (iii) does so in accordance with, and under the guidance of, values contained in the universe of human ideas and (iv) by means of norms (also belonging to the universe of human ideas) and their enforcement in the universe of actual reality.

In the following we shall look at (i)–(iv) in more detail.

6.4 Instituting Legislators

The universe of mere possibilities is that strange, heavenly and infernal, tempting and horrifying universe where all novels and plays of mankind are enacted, all music performed by virtuosi and the most excellent wines tasted—as well as the universe where Hitler's Holocaust (which once belonged to the universe of actual natural reality) is going on forever, together with the devastating wars. It is the universe where our private hopes, delights and fears are fulfilled beyond space and time. It is the ontological universe where anything (save logical contradictions) could be real, but is not. It is the Garden of Eden, and our filthy backyard. It is the repository of mankind.

What, then, can justify a legislator to dispose of this fateful universe, surrounding the real life of mankind, and allow a piece of it to intrude upon real life?

First of all, of course, because a piece of actual reality might be far worse than a piece of mere possibilities. Wars, murders, theft and neglect of children belong to real life, but peace, non-violence, safety and caring are possible. We are indeed all engaged in the project of creating reality out of possibility.

This justifies the instituting of legislators. But, certainly, it does not justify any legislator whatsoever having the power to do anything he likes.

I adhere to a humanistic theory of law. By that I mean the conception of law as an artefact, a creation of human culture. Nothing even similar to convincing reasons has ever been provided for the thesis that legal norms are immanent in (biological) human nature (save in the utterly trivial sense that legal rules usually have the function of guaranteeing peace and safety in human interaction—after all, laws are for human beings, not for wolves or angels), neither for the thesis of theocratic voluntarism to the effect that legal norms are expressions of the will of some god.

History is not unfamiliar with legislative power held by one single person. But usually legislation is a collective enterprise. Even customs with the status of law are created by individuals in a complex collective endeavour over perhaps a very long span of time, although these individuals are unknown to us.

So the normative mechanism is entirely in our hands. In this vast space of freedom our responsibility is by no means insignificant.

6.5 Normative Mechanisms

Let us now turn our attention to the normative mechanism itself.

One part of that mechanism might seem to belong to the universe of human ideas entirely. What I have in mind is the relationship between value and norm. The idea that values in some way or another *justify* norms and also have an impact on their formulation seems reasonable. What is, e.g., the relation between the evaluation

(v) The life of a human being is valuable

and the norms

(n) Thou shalt not kill

and

(n') If somebody wilfully kills another person, he shall be sentenced to life imprisonment?

First of all, we get an impression that the norms do not "cover", as it were, the whole of the value. Many other norms corresponding to the same value could be formulated, e.g.,

(n^*) You shall take care of yourself

and it appears to be utterly difficult, or even impossible, to formulate one single norm which actually covers the whole value. On the other hand, it seems obvious that (v) is the value that justifies each of (n), (n') and (n^*), and it is hard to imagine more specific values, independent of (v), covering each norm but none other.

Be that as it may, although both values and norms are entities belonging to the universe of human thought, the process of justification cannot take place altogether within that ontological universe. In order to, e.g., justify (n) by means of (v) we must make an excursion into the universe of mere possibilities, and perhaps also into the universe of actual reality. (But note that, e.g., the killing of John F. Kennedy *now*, in 2018, belongs to the universe of mere possibilities. No killing of John F. Kennedy fills the temporal-spatial room of, say, March 1, 2018, Dallas). To make the justification in question conclusive, we must add the premise

(p) If a person kills another person, the value of the killed person's life is violated which premise is a kind of induction from events that have taken place in the other ontological universes.

In the case of (*n'*)—which is a hypothetical norm—we notice that what is regulated is not killing at all, but the judge's sentencing the murderer to life imprisonment. That the justification of such a norm must take phenomena in the other ontological universes into consideration is obvious.

The very *raison d'être* of a norm is the achievement of its goal. The goal can be conceived of as an event in the universe of mere possibilities. A norm is *expedient* if its observance in the universe of actual reality transfers the goal from the universe of mere possibilities into the universe of actual reality. To *justify* a norm is (i) to give reasons for its goal being valuable (and more valuable than its probable negative side-effects), and (ii) to give reasons for its expediency.

6.6 The Enforcement of Norms

How do we transfer desired states of affairs from the universe of mere possibilities to the universe of actual reality or, vice versa, undesired states of affairs from the universe of actual reality to the universe of mere possibilities by means of norms and their enforcement?

As a matter of principle, the answer is easy, and consists of two steps: (1) that the legislator sees to it that the norms are expedient, and (2) that the norms are actually followed by the public and by the norm-applying authorities. To follow an obligatory norm is to do what is obligatory and to follow a prohibition is not to do what is prohibited, otherwise the norm is broken. A genuine permission is always followed (it cannot be broken).

It is *a utopian ideal* that the transformation will take place by itself, without any norm, as an effect, perhaps, of the inherent goodness of man. It is *a legislative ideal* that the transformation in question takes place as an effect of the mere existence of the norm. But in real life, as we all know, this is seldom the case. For the goal to be achieved, enforcement of the norm is necessary. That the goal is actually achieved by means of enforcement we might call *a judicial ideal.*

The enforcement of law has as an underlying condition the idea that the norm is only one component—and in some situations a rather insignificant component at that—in the complex mechanism aimed at safeguarding law-abiding behaviour.

Enforcement of law can be said to consist of two levels: the level of administration (application) of law, and the level of execution of law. Both levels can be analysed in terms of our ontological universes.

Let us in a schematic form, and by means of an example, try to establish the relations between different ontological universes with respect to the application of law.

We use the following line of reasoning as a starting point.

(1) Anyone who, in a way that might obstruct a restoration, meddles with something that has been taken away from another person by a criminal action, shall be punished for receiving stolen goods to at the most 2 years of imprisonment
(2) Anyone who receives a receipt concerning stolen goods which has been deposited in a railway station's cloak room, shall be punished for receiving stolen goods to at the most 2 years of imprisonment
(3) Person X has received a receipt concerning stolen goods which has been deposited in a railway station's cloak room
(4) X shall be punished for receiving stolen goods to at the most 2 years of imprisonment
(5) X is sentenced to 1 month of imprisonment for receiving stolen goods.

Sentence (3) describes the case at hand for the judge to decide. His first task, from the viewpoint of principle, is, by evaluation of the evidence, to establish whether the state of affairs described in (3)—an element in the universe of mere possibilities—once belonged to the universe of actual reality. Only if he, correctly or not, finds that it has, is there any reason to go further in the process of application. Evaluation of evidence is an activity to no small degree regulated by (second order) legal norms.

The next step is to decide whether the norm (1) is applicable to the state of affairs described in (3) or not. In the language of lawyers this process is often referred to as interpretation. If the judge finds that (1) is applicable, (the result of) the interpretation is norm (2).

We see, that (4) does not logically follow from premises (1) and (3). But (4) follows logically from premises (2) and (3). (2) is the norm that our judge in fact *applies*. Application *sensu stricto* is to draw a conclusion of type (4) from sentences of type (2) and (3). All three sentences express norms (belonging to the universe of human ideas), but the mental action consisting in drawing the conclusion belongs to the universe of actual reality. Application *sensu stricto* is the third step in the application of law *sensu largo*.

By pronouncing sentence (5), the very judgment, the judge fulfils what he is ordered to do in norm (4). He fulfils it by pronouncing a *performative* sentence, (5). This last step in the administration of law, or application of law *sensu largo*, we can call the choice of (individual) legal consequence. Since the possibilities of judgment are many—the judge could have sentenced X to 1 year of imprisonment instead –, he must give arguments for his decision, e.g., that the culprit is a young person. In making choices of this kind, the judge uses elements from the universe of mere possibilities.

Let us finally turn to the execution of law. The executor starts where the judge stops, viz. at sentence (5). The executor (in our example consisting of the police and the prison authority) shall see to it that what is sentenced in the judgment is also realised; in our example that X is actually held in prison for 1 month. The theme, as it were, of sentence (5)—X is held in prison during 1 month—belongs at the time of the sentencing to the universe of mere possibilities, but during the month that the sentence is served, the state of affairs is actually realised. It has been transferred from the universe of mere possibilities to the universe of actual reality.

Such a realised state of affairs can be the very goal of the legislator. But realised law is usually a kind of second best state of affairs, serving in its turn as one cause among others for achieving the ultimate goals, still belonging to the universe of mere possibilities.

6.7 Kelsen's Norm-Exclusiveness

For epistemological reasons it was important for Kelsen to formulate a pure theory of law, i.e., a well-founded conception of the legal system as a system of norms, ontologically independent of what I have called the universe of natural reality. The legal system is a self-contained set of norms, being a system in virtue of its basic norm. Legal norms belong ontologically to a universe of norms.[7] In my conception, this universe of norms belongs to the universe of ideas, which, in turn, belongs to the universe of artificial reality.

Crucial in Kelsen's effort is the idea of the *Stufenbau*, i.e., a kind of ordering of legal norms, an idea which Kelsen borrowed from Adolf Julius Merkl.[8] The relation between a norm on a later stage in the ordering and a corresponding norm on an earlier stage is that the former has (genetically) come about by means of the latter. Let me give an example. The act-in-the-law

(a) X is imprisoned for 2 years

is valid because it is performed in accordance with the individual norm (in a judgment)

(1) X shall be imprisoned for 2 years.

(1) is valid because it has been created in accordance with

(2) If someone has stolen something, he shall be imprisoned for at least 6 months and at the most 3 years.

(2) is valid because it has been created in accordance with provisions in a constitution

(3) C_n.

(3) is valid because it has been created in accordance with the preceding constitution

(4) C_{n-1}

and so on, until we reach the historically first constitution in a chain of legal continuity

[7]A thoroughly performed study of Kelsen's pure theory of law is Bindreiter (2003). Here we also find many valuable references.

[8]Merkl (1917).

(5) C.

But why is C valid? According to Kelsen because the lawyers postulate that it shall be valid. In order to preserve the normative status of the entire legal system, which is important for Kelsen for ontological and epistemological reasons, he conceives of this postulate as a norm, the basic norm, which could be formulated

(BN) C shall be valid.

And hence, all later members of the chain (the *Stufenbau*) are valid, down to the act-in-the-law (a).

It should be clear from what I have said in the foregoing chapters that I fully agree with Kelsen that legal systems are systems of norms exclusively. It should, however, also be clear from what I have said in Sects. 3.3 and 6.1 that I do not adhere altogether to Kelsens's ontological and epistemological points of departure.

Let us make a slight logical reconstruction of the *Stufenbau*, which, I think, will render it a bit clearer. We structure a non-momentary legal system, *S*, in the following way, which reflects the structure of legal systems belonging to well-developed legal orders.

(i) *S* contains norms specifying who the legislators of *S* are (*NL*)
(ii) *S* contains norms specifying the procedures the legislators shall follow when legislating (*NP*)
(iii) *S* contains norms specifying who the law-appliers of *S* are (*NA*)

In addition to (i)–(iii) *S* of course contains the usual bulk of "ordinary" legal norms (*N*). In this connection we follow Kelsen in regarding these norms as addressed to legal functionaries.

Let us now regard the legal system *S* as a structure $S = \langle NL, NP, N, NA \rangle$. We can then imagine a *Stufenbau* within *S*, where each stage has the same structure (for the sake of example a four-level hierarchy SS, SS', SS'', SS'''):

$$SS = \langle SNL, SNP, SN, SNA \rangle$$
$$SS' = \langle SNL', SNP', SN', SNA' \rangle$$
$$SS'' = \langle SNL'', SNP'', SN'', SNA'' \rangle$$
$$SS''' = \langle SNL''', SNP''', SN''', SNA''' \rangle.$$

The genetic order between these stages is: SS''' is the lowest one, SS'' the immediately higher stage in relation to SS''', SS' the immediately higher stage in relation to SS'', SS the immediately higher stage in relation to SS' and also the highest stage of the hierarchy. SS''' could be the stage of the application of law, SS'' the stage of "ordinary" legislation, SS' the stage of constitutional legislation and SS the stage of introducing the historically first constitution.

(1) *Stage SS.*

- Legislators: The authors of the first constitution ("the founding fathers").
- Procedures of legislation: Do not exist or exist *ad hoc*, since this is the first constitution.

- The norms created: The first constitution.
- Norm-appliers of the first constitution: Later constitutional legislators.

(2) *Stage SS′*.

- Legislators: Constitutional legislators.
- Procedures of legislation: Contained in the first constitution.
- The norms created: A later constitution, *c*.
- Norm-appliers: Legislators of "ordinary" legislation (civil law, criminal law etc.).

(3) *Stage SS″*.

- Legislators: Legislators of ordinary legislation.
- Procedures of legislation: Contained in *c*.
- The norms created: Ordinary legislation.
- Norm-appliers: The judges.

(4) *Stage S‴*.

- Legislators: Legislators of individual legal norms (the judges).
- Procedures of legislation: Contained in ordinary legislation (the applicable rules, procedural law etc.).
- The norms created: Individual legal norms.
- Norm-appliers: Executive authorities.

Let us now have a look at the genetic relations between these stages in our *Stufenbau*. We find that the norm-appliers of *SS* are the legislators of *SS′* and that the norms created at level *SS* are the procedures of law-creation at stage *SS′*. The norm-appliers of *SS′* are the legislators of *SS″* and the norms created at stage *SS′* are the procedures of law-creating at stage *SS″*. The norm-appliers of *SS″* are the legislators of *SS‴* and the norms created at stage *SS″* are the procedures of law-creating at stage *SS‴*. This fits well with Kelsen's firmly held conviction that law-applying is also law-creating.

Merkl-Kelsen's *Stufenbau* is a brilliant theory of the structure of legal systems. It is one of the most interesting results of twentieth century jurisprudence, perhaps only matched by Hohfeld's theory of jural relations. However, I find it questionable in the following respects.

My doubts concern the ontological theory that Kelsen attaches to the *Stufenbau*. The ontology he infuses into the *Stufenbau* and the *Stufenbau* itself are not logically connected—one can very well accept the *Stufenbau* theory without accepting Kelsen's ontological aspect regarding it. In fact, I think one should.

Kelsen separates two ontological universes, natural reality and ideal reality.[9] These two correspond roughly to what I have called natural and artificial reality. Concerning the extension of ideal reality Kelsen says: "One can argue over whether

[9]Kelsen (1996), p. 15.

the opposition between the natural and the ideal coincides with the opposition between natural reality and value, between 'is' and 'ought', between causal law and norm, or whether the realm of the ideal is indeed broader than the realm of value, of 'ought', of norm."[10] For my part, I see no reason whatsoever for excluding human ideas other than evaluative or normative ones from the realm of ideal, or artificial, reality. And I can find no reason why normative ideas would not exist in the same sense as all other human ideas exist. Neither do I, therefore, see any need of a certain "form of existence" with respect to normative ideas. For Kelsen, however, there is such a special form of existence for norms, viz., validity.

It seems to me that Kelsen in his Pure Theory of Law operates with two different concepts of validity—one for ontological purposes, the other for juridical purposes—and that he confuses the two concepts in an attempt to kill two birds with one stone.

Let us call the first one *the ontological concept of validity*. It pertains to the question of what a norm is, i.e., to validity as existence in the normative sphere. It is to be noted that Kelsen assigns also evaluations to this ontological realm—"the realm of value, of 'ought', of norm". What, then, characterises the special kind of existence that Kelsen calls validity? Kelsen is not easy to grasp here. On the one hand, a legal norm does not belong to the temporal-spatial realm but on the other, Kelsen seems to think, it begins to exist at one point of time and ceases to exist at a later one. With respect to both legal and moral norms, *validity is attributed to them by human beings*. Their existence is in the hands of mankind. Moreover, a norm can exist for one human being but not for another at the same time.

Let me try to give an elucidation of Kelsen's ontology of norms as I have understood it. It can be summarised in the following 11 Kelsenian theses.

(T1) The form of existence of norms is validity. A norm exists if and only if it is valid.
(T2) That a norm is valid means that it is binding.
(T3) Hence, that a norm exists means that it is binding.
(T4) "Ought" (*Sollen*) as such is a form of existence.
(T5) Hence, "ought" is validity and bindingness.
(T6a) Norms are expressions of will.
(T6b) Norms are the meaning of acts of will.
(T7) The validity of any norm stems from another norm being its basis of validity (*Geltungsgrund*)—not from some factual state of affairs.
(T8) The basis of validity is a basic norm (*Grundnorm*).
(T9a) The basic norm is presupposed, not posited. At the same time some people can presuppose the basic norm and others not. To presuppose the basic norm is to interpret the subjective meaning of the act of will causing the first constitution as an objective meaning.
(T9b) The basis of validity is hypothetical (or fictional).

[10] Kelsen (1996), p. 15.

(T10) Basic norms transport, immediately or mediately, validity to other norms.
(T11) The validity and the efficacy of a norm are different, although interrelated, things.

(T1) must be taken most seriously. It is constantly repeated by Kelsen. Although his main purpose is to uncover the epistemological foundation of legal cognition, this enterprise is based upon an elaborate ontological standpoint—proper enough, since ontology precedes epistemology. My doubts concerning Kelsen's ontology rest on three basic objections.

I. Norms have no unique ontological status. They do not need any special "form of existence"—just as questions or interjections do not have any special form of existence. They are all human ideas and exist as such. What distinguishes norms from other human ideas is not an ontological matter. (Cf. Sects. 3.3 and 6.1.)
II. There is no ontological need for a basic normative idea, a basic norm, transporting validity to other norms. If a norm exists, it seems reasonable to think that it exists ontologically independent of other norms, in actual or hypothetical reality. If we accept Kelsen's thesis that the basic norm is presupposed, why could not every separate norm be presupposed and hence exist? The idea of a *Stufenbau* transporting validity might be plausible as a juridical idea but not as an ontological one. But what is more, there is no reason for thinking that a norm can exist (directly or indirectly) if and only if it is presupposed—after all, other human ideas, such as Einstein's theory of relativity or Descartes' *Cogito ergo sum*, exist without being "presupposed". It seems to be enough that the norm appears or can appear in persons' minds.

    Kelsen is ambiguous on the issue whether the basic norm itself belongs to the legal system it is a basis of or not.[11] Perhaps this ambiguity has its roots in Kelsen's vacillating between an ontological and a juridical concept of validity. From the viewpoint of ontology it is reasonable to place the basic norm outside that system, from a juridical viewpoint, however, inside it.
III. The realm of normative existence is wider than that of normative validity. Also norms no longer, or not yet, juridically valid can exist as thought contents. For that reason it is not appropriate to identify existence with validity. Furthermore, one might ask, what is the ontological nature of the phenomenon that exists "before" validity is assigned to a legal system—and which phenomenon becomes valid by people's presupposing the basic norm? Kelsen refers to that phenomenon as the "empirical data", which are interpreted (presupposed) as law.[12] These data can be nothing but, in the first place, some statutory material. But this statutory material (i) no doubt exists and (ii) no doubt has a normative character. It is loaded with normative ideas formulated in a structure of legal rules containing normative modalities. Then it seems strange to think that these normative ideas, merely by being "presupposed" by someone, all of a sudden

[11]Kelsen (1964–65), p. 1151.
[12]Kelsen (1996), p. 58.

begin to exist. Less strange is to think that they become valid in the juridical sense. Hence also on this point Kelsen seems to vacillate between an ontological and a juridical concept of validity.

Let us now turn to *the juridical concept of validity*. Here we should take note of Kelsen's ideas about the different behaviour of the basic norm in moral and in juridical thinking, respectively. The relation between a moral basic norm and a corresponding moral norm based on it is a matter of content. The relation between them is a relation between particular (the moral norm) and universal (the basic norm). For instance, "Thou shalt not lie" derives from a basic norm of honesty. But the relation between a legal norm and its corresponding basic norm is not a matter of content. It is a genetic relation, where the norm can have any content whatsoever which is possible to express in a norm. A legal norm is valid if (i) the basic norm is "presupposed" by the law-appliers in their work and (ii) the legal norm is produced in the way the basic norm states that the norm shall be produced.[13] It seems to me that the term "basic norm" expresses different concepts in (i) and (ii) respectively. No doubt the concept "basic norm" figuring in (ii) is a juridical concept. With respect to the juridical function of the basic norm described in (ii), it can be conceived of either as a norm of competence or as a duty-norm. Kelsen does both.[14]

My objections to Kelsen's version of the juridical validity concept are the following. First it could be argued that the idea of presupposition is a rather trivial one. Is it not self-evident for the functionaries of the legal order that they shall do their job? After all, doctors, taxi drivers or farmers do not seem to need "a basic norm" to the effect that they shall cure people, transport them or provide them with food.

More important, Kelsen's theory that official law-appliers (consciously, or what is far more probable, unconsciously) see as their duty to apply (regard as valid) those norms which are, in a mediate way, genetically derived from the first constitution—this duty being explicitly formulated as the basic norm—is in my opinion mistaken. Judges do nothing of the sort. They don't give a damn for the first constitution, and if they are made conscious of such a basic norm they would surely not admit that it gives a correct description of how lawyers think and argue. This is blurred in Kelsen's *Stufenbau* theory, and this is a consequence of the *Stufenbau* structure being intended to fulfil two different functions—the ontological one of transporting validity as existence and the juridical one of transporting competence to produce juridically valid norms. But the model of *Stufenbau* plus basic norm in the latter function does not, as far as I can see, give an adequate description of actual juridical thinking.

Validity for lawyers pertains to the rules they shall apply. A judge setting about to apply a statutory provision to a case is satisfied if the provision is in force

[13]Kelsen (1935), p. 517 ff.

[14]Kelsen (1960), pp. 196 f and 203 f.

(promulgated and not abrogated) and not obsolete. If he is setting about to apply a precedent he is satisfied if the precedent is in an analogous way "valid". Only in cases involving judicial review is the constitution in force actualised. In fact, Kelsen's *Stufenbau* consists of two different structures, one vertical (momentary) and one horizontal (diachronic, historical). The latter is not hierarchical at all, but a sequence in time of successive constitutions on the same "hierarchical level", the highest. All but the latest of these constitutions are no longer valid and it seems strange from a juridical viewpoint to assume that lawyers would ascertain the validity of the norms they are contemplating to apply by means of non-valid rules. Of course, a statutory provision in force can be valid even if it is produced in accordance with a later abrogated constitution. But this is not a horizontal but a vertical (hierarchical) relation. In my example above (p. 117 f.) the vertical *Stufenbau* includes (a) and levels (1)–(3), the horizontal one stages (3)–(5). Kelsen's *Stufenbau* is in fact a construction at an angle of 90°. The shift from a vertical to a horizontal sequence occurs at level (3), the actual constitution. My point is that "the total" *Stufenbau* might be considered relevant from an ontological viewpoint (although I for my part reject it) but that the horizontal (historical) part of it is irrelevant from a juridical viewpoint by not adequately mirroring actual juridical thinking.

Hart's rule of recognition is often treated together with and compared to Kelsen's basic norm. But there are obvious differences between them. First of all, Hart is not philosophically committed to introduce his fundamental norm in the way Kelsen is for ontological and epistemological reasons. Secondly, the rule of recognition is manifestly a member of the legal system. Therefore it seems somewhat strange that Hart insists on regarding the rule of recognition as one single rule—contrary to what he calls "rules of change" and "rules of adjudication", which are subsets of rules within the system. What would Hart lose if he, instead of a single rule of recognition, included in the legal system a subset of legal rules, rules of recognition,—which, in fact, would coincide with the doctrine of legal sources actually informing the functionaries' handling of the system? That would present us with a more adequate and realistic rendering of juridical thinking. Assuredly, most such doctrines are rather poor but in spite of that, if we would take the trouble to spell out the rule of recognition of this or that legal system, we would no doubt end up with a grotesquely complicated rule full of conjunctions and disjunctions, principal rules and exceptions. Why this insistence on basing the validity of the legal system on one single norm?

References

Bindreiter U (2003) Why Grundnorm? A treatise on the implications of Kelsen's doctrine. Springer, Berlin

Hage J (2015) The (onto)logical structure of law: a conceptual toolkit for legislators. In: Araszkiewicz M, Pleszka K (eds) Logic in the theory and practice of lawmaking. Springer, Berlin, pp 3–48

Kelsen H (1935) The pure theory of law. Law Q Rev 51:517 ff

Kelsen H (1960) Reine Rechtslehre, 2nd edn. Mohr Siebeck, Heidelberg
Kelsen H (1964–65) Professor Stone and the pure theory of law. Stanford Law Rev 17:1128–1157
Kelsen H (1996) Introduction to the problems of legal theory (trans: Litschewski Paulson B, Paulson SL). Oxford University Press, Oxford
Lewis D (1987) Counterfactuals. Harvard University Press, Cambridge
Merkl AJ (1917) Das Recht im Lichte seiner Anwendung. Helwing, Hannover
Moore MS (1988–89) The interpretive turn in modern theory: a turn for the worse?. Stanford Law Rev 41:871–957
von Wright GH (1963) Norm and action. Routledge, Abingdon

Chapter 7
The Juridical Topology: Some Basic Concepts

7.1 Introduction

In Sect. 2.9.2 above, we presented, by means of an example, the morphological structure of an ordinary regulative rule in the following manner

(*r*) If the seller due to delay on the part of the buyer has had costs for the proper care of the goods, the buyer shall pay damages for those costs.

We divided *r* into the different elements:

(1) *the requisites*: "due to delay on the part of the buyer the seller has had costs for the proper care of the goods"
(2) *the legal consequence*: "the buyer shall pay damages for those costs"

and the legal consequence into

(3) *the normative modality*: "shall"
(4) *the norm-theme*: "the buyer pays damages for the costs".

This is a normative structure. Rules with this structure—and rules with the structures rendered by way of standard forms for the different types of legal rules presented in Chap. 2—shall be applied to, or in other ways operate on, *states of affairs*, belonging to actual or hypothetical reality. Legal rules map a landscape of reality. For that reason I call concepts characterising states of affairs in these ways related to legal rules *topological concepts*. In this chapter I shall try to clarify some basic topological concepts.[1]

[1]From what follows it should be obvious that I do not use the term "topological" in the same sense as in Müller-Mall (2013).

Å. Frändberg, *The Legal Order*, Law and Philosophy Library 123,
https://doi.org/10.1007/978-3-319-78858-6_7

7.2 Legal Case, Operative Fact, Potential Operative Fact

A legal state of affairs (*a legal case*) is either (i) *an operative fact* or (ii) *a potential operative fact*. Operative facts are necessarily tied to legal rules. An operative fact relative to rule *r* is a state of affairs such that the law-applying authorities generally regard *r* as applicable to it. By "potential operative fact" I mean a state of affairs that is not an operative fact but is legally relevant, i.e., a legal case that the law-applying organs by virtue of the prohibition of denial of justice (*déni de justice*) must take into consideration if actualised. A potential operative fact is a legal case that could be an operative fact. (As a concession to common juridical usage, I let the term "fact" cover also only alleged states of affairs.) As you see, I use the term "case" in a wider sense—not in the narrower sense of "litigation". The term is used in both senses in juridical thinking.

Alchourrón and Bulygin make an important distinction between *generic* and *individual cases*, presented here in my terminology.[2] Let us form the set O_r of all operative facts relative to a rule, *r*. The elements of O_r we call *individual operative facts*. Subsets of O_r we call *generic operative facts*. For an operative fact to be an individual operative fact it must be in some way unique in the spatial-temporal realm, implying that the parties involved must be (named) individual persons. Examples of individual operative facts: (i) "Jones did not fetch the cow Rosita which he had bought from Smith at the time agreed and that cost Smith ten thousand kronor extra for the care of Rosita" and (ii) "Ruritarian Airlines did not pay the purchase money of one hundred million dinars for the purchase of two aeroplanes from Flying Fox Ltd., which because of the costs for taking care of the planes during the delay contributed to the company's going into bankruptcy". Examples of generic operative facts: (i) "buyers do not take into possession the goods purchased at the time agreed, leading to costs for the seller's taking care of the goods during the delay", (ii) "buyers do not pay the purchase money in due time, leading to costs for the seller's taking care of the goods during the delay" and (iii) "[the fact that] due to delay on the part of the buyer the seller has had costs for the proper care of the goods". The examples show that generic operative facts can be more or less genetic. (iii) is *maximally genetic*. It is the set O_r. (i) and (ii) are proper subsets of O_r.

It must be observed that the distinction generic—individual is not identical with the distinction actual—hypothetical reality. An individual case can have actuality at time *t* although being hypothetical at the later time *t'* (e.g., the time when the case is tried at a court of law), or have only hypothetical reality at any time, even *t*, in which case it has never occurred. Hopefully, the former is generally the case in our courts of law. The cases described by the requisites of statutory provisions as well as invented examples in legal text books are for the most part genetic, hypothetical cases.

Legal rules describe generic cases. Individual legal norms describe individual cases.

[2] Alchourrón and Bulygin (1971), p. 27-30. Cf. Austin (1911), p. 1002 and the distinction between generic and individual actions in von Wright (1963), Ch. III, Section 2.

7.3 The Structure of Legal Cases

Let us elaborate a little on the structure of legal cases. Generally speaking, the requisites of a legal rule express two things: (i) they describe some kind of relation and (ii) they state what kinds of individuals between whom this relation exists.

An example: The requisite "The seller is in delay delivering the goods to the buyer" can be structured as a relation, R, "being in delay delivering the goods" between sellers (S) and buyers (B): R(S,B). In this section we shall elaborate a bit on such relations. In order to attain a higher degree of preciseness in this endeavour I shall use some elementary set theory and theory of relations. (The reading of this section is not necessary for the understanding of what follows after it. It can be passed over by readers not interested in a closer analysis of the structure of legal cases.)

Let us call the totality of the requisites of a legal rule *a requisite proposition* (*rp*). To each *rp* corresponds *an rp-structure* (*RPS*) $= \{<U,K,L,R>\}$ where U, K and L are non-empty sets of individuals, R a relation over U, ($R \subseteq UxU$), and $K \subseteq U$ and $L \subseteq U$. (We do not exclude the case $K = L$.) R is the relation described in *rp*, K a subset of its domain and L a subset of its counterdomain. In our example R is the relation "being in delay delivering the goods", K the set of sellers and L the set of buyers. The set of individuals U is kept constant. (For the sake of simplicity we take only binary relations into consideration here. That is of course a rather rough rendering of many requisite propositions. But if one wishes, it is easy to use ternary or higher *n*-ary relations, which could be necessary, e.g., within the law of property.)

Given an *rp*-structure $RPS = \{<U,K,L,R>\}$ relative to a rule, r, the material set of operative facts M_r, is the intersection of the relation R and the Cartesian product KxL:

$$M_r = R \cap (KxL).$$

Examples: (1) The material set of operative facts relative to the rule "If the seller due to delay on the part of the buyer has had costs for the proper care of the goods, the buyer shall pay damages for those costs" is the intersection of "the delay relation" and the Cartesian product of the set of buyers and the set of sellers. (2) For the rule "If someone improperly subjects animals to suffering, he shall be punished for cruelty to animals to imprisonment for at most two years" the material set of operative facts is the intersection of the relation "being cruel to" and the Cartesian product of men and animals.

Let us now formulate the following requisite propositions:

(i) The seller is in delay with delivering the goods to the buyer.
(ii) The seller Jones is in delay with delivering the sold cow Rosita to buyer Smith.
(iii) The lessor is in delay with delivering the leased goods to the lessee.
(iv) Gray is lashing his dog Pluto.

These four requisite propositions describe relations which, in a semi-formalised manner can be rendered:

(i') Delay (seller, buyer).
(ii') Delay (Jones, Smith).
(iii') Delay (lessor, lessee).
(iv') Being cruel to (Gray, Pluto).

In the rp-structure of (i) and (ii) *K* is the set of sellers, *L* is the set of buyers and *R* is the delay-relation. In (ii) *R* operates over an element in the set *KxL*, viz., <Jones, Smith>. (ii) describes an individual case. In (i) *R* operates over all elements in *KxL*. It describes a generic case.

Suppose now that there is a legal rule analogous to the rule about delay on the part of sellers with the same legal consequence *mutatis mutandis* when a lessor is in delay with delivering the leased goods to the lessee. (iii) is the requisite proposition of that rule. The rp-structure of this requisite proposition contains the set of lessors, K', the set of lessees, L', and the delay-relation *R*. The rule about purchase and the rule about lease are similar in that they both contain the delay-relation. But *K* and *L* in the former are not identical with K' and L' in the latter. In fact, *K* and K' as well as *L* and L' are disjoint sets. The rp-structure of the lease rule can be rendered $S' = \{<U, K', L', R>\}$.

As for the cruelty-to-animals rule the rp-structure can be rendered $S'' = \{<U', K'', L'', R'>\}$, where K'' is the set of human beings, L'' the set of animals and R' the cruelty-relation. (iv) is an element in the set $K''x\,L''$, viz., <Gray, Pluto>.

Every element in a material set of operative facts is, as I have said before, an individual legal case. Such cases are, for instance, the couple ordered by means of the delay-relation (<Jones, Smith>) and the couple ordered by means of the cruelty-relation (<Gray, Pluto>). Hence <Jones, Smith> $\varepsilon\ R \cap (KxL)$ according to the requisite proposition (i).

Our concept "rp-structure" can also be used in the following manner. Suppose that something has occurred: a seller has not delivered the goods in due time, a person has stabbed a rival with a knife and the rival dies. Then we have a course of events in reality, a set of *circumstances*:

$$C = \{c_1, \ldots, c_n\}.$$

Now such a course of events is tried by a court of law. Parties and witnesses make a lot of assertions about *C*. Let us call the set of circumstances in that way presented to the court "*introduced circumstances*"

$$IC = \{ic_1, \ldots, ic_m\}.$$

No doubt, *IC* is in most cases not a subset of *C* due to the fact that parties and witnesses might have forgotten what they actually have noticed or lie about it.

Among the elements of *IC* some are satisfactorily proved, others not. We get a set of *proved circumstances*

$$PC = \{pc_1, \ldots, pc_k\}.$$

Given *IC*, the judge finds the legal rule *r* relevant. It might seem directly applicable to *IC* or a plausible candidate for analogical use on *IC*. Let us assume the former.

Let *r* have the rp-structure $S = \{<U,K,L,R>\}$. Let us then regard *S* as *a principle of selection* with respect to *IC*. By that I mean that the judge investigating whether *r* is applicable to *IC* must answer the question: Is there in *IC* a state of affairs, *IC**, containing an individual *x* such that $x \varepsilon K$ and an individual *y* such that $y \varepsilon L$, and such that *R* exists between *x* and *y*? If this question is answered in the affirmative, i.e., if $IC^* \subseteq IC$, we can say that *S* has structured, or ordered, circumstances in *IC* for the purpose of applying *r* to the present case.

In order for the judge to pronounce a judgment in accordance with the legal consequence of *r*, two conditions must be fulfilled (we disregard the possibility that there could be reason to perform a reduction of *r* or even to regard it as obsolete):

(1) It *shall* be the case that $IC^* \subseteq PC$. This means that the existence of *IC** must have been satisfactorily proved in accordance with the rules of burden and standard of proof.
(2) It *shall* be the case that $IC^* \subseteq IC$. This means that the judge must base his judgment only on circumstances presented at the main hearing ("the principle of immediacy" in procedural law).

The part of juridical topology that investigates the structure of legal cases could be called "microtopology".

7.4 Ontologically Mixed Cases

Very often cases, e.g., those tried in courts of law, do not have the character of being exclusively "brute (natural) facts". More often than not they are combinations of brute facts, individual legal positions and individual acts-in-the-law. Neither it is impossible that such a case in its totality is an individual legal position. An example of a case being a brute state of affairs altogether is "[the fact that] A has stabbed B to death". An example of a case being a mixture of an individual legal position and a brute fact is "[the fact that] C owns the land L and D has cut down trees on L". An example of a case being a mixture of an individual legal position and an individual act-in-the-law is "[the fact that] C owns the land L and C sells L to E". An example of a case being a pure individual legal position is "[the fact that] C is the owner of L", e.g., when the validity of such an alleged position is under dispute in a court of law and a declaratory judgment is required. We can also talk about generic brute facts and legal positions.

"Act-in-the-law" (in German *Rechtsgeschäft*) is a praxeological concept.[3] I conceive of such an act as an act which (i) if performed changes a legal position or preserves a legal position which would otherwise expire, and (ii) is defined by rules in the legal system for the very purpose of doing so. Acts-in-the-law are more often than not oral or written acts of a performative character, e.g., offers and acceptances, pronouncing of a judgment and promulgation of a statute, but they can also be physical acts, e.g., tradition of a thing and restoration of borrowed goods. Clause (ii) rules out criminal and negligent acts, which acts also change legal positions.

Brute facts (brute states of affairs) belong to natural actual or hypothetical reality. Individual legal positions belong to artificial actual or hypothetical reality. Acts-in-the-law belong as qualified by legal rules (e.g., an act qualified as an offer or an acceptance) to artificial actual or hypothetical reality, but the substratum ("the brute act") of the acts-in-the-law (e.g., the emission of certain sound waves, the inscription of signs on a paper or one person's handing over of a bracelet to another) belong to natural actual or hypothetical reality.

There is a fascinating interplay between these components of a legal case and the normative phenomena we call "legal rules". We refer to such relations between rules and cases as *topological relations*. This brings us to the next section.

7.5 Topological Relations: Single-System Static and Dynamic Topology

The juridical topology can be systemised in the following way:

1. Single-system topology
   a. Static
   b. Dynamic
2. Multi-system topology.

Single-system topology concerns the relation between legal case and legal rule when the legal system itself is considered constant– or, in other words, when all rules involved belong to one and the same system. In single-system static topology the legal rule(s) and the legal case are considered constant as well. A course of events is frozen at a certain point of time just like a photograph freezes a certain moment. The relation between rule and case is either a one-to-one relation or a many-to-one relation. This is so because more often than not a single case is not "solved" (qualified, defined) by one rule only, but a cluster of many rules. An example of a single-system static relation between a rule and a case is the relation between a provision punishing theft and an act of stealing. In single-system dynamic topology

[3]The concept is investigated more thoroughly in Spaak (1994), p. 104–118.

the legal rule and the legal case are not considered as constant; many rules and cases are involved although the legal system itself, to which the rules involved belong, is held constant. The relation between rule and case is a many-to-many relation.

Multi-system topology concerns the relation between legal case, legal rule and legal system. In multi-system topology the rules involved belong to two or more different legal systems. It deals in the first place with some important kinds of norm conflicts. Basic concepts of multi-system topology will be investigated in Chaps. 11 and 12.

The topological interplay between rules and cases is most prominent in one-system dynamic topology. The occurrence of brute facts qualified as something legally relevant by legal rules (BL-facts, for short) and the performance of acts-in-the-law are the dynamic elements in legal life, the motor in the legal machinery.

BL-facts and acts-in-the-law intervene between legal positions. For example, a person, x, is in position p according to rules R. Then BL-fact bl occurs at time t, and in pursuance of rules R' position p' is substituted for p. From time t x is in p'. At a later time t' x performs the act-in-the-law a, whereby p'' in pursuance of rules R'' is substituted for p'. From time t' x is in p''. The transition from p to p' and from p' to p'' is brought about by the dynamic factors BL-fact bl and act-in-the-law a. A concrete example of this could be the following course of events:

(i) x does not own real estate e (which is a legal position)
(ii) *x:s* father y dies (BL-fact)
(iii) x owns e (by inheritance from y)
(iv) x leases a flat in e to z (act-in-the-law)
(v) *x:s* right of disposition of e is limited in favour of z.

7.6 Evidentiary Fact

There are some concepts that, although not topological themselves, stand in a necessary relationship to such concepts. One important such concept is *evidentiary fact.*

"Evidentiary fact" is a key concept in the intellectual structuring of the field of juridical thinking that concerns evaluation of evidence. An evidentiary fact is usually thought of as a state of affairs the existence of which—i.e., that it once belonged to actual reality—directly or indirectly is used as an argument for the existence of an operative fact—i.e., that the operative fact once belonged to actual reality.

In fact, this thought is misleading. Strictly speaking, propositions such as "Smith murdered Jones" or "Brown offered to buy Adams's old Mercedes" can never be proved. That follows *per definitionem* the way the juridical conceptual framework is constructed. "Murdering" and "offering" are qualifications (labelling) of brute states of affairs, not the brute states of affairs themselves. The corresponding brute state of affairs of such qualifications, their *substratum*, is, e.g., "Smith killed Jones" and "Brown said to Adams: 'You can buy my car, if you like'". It is such substrata that shall be proved; they are *the theme of proof.* The legal characterisation of them, on the other hand, is a matter of interpretation. When in this connection I talk about operative facts, what I have in mind are their substrata.

What shall be proved is ultimately an operative fact which we can call *the basic theme of proof.* A state of affairs used as an argument for or against the basic theme of proof is an evidentiary fact. Evaluation of evidence is, like interpretation, a matter of rational argumentation. "Arguments are appeals to rationality in the light of the facts", as Naess brilliantly puts it.[4] Also an evidentiary fact might be in need of being proved, hence becoming a (non-basic) theme of proof. For this purpose some "second order" evidentiary facts must be mobilised—and so on (sometimes called "facts affecting the weight of evidence").

The weight of evidence is a function of two circumstances: tenability and relevance.[5] The degree of tenability of an evidentiary fact is the same as the probability that it is true. The relevance of an evidentiary fact concerns its weight as a proof of the theme of proof. Tenability is independent of the relation between evidentiary fact and theme of proof. Relevance, however, is such a relation (not to be investigated here). For the theme of proof "Anderson killed Smith" the evidentiary fact that Anderson's fingerprints are found on the weapon that killed Smith has a greater relevance as a proof of the theme than a statement by a seer of visions to the effect that Anderson stabbed Smith to death.

Evaluation of evidence is to test arguments *pro et contra* the theme of proof with respect to tenability and relevance. A fruitful instrument by which arguments, including arguments for the purpose of evaluation of evidence, can be tested is what Naess calls "a *pro-et-contra* survey", i.e., a list of arguments for and against the basic theme of proof as well as arguments for and against arguments of the first kind.[6] In that way we get pro-pro, contra-pro, pro-contra, contra-contra, pro-pro-pro arguments, etc.

Let me give an example. Friday 28 February, 1986, at 11.21 p.m., Swedish Prime Minister Olof Palme was shot to death in central Stockholm when he and his wife, Lisbet Palme, were on their way home after a visit to the cinema. Mrs. Palme got a slight gunshot injury in her back. After some time a man, CP, was suspected of having committed the crime. He was convicted of murder by the district court of Stockholm but acquitted by the court of appeal. Here are some of the relevant arguments concerning the evaluation of evidence, ordered according to a *pro-et-contra* survey à la Naess. (BTP is the basic theme of proof, P a pro-argument, C a contra-argument, $\mathrm{P}_1 P_1$ and $\mathrm{P}_2\ P_1$ pro-pro-arguments (for P_1), $\mathrm{C}_1\mathrm{P}_1$ a contra-argument (against P_1) etc.) I will not comment on the tenability and relevance of the arguments. The purpose of my example is to elucidate the conceptual relation between "operative fact" and "evidentiary fact".

---

[4]Naess (1966), p. 97.

[5]Naess (1966), p. 108–110.

[6]Naess (1966), p. 106–108.

- BTP: CP shot Olof Palme to death in place *p* at time *t*.
- P_1: At a confrontation Mrs. Palme pointed out CP as the man who turned up behind her just after the shot.
- P_1P_1: Mrs. Palme observed a concordance between certain features of the face belonging to the man she pointed out at the confrontation and of the man she saw at the place of the murder.
- $P_1P_1P_1$: Mrs. Palme has good qualifications as a trained psychologist to make observations of the relevant kind (an argument put forward by herself).
- C_1P_1: The confrontation took place almost 3 years after the murder and Mrs. Palme's visual picture could have been influenced during this time.
- C_2P_1: Mrs. Palme was shocked and frightened at the time of the observation.
- C_3P_1: It is important to be wary when evaluating identity evidence.
- $P_1C_3P_1$: /Reference to a report presented by the so-called Devlin Commission in Great Britain 1976./
- P_2: CP has admitted that he was in the neighbourhood at the time of the murder.
- P_3: CP has occasionally expressed feelings of hatred toward Olof Palme.
- C_1P_3: CP has on other occasions also showed admiration of Palme.
- Etc.
- C_1: There are no indications that CP had access to a gun.
- C_2: Several witnesses near the place of the murder have given contradictory statements regarding the man they thought behaved strangely.
- C_3: A witness, AA, saw CP at a place very far from the place of the murder at the crucial time.
- $P_1\ C_3$: AA had no reason whatsoever to protect CP.
- C_1C_3: AA has on several occasions changed his mind.
- Etc.

Conclusion. Operative facts (positions, acts-in-the-law, legally interpreted brute facts) have a substratum of brute facts. Basic themes of proof are such substrata. Evaluation of evidence is (i) to evaluate the tenability and the relevance of arguments for and against the basic theme of proof, (ii) to weigh these arguments against each other and (iii) to decide whether the basic theme of proof is proved satisfactorily or not (a decision that judges are under a duty to make). The relation between the theme of proof (TP) and an evidentiary fact (EF) can be a matter of causation, either in the direction that TP caused EF (e.g., when TP is the fact that a car had a certain speed and EF is the fact that skid-marks measured up had so and so many metres in length) or in the direction that EF caused TP (e.g., when EF is the fact that a driver drove on the wrong side of the road and TP is the death of a meeting driver). Sometimes an evidentiary fact is an inductive generalisation, such as $P_1C_3P_1$.

Juridical thinking is basically argumentation. Within the framework of application of law, this applies to evaluation of evidence (arguing pro et contra themes of proof) as well as to qualification, or interpretation, of law (arguing pro et contra themes of interpretation).

7.7 Normativised Fact[7]

Let us now turn to the topology corresponding to legal consequences. In the example used in Sect. 7.1 for describing the morphological structure of an ordinary regulative rule we found that the legal consequence of the rule (given that a seller has had costs due to delay on the part of the buyer) was

(1) "the buyer shall pay damages for those costs"
    which could be split up into
(2) the normative modality: "shall"
    and
(3) the norm-theme "the buyer pays damages for those costs".

Just as requisites describe operative facts, so norm-themes describe what I shall call *normativised facts.* Such facts can be individual or more or less general.

Examples:

(i) "that buyer Smith pays damages to seller Jones for costs due to Smith's delay in fetching the sold goods"
(ii) "that buyers of cars from car dealers pay damages for costs due to delay in fetching the bought cars"
(iii) "that buyers pay damages to sellers for costs due to delay on the part of the buyers".

An individual normativised fact corresponding to the prohibition "If a car is driven where there is a speed limit this limit may not be exceeded" is, e.g.,

(iv) "that Brown when driving his car on E 4 exceeded a speed limit of 120 km/h by driving 160 km/h" (the thing forbidden).

To the permission "If you drive an emergency vehicle on duty you may exceed speed limits" corresponds, e.g., the individual normativised fact

(v) "that ambulance driver Adams when driving his ambulance on E 4 in order to bring a badly injured person to hospital exceeded a speed limit of 120 km/h by driving 160 km/h" (the thing permitted).

In this connection I would like to make a distinction between categorical and hypothetical legal positions. Categorical positions "mirror" legal consequences, for example

(a) A is in the position that A owns real estate E.
(b) Judge J is in the position that J shall sentence thief T to imprisonment.
(c) B is in the position that B is married to C.

[7] I take the liberty to enrich the English language with the neologism "to normativise" for the act of making something obligatory, prohibited or permitted.

Hypothetical legal positions "mirror" legal rules or sets of legal rules, for example

(a′) A is in the position that if A buys real estate E at *t*, then A owns E as from *t*.
(b′) Judge J is in the position that if J has found T guilty of theft, then J shall sentence T to imprisonment.
(c′) B is in the position that if B is lawfully wedded to C at *t*, then B is married to C as from *t*.

It is important to be observant of the fact that also phenomena such as (a′)–(c′) are legal positions.

Just as lawyers can create new norms by operating on sets of operative facts they can also do so by operating on sets of normativised facts. We shall return to this in Chap. 8.

7.8 Topological Spheres

One way of doing justice to all things lawyers can do—and do—with legal rules is to discern different *topological spheres*, i.e., sets of cases that in different ways can be affected by legal rules. In this concluding section I shall construct a typology of such topological spheres, all concerning different relations between requisites and cases. They will all be used in subsequent chapters for the purpose of illuminating what lawyers do with legal rules. The following four spheres seem to me indispensable.

Sphere 1. The Linguistic Sphere of Cases (L) A linguistic sphere, *L*, of a legal rule, *r*, is the set of cases covered by the requisites of *r* with respect exclusively to ordinary semantic understanding of them, i.e., if they are interpreted in accordance with ordinary use of language. *L* comprises two, juridically most important, subsets: (i) *the certain set of L* (*CL*), i.e., the set of cases which without any doubt whatsoever are covered by the wording of *r*, and (ii) *the uncertain set of L* (*UCL*), consisting of the cases as for which it is uncertain whether they are covered by the wording of *r* or not, due to the general vagueness of natural languages.[8]

Sphere 2. The Sphere of Operative Facts (OF) The sphere of operative facts, *OF*, of *r* is the set of cases to which *r* is actually applied. To be sure, such relations can change in the course of the time, so strictly speaking they should be equipped with time-indices such as, e.g., "cases of type *C* do not belong to *OF* at time t_1 but belong to *OF* at t_2".

A sphere of operative facts is more precisely an intersection of three different sets of cases.

[8]This distinction has been well known for a long time. We find one of its first formulations in jurisprudence in Heck (1932), p. 52. Heck distinguishes between *Begriffskern* ("the nucleus of the concept", my *CL*) and *Begriffshof* ("the halo of the concept", my *UCL*). Cf. Hart (1994), p. 128 about "the open texture" of legal rules.

(1) *The material set of operative facts (M). M* of *r* is the set of operative facts (as defined in Sect. 7.2) that the law-applying authorities find *r* applicable to exclusively with respect to the content of *r*. It is obvious for lawyers that $M \neq L$. (2) *The spatial set of operative facts (S). S* is the set of cases to which *r*, belonging to the legal system *LS*, is applicable according to rules in *LS* exclusively with respect to the geographical location of these cases. For instance, a theft shall not be tried and punished in Sweden if it is committed in Beijing by a Chinese citizen who has never set foot in Sweden. (3) *The temporal set of operative facts (T). T* is the set of cases to which *r*, belonging to *LS*, is applicable according to rules in *LS* exclusively with respect to when these cases took place. For instance, *r* is not applicable to case *c* if, according to the transitional law of *LS*, *r* is not applicable to cases that have taken place before *r* has come into force and *c* is such a case.

OF can now be defined as the cases which belong to all three of *M*, *S* and *T* (their intersection). $OF = M \cap S \cap T$.

Sphere 3. The Sphere of Influence (I) I of *r* is the set of potential operative facts relative to *r*, i.e., cases that are not operative facts but legally relevant in a way that makes *r* come to the fore.

The fact that members of *I* can be relevant is a consequence of what might be called "the application dilemma" confronting judges. The "dilemma" is the following. On the one hand, the judge is under an obligation to decide every case of a legal character that is submitted to him (given that the formal requirements such as jurisdiction are met)—the prohibition of denial of justice. On the other hand, the fact that the judge is under a duty to decide does not mean that he is free to go his own way in situations where the law is obscure or even silent. He is bound by loyalty to the existing legal system: he shall interpret the law, or create a new norm, "in the spirit of the law". The judge has to decide, but the law is silent. As, in such situations, he cannot apply a legal rule directly, he uses the legal system in an indirect, or mediate, way, thereby being, in a more remote manner, loyal to the existing law, and, at the same time, not violating the prohibition of denial of justice. As a consequence, a statutory provision can have *a sphere of influence* at time *t* exceeding both its linguistic sphere of cases and its material set of operative facts at *t* by means of extensions and analogies. In that way legal rules might exert a kind of long-range effect extending far beyond what could reasonably be called its linguistic sphere. But it might also happen that the judge does not apply a certain statutory provision to a case that, without any doubt whatsoever, falls under the provision (to use a modern term, he makes a reduction of (the linguistic sphere) of *r*).

The concept "sphere of influence" is instrumental for the understanding of a phenomenon that we can call *law-glide*, which sometimes happens to statutory provisions. This means that over time their spheres of operative facts can come to differ from their linguistic sphere of cases. While the latter is constant, until the legislator abolishes or changes it, the former undergo a change. Suppose, for instance, that a supreme court applies statutory provision *sp* to cases where it is highly dubitable that they fall under "the linguistic meaning" of *sp*, in that way extending its sphere of operative facts. Strictly speaking, a norm *n* other than *sp* has thereby been created by the court—although when in the future n is applied to such "new" cases this is generally regarded as an application of *sp*.

Sphere 4. The Sphere of Operation (O) The union of the sphere of operative facts and the sphere of influence we call *the sphere of operation*, O, (of a rule r): $O = OF \cup I$. While OF and I are subsets of O ($OF \subseteq O$, $I \subseteq O$), L is not. If courts of law in general do not apply r to some members of UCL (by a restrictive interpretation of r), or not even to some members of CL (by reduction), these members are not members of O. The courts have removed them from O, to which they belonged when r came into force. We can say that O is the universe of discourse for r.

All this makes the family of topological J-concepts rather comprehensive. It includes the concepts presented in the present chapter as well as what I shall call "the genetic-topological relations" investigated in Chaps. 8 and 9. Furthermore, different kinds of conflicts between legal rules are caused by the fact that the sphere of operative facts of one rule intrudes into the sphere of operative facts of another rule—which makes concepts pertaining to conflicts between legal rules topological concepts (to be investigated in Chap. 10).

Basic topological concepts pertaining to the spatial set (or, in other words, concepts about the juridical handling of private international law) will be investigated in Chap. 11 and basic topological concepts pertaining to the temporal set (or, in other words, concepts about the juridical handling of transitional law) are studied in Chap. 12.

References

Alchourrón CE, Bulygin E (1971) Normative systems. Springer, Berlin
Austin J (1911) Lectures on jurisprudence or the philosophy of positive law, vol II, 5th edn. J. Murray, London
Hart HLA (1994) The concept of law, 2nd edn. Oxford University Press, Oxford
Heck P (1932) Begriffsbildung und Interessenjurisprudenz. J.L.B. Mohr, Tubingen
Müller-Mall S (2013) Legal spaces. Towards a topological thinking of law. Springer, Berlin
Naess A (1966) Communication and argument. Allen & Unwin, Crows Nest
Spaak T (1994) The concept of legal competence. Dartmouth Publishing Co Ltd, London
von Wright GH (1963) Norm and action. Routledge, Abingdon

Chapter 8
Genetic-Topological Norm-Relations

8.1 Introduction

The legal system is something that shall be used. It is a means, an instrument, for achieving peace and a reasonable amount of order in society. The conceptual clarification of this fact can take its point of departure in two fundamental relations, one topological (*"top"*) and one teleological (*"tel"*; *r* is a legal rule, *c* a legal case and *g* a social goal such that *r* is meant to be a means of achieving *g*):

- (*top*) *r* is applicable to *c*, and
- (*tel*) if *r* is applied to *c*, then *g* is achieved.
- *Tel* serves as a justification of *top* (and of *r*). Hence the norm
- (top_n) *r* shall be applied to *c*.

The purpose of the present chapter is to clarify the relation *top* a bit more precisely. The relations *tel* and top_n will be investigated in Sect. 9.3.4.

Usually *c* belongs to the sphere of operative facts, *OF*, of a rule. However, *r* can also at time *t* be applied to a case that does not belong to *OF* but to the sphere of influence, *I*, of *r*. If that happens, *c* is thereby removed from *I* to *OF* at *t*.

The scope of *I* is a matter of contingency. It differs with respect to different legal orders. The margin given to judges subject to the prohibition of denial of justice to exceed the strictly literal meaning of legal rules is not the concern of juridical topology. It is determined by the juridical methodology (the juridical technique of argumentation) prevailing among judges. Such methodologies vary more or less from one legal order to another. Common to them all is that they allow for exceeding the principles of strict legalism but are limited by the principle of broad legalism, the exceeding of which is prohibited. In another work[1] I have formulated three principles of strict legalism, which I repeat here:

[1]Frändberg (2014), p. 59 ff.

Å. Frändberg, *The Legal Order*, Law and Philosophy Library 123,
https://doi.org/10.1007/978-3-319-78858-6_8

(L1) A legal rule shall always be followed (applied) by the law-applying functionaries to whom the rule is addressed when adequate operative facts are present.

(L2) A legal rule shall never be followed (applied) by the law-applying functionaries to whom the rule is addressed when adequate operative facts are not present.

(L3) A legal rule shall always be followed (applied) adequately with respect to its norm theme by the law-applying functionaries to whom the rule is addressed.

I formulate the principle of broad legalism thus:

(L4) For the law-applying functionary to comply with the legal system when deciding an individual case, he must consider the legal system in its totality as well as its underlying value basis (its teleology, or axiology). He shall be loyal to "the spirit of the law".

A description of what judges do with cases in *I*—a study, if you like, of how to do things with rules—involves in fact both morphological and topological elements. From a morphological viewpoint relations between legal rules are involved, from a topological viewpoint relations between rules and cases are involved. The morphological relations are *genetic relations*: rule r' is created some way or another by means of rule *r*. Hence the term "genetic-topological norm-relations" (in the following *GT- relations*).

GT-relations are relations between a rule *r*, a case *c*, another rule r' and, for some GT-relations another case, c'—for instance:

(1) r' applied to *c* is a restrictive interpretation of *r* applied to *c*
(2) r' applied to c' is analogous to *r* applied to *c*.

The set of GT-relations contains eight such relations (and with variations of them 32). When describing these relations I fall back on an, at least partially, well-established juridical family of concepts, which I clarify and present in a more logically stringent way than is usually the case. The eight GT-relations are the following:

(i) n' is an application proper of *n*
(ii) n' is a precisation of *n*
(iii) n' is analogous to *n*
(iv) n' follows *e contrario* from *n*
(v) n' is a reduction of *n*
(vi) n' makes *n* obsolete
(vii) n' is an extensive interpretation of *n*
(viii) n' is a restrictive interpretation of *n*.

(i)–(viii) are, taken together, our *clarificandum.*

In accordance with the separation between the topological and the methodological aspect of GT-relations we must make a distinction between *the result of an application of r* (e.g., an analogy) and *the principles guiding the choice of this result.*

In this chapter our concern is exclusively the former. To both is tied a special family of concepts, to the former the GT-relations, to the latter the principles of interpretation (to be investigated in Chap. 14). Between members of the two families there are close relationships. Thus, e.g., the use of a consequentialist (teleological) principle might result in an analogy, the use of a systemic principle in an *e contrario* result.

What judges apply are legal rules. But what is the result of an application of a legal rule? The answer is: a legal norm.

From the viewpoint of the application of legal rules a distinction between two kinds of legal rules—*basic rules* and *rules of application*—plays a crucial role in our clarification of the GT-relations. I shall explain the distinction by means of an example. Take the following line of reasoning:

(1) Anyone who, in a way that may obstruct a restoration, meddles with something that another person has been deprived of by a criminal action, shall be punished for receiving stolen goods to at most 2 years of imprisonment
(2) Anyone who receives a receipt concerning stolen goods which has been deposited in the cloakroom of a railway station, shall be punished for receiving stolen goods to at most 2 years of imprisonment
(3) Person X has received a receipt concerning stolen goods which has been deposited in the cloakroom of a railway station
(4) X shall be punished for receiving stolen goods to at most 2 years of imprisonment.

Assume that (3) describes the case at hand for the judge to decide. Assume further that (1) is a legal rule expressed in some statutory provision. The problem for our judge is to decide, by statutory interpretation, whether (1) is applicable to (3) or not. Then the result of his interpretation is rule (2).

We see that (4) does not follow logically from premises (1) and (3). But (4) follows logically from premises (2) and (3). (2) is the rule that our judge in fact *applies*. Therefore (2) is a rule of application. But (2) is an interpretative result of (1). (1) is a kind of basis for (2). Therefore (1) is a basic rule. With the help of one or more basic rules a rule of application is constructed by means of interpretation. Any instance of judicial application of legal rules to cases can be reconstructed in this way.

A rule of application is in relation to a basic rule an interpretation of the latter. It is the result of an interpretation (rule of application ex post). A rule of application is in relation to inferences of the kind just exemplified the major premise in such inferences (rule of application ex ante). In this sense the rule of application is a subsumption rule (see Sect. 13.3.2 below).

GT-relations are relations between basic rules and rules of application. The act of constructing a rule of application by means of one or more basic rules is traditionally called "qualification" or "interpretation" (concepts to be investigated in Sects. 13.3 and 14.3 below). In our example the GT-relation between the basic rule (1) and the rule of application (2) is an extensive interpretation (or perhaps even an analogy) since it could be argued that X has not "meddled" with the stolen goods at all, only with the receipt.

Our task here is to bring the GT-relations into some kind of system. We are looking for a homogeneous model of representation, which enables us to define them within one and the same conceptual framework, thereby letting their mutual relationships stand out more clearly. This conceptual framework will be constructed by means of elementary set theory.

We define our GT-relations in terms of set-theoretical relations between spheres of operative facts, i.e., between the sphere of operative facts, OF, of a basic rule r and the sphere of operative facts OF' of a corresponding rule of application r'—and, in a similar way, between the set of normativised facts N of r and the set of normativised facts N' of r'. Given a certain rule, e.g., a statutory provision, another rule can be constructed, where the sphere of operative facts and the set of normativised facts of the two rules stand in some GT-relation to each other. The act of qualification by which the latter is constructed by means of the former can from a topological viewpoint be described in terms of set-theoretical manipulations with spheres of operative facts and sets of normativised facts respectively. We shall find that there are several different precisation, analogy, reductive, etc., GT-relations.

In Sect. 8.2 we define 16 different varieties of the relations (i)–(iii)—application proper, precisation and analogy. Our idea is that these relations are exactly determined by "underlying" set-theoretical relations between spheres of operative facts and sets of normativised facts. These 16 GT-relations we call *the spectrum of a (basic) legal rule.*

In Sect. 8.3 we define another 16 GT-relations, (17)–(32), now varieties of the relations (iv)–(vi). We use the same set-theoretical device as we used with respect to (1)–(16), i.e., (17) corresponds to (1), (18) to (2), etc. But the relations (17)–(32) are in addition to that also characterised by reversing the normative modality of the legal consequence of the basic rule into its "opposite" in the legal consequence of the rule of application, i.e., we are reversing "may" or "shall" into "must not" (prohibition) or "must not" into "may" or "shall". If r allows action a, r' forbids action a', and if r forbids a, r' allows a' (where a certain kind of relation exists between a and a'). In this way we get various concepts of *desuetude*, *e contrario* and *reduction.* The relations (17)–(32) constitute *the antithetic spectrum of a basic rule.* An example: If we conclude from the norm "Motor traffic forbidden" to the norm "Cycling permitted" (the latter standing in an *e contrario*-relation to the former: the conclusion is, of course, not logically binding), we have moved to the antithetic spectrum of the prohibition, which also belongs to its sphere of influence.

In section "Extensive and Restrictive Interpretation" the GT-relations (vii) and (viii) are defined as marginal cases of (ii) (or (i)) and (iii), and of (iv) and (v) respectively.

8.2 The Spectrum of a Legal Rule: GT-Relations 1–16

Let us, for the sake of simplicity, talk about *F-sets* for spheres of operative facts and *N-sets* for sets of normativised facts. In this section we shall investigate the precisation and analogy relations between legal rules. We talk of a basic rule, *r*, its F-set, *F*, its N-set, *N*, and about a rule of application, r', with F-set F' and N-set N'.

Set-theoretical operations can be performed on both F-sets and N-sets. We can pick out subsets, form unions, form a set disjointed from another set, etc. The results of such operations are different set-theoretical relations between sets. Of interest here are the following four relations between F-sets and between N-sets respectively.

I. *Identity* (id): $F' = F$; $N' = N$.
II. *Specification* (spec): $F' \subset F$; $N' \subset N$ (i.e., F' is a proper subset of *F*, N' of *N*).
III. *Expansion* (exp): $F \subset F'$; $N \subset N'$.
IV. *Disjunction* (dis): F' and *F*, and N' and *N* are disjoint sets (i.e., they have no element in common: $F' \cap F = \phi$, where "ϕ" is the empty set).

Suppose that F' *id F* and N' *spec N*. This means that F' is identical with *F* and N' is a proper subset of *N*. On the basis of a rule, *r*, to which *F* and *N* correspond we have got another rule, r', to which F' and N' correspond.

By means of this simple set-theoretical device the following 16 possible GT-relations between basic rules and rules of application can be formulated. Together they constitute *the spectrum of a basic rule.*

Relation between F- and N-sets		*GT-relation*
(1)	*F′ id F; N′ id N*	r' is identical to (an application proper of) *r*
(2)	*F′ id F; N′ spec N*	r' is a N-precisation of *r*
(3)	*F′ id F; N′ exp N*	r' is N-analogous to *r*
(4)	*F′ id F; N′ dis N*	r' is N-analogous to *r*
(5)	*F′ spec F; N′ id N*	r' is a precisation of *r*
(6)	*F′ spec F; N′ spec N*	r' is a precisation of *r*
(7)	*F′ spec F; N′ exp. N*	r' is N-analogous to *r*
(8)	*F′ spec F; N′ dis N*	r' is N-analogous to *r*
(9)	*F′ exp F; N′ id N*	r' is a generalising analogy of *r*
(10)	*F′ exp F; N′ spec N*	r' is a generalising analogy of *r*
(11)	*F ′exp F; N′ exp N*	r' is a generalising analogy of *r*
(12)	*F′ exp F; N′ dis N*	r' is a generalising analogy of *r*
(13)	*F′ dis F; N′ id N*	r' is a disjoint analogy of *r*
(14)	*F′ dis F; N′ spec N*	r' is a disjoint analogy of *r*
(15)	*F′ dis F; N′ exp N*	r' is a disjoint analogy of *r*
(16)	*F′ dis F; N′ dis N*	r' is a disjoint analogy of *r*

Examples and commentaries:

(*Ad 1*) This GT-relation is, of course, trivial. It is a marginal case in the spectrum of *r*. It amounts to the fact that the basic rule and the rule of application are identical or, in other words, that the basic rule is applied "directly" to a given case. (It must be emphasised that two rules can be identical without being expressed linguistically in exactly the same way.)

(Ad 2) Suppose that we have a rule to the effect that acts belonging to *F* are punished within the latitude 1–10 years of imprisonment. *N*, then, is the set of facts where persons having committed some act belonging to *F* undergo imprisonment within the latitude. But suppose further that according to a rule developed in court practice the maximum penalty for F-crimes is 8 years imprisonment. While F' is identical to *F*, N' is a proper subset of *N*. r' is a N-precisation of *r*.

(Ad 3) In our example of (2) *r* is N-analogous to r'. (See further our commentary ad (7).)

(Ad 4) With respect to the rules

- (*r*) If the buyer is liable for considerable overdue payment, the seller may cancel the contract

  and

- (r') If the buyer ... payment, the seller is entitled to damages

r' is N-analogous to *r* (and *r* to r' since this analogy relation is symmetrical).

(Ad 5.) In this example r' is a precisation of *r*:

- (*r*) If the same goods are sold to two buyers, the buyer who bought the goods first shall keep it

  and

- (r') If the same goods are sold to two buyers and the second buyer has not got possession of the goods in good faith, the first buyer shall keep it.

  (See also the commentary to (7).)

(Ad 6.) In this example, r' is another kind of precisation of *r*:

- (*r*) If anyone commits a robbery, he shall be sentenced to at most 8 years' imprisonment

  and

- (r') If anyone commits a robbery but there are extenuating circumstances with respect to the culprit, he shall be sentenced to at most 4 years' imprisonment.

(Ad 7.) As an example of this GT-relation I shall use a case from 1969 decided by a Swedish court of appeal (referred to here as "the boat case"). Person A had, under the influence of drink, in his motorboat collided with a buoy, to which a sailing boat was attached, with the consequence that the sailing boat was damaged. After the collision, A left the place without supplying information as to his identity. The prosecutor argued that A had violated a

provision in the Swedish maritime law, to the violation of which a criminal penalty was tied:

- (*r*) If vessels collide, each master shall inform the other of the name of the vessel, its home port, its port of departure and its port of destination.

The prosecutor's claim was rejected by the court. However, there was a dissident, P, who assented to the claim. P's vote is interesting, since it provides us with an example of GT-relation (7).

The judges disagreed as to whether small boats of this kind were "vessels" or not, i.e., whether the set of collisions between small boats is a proper subset of the set of collisions between vessels or whether these two sets were disjoint.

In his vote P argued that there was a great demand for a rule applicable to small boats for the same purpose as that of *r* with respect to vessels, and he added: "There is nothing to prevent letting the provision in the maritime law also include small boats. It is true that such boats often have no names and the duty to supply the information can also in other respects be difficult to literally be complied with. *However, the purpose of the provision would be fulfilled if the master gives such information that any difficulties to identify him or the boat do not arise*" [my transl. and italics].

So the rule P applies is this:

(r') If small boats collide, each master shall give the other such information that any difficulty to identify them or their boats does not arise.

Let us assume that collisions between small boats is a proper subset of collisions between vessels, i.e., that $F' \subset F$. Moreover, $N \subset N'$. For every action in *N* is such that it amounts to giving such information that any difficulty to identify the master or his boat does not arise, but there are actions in N' that are not members of *N*, e.g., to give a permanent address or telephone number to the place of work. What P does is in fact to construct a rule of application that stands in GT-relation (7) to the provision in the maritime law.

(*Ad 8.*) An example of this N-analogy is the following:

- (*r*) If anyone buys sex, he shall be sentenced to at most 1 year's imprisonment
- (r') If anyone buys sex but there are extenuating circumstances, he shall be imposed a fine.

(*Ad 9–12.*) The generalising analogies are treated in Sect. 9.2.1 for reasons given there.

(*Ad 13.*) Let us first make a distinction between trivial and non-trivial disjunction between N-sets. Suppose that someone on the basis of

- (*r*) If the buyer does not pay the purchase money on the day of maturity, the seller may cancel the contract
- (r') If the lessee does not pay the rent on the day of maturity, the lessor may cancel the contract.

Here F and F' as well as N and N' are disjoint: According to the very legal systematics there is no agreement that is both a purchase and a hire contract. Hence, nobody can be both a lessor and a seller with respect to the same agreement. (Another aspect is that it can be a state of uncertainty as to whether a certain agreement is a purchase or a hire contract.)

However, the fact that N and N' are disjoint here is trivial in the sense that it is, so to speak, a direct consequence of the fact that F and F' are disjoint. If the buyer does not pay, it is of course the buyer who is subject to cancellation while, if the lessee does not pay, it is the lessee who is affected. But apart from this resulting effect the relation between buyer and seller according to the legal consequence of r (cancellation) is identical with the relation between lessor and lessee according to the legal consequence of r' (Sect. 9.2.1). In order to separate this kind of disjoint relations from more interesting ones, I take the liberty here to look upon the trivial disjunction as an identity relation with respect to N-sets. For that reason we say that r' in our example stands in GT-relation (13) to r. (13) is the standard relation with respect to what I shall call "institutional analogy" (Sect. 9.2.1).

Let us return to the boat case. Given that the sets of vessels and of small boats are disjoint but that notwithstanding the maritime law is applied also to small boats, the rule of application would then be

(r') If small boats collide, each master shall inform the other of the name of his boat, its home port, its port of departure and its port of destination.

Here r' stands in GT-relation (13) to r (the rule in the maritime law).

(*Ad 14.*) Also legislators think in terms of analogies. As a consequence of the outcome of the boat case a statutory provision was issued very similar to the rule applied by dissident P. When regulating boat traffic, the legislator made an analogy from an existing provision regulating motor traffic. This is an example of the fact that also legislators sometimes "think in analogies". (Admittedly, the term "rule of application" is not fully appropriate in legislative situations but I do not want to complicate my terminology further by introducing a special term for legislative analogies.) The provision concerning motor traffic reads (somewhat shortened):

- (r) A road user who has been involved in a traffic accident and, by leaving the scene of the accident, has evaded giving his name and domicile, or has neglected to report the occurrence, shall be sentenced to at most 1 year's imprisonment or fines.

The new provision concerning boat accidents reads:

(r') Anyone who has been involved in a boat accident evading --- [= r] --- occurrence, shall be sentenced to fines or at most 6 month's imprisonment.

The sets F and F' were intended to be disjoint. The set N' is a proper subset of N. Hence, r' stands in GT-relation (14) to r.

(*Ad 15.*) In the example of (14) r stands in GT-relation (15) to r'. Let us also take a look at dissident P's solution of the boat case under the assumption that the set of small boats and the set of vessels are disjoint. Then the rule applied by P (see ad (7)) stands in GT-relation (15) to the rule in the maritime law.

(*Ad 16.*) Let us still assume that the set of small boats and vessels are disjoint. Then, of the following two rules, r' stands in GT-relation (16) to r.

- (r) If vessels collide, each master shall inform the other of the name of his vessel, its home port, its port of departure and its port of destination.
- (r') If small boats collide, each master shall inform the other of his name and domicile.

It might seem that GT-relation (16) is "wide-open" in that any rules r and r' having disjoint F- and N-sets (but the same modality) stand in this relation to each other. But then it must be borne in mind that we the whole time are operating within a given universe of discourse, viz., the sphere of influence of the basic rule.

8.3 The Antithetic Spectrum of a Legal Rule: GT-Relations 17–32

In this section 16 more GT-relations, (17)–(32), are defined. They form *the antithetic spectrum* of r. These GT-relations are variations of concepts (iv)–(vi)—*e contrario*, reduction and obsolescence (desuetude)—presented as our *clarificandum* in Sect. 8.1.

As we explained already in that section, the set-theoretical relations between the F-sets and N-sets, respectively, are the same as with respect to the spectrum of a rule, i.e., (17) = (1), (18) = (2), etc. But the GT-relations (17)–(32) are, in addition to that, characterised by a further quality: the normative modality in the legal consequence of r is in r' exchanged for the "opposite" modality. The antithetic quality of a GT-relation is such a "normative state of opposition". Such reversals can take place in both directions: from permission or obligation to prohibition, or from prohibition to permission or obligation. Reversing of modalities in this way is symbolised "P//F". In Sect. 8.1 we also emphasised that these GT-relations are no logical inferences: r' does not follow logically from r.

It is often said, a bit stereotypically, that legal orders handled in conformity with the law-state values are informed by the idea that everything that is not explicitly forbidden is permitted.[2] The typical antithetical use of legal rules would then amount

[2]Which reminds us of the old 19th century joke: In England everything is permitted that is not forbidden, in Germany everything is forbidden that is not permitted, in Russia everything is forbidden even if it is permitted and in France everything is permitted even if it is forbidden.

to issuing permissive rules of application by means of forbidding basic rules. This idea comes very close to a variation of the idea of the completeness of the legal system: every action is regulated by the legal system completed with the principle just mentioned. Then every action is either forbidden or permitted (or obligatory) according to the legal system.

However, there are also modality exchanges in the opposite direction. Suppose, e.g., that a Code of Procedure includes a provision to the effect that granting leave to appeal is permitted only under circumstances c_1 or c_2. Then it is forbidden to grant leave to appeal when neither c_1 nor c_2 has occurred.

Also reduction, i.e., a court making on its own an exception from a rule for a case to which the rule without any doubt whatsoever is applicable, involves a change of modality, e.g.,

(*r*) It is forbidden to bring dogs into the cemeteries of the town.
(*r*′) It is permitted to bring guide dogs into the cemeteries of the town.

Here are the antithetic GT-relations:

Relations between F- and N-sets	*Reversed modality*	*GT-relation*
(17) = (1)	P//F	*r*′ makes *r* obsolete
(18) = (2)	"	*r*′ is a N-reduction of *r*
(19) etc.	"	*r*′ is N-*e contrario* to *r*
(20)	"	*r*′ is N-*e contrario* to *r*
(21)	"	*r*′ is a reduction of *r*
(22)	"	*r*′ is a reduction of *r*
(23)	"	*r*′ is N-*e contrario* to *r*
(24)	"	*r*′ is N-*e contrario* to *r*
(25)	"	*r*′ is *e contrario* to *r*
(26)	"	*r*′ is *e contrario* to *r*
(27)	"	*r*′ is *e contrario* to *r*
(28)	"	*r*′ is *e contrario* to *r*
(29)	"	*r*′ is *e contrario* to *r*
(30)	"	*r*′ is *e contrario* to *r*
(31)	"	*r*′ is *e contrario* to *r*
(32) = (16)	"	*r*′ is *e contrario* to *r*

Examples and commentaries (I shall not bore my readers by giving examples of each antithetic GT-relation but only of the most important):

(*Ad 17.*) In a Swedish statutory provision from 1734, still in force, pawn agreements must be in writing and attested. However, in court practice this provision has fallen into desuetude. Nowadays, oral pawn agreements are valid. The rule

– (*r*) If an oral unattested pawn agreement is concluded, the pawnee may not redeem the pawn

has been made obsolete by the rule

- (*r*′) If an oral unattested pawn agreement is concluded, the pawnee may redeem the pawn

(*Ad 21.*) GT-relation (21) is the typical reduction relation. As an example, let us choose another Swedish statutory provision from 1734, still in force. The rule

- (*r*) If anyone sells the same goods to two different buyers, the later buyer is not entitled to keep the goods

  has been reduced in court practice by the rule
- (*r*′) If anyone sells the same goods to two different buyers and if the later buyer in good faith has got possession of the goods, he is entitled to keep it.

  Let us once more return to the boat case (see the example ad (7)) and assume that the set of collisions of small boats is a proper subset of collisions of vessels. The majority of the court of appeal applied the rule
- (*r*′) If small boats collide, it is permitted for their masters to leave the spot without informing the other of the name of his vessel, its home port, etc.

  thereby reducing the provision in the maritime law
- (*r*′) If vessels collide, it is forbidden for their masters to leave the spot without informing etc.

  In the Act 1928 on the Right of Swedish Lapps to reindeer pasture (now abrogated) we find the following provision:
- (*r*) If a dog is found while chasing or otherwise molesting reindeer, being in an area where reindeer at the time may be sent out to pasture, the dog may be killed.

The nomadic Lapp family B moved with their reindeer alongside the slope of the Gotko massif in Lapland, as did the nomadic Lapp family S. The two herds clashed. A member of family S shot a dog belonging to a member of family B. The owner claimed damages for the dog. The defendant answered that he had a right, according to *r* to kill the dog, which, he claimed, had molested some of his reindeer. The Supreme Court seems to have accepted this as a fact.[3] Then, according to the literal meaning of *r*, the defendant must have been in his right to kill the dog—which, without any doubt whatsoever was a dog, not a bear or an angel. The court, however, decided in favour of the plaintiff. Why? Since in the preparatory work of an act of 1886, which was the statutory predecessor of the 1928 act, it was stated that the purpose of the provision was to protect the Lapps from dogs belonging to the domiciled population, whose dogs were a great nuisance at the time, not to protect

[3]Nytt Juridiskt Arkiv – NJA – (1961), part I, p. 98. (NJA, part I, contains reports of Supreme Court precedents.)

them from dogs belonging to other nomadic Lapps. (This is, by the way, an example of the great importance Swedish courts of law have attached to the legislative preparatory material over the last 70 years or so.)

(*Ad 29.*) GT-relation (29) is the typical *e contrario* relation. For example, the rule

- (r') If a trade union is bound by a collective agreement and if another trade union carries out an illegal strike, the former may not carry out a strike in order to assist the latter

  stands in an *e contrario* relation to
- (r) If a trade union is bound by a collective agreement and if another trade union carries out a legal strike, the former may carry out a strike in order to assist the latter.

The boat case provides us once more with an example. Under the assumption that the set of small boats and the set of vessels are disjoint, r and r' in the example given ad (21) stand in an *e contrario* relation to each other.

Let us now make some more general commentaries.

(1) Reduction relations are common for the simple reason that every exception is a reduction of its principal rule.
(2) Obsolescence (desuetude) can be seen as a marginal case of reduction. That r' makes r obsolete means in fact that r' is a "total exception" to r, i.e., that the exception completely invalidates its principle rule. All that is left of an obsolete provision (a provision still in force but no longer valid) is an empty shell in the shape of a linguistic formulation in a statute book.
(3) It is also possible to regard the reduction relations (and, hence, obsolescence) as a special category of *e contrario* relations, viz., such *e contrario* relations where one rule has the fatal quality of partially (or, with respect to obsolescence, totally) eliminating another from the system of valid rules. With respect to *e contrario* relations (25) and (27), r' not only makes r obsolete but also "expands in the antithetic direction" in relation to r. Radical changes in legislation, court practice and legal doctrine might be described in terms of these two GT-relations.
(4) In order to be able to distinguish between reduction and precisation – as well as between analogy and *e contrario* relations—it is necessary to make an antithetic exchange of modality in addition to set-theoretical operations on F- or N-sets.
(5) When a court of law passes *a judgment of dismissal upon the merits* it always uses a rule *e contrario* in order to establish the rule of application which results in the dismissal.

The boat case shall for the last time supply us with an example. In this case the district court held that the set of small boats and the set of vessels are disjoint. From the rule

(r) If vessels collide and a master leaves the spot without informing, etc., the court shall sentence him to punishment according to § 294 of the maritime law

The following rule of application was established *e contrario*:

(r') If small boats collide and a master leaves the spot without informing, etc., the court may not sentence him to punishment according to § 294 of the maritime law.
r' is the rule applied by the court and its application resulted in the dismissal.

It is to be noted that, *logically*, there are no stronger reasons to pronounce a judgment of dismissal than to pass a verdict of guilty by means of a rule constructed by analogy from a criminal law provision. But the immense importance of compliance with the legality principles when handling criminal law urges an *e contrario*-use of criminal law to take precedence over an analogical use of them.

Extensive and Restrictive Interpretation

In this section we shall clarify the GT-relations

(vii) r' is an extensive interpretation of r
(viii) r' is a restrictive interpretation of r.

Let us as an example use another case from the Swedish Supreme Court.[4] The case concerned two hotels in Stockholm where each room contained a radio set connected to a communal aerial system and in one of the hotels there was a TV-set in each room. Section 2, para. 1 of the Copyright Act of 1960 specifies what is included in a copyright. *Inter alia* there is included an exclusive right to make the work, e.g., a musical composition, available to the public. Section 2, para. 3 informs us that a work "is made available to the public when it is performed publicly". The organisation of composers claimed damages from the hotel company on the ground that music without the authors' permission had been performed publicly by means of the radio and TV-sets (in the rather peculiar sense of the term "perform" in the Copyright Act). The interpretation of the term "performed publicly" is open to doubt in this case, making it a "hard case". The district court decided for the defendant. This was not a matter of public performance. The Supreme Court, on the other hand, decided for the plaintiff (also in this case by reference to the preparatory works).

It is obvious that the limits of the scope of the F-set of the basic rule in the Copyright Act are indefinite. This indefiniteness can be described in the following manner.

(a) In the solution of the district court the indefiniteness lies in the fact that it cannot be ascertained whether the court is making an *e contrario-use* of the basic rule or is making a *reduction* of it.
(b) In the solution of the Supreme Court the indefiniteness lies in the fact that it cannot be ascertained whether the court is making a *precisation* (or an application in the proper sense) of the rule or is using it *analogically*. (Moreover, after the decision by the Supreme Court it is clear that the case belongs to the sphere of operative facts of the provision—the court has "read the case into" this sphere.)

[4]NJA (1980), p. 123 ff.

We say that the district court chose a restrictive interpretation of the rule, while the Supreme Court chose an extensive interpretation.

Hence, that r' is *a restrictive interpretation of r* means that it is uncertain which of the following GT-relations holds between r' and r: (1) r' stands in an *e contrario* relation to r or (2) r' is a reduction of r. That r' is *an extensive interpretation of r* means that it is uncertain which of the following GT-relations hold between r' and r: (1) r' is a precisation (or an application proper) of r or (2) r' is analogous to r. In other words, extension is a marginal case of precisation (application proper) and of analogy, while a restrictive interpretation is a marginal case of *e contrario* and of reduction. We do not know whether we are doing the one or the other.

Quite another uncertainty arises when a court of law shall make *the choice* between an extensive and a restrictive interpretation. But this uncertainty is of a legal-political nature and has nothing to do with the definition of the concepts in question. The legal-political choice is about whether to choose a solution within the spectrum of the basic rule or within its antithetic spectrum. In the choice between an extensive and a restrictive interpretation in criminal law, the legality idea, in the form of the principle *in dubio pro reo*, gives the preference to the latter.

Reference

Frändberg Å (2014) From Rechtsstaat to Universal Law-State. Springer, Berlin

Chapter 9
On Analogical Use of Legal Rules

9.1 Introduction

The purpose of this chapter is to clarify the juridical concept "analogy".

The term "analogy" is used in several different sciences. In mathematics it signifies a similarity relation of the kind that exists between, e.g., the numbers 2/6 and 3/9 (isomorphism). In zoology the term "analogical organs" signifies organs in animals with the same function, e.g., gills in fishes and lungs in mammals. In linguistics one talks about analogical formation of linguistic expressions: the verb "telephone" was at the time formed by analogy with the verb "telegraph" and hence inflected in the same way (e.g., "telegraphed"—"telephoned").

Analogy relations were studied already in classical antiquity. In his Nicomachean Ethics Aristotle uses a term ἀναλογία (analogía) in a sense that comes close to the mathematical one.[1] In the scholastic, not least the thomistic, philosophy, different concepts of analogy were intensely discussed.[2]

Already Aristotle made a distinction between "analogy" in the sense of a certain kind of similarity relation and the so-called analogism, i.e., the analogy usually regarded as a part of inductive logic (and which Aristotle calls παράδειγμα (parádeigma). The ancient Greeks were fully aware of the fact that inductive analogy does not possess the necessity which informs the deductive conclusion.

The juridical analogy was no unknown phenomenon to the Roman lawyers: *Ubi eadem est legis ratio, ibi eadem est legis dispositio.* Also the idea that it is improper to analogise from legal provisions being exceptions from other legal provisions is a Roman idea.[3] The use of the term "analogy" itself in juridical thinking was probably introduced by scholastic writers of the medieval period.

[1] In Book 5, where it plays a crucial part in his analysis of distributive justice. See also Dorolle (1949), p. 1 ff. and Hart (1994), p. 299 f.

[2] See Bocheński (1948), p. 424 ff.

[3] See Fabreguettes (1914), p. 374.

Å. Frändberg, *The Legal Order*, Law and Philosophy Library 123,
https://doi.org/10.1007/978-3-319-78858-6_9

Among jurisprudential classics it is above all Austin who has an interesting discussion about the juridical analogy concept.[4] From the more modern literature on the topic mention can be made of works by N. Bobbio,[5] T. Heller,[6] C. Alchourrón,[7] García Mendez,[8] Klug[9], Cross and Harris[10] (with respect to analogies from rules expressed in precedents), S. Brewer[11] and J. Hage.[12] A work of high quality is a recent monograph by D. Reidhav.[13]

At this point it can be appropriate to give some examples of analogies between norms.

(1) Suppose that we find a sign on a beach saying: "Bathing suits prohibited!"[14] On the beach two gentlemen suddenly appear, one naked, the other wearing a dinner jacket and a pair of elegant trousers. What does the sign say with respect to this situation? Neither of the two men is in fact wearing a bathing suit. Is it permitted for one of them to stay but not for the other (and, if so, which one?), or is it permitted or prohibited for both of them? Let us suppose that the beach belongs to a religious association of the more prudish kind. Probably the nude gentleman must leave (by analogical use—*a fortiori*!—of the prohibition) while the well-dressed one is allowed to stay (by *e contrario* use of it). Suppose, on the other hand, that the beach is owned by the local nudist colony. Then it is fairly reasonable to presume that the naked gentleman is allowed to stay (*e contrario*), while the man wearing the dinner jacket must take his leave (analogically).

And now some more legally relevant examples.

(2) In 1970, a murder was committed on an iceberg floating around in arctic waters, on which an American arctic station was situated. The US department of justice argued that the murderer should be tried according to a statute applicable to crimes committed on board ships in international waters.[15]

(3) According to the Swedish Inheritance Tax Act of 1941 (now abrogated) associations for strengthening the defence of the country or for the promotion of the care of children, youth and old or sick people, or for the promotion of education and research, were exempted from inheritance tax. In a case from 1973 the

[4]Austin (1911), Vol. II, pp. 1001–1020.

[5]Bobbio (1938).

[6]Heller (1961).

[7]Alchourrón (1965), p. 5 ff.

[8]García Máynez (1965), p. 115 ff.

[9]Klug (1966).

[10]Cross and Harris (1991).

[11]Brewer (1966).

[12]Hage (2005).

[13]Reidhav (2007).

[14]The example is an elaboration of an example in Ross (1959), p. 153.

[15]Article in the Danish daily *Politiken*, 1 August 1970.

situation was this. In a testament a great amount of money went to the Swedish Society for Rescue of Shipwrecked People for acquisition of a life-saving cruiser. The society claimed exemption from tax liability. The court of appeal agreed, thereby making an analogy from the inheritance act.

(4) According to a rule in the former Swedish penal code, careless handling of "poison or similar [substances]" was punishable. The Supreme Court used this rule to punish a person who had handled a radioactive iridium isotope carelessly.[16]

(5) According to the Swedish Contract Act, acts-in-the-law that have come about by usury are invalid. The contract act comprises exclusively only acts-in-the-law belonging to the law of property, not acts belonging to family law. That notwithstanding, the Supreme Court declared a contract concerning distribution of marital property invalid, since it had come about by means of usury on the part of the husband.[17] Here an application proper was impossible due to the very legal systematics. This kind of analogy I call *institutional analogy* (see further Sect. 9.2.1 below).

(6) In the former penal code of Sweden there was a provision saying: "Anyone who buys a thing which a person was deprived of by means of crime ... shall be punished for receiving stolen goods ...". The provision added: "If the offender did not realise but had reasonable ground to presume a crime, he shall be punished for a [so-called] misdemeanour with respect to receiving stolen goods...".

    B sold a rented car to P, who had reasonable ground to presume that B was not the owner of the car. The provision was not applicable, since the owner was not deprived of the car by a crime—the car was hired. This notwithstanding, both the district court and the court of appeal found P guilty of such misdemeanour (an example, by the way, of analogical use of criminal law to the detriment of the defendant, thereby violating the prohibition of analogy *in malam partem* in criminal law). The Supreme Court, however, took a more legalistic stand and dismissed the claim with reference to the very wording of the provision.[18]

(7) I have already drawn our attention to the fact that legislators, too, "think in analogies". For example, when a Swedish statute concerning liability in connection with air traffic was issued in 1922, the extant statutes concerning liability in connection with railway and automobile damages were models.

Let us, after these samples of juridical analogies, make some preliminary definitions.

(i) By *analogy* we mean a certain relation between legal rules. We say that a rule r' is analogous to another rule r if a relation of a certain kind holds between them.

[16] NJA 1959, p. 254.
[17] NJA 1965, p. 345.
[18] NJA 1957, p. 44.

Or, to be more precise, that this kind of GT-relation holds between rules and cases:

(AN) r' applied to c' is analogous to r applied to c,

where $r' \neq r$ and $c' \neq c$.

(ii) By *analogous use of a rule r* we mean the establishing of a rule r' which is analogous to r.
(iii) By *analogy argumentation* we mean the reasons for analogical use of a rule.

In Sect. 1.3 I presented some (which I labelled) juridical modes of thinking. One extremely important such mode, deeply ingrained in juridical thinking, is the similarity thinking. The analogy thinking is a variation of the similarity thinking. The juridical analogy is a similarity relation between something *in* the law, and something *outside* the law, but in some way or another *affected by* the law. The juridical analogy argumentation establishes a topological nucleus (r', c') by means of another, "existing" topological nucleus (r, c). *The result* of such an argumentation can be described in terms of certain GT-relations—let us refer to them collectively as *the formal analogy-relation. The justification* of the making of an analogy—the analogy argumentation—can be described in terms of a similarity relation, let us call it *the material analogy-relation.* In Chap. 8 we found that, within the spectrum of a legal rule, GT-relations (3), (4) and (7)–(16) were (different kinds of) analogies. An analogy either expands the sphere of operative facts of a rule (generalising analogy) or creates an entirely new "parallel" rule with its own sphere of operative facts (disjoint analogy). In both cases one "goes outside" a given sphere of operative facts. With respect to the other GT-relations we do not talk about analogies even if this result also is based on a similarity argument. That any one of the relations (3), (4) and (7)–(16) holds we regard as a necessary condition for a GT-relation to be an analogy-relation, let us call it *the formal analogy-condition.*

Another necessary condition for a relation to be an analogy-relation is (i) that it is based on a similarity argument and (ii) that the similarity referred to in the argument is decisive, i.e., that it outweighs the reasons for not applying the actual rule beyond its sphere of operative facts. We call this condition *the material analogy-condition.* Both conditions will be investigated in this chapter.

The following three questions, it seems to me, are of particular interest in a discussion of analogical use of legal rules, and we shall try to give an answer to them in this chapter.

1. What would a satisfying clarification of "analogy" look like with respect to how the term is used in juridical discourse?
2. Is there any method (technique) for analogical use of legal rules?
3. Why are legal rules used analogically?

This chapter is outlined as follows. In Sect. 9.2 we investigate the formal analogy-condition. Section 9.2.1 deals more thoroughly with analogies as GT-relations, Sect. 9.2.2 with analogies described in terms of manipulations with requisites. In Sect. 9.3 we study the material analogy-condition, i.e., the role of reference to similarity in analogy argumentation. After an introduction (Sect. 9.3.1), in Sect. 9.3.2 some general remarks about analogies in inductive reasoning are made, later to be used as a means of illuminating the juridical one. Sections 9.3.3, 9.3.4, 9.3.5 are the crucial ones. Here we try to get a firmer grip on the role of the similarity concept in juridical analogy argumentation. This concept is conceived of as a relation, the material analogy-relation. In order to clarify this relation we introduce the concepts "similarity set", "analogy set", "legal basis" and "analogy-basing property". In Sect. 9.3.6 we make some remarks on the formal properties of analogy-relations. In Sect. 9.4, finally, we try to answer questions 2 (Sect. 9.4.2) and 3 (Sect. 9.4.3).

9.2 The Formal Analogy-Relation

9.2.1 More About Analogies as GT-Relations

In this subsection we shall occupy ourselves with some more complicated analogical GT-relations. First we shall take a look at co-operation and competition between different basic rules for analogisms. After that we give examples of situations where one and the same rule is used as a basic rule for the construction of more than one analogical rule of application. Then we describe some, let us call them, composite analogy-relations. Furthermore, collisions between rules can also occur as a consequence of the analogical use of a rule: by constructing a rule r' analogically from r, another rule, r'', may be reduced by r'. Finally, we explain the distinction between generalising and disjoint analogy and introduce the concept "institutional analogy" to describe the result of creating rules within the range of a certain legal institution (e.g., leasing of goods) by analogical use of rules belonging to another legal institution (e.g., sale of goods). (It is to be observed that the term "institution" is ambiguous: it might connote (i) a certain kind of organisation, e.g. the National Administration on Road Safety or Volvo Ltd., or (ii) a certain set of legal rules held together by their content, e.g., [the law of] marriage, leasing of goods, tort, trust, limited liability companies, crime against property, etc. Here the term is of course used in the latter sense.)

That two (or more) basic rules (r_1, r_2, ... r_n) are *co-operative basic rules of analogy* for another rule, r', means that r' can be established by means of each of r_1, r_2, and ... and r_n alone. Such co-operative rules are sometimes also mutually analogous to each other. We are likely to assume that the reasons for creating r' have greater weight the greater the quantity of basic rules that can be mobilised for making such an analogy. But it could not be claimed that that would always be the case.

Co-operative basic rules of analogy are especially interesting in the law of contracts. Suppose that we have the legal institutions (types of contracts) C_1 and C_2 and the rules r_1 ($r_1 \subset C_1$) and r_2 ($r_2 \subset C_2$), where r_1 and r_2 regulate "the same" thing in "the same" way, e.g., delay, within each institution. Suppose, further, that there is a third type of contract, C_3, which lacks a rule pertaining to this thing. It might then be thought reasonable—or even experienced as an obligation—to incorporate, by precedent or legislation, a rule, r', into C_3 by using r_1 and r_2 as co-operative basic rules of analogy for the creation of r'. For both practical reasons and for the sake of legal certainty this can be justifiable. In that way, r_1, r_2 and r' can be conceived of as giving expression to a general principle within the law of contracts. We find a striking example of the use of co-operative basic rules of analogy in a Swedish work on hire contracts concerning movables.[19] This institution is almost completely unregulated by statutory provisions in Sweden. Sundberg uses the statutes then in force about, on the one hand, rent and leasehold of real property and, on the other, sale of goods as co-operative bases of analogy-making within the field of hire of movables.

But two or more rules belonging to different legal institutions may also compete about being an analogy base with respect to another institution where the situation in question is unregulated—let us call these rules *competing basic rules of analogy*. In this case the competing rules have different solutions to the situation. It is hard to say anything substantial in general terms about the choice of applicable basic rules in such situations. The circumstances in different cases where such a choice might come up are too dissimilar for that to be possible. For instance, a sale of goods act stipulates annulment *ex tunc* and a usufruct act annulment *ex nunc*. Which act is most appropriate as a basic rule of analogy with respect to hire contracts?

It can also be the case that one and the same rule is an analogy basis for two or more different rules of application—let us call such a rule *a multi-basic rule of analogy*. In the Swedish Contract Act there is a provision saying that a declaration of intention conveyed by telegram or by a messenger, which declaration has been distorted by the conveyer, is not binding for the sender. But this applies only if the sender informs the addressee about the distortion without undue delay after he has learnt about the distortion—a so-called passivity rule; estoppel by laches. This rule has been used by a Swedish scholar to recommend two other passivity rules, using the provision as an analogy basis for both.[20] One rule concerns the situation where a proxy with an oral authority distorts the sender's declaration of intention, the other where the sender's declaration of intention is based on an erroneous assumption.

Moreover, there is a further variation of the juridical analogy thinking, viz. analogies based on different components of different basic rules—we can call rules such created as *compositely analogical rules*. The requisites of the rule created analogically can be taken from different existing rules, or the requisites can be taken from one rule and the legal consequence from another. Let me give an example.[21] A rule in the Swedish Contract Act says

(r_1) If somebody has given a declaration of intention, which due to error has got another content than the one intended, and the person to whom the declaration

---

[19]Sundberg (1966) – The work is unfortunately only available in Swedish.

[20]Karlgren (1965), p. 114 f. – Also this work is unfortunately only available in Swedish.

[21]Karlgren (1965), p. 194 ff.

of intention was addressed understood, or should have understood, the error, then the former is not bound by the content of the declaration of intention.

More often than not, however, the parties do not want the contract to be invalid. Usually each party wants the contract to be valid, albeit according to his interpretation of it. But which rule should apply when this is the case?

Another rule in the Contract Act says:

(r_2) If an answer to the effect that an offer is accepted due to addition, restriction or reservation is not in accordance with the offer, *and* the person who gave the answer considers it to be in accordance with the offer (and the addressee must understand that), *and* if the addressee, if he does not want to accept the answer, not without undue delay notifies the other hereof, then a contract according to the content of the answer has come about.

For the case that both parties want the contract to remain valid Karlgren establishes the following rule:

(r') If somebody who has given a declaration of intention ... should have understood the error [= r_1] *and* the person to whom the declaration of intention is addressed not without undue delay notifies the person who gave the declaration that he does not want to accept the content of the declaration of intent, then the contract is valid according to the content intended by the person who gave the declaration of intention.

As we see, r' is constructed by a requisite taken from r_1 and another taken from r_2. The legal consequence is taken from r_2.

It is to be observed that, although r_1 provides r' with a requisite, r' is not analogous to r_1. In fact r' stands in GT-relation (21) to r_1. But r' is analogous to r_2 (GT-relation (13)).

This example, then, also illustrates another, not uncommon juridical phenomenon. Creating a rule analogically from some rule or rules in the legal system often has the consequence that another rule in the system is reduced. One rule pushes away another. For instance, in our example just given r_1 is reduced by r' as a consequence of the creation of r' analogically by means of r_2.

Within the spectrum of a (basic) legal rule (Sect. 8.2) we made a distinction between generalising analogies (GT-relations (9)–(12)) and disjoint analogies (GT-relations (13)–(16)). As for generalising analogies: $F \subset F'$; as for disjoint analogies: $(F' \cap F)=\phi$.

However, GT-relations (9)–(12) can be conceived of as "spurious" analogies.

The reason for that is it could be said that such an operation does not result in another rule r', analogous to r, but in the fact that r has been included in a more general rule, r'. r' has been substituted for r. From now on we regard—with the exception of the N-analogies—only GT-relations (13)–(16) as *analogies.* For GT-relations (9)–(12) we use the term *generalisation*, identical neither to analogy nor to extensive interpretation (Sect. 8.4). The methodological implications of this will be investigated in Sect. 9.4.2.

This leads us on to a phenomenon in juridical analogy thinking that I shall call *institutional analogy*. An analogy relation between two rules, r and r' is an institutional analogy if and only if (i) F and F' are disjoint sets and (ii) the cause of that disjunction lies in the established systematisation of law itself. Examples: r pertains to purchase and r' to hire, r to contracts within the law of property and r' to contracts within family law, r to complicity with respect to crime against property and r' to complicity with respect to crimes of type forgery.

Let us also introduce the concept *isomorphic institutional analogy* (a concept we will use in our investigation of the technique of analogical use of rules in Sect. 9.4.2). Take the rules

(r) If the seller delays considerably in delivering the goods, the buyer may cancel the contract

and

(r') If the lessor delays considerably in delivering the goods, the lessee may cancel the contract.

Let the rp-structure of r (see Sect. 7.3) be $S=<U,K,L,R>$ and the rp-structure of r' be $S'=< U,K',L'R>$. The relation of isomorphic analogy holds between r and r'. That means that the R-relations in their rp-structure are identical ("delaying considerably in delivering the goods") while K and K' and L and L', respectively, are disjoint sets within "the universe of discourse", U, due to the established systematisation of law: K being the set of sellers, K' the set of lessors, L the set of buyers and L' the set of lessees.

Isomorphic analogies are, so to speak, "pure" analogies: for each requisite in r there is a corresponding requisite in r'. But it also happens that, when creating a rule by means of an institutional analogy, the result is a non-isomorphic analogy, i.e., one sets limits to "the analogy effect" by adding another requisite to the rule thus created (see further Sects. 9.2.2 and 9.4.2).

9.2.2 *Analogical and Other Uses of Rules Described in Terms of Manipulations with Requisites*

So far we have regarded analogies from a topological viewpoint. But it is possible to regard them also from a purely morphological viewpoint: analogy as a result of manipulations with requisites.

Of the requisites of a legal rule some designate the K-set, some the L-set and some the R-relation. However, this is not necessarily always the case. The K- or L-set can be so specified by the place of the rule in a certain statute, or part of a statute, that these sets do not need to be explicitly indicated in the rule in question. The R-relation is usually the most complicated element of the rp-structure. It is often composed of what reasonably can be regarded as many different requisites. Sometimes it can be a bit arbitrary to decide which phenomena shall be assigned to the K-set, the L-set or the R-relation, but usually this comes quite naturally.

Let us have a look at juridical manipulation with requisites not only with respect to analogy but, by way of comparison, also with respect to generalisation and reduction.

I. Analogy in this perspective means *exchange* of a requisite: one requisite is substituted for another. r has the requisites $a\&b\&c$, r' gets the requisites $a\&b\&d$. This is obvious with respect to institutional analogies but holds for other analogies as well. An example.[22] A provision then in force in the Swedish Code on Parents and Children stipulated that a father to a child born out of wedlock should contribute to the maintenance of the mother 6 weeks before and 6 weeks after the delivery. This provision was applied analogically to a situation where no delivery had taken place—the pregnancy had been terminated by an abortion. The requisite "father to a child born out of wedlock" was in the rule of application exchanged for "a man has made a woman to whom he is not married pregnant and the pregnancy has been terminated by an abortion".

II. Generalisation means *an elimination* of a requisite. r has the requisites $a\&b\&c$, r' gets the requisites $a\&b$. An example.[23] A provision then in force in the Swedish exchange regulation stipulated that, when a person had been sentenced to punishment for currency offence, the currency illegally imported could be confiscated. An American citizen, S, had, with the help of a deck steward on a Swedish passenger liner, tried to import money, wrapped in a parcel, into Sweden. However, S could not be sentenced to punishment since he was not subject to Swedish jurisdiction (he was a foreign citizen not residing in Sweden).That notwithstanding, the Supreme Court confiscated the money, thereby eliminating the requisite "has been sentenced to punishment".

III. A kind of hybrid form of analogy and generalisation is *weakening* of requisites. Take "the abortion case" just mentioned. The rule of application there could be rendered either

(r'_1) Has a man made a woman to whom he is not married pregnant, and has the pregnancy been terminated by an abortion, he shall contribute to the maintenance of the woman, etc.

which is an analogy, or

(r'_2) A father to a child born out of wedlock *or* a man who has made --- [= r'_1] shall contribute, etc.

which is a generalisation. However, this kind of generalisation is weaker than the one presented under II. There a requisite was eliminated, here it is only weakened. It

[22] NJA 1951, p. 265.

[23] NJA 1953, p. 524.

is weakened by the establishing of *a disjunction*—a new requisite is introduced and coupled to the existing one by making a disjunction of them.[24] In "the confiscation case" the requisite "has been sentenced to punishment" could after this judgment be disregarded by the courts of law, since the judgment was a precedent. But neither of the alternatives in r'_2 can be disregarded.

Now the question arises: Which one of r'_1 and r'_2 is "the correct" rendering of r'? The answer I think is: Both are. In certain situations it comes natural to use the one, in other situations the other.

IV. Precisation and reduction both mean *the addition of* a requisite. *r* has the requisites *a&b*, *r'* gets the requisites *a&b&c*. The difference between precisation and reduction is that the latter has a reversed modality. As we see in our schemata, to the precisation relations (5) and (6) correspond the reduction relations (21) and (22).

An example. Take the rules

(*r*) If the same goods are sold to two buyers, the buyer who bought the goods first shall keep it

and

(*r'*) If the same goods are sold to two buyers *and* the second buyer has not got possession of the goods in good faith, the first buyer shall keep it

and

(*r''*) If the same goods are sold to two different buyers *and* the second buyer has got possession of the goods in good faith, the second buyer shall keep it [= the first buyer may not keep it].

Of these rules, *r'* is a precisation of *r* by the addition of the requisite "the second buyer has not got possession of the goods in good faith" and *r''* is a reduction of *r* by the addition of the requisite "the second buyer has got possession of the goods in good faith".

Another example of reductive addition of a requisite to a statutory provision is "the dog case" (see Sect. 8.3 above). The rule of application reads (the requisite in italics is added to the statutory provision):

(*r'*) If a dog *which is used in the Lapps' reindeer keeping* is found while chasing or otherwise molesting reindeer, being in an area where reindeer at the time may be sent out to pasture, the dog may not be killed.

Since the analogy argumentation can be described in terms of manipulations of requisites, what is being exchanged can either be the R-relation or the set of individuals to which this relation holds (*KxL*) or both. The same applies *mutatis mutandis* to generalisation, precisation and reduction.

---

[24] Cf. Heller (1961), pp. 71 and 84; Tammelo (1969), p. 129.

9.3 The Material Analogy-Relation: Similarity and Analogy Argumentation

9.3.1 Introduction

The formal analogy-relation we regarded as a necessary condition for a GT-relation between rules to be an analogy-relation. Genuine analogy-relations were, with the exception of the N-analogies (see Sect. 9.3.5 in fine below), GT-relations (13)–(16). The other necessary condition is that a material analogy-relation holds. Here the concept "similarity" comes to the fore. Together these two conditions are sufficient. (When clarifying the similarity relation we leave the complex analogy-relations investigated in Sect. 9.2.1 out of account.)

So the two necessary and together sufficient conditions for the relation "r' applied to c' is analogous to r applied to c" to hold are these:

(i) That one of the GT-relations (13)–(16) holds between r' and r.
(ii) That c' and c are elements of *a similarity set* constituted by *an analogy-basing property*.

In the present section my aim is to clarify condition (ii).

That the juridical concept "analogy" is closely bound to the concept "similarity" is regarded in the literature as something more or less self-evident. Sometimes we hear the idea that analogy and similarity are roughly the same thing, sometimes that analogy is a special kind of similarity[25] and sometimes that an analogy depends on, or is justified by, similarity between certain entities.

Our clarification of the function of the similarity concept in juridical analogy argumentation is in the first place founded on the last-mentioned idea. I see the analogy as a relation between legal rules justified by a certain kind of similarity between legal cases. This similarity is so fundamental that we include it in our definition of the analogy-relation. This idea is expressed in a precise manner by García Máynez[26]:

> [Wir können sagen] dass die Füllung einer Lücke auf dem Wege der Analogie nur gerechtfertig ist, wenn folgende Bedingungen gegeben sind:
>
> 1) die Ähnlichkeit zwischen dem unvorgesehenen Fall und dem analogen, vorgesehenen muss auf einem gemeinsamen Element M beruhen, das für den vorgesehenen Fall die Anwendung einer bestimmte Rechtsfolge rechtfertigt;
>
> 2) die Zuschreibung auf den unvorgesehenen Fall einer Folge, die das Gesetz mit dem analogen, vorgesehenen verknüpft, muss ebenfalls in dem gemeinsamen element M begründet sein;

[25] So Austin (1911), Vol. I (Lecture V), p. 167: "Analogy is a species of resemblance". However, a little bit later he introduces another analogy concept, where "resemblance is opposed to analogy". In many European languages it comes natural to use "analogous" as synonymous with "similar". Sometimes "analogous" is used in the same sense as "isomorphous". See further Heller (1961), p. 7 ff.

[26] Garcia Máynez (1965), p. 118.

3) in dem unvorgesehenen Fall darf nichts vorhanden sein, das verhindern würde, auf Grund des gemeinsamen Elements M die für den analogen, vorgesehenen Fall bestimmte Vorschrift auf diesen speziellen Fall anzuwenden.

The basic ideas expressed in this quotation have inspired the development of the theory presented in this section.

9.3.2 The Argument from Analogy in Inductive Logic

Outside juridical thinking we meet an analogism usually treated in works on inductive reasoning.[27] Sometimes the analogy is regarded as a variation of induction, sometimes as something closely related to induction[28] and sometimes as something quite different from induction.[29] I think it is of some interest to compare this analogism—*the inductive analogy*—with the juridical one, especially with respect to the role similarity plays in these two kinds of argumentation.

To be sure, also inductive analogy has a place in juridical reasoning, viz., within the evaluation of evidence. Let us take an example from Schneider.[30] A witness asserts in a cruelty to animals case: "I saw the accused lash the dog. The animal was in great pain". As an answer to the judge's question how he knew that the dog was in pain, the witness says: "Because the dog howled awfully".

The various steps in this analogy argumentation are:

(1) If a human being is whipped and she screams, she experiences pain.
(2) Human beings and dogs are biologically similar.
(3) Hence: If a dog is whipped and she screams she experiences pain.
(4) A dog's scream is called howling.
(5) Hence: If a dog is whipped and she howls she experiences pain.

This is an inductive analogy: As a reason for claiming that the dog has a certain property that also human beings have, similarities between dogs and human beings in other respects are referred to.

In the present section I shall give a short presentation of what I regard as the essential thing about the inductive analogy. This will in the subsequent sections be compared with the juridical analogy.

It is common to look upon the inductive analogy as a coupling together of an inductive and a deductive line of reasoning. Thus, the analogism

---

[27]See, e.g., von Wright (1951), p. 254 ff. and von Wright (1957), p. 134 ff. On induction in general see further Hacking (2001); Kyburg, Jr. (1970) and Rosenkrantz (1981). As the titles suggest, there is a close connection between induction and probability. Another closely related concept is "confirmation".

[28]See von Wright (1951), p. 264.

[29]See Lindenbaum Hosiasson (1941), p. 351 ff.

[30]Schneider (1965).

(1) s_1 *is a, b, c*
(2) s_2 *is a, b*

---

(3) s_2 *is c*
can be brought up in the induction

(1′) s_1 *is a, b, c*
(2′) s_1 *is s*

(3′) *Every s is a, b, c*
and the deduction
(3′) *Every s is a, b, c*
(4′) s_2 *is s*

(5′) s_2 *is a, b, c.*

Modern inquiries into induction and inductive analogy are built on an understanding of the fact that they include a probabilistic element and, for that reason, probability theory is needed for their explication.[31] Such an explication has been given by, among others, von Wright.[32] The essential things in inductive analogy are, according to him, the following.

(1) From the fact that two states of affairs ("things"), *x* and *y*, are similar with respect to the properties $A_1, \ldots, A_n$ and that *x* moreover has the property *B*, we conclude that also *y* has the property *B*.
(2) The probability of the conclusion in an analogism (e.g., "*y* has the property *B*") is greater the greater the number of similarity properties ($A_1, \ldots, A_n$) there are with respect to the compared states of affairs *x* and *y*. (But von Wright does not claim that the probability of the conclusion is a function *exclusively* of the size of *n*.)
(3) That the analogism seems convincing is due to the fact that we suspect some kind of *connection* between the existence of the properties $A_1, \ldots A_n$ and the property *B* of some state of affairs. The former properties are conceived as being some way or another "responsible" for the existence of the latter.
(4) This "responsibility relation" is analysed in terms of sufficient (or perhaps even necessary and sufficient) conditions. If the set of similarity properties $A_1, \ldots A_n$ (probably) contains an element that is a sufficient condition of *B*—or many elements which together make up such a condition—the existence of the similarity properties show that the state of affairs in question also has property *B*.
(5) The probability that $A_1, \ldots, A_n$ contain a sufficient condition of *B* is greater the greater *n* is.

It is obvious, as von Wright emphasises, that the *number* of similarity properties cannot alone be decisive of the credibility of an inductive analogism. If we have two

---

[31]This is evident from the titles of the works mentioned in n. 27. See also Carnap (1950), § 110 D.
[32]See von Wright (1957), p. 134 ff.

different states of affairs, s_1 and s_2, of which s_1 has property *B*, we cannot, if we want to investigate whether also s_2 has property *B*, content ourselves with considering the number of properties common to s_1 and s_2. For it is possible that, among the properties of s_1, there could be one, *C*, that is not a property of s_2 and that in all probability is a sufficient condition of *B*. Then it can be called into question that there is a sufficient condition of *B* among the similarity properties. Or it might be the case that among the properties of s_2 there is one, *D*, which, with a high degree of probability, is a sufficient condition of *non-B*.

In the following I shall make some reflections about the probabilistic element in the inductive analogy and about the significance of factors of the kind just mentioned. My purpose is to use these reflections as a basis of a comparison between the inductive and the juridical analogy (which we, *ex hypothesi*, for the present regard as two different things).

Our reasoning will be illustrated by means of some variations on an example, where we compare two situations, s_1 and s_2, in which a patient undergoes a dental treatment. s_1 and s_2 have some properties in common. The set of these properties we call *the similarity basis*. In our example the question is if one should attribute to s_2 a property that we know belongs to s_1, namely that the patient experiences pain. The proposition that s_1 has this property we call *the analogy theme*. States of affairs in (properties of) s_1 and s_2 are indicated by letters *a, b, c*, etc., in accordance with the following:

- $a =$ that the dentist is drilling in the patient's tooth
- $b =$ that the patient wriggles in the chair
- $c =$ that the dentist has an attractive nurse
- $d =$ that the patient dislikes the sound of the drill
- $e =$ that the patient is seized with a cramp in his leg
- $f =$ that the tooth is frozen
- $g =$ that the patient experiences pain.

The proposition that *g* is the case is the analogy theme. The propositions that each of *a*–*g* is the case are logically independent of each other. (In the example we disregard that pain can vary in intensity. We assume that this is not the case here.)

The central concept in our clarification of the inductive analogism is "sufficient condition". In order for the analogism to be convincing it must be probable that the similarity basis contains a sufficient condition of the state of affairs that is indicated by the analogy theme.[33]

An analysis of the most complicated relation "*x* is probably a sufficient condition of *y*" presents considerable difficulties. My attempt at a clarification here is an attempt to formulate an intuitive conception in a more explicit way.

First we can observe that the concept "sufficient condition" is relative in the sense that *x* can be a sufficient condition of *y* (abbreviated "*xSCy*") within the set of states

[33]About the importance, in the inductive analogism, of the probability of something being a sufficient condition of something else, see von Wright (1957), p. 134 f.

of affairs F_1 but not within the set of states of affairs F_2. Hence, the relation we shall clarify includes some set of states of affairs, F, such that $xSCy$ in F.

The intuitive conception of the "sufficiency" is, I guess, that x on its own shall "manage to" establish the existence of y in F, i.e., that the conditioned circumstance exists as soon as the conditioning circumstance exists independent of other actually existing circumstances in F. Sufficiency is an independence of sorts.

Now let us, which is conceivable, include the probabilistic element in the very definition of $xSCy$ in F, or, in other words, compare the probability of y in various situations where x exists. We can express this idea in a little more precise and technical way like this:

Hypothesis: $xSCy$ in F. $F = \{x, y, f_1, \ldots, f_k\}$.

We form the set $S = F \neg \{x, y\}$, i.e., $S = \{f_1, \ldots, f_k\}$. (The symbol "$\neg$" is read "minus".)

Moreover, (i) let $Z = \{z_1, \ldots, z_k\}$ be the power set of S[34] and z_i any element in Z ($z_i \in Z$), and (ii) let "$Pr (B/A)$" be a conditional probability symbol which is read "the probability of B given A". We can now formulate the condition

$$xSCy \textit{ in } F \text{ only if } Pr\left(y/x, \sim z_i\right) \geq Pr\left(y/x, z_i\right).$$

(The formula is read: "x is a sufficient condition of y in F only if the probability of y given x but not z_i is at least as great as the probability of y given x and z_i".)

The condition says that the probability of y given x and any other combination of circumstances in F apart from x and y cannot be greater than the probability of y given x when this combination is not present. For if the probability became greater when such a combination were introduced in the presence of x, it would not be probable that x is a sufficient condition of y. If $xSCy$, z_i cannot have an influence on the probability of y being the case when x is the case. That is what "sufficiency" means. (If also z_iSCy is the case, "=" can be substituted for "$\geq$".) x can, of course, be a conjunction of factors, e. g., $x = x_1 \,\&\, x_2 \,\&\, x_3$. Then each of x_1, x_2 and x_3 is a part of a sufficient condition of y.

Let us now turn to the example with the dental patient. We shall regard the following seven situations.

(1) $s_1 = \{a, b, c, g\}$
$s_2 = \{a, b, d\}$
The similarity basis $= \{a, b\}$.

Suppose that, as a matter of fact, neither c in s_1 nor d in s_2 influences the patient in any way from the viewpoint of pain. Then c and d are *irrelevant factors*. (So they will remain in the following examples as well.) Hence, the credibility of the analogy theme depends on the probability of there being a sufficient condition of g in the similarity basis.

The example also shows that the strength of the analogy argument does not exclusively depend on whether there is a sufficient condition in the similarity basis

[34] The power set $P(S)$ of a set S is the set of all subsets of S, including S and ϕ. So if $S = \{x, y\}$, $P(S) = \{\{x\}, \{y\}, \{x, y\}, \phi\}$.

that *causes* the analogy theme. Suppose that we find that $\{a, b\}$ is a sufficient condition of *g*. Of these two factors in the similarity basis it makes sense to say that *a* is the cause of *g*. But it does not make sense to say that *b* is (a component of) the cause of *g*. On the contrary, *g* is the cause of *b*. But it still might be reasonable to claim that the probability of *g* given *a & b* is greater than the probability of *g* given only *a*: *Pr (g/ab) > Pr (g/a~b)*. So we must separate the factors *causing* the pain from other factors making the presence of the pain probable.[35]

(2) $s_1 = \{a, b, c, e, g\}$
$s_2 = \{a, b, d\}$
The similarity basis $= \{a, b\}$.

In this case it can be difficult to decide whether the similarity basis contains a sufficient condition of *g*. For we are likely to assume either that *e* alone is a sufficient condition of *g* while $\{a, b\}$ is not, or that neither *e* nor $\{a, b\}$ separately is alone a sufficient condition of *g*, but that *e* and $\{a, b\}$ together are. In both cases an analogism is unfounded. It is well-founded only if $\{a, b\}$ alone is a sufficient condition of *g*—and then it does not matter if also *e* alone is a sufficient condition of *g*. An analogism is well-founded only if the following condition is fulfilled:

Pr (g/ab~e) $\geq$ *Pr (g/abe)*.

(3) $s_1 = \{a, b, c, e, g\}$
$s_2 = \{a, b, d, e\}$
The similarity basis $= \{a, b, e\}$.

Suppose that $\{a, b\}$ and *e*, respectively, are separately a sufficient condition of *g*. According to our condition, the strength of the analogy argument is not augmented because the similarity basis contains two separate sufficient conditions of the analogy theme compared to the case where only one sufficient condition is present. For *Pr (g/ab~e) = Pr (g/abe) = Pr (g/~a,~b, e)*.

(4) $s_1 = \{a, b, c, g\}$
$s_2 = \{a, b, d, e\}$
The similarity basis $= \{a, b\}$.

If it is probable that $\{a, b\}$ and *e*, respectively, are sufficient conditions of *g*, one can as an argument for the existence of *g* in s_2 refer to an analogy from s_1 as well as the presence of *e*. But referring to both does not augment the strength of the argument compared to referring to only one of them.

(5) $s_1 = \{a, b, c, f, g\}$
$s_2 = \{a, b, d\}$
The similarity basis $= \{a, b\}$.

[35]This is often the situation in the evaluation of evidence. For example, from the fact that skid marks of a certain length are measured we conclude that the car that made them had the speed *s* km/h. And the speed is (a component of) the cause of the skid marks.

(6) $s_1 = \{a, b, c, f, g\}$
$s_2 = \{a, b, d, f\}$
The similarity basis $= \{a, b, f\}$.

With respect to these two situations suffice it to say that in (5) the existence of *f* in s_1 but not in s_2 does not augment the strength of the analogy argument. For *g* is present in s_1 and $\{a, b\}$ can very well be a sufficient condition of *g* even in the presence of *f*.

(7) $s_1 = \{a, b, c, g\}$
$s_2 = \{a, b, d, f\}$
The similarity basis $= \{a, b\}$.

Here we have a circumstance, *f*, in s_2, which is not present in s_1 and which can be suspected to be *a negative factor*. This means that $\{a, b\}$ can very well be a sufficient condition of *g* in s_1 but, if *f* is introduced, *g* does not occur. The drilling can be a sufficient condition of the pain in the absence of freezing the tooth, but if the tooth is frozen, the pain does not occur. This is an example of the fact, mentioned above, that something, *x*, can be a sufficient condition of something else, *y*, in certain circumstances but not in others. If we analogise in our example, we must be able to make it probable that *abSCg* also in the presence of *f*.

9.3.3 Similarity Sets and Analogy Sets

Cases of interest in juridical analogy argumentation are situations belonging to sets in a certain way generated by cases belonging to the sphere of operative facts of a legal rule (so-called equivalence classes). In our connection we call them (juridically relevant) *similarity sets.* The elements of such sets belong to the sphere of influence of the rule. Between the elements in similarity sets there exists a similarity in some certain, specified respect. This idea, being a corner-stone in our theory, has the following signification.

The relation "is similar with respect to *b*" (where *b* is a variable over some specified set of properties) is a so-called *equivalence relation*, i.e., it is reflexive, symmetric and transitive.[36] (It is reflexive since *x* is similar with respect to *b* to *x* itself, it is symmetric since, if *x* is similar to *y* with respect to *b*, *y* is similar to *x* with respect to *b*, and it is transitive since if *x* is similar to *y* with respect to *b* and *y* is

[36]Among philosophers and jurisprudents there is no consensus that the similarity relation is an equivalence relation. According to Carnap (1969), Ch. A, 11, a relation is "a *similarity relation* if it is symmetrical and reflexive and an *equivalence* if it is also transitive". On the other hand, Alchourrón (1965), p. 21; and Segerberg (1971), p. 150, regard similarity as an equivalence relation (although Segerberg does not take it completely for granted). Hilpinen (1969), p. 189, argues that some, but not all, similarity relations are equivalence relations. It comes natural to me to regard our relation "similar with respect to *b*" as an equivalence relation. The analogy relations, on the other hand, are no equivalence relations (see Subsection 9.3.5).

similar to z with respect to b, then x is similar to z with respect to b.) Let E be an equivalence relation in some set, M. For x ($x \in M$) we can now form the set $[x]$, that we call *the E-equivalence set generated by x*, such that ("$\leftrightarrow$" reads "if and only if")[37]:

$$y \in [x] \leftrightarrow (y \in M \& xEy).$$

Suppose that we have a legal rule, r, its sphere of operative facts, R, and a case c ($c \in R$). Suppose further that c has a property g that is of particular legal interest, e.g., in a court trial. (g is, e.g., the property "negligent handling of dangerous chemical substance" and the trial concerns a case c'($c' \notin R$), also having the property g. *The g-equivalence set generated by c*, $[c_g]$, then, is the set of all cases having the property g, *however different these cases might be in other respects.* We say that $[c_g]$ is *the (g-)similarity set for c* ($c \in R$). For every case c in a sphere of operative facts R we can form similarity sets of this kind.

Thus, $[c_g]$ is the set of all cases having the property g in common. Among such properties some are of special interest to us, let us call them *analogy-basing properties.* The presence of such properties gives cause for creating a rule by analogy from another rule in a way that will be investigated in Sect. 9.3.5.

Suppose that we have a rule r, its sphere of operative facts R, a case c ($c \in R$) and the similarity set $[c_g]$. We also have two cases, c' ($c' \notin R$) and c'' ($c'' \notin R$). The juridical problem is whether we shall construct rules analogical to r for cases c' and c'' or not. Suppose that c'' has a property h making it inappropriate to analogise from r with respect to c'' (h is a so-called *negative instance*) while no such property is present in c'. So the solution to the problem would be to construct a rule analogous to r for c' but not for c'', and perhaps instead a rule created *e contrario* to r for c''. But another solution with respect to c'' could also be to construct a rule r'' for c'' containing an additional requisite restricting its sphere of operative facts and thereby decreasing the disadvantage of h. We shall presently come back to this.

The set of cases in $[c_g]$ for which a rule r' is constructed by analogy from r we call *the (g-)analogy set for c* ($c \in R$). For such analogy sets we use the variable AN_r.

Hence, an analogy set is always a subset of some similarity set $[c_g]$, where $c \in R$. On the other hand, AN_r and R are always disjoint. The case that $AN_r = [c_g]\ R\ [c_g$ minus $R]$ we call *maximum g-analogy relative to c* ($c \in R$).

A word must also be said about the relation between R and $[c_g]$, where $c \in R$. It is not necessarily the case that $R \subseteq [c_g]$. For there might be cases in R which lack the analogy-basing property g constituting the similarity set of which AN_r is a subset.

Moreover, an illuminating concept in this connection is *deontic distance*, suggested by Segerberg.[38] Deontic distance is a relation over possible situations and is intended to capture the idea of similarity gradation: a case c' can be more similar to another case c than a case c'' is similar to c:

[37]See Suppes (1967), p. 218 f.

[38]Segerberg (1971), p. 150.

> A possible situation may be similar to another with respect to certain features, and not similar with respect to others. Of two possible situations that are both similar to a third, one may be more similar to the third than the other is. Suppose it were meaningful to talk about the 'deontic distance' between possible situations. The two situations would be similar to some degree whenever the deontic distance between them would be finite; the deontic distance between two situations would be zero if and only if they would be completely similar from a deontic point of view (that is, with respect to every set of deontically relevant features); a situation u would be more similar to a situation w than a situation v would be if and only if the deontic distance between u and w would be smaller than that between v and w; and so on.

As Segerberg points out, the idea of deontic distance is a bit fanciful and he does not make any attempt to present some kind of "normative gradation" over sets of possible situations. We shall not make any such attempt either. We content ourselves by saying that the normative distance between legal cases in a similarity set has to do with the weight as an argument the negative features (instances) of the cases compared have—a case c' is closer to a case c than a case c'' if and only if the weight as an argument of the negative features of c' relative to c is lower than the weight as an argument of the negative features of c'' relative to c.

Let us illuminate this idea by means of some examples. Think of a similarity set $[c_g] = \{c, c_1, c_2, c_3, c_4, c_5, c_6\}$. Over $[c_g]$ the relation "deontic distance" holds in the way that c_1 is closer to (more similar to) c than c_2 is, etc. Suppose that $\{c, c_1, c_2\} \subseteq R$ (i.e., that c, c_1 and c_2 belong to the sphere of operative facts of rule r). Suppose further that c_3 and c_4 are similar to c to such a high degree that a rule r' is created for these cases by analogy from r. That means that we have constructed *an analogy set* AN_r ($AN_r \subset [c_g]$): $AN_r = \{c_3, c_4\}$.

For instance, c and c_1 are clear cases of "motor traffic injury" according to some statutory provision. c is a case where a car has run into a pedestrian, c_1 a case where one car has run into another, whose driver has been injured. c_2 is a case where a car has made a jerk forward in a garage and squeezed a person against a wall. This is not a clear case of traffic damage but it has been incorporated in R by a precedent. c_3 is a case where a person has slipped off a bus stationary at a bus-stop, c_4 a case where a person has been accidentally pushed out of a bus stationary at a bus-stop. c_3 and c_4 are hardly traffic injuries but let us imagine that some courts apply the provision in question analogically to these cases.

Let us now turn to a more complicated situation. Suppose that, with respect to case c_5, the presence of the similarity property is an argument for creating an analogical rule for this case. However, opposite considerations in the form of the presence of negative instances justify *a modification* of such an analogically created rule. It can then be reasonable to add a requisite to this rule in order to restrict its sphere of operation. For instance, a person has got caught in the closing doors of a bus when trying to enter it and has been injured. A court applies a rule analogous to the provision but with the addition of the requisite "and if the driver did not check whether someone was entering when closing the doors". Such a modification can also consist in changing the norm-theme of the analogical rule in some respect (as was done in the boat case (Sect. 8.2, GT-relation 7).

Finally, suppose that, with respect to case c_6, it is the case that the argumentative weight of negative instances—or, in other words, the deontic distance—is so great that it supersedes the argumentative weight of the similarity property. Then it is not justified to construct a rule analogous to the provision for c_6 but rather to use it *e contrario.* For instance, a person jumps intentionally off a bus in motion.

9.3.4 Legal Bases

Now we are able to formulate a preliminary definition of the concept "analogy-basing property".

Let r be a basic rule for the analogous rule r', $c \in R$ and $c' \in R'$. That a similarity property, g (or a conjunction of such, g_1 & ... g_n), of c and c' is an analogy-basing property with respect to c' means that g *justifies* the construction of r'. Reference to g, then, must be so strong an argument that it supersedes the argumentative value of every property h (or conjunction of properties h_1 & ... h_m) of c', whose existence is to the disadvantage of constructing r'.

This preliminary definition will be elaborated on in Sect. 9.3.5. But in order to be able to do such an elaboration we must introduce the concept *legal basis* (German *Rechtsgrund).*

There is an idea that I am inclined to regard as something of a juridical axiom: Every legal rule is *a means*, an instrument, of attaining a social state of affairs. The legal order is no end in itself. This state of affairs is a state desired by the law-giver. This axiom, or postulate, can also be formulated like this: To every legal rule, r, corresponds a desired social state of affairs, s, such that r is an instrument of achieving s. One further formulation would be: Every legal rule is warranted by a legal basis. It seems to me that if this postulate is not accepted, rational juridical argumentation is impossible. In this subsection we shall try to clarify the relation "r is a means of attaining s". The concept "legal basis" is not a topological concept but a teleological one. However, it is fundamental to topologically involved concepts such as "if r is applied to *case* c, s will probably follow".

One can imagine studying some legal order from a rather special point of view. Given information concerning the content of its legal rules (the law), together with statements given by the legislator (e.g., in the preparatory material), we can, with varying degrees of probability, form an idea of the legislator's conception of the nature of *the ideal society.* Every legal order conveys—albeit dimly and ambiguously—a picture of an ideal society. We can talk about the ideal society S relative to the legal order L. Let us call S *the utopia of* L.

To every rule in L we can attribute an ideal social state of affairs. The "total" social state of affairs prevailing if the ideal state of affairs relative to all rules in L prevails is the utopia of L.

When we talk here about an ideal society this refers, as the reader has seen above, to the legislator's conception of it. Nothing prevents such a utopia from being of the most evil kind from a moral viewpoint—such as, e.g., the Nazi utopia as it stands out in the legislation of the Third *Reich*.

But a legal order does not only convey the image of a utopia. Often we can, with a no small degree of certainty, make assertions of a more sophisticated nature. More often than not particular rules (or sets of such) can be assigned to *preference orders* over social states of affairs desired by the legislator. The legal rules "rank" different social states of affairs from the ideal to the next best, to the next to next best, etc. Such preference orders are, as we shall see, of a certain significance when we try to establish the purpose of legal rules.

Let us illustrate this idea by some examples.

(1) The ideal state of affairs corresponding to a provision punishing theft is, of course, the society where no thefts occur. But relative to the provision (together with the law of procedure and the adherence to the value of legal security) the following order of preference can be made:

  (i) The society where no one steals and no one is punished for stealing.
  (ii) The society where stealing occurs and the thieves are punished for it.
  (iii) The society where stealing occurs and the thieves are not punished for it.
  (iv) The society where no one steals and people are punished for stealing.

  (Of course, according to the preference order a society is better the least thefts are committed in it and a society is better the more thieves are punished in it.)

(2) The ideal state of affairs corresponding to the rule "If anyone intentionally or by negligence damages another person's property, he shall pay damages for it" is the one where no damages on somebody's property are caused intentionally or by negligence. With respect to the rule, we can also single out the next best state of affairs, viz., the best state *when such a damage has already occurred*—i.e., the state where, when a damage has occurred, it is compensated for.

(3) Sometimes it is not totally obvious which ideal state of affairs corresponds to a given legal rule. Take, e.g., a provision in some sale of goods act to the effect that, if the price is not included in the agreement, the buyer shall pay what the seller requests when this is not undue. That the ideal state would be the state where the parties always agree upon the price is not likely. Rather it is the state where the price is always due—a manifestation of the old honest Roman principle *suum cuique tribuere.*

(4) With respect to such rules in the social assistance legislation that allot assistance to people in certain circumstances we can, generally speaking, establish the preference order:

  (i) The society where no one needs social assistance
  (ii) The society where all in such circumstances get social assistance.

It is to be noted that, unlike, e.g., criminal law and the law of torts, the social assistance legislation is not suitable for (nor intended to) achieving the ideal state of affairs. Its function is exclusively reparative.

The instrumental function of legal rules is often a complicated matter. More often than not they have several different functions. This is sometimes associated with the fact that a given rule zeros in on different steps in a preference order. A typical example is rules in civil law that have both a preventive and a reparative function, such as the law of torts. If we take a look at the preference order in two steps in example (2), it could be said that the reparative function pertains to the lower step in the preference order, i.e., the interest of compensating the victim once the damage has occurred. But the rule in the example also has a preventive function—it is aimed at preventing the tort-feasor and others from causing damages in the future. But this function is part of the aim to realise the ideal state of affairs that damages are not caused intentionally or negligently at all. It is probably not uncommon that the instrumental function of legal rules is spread over a preference order—something we must bear in mind when we discuss the purpose of a legal rule. Considering the function of legal rules to attain ideal social states of affairs we can, a bit aphoristically, say that every legal system has as its ultimate purpose to make itself superfluous. It seeks to attain its utopia.

But, we can ask ourselves, is it really the case that we can attach a desirable state of affairs to *every* legal rule? Is it, for instance, meaningful to say that the law of inheritance has a utopia? I think we can answer this question in the affirmative, if we take into consideration that utopias can sometimes be of a rather modest kind. The utopia of the law of inheritance, then, can be said to consist in having a certain amount of certainty with respect to property. With respect to optional rules, they can be regarded as an abandonment on the part of the legislator of his claim of monopoly for his own preferences.

Now we take a further step closer to the concept "legal basis". We have a rule r, its sphere of operative facts R and its set of normativised facts N. To each individual operative fact in R corresponds one or more individual normativised facts in N. Let c be any individual operative fact (case) in R. Then we can introduce a concept "*individual normativised fact in N corresponding to c*". This is done in the following ostensive manner.

Suppose that we have the rule

(r) If anyone has negligently damaged another person's property, he shall pay damages to the victim.

r contains the requisites "someone has negligently damaged another person's property" and the normativised fact "the tort-feasor pays damages to the victim". The following members of R are individual operative facts:

(c_1) Smith has negligently damaged Jones' power lawn mower
(c_2) Brown has negligently damaged White's bicycle.

The following members of N are individual normativised facts:

(n_1) Smith pays 1.000 kronor as damages to Jones
(n_2) Smith pays 2.000 kronor as damages to Jones
(n_3) Brown pays damages to White.

We see that n_1 and n_2 are both individual normative facts corresponding to c_1 but this is not the case with respect to n_3. On the other hand, given r and c_2, n_3 is a normative fact corresponding to c_2.

Given a certain rule r and a certain individual operative fact c in R, we can pick out the set of individual normativised facts in N, say N_c, corresponding to c. Let $n_c \in N_c$. We say that n_c is an individual normativised fact corresponding to c. By means of this concept we can then define a concept "*satisfaction of a legal rule*", which is essential for being able to define the concept "legal basis". In order to do so we must introduce a symbol "**&**" which is not an ordinary conjunction but a conjunction with a temporal flavour, reading "and, simultaneously or later," or "simultaneously or followed by".

Let n_c be an individual normativised fact corresponding to case c. Then c **&** n_c is *a satisfaction of r.*

Examples of satisfactions of legal rules related to the examples given:

(1) that Smith negligently damages Jones' power lawn mower and then pays 1.000 kronor as damages to Jones.
(2) the situation that Smith negligently damages Jones' power lawn mower is followed by the situation that Smith pays 2.000 kronor as damages to Jones.

(1) and (2) are examples of satisfactions of obligatory rules. In the case of prohibitions satisfactions have another shape. Take the prohibition

(r') If a car is driven on a road where there is a speed limit, it is prohibited to exceed the limit.

If c' is "driver Black drives his car on a road where there is a speed limit of 100 km/h" and $n'_{c'}$ is "Black drives his car at 120 km/h" (corresponding to the norm theme "the limit is exceeded"), the satisfaction of r' is c' **&** *not-*n_c'.

With respect to genuine permissions the satisfaction is trivial. Take the permission

(r'') Cycling is permitted on Hickory Road

If c'' are circumstances where it can be actualised to cycle on Hickory Road and $n''_{c''}$ is "Davis cycles on Hickory road", then the satisfaction of r'' is c'' **&** *either* $n''_{c''}$ *or not-*$n''_{c''}$.

After these preliminaries we are able to define the concept *legal basis.* As has already been emphasised, to every legal rule corresponds one or more desired social states of affairs. We can formulate propositions describing such states of affairs.

Let r be the obligatory rule in our example just given. To r corresponds, e.g., the following proposition describing a desired state (relating to the reparative function of the law of torts):

(*PDS*) The victim is compensated for the damage caused by the tort-feasor.

The following propositions are specifications of *PDS*:

(pds_1) The victim Jones is compensated for the damage to his power lawn mower caused by Smith.

(pds_2) The victim White is compensated for the damage to his bicycle caused by Brown.

In the same way as we connected an individual normativised fact with its corresponding individual operative fact (case), we can connect an individual operative fact with its corresponding individual desired state of affairs. In our example, pds_1 corresponds to c_1 but not to c_2, while pds_2 corresponds to c_2 but not to c_1. We can form the concept "*a desired state of affairs corresponding to an operative fact*" relative to a given legal rule.

A legal basis for a rule *r* is a causal relation between a satisfaction of *r* as the cause and a corresponding desired social state of affairs as the effect.

Let "→" signify such causal relations. They will not be subject to a closer analysis here. They can appear in different shapes. Suffice it to say that they can be sufficient conditions or parts of such, or necessary conditions. They might also be direct or indirect causes.

Legal bases always have the following structure (*sat* is any satisfaction of a rule *r* and *s* any desired social state of affairs corresponding to an operative fact of *r*):

(lb) $sat \rightarrow s$

Or, more realistically rendered,

(lb') *It is probable that:* $sat \rightarrow s$

where the degree of probability as an empirical phenomenon of course varies from one legal basis to another. Example: The case that Smith has negligently damaged Jones' power lawn mower, and then pays 1.000 kronor to Jones, is the (probable) cause of Jones being compensated for the damage of the mower caused by Smith. This legal basis is of a reparative character. A legal basis of a preventive character would be: The case that Smith has negligently damaged Jones' power lawn mower, and then pays 1.000 kronor to Jones, is the probable cause that Smith (individual prevention) or others (general prevention) do not act negligently in the future.

Our concept "legal basis" captures, I think, the intuitive idea that legal rules are motivated, or justified, by legal bases—which reasonably must mean that, if the legal consequence "is realised" when a corresponding operative fact has occurred, there then follows (with a higher or lower degree of probability) a desired social state of affairs.

Just as we distinguish between individual and (more or less) general legal rules, and between individual and (more or less) generic operative facts (cases) and normativised facts, we can also distinguish between individual and (more or less) generic satisfactions, desired social states of affairs and legal bases. A legal rule, a case, a normativised fact, a satisfaction, a desired social state of affairs and a legal basis that are all of them individual, or have the same degree of generality, can be said to dwell on *the same topological level.* From the legislators' viewpoint it is not individual legal bases that are of interest but generic (general) ones.

Finally, in order to clarify the concept "analogy" we need one last distinction, viz., one between *positive* and *negative legal bases.* A positive legal basis is simply a legal basis warranting a *desired* social state of affairs, while a negative legal basis is a legal basis warranting an *unwanted* (bad) state of affairs. For it might well be the case that the application of *r* to *c* has certain negative consequences such that either these consequences are outweighed by the positive ones or, on the contrary, the former outweigh the latter.

In the case that a positive legal basis, *pb*, of a rule outweighs every negative legal basis of that rule, we say that *pb is a dominant positive legal basis* of the rule. A more precise formulation of our juridical postulate would then be: Every legal rule is (explicitly or implicitly) warranted by a dominant positive legal basis of the rule. (Correspondingly we can speak of dominant negative legal bases.)

9.3.5 Analogy-Basing Properties

In Sect. 9.1 we put forward two necessary conditions for the existence of an analogy relation between two rules, a formal one and a material one. Here we are occupied with the material condition—or, in other words, the similarity condition. In order to clarify this condition we need the concept *analogy-basing property*, defined in a preliminary way in the foregoing subsection. In our analogy theory this concept plays the same role in the juridical analogy argumentation as the concept "the sufficient condition for the analogy theme included in the similarity basis" plays in an inductive analogism. A (rational) inductive analogism is based on an estimation of probabilities while a (rational) juridical analogism is based on both evaluations of social states of affairs and estimations of the probability of legal bases.

Our analogy theory is based on the idea that the similarity properties that motivate an analogical use of a legal rule cannot be any similarity properties whatsoever. *A similarity property fulfilling that purpose must be such that it warrants a dominant positive legal basis of the rule created analogically.* To use the concept "analogy" in connection with any arbitrary similarity property whatsoever violates our juridical axiom that every legal rule is a means of attaining a social state of affairs. Similarities of interest with respect to the juridical use of legal rules analogically have a final (teleological) character. A similarity property warranting a dominant positive legal basis is an analogy-basing property.

The relevant similarity properties do not need to be "internal" ones. More often than not they are relations between the phenomena compared and the phenomena external to them, not least causal relations—and among such causal relations especially such where the function of the compared phenomena is to attain states of affairs of the same kind. (It must be observed that this is another kind of function than the functions of *legal rules* mentioned in the previous paragraph.) For example, according to a provision in an old Swedish criminal code, no longer in force, it was a crime to raise a highly dangerous weapon against someone. This provision was applied by courts of law to, among other things, a blow on the head with a hammer, the throwing of a flat iron, a blow with a shovel and a blow with an iron strip. In certain circumstances a loaded pistol, a hammer, a flat iron, a shovel and an iron strip can have the same function, viz., to put someone in mortal danger. This function of the objects enumerated can be used as an analogy-basing property.

Let us define "analogy-basing property" in the following six steps:

(1) Let (i) c be a case in the sphere of operative facts of rule r, (ii) n a normativised fact corresponding to c, (iii) lb (= $(c \mathbin{\&} n) \rightarrow s$) a legal basis of r and (iv) g a property of c.
(2) We form the similarity set $[c_g]$—however different its members may be apart from having the property g.
(3) For every case, c_i, in $[c_g]$, we can formulate a rule, r_i, corresponding to r in the sense that r_i attaches *the same* legal consequence to c_i as r attaches to c. Here we take identity in the broader sense of allowing such trivial consequence changes *mutatis mutandis* as was described in our commentary to GT-relation (13) in Sect. 8.2 above. Hence we get a set of legal rules, L:

r_1, where n_1 is attached to c_1
r_2, where n_2 is attached to c_2
---
r_n, where n_n is attached to c_n.

In the same manner we form the set LB of legal bases of $r_1, \ldots, r_n$ corresponding to lb:

lb_1: $(c_1 \mathbin{\&} n_1) \rightarrow s_1$
lb_2: $(c_2 \mathbin{\&} n_2) \rightarrow s_2$
---
lb_n: $(c_n \mathbin{\&} n_n) \rightarrow s_n$.

(4) We say that g is a *relevant positive similarity property of* c if and only if the existence of g makes each one of $lb_1, \ldots, lb_n$ a positive legal basis of $r_1, \ldots, r_n$ respectively—however weak the positive value of the legal basis as an argument may be. That is to say, as soon as a case c' has the property g there is a positive legal basis for constructing a rule r' by analogy from a rule r, regulating cases with property g, by connecting c' with the legal consequence of r. Our reason for using the concept "relevant positive similarity property" of "the analogy-basing" case is this. Suppose that, with respect to two rules, r_1 and r_2, it is argued that r_1 applied to case c_1 is analogous with r_2 applied to case c_2. Suppose further that h is a similarity property of c_1 and c_2. But the existence of h in the two cases does not necessarily mean that h warrants (motivates) the analogy. For h can, from the viewpoint of analogy, be a totally indifferent or even a negative factor.

This criterion, then, is to the effect that, for *every* hypothetical rule regulating cases in the same way as r regulates c, there is a positive legal basis, however weak it might be compared to possible negative legal bases.

(5) Let (i) c' be a case in the (would-be) set of operative facts of a rule r', (ii) lb' (= $(c' \& n') \rightarrow s'$) a legal basis of r', and (iii) g be a property of c' as well as of c.
(6) We say that the similarity property g that c and c' both have in common is *an analogy-basing property of* c' relative to r' if and only if

   (i) $r' \in L$ and $lb' \in LB$
   (ii) g is a relevant positive similarity property of c
   (iii) lb' is a dominant positive legal basis of r'.

Clause (iii) is to the effect that the legal basis constructed by means of g *just in this case* (c') is a dominant legal basis for r', i.e., it takes precedence over possible negative legal bases.

Our account in the present chapter up to now can be seen as a kind of recursive definition of the juridical concept "analogy". Now we are able to take the last step of this definition.

(*DEF. JURIDICAL ANALOGY*)

I. Let

   (i) c be a case in the sphere of operative facts of rule r
   (ii) c' be a case in the sphere of operation of rule r'
   (iii) g (g_1 & ... & g_n) be a similarity property of c and c'.

II. r' as regards c' is analogous to r as regards c relative to g if and only if

   (a) r' stands in some of GT-relations (13)–(16) to r; and
   (b) g is an analogy-basing property of c' with respect to r'.

It is evident from the definition that it is possible that r' applied to c' can be analogous to r applied to a case c_1 in the sphere of operative facts of r without necessarily being analogous to another case, c_2, in that sphere. Furthermore, r' applied to c' can be analogous to r applied to c with respect to property g without necessarily being analogous with r with respect to some other property, h, of c. Consequently, our concept "analogy" is a rather flexible one.

Let us now concretise our definition by means of an example.

(r) Anyone who buys a thing that is deprived a person by means of crime shall be punished for receiving to .... If the offender did not realise but had reasonable ground to presume a crime, he shall be punished for misdemeanour with respect to receiving to....

(c) A has bought a car from B who had stolen it from C and A had suspected that B had stolen it.

(lb) (It is probable that) if someone has bought a thing that is deprived a person by means of crime and then is sentenced to ..., the safety of ownership (and some other rights) is maintained.

Now a court of law (cf. Sect. 9.1 example (6)) applies a rule created analogically from (r)—as did the district court and the court of appeal in the example—to the case

(c') D has bought a car from E who had rented it from F and D had suspected that E was not the rightful owner.

The analogically created rule can be formulated like this

(r') Anyone who buys a thing that the seller has leased from another person and the buyer did not realise it but had had reasonable ground to presume that the thing was leased, he shall be punished for misdemeanour with respect to receiving to...

and its legal basis like this

(lb') (It is probable that) if someone has bought a thing from a person who has leased it and then is sentenced to ..., the safety of ownership is maintained.

The similarity property, g, of c and c' could be described in so many words: illegal dispossession.

Now we confront the example with our analogy definition. Clause (a) is fulfilled since r' stands in GT-relation (13) to r. Let us then examine the example with respect to clause (b).

We form the similarity set $[c_g]$ of cases of illegal dispossession, of which, of course, both c and c' are elements. Then we formulate a set of legal rules, L, for the cases of $[c_g]$, e.g., r itself, r' and

(r'') Anyone who buys a thing that the seller has borrowed from another person and the buyer did not realise it but had had reasonable ground to presume that the thing was borrowed, he shall be punished for misdemeanour with respect to receiving to....

We form the set LB for the rules in L corresponding to lb, e.g., lb itself, lb' and

(lb'') (It is probable that) if someone has bought a thing from a person who has borrowed it and then is sentenced to ..., the safety of ownership is maintained.

For g to be a relevant positive similarity property of c the existence of g must make every legal basis in LB a positive one—however weak it may be. That this is the case with respect to lb seems obvious, and with respect to lb' and lb'' as well (the district court and the court of appeal even seem to have regarded lb' as a dominant one).

The next step will be to investigate whether g is an analogy-basing property of c' with respect to r'. Clauses (i) and (ii) of the definition of this concept are fulfilled. But is lb' a *dominant* positive legal basis for r' or not? The examination of this question can be performed in the same manner as the examination performed with respect to the seven cases of inductive analogism ("the dentist situations") presented in Sect. 9.3.2 above. This comparison shows that there can be indifferent similarity properties (like in situation (1), for instance, the similarity property b might be indifferent from the viewpoint of analogy) and that the existence of a property h in c but not in c'

can make it difficult to ascertain whether *g* is an analogy-basing property of *c*′ (cf. situation (2)).

Situation (3) points out a difference between the inductive and the juridical analogy argumentation. While in the inductive analogy reasoning the existence of two different, and each of them sufficient, conditions for the analogy theme does not add to the strength of the argumentation compared to if only one of them exists; in the juridical analogy reasoning the opposite seems to be the case. The same goes for situation (4). The existence of a negative property in *c* but not in *c*′ (cf. situation (5) with respect to property *f*) can be said to characterise an analogy argumentation *a fortiori*.

Of particular interest is the juridical equivalent to situation (7), i.e., cases where there are negative properties (or, in other words, properties warranting negative legal bases) in *c*′ which are not present in *c*. In our example such a negative property, *h*, is the relation between *c*′ and *r* to the effect that *c*′ is not covered by the wording of *r*. *h* motivates the negative legal basis

(*lb*′/*neg*) (It is probable that) if (someone has bought a thing from a person who has leased it and) a provision in a criminal law is applied analogically to this situation to the disadvantage of the defendant, the legality principle will be violated and, hence, the legal certainty and the legal security of the defendant will be set aside.

In our example the district court and the court of appeal did not let *lb*′/*neg*—or any other negative legal basis—take precedence over *lb*′. They regarded the latter as a dominant legal basis of *r*′. *According to our definition, they made a juridical analogy from r*. The Supreme Court, on the other hand, was on the side of the Law-State and let *lb*′/*neg* take precedence over *lb*′. It used *r e contrario*.

Some words must finally be said about the *N-analogies*, i. e., the analogies made not from cases but from normativised facts—in the first place GT-relations (3), (4), (7) and (8).

Among the components of the legal rule the very instrumental function is located in the legal consequence—the realisation of which is intended to achieve a desired social state of affairs. No wonder then that lawyers at times manipulate the legal consequences in order to make them as effective as possible for realising the purpose of the rule. An example is the dissident P's modification of the legal consequence in the boat case (Sect. 8.2 example (7)). For the GT-relations where the legal consequence of a rule, *r*, is modified by expansion or disjunction of its N-set we can use the term "legal consequence analogy".

My clarification of the juridical concept "analogy" makes that concept a teleological (final) one. Against this can be objected that phenomena that in ordinary juridical linguistic usage are called "analogies" do not at all have a teleological character. Courts sometimes content themselves with phrases like "must be regarded as on equality with...", "must be applied correspondingly to the present case" and the like—or they pretend, or perhaps even believe, that they are doing an application proper of a rule. To this objection can be responded that such phrases can be conceived of as a kind of standardised abbreviations behind which teleological similarity arguments are hidden. But here, after all, as well as with respect to so many other juridical decisions, we must often remain in a state of uncertainty as to the real motives behind a given standpoint.

9.3.6 Some Remarks on the Formal Properties of Analogy Relations

In this section a few words will be said about the formal (logical) properties of the analogy relations, among which I here include also the generalising GT-relations (9)–(12). For the sake of simplicity we here refer to them all as analogy relations.

We have already stated that the relation "similar with respect to ..." is an equivalence relation, i.e., it is reflexive, symmetric and transitive (Sect. 9.3.3).

An examination of the formal properties of the analogy relations shows the following. For every analogous rule, r', it is the case that either its set of operative facts or its N-set is (i) a specification, (ii) an expansion or (iii) a disjunction of the corresponding set of the basic rule r. Since both specification and expansion are "proper subset-relations" and both the proper subset-relation and the disjunction are irreflexive, it follows that a rule cannot be analogous to itself.

Furthermore, the proper subset-relation is asymmetric, while the identity relation and the disjunction are symmetric. Hence, analogy relations (4), (13) and (16) are symmetric while the rest are asymmetric.

The converse, S, of a relation R is a relation such that, for all x and y, xSy if and only if yRx. For instance, the converse of "bigger than" is "smaller than" and "x sells a car to y" is the converse of "y buys a car from x". So we find that the converse relations to (4), (13) and (16) are (4), (13) and (16), respectively, since they are symmetric. As for the remaining relations we find that:

(i) The converse of (3) is (2)
(ii) The converse of (7) is (10)
(iii) The converse of (8) is (12)
(iv) The converse of (9) is (5)
(v) The converse of (10) is (7)
(vi) The converse of (11) is (6)
(vii) The converse of (12) is (8)
(viii) The converse of (14) is (15)
(ix) The converse of (15) is (14).

As a consequence we cannot for every analogy relation use expressions like "two rules analogous to each other" or "the two analogous rules r and r'". As for relation (3), (9), and (11), while r' is analogous to r, r is not analogous to r' but instead a precisation of it. Strictly speaking we can only say that two rules are analogous to each other if they stand in one of the symmetric relations (4), (13) and (16) to each other. As for the remaining relations—(7), (8), (10), (12), (14) and (15)—r and r' are indeed analogous to each other, but r' is *not* analogous to r *in the same sense* as r is analogous to r'. For the sake of clarity I find it valuable to call attention to these logical relationships.

9.4 The Technique and Ideology of Analogical Reasoning

9.4.1 Introduction

In the introduction to the present chapter we set ourselves the task of presenting answers to the following questions:

1. What would a satisfying clarification of "analogy" look like with respect to how it is used in juridical discourse?
2. Is there any method (technique) for analogical use of legal rules?
3. Why are legal rules used analogically?

Our answer to 1 is presented in the previous sections. In this final section we shall, quite briefly, occupy ourselves with questions 2 and 3.

In Sect. 9.4.2 we give an answer in an affirmative direction to question 2. The important thing we try to show there is that "analogical use of legal rules" is not a name of a principle of interpretation; it is *a technique for creation of (new) legal rules*—if you like, a principle of legislation within the framework of the administration of justice. This technique has two fundamental components: generalisation and separation of rules.

In Sect. 9.4.3 we argue that the use of analogies in juridical thinking can be explained as a way of mediating between two potentially conflicting fundamental principles governing the administration of justice, a conflict that sometimes places the judge in a kind of dilemma: the principle of loyalty and the prohibition of denial of justice (*non liquet*). Reasoning by analogy shows a way out of this dilemma.

9.4.2 The Technique of Analogical Reasoning

We conceive of the creation of rules by analogy as a process in two steps: rule generalisation[39] and rule separation.

By rule generalisation is meant that one hypothetically (tentatively) propounds a rule, r^*, being a generalisation of an (existing) rule r, for all cases with some property, g—or, at least, a rule in that direction. Such a generalised rule we call *a model rule.*

The idea that the analogical use of legal rules includes a generalisation is clearly expressed in the following statement by Austin:

> The cases which the law omits (but which fall within its principle), and the cases which fall within its principle, and which it actually includes, are *analogous.* Or (changing the expression) they are resembling cases, *with reference to that common principle*, in spite of

[39]Here "generalisation" refers to an action while in Chapter 8 it referred to a certain type of GT-relations. The result of a generalisation in the former sense can be described in terms of a generalisation in the latter sense. Here the term is used in the former sense.

> the differences by which they are distinguished when viewed from other aspects. And, since they are resembling cases with reference to the principle of law, *analogy* [...] is said to require, that the law should be applied to *all* of them in an equable or uniform manner.[40]

In many situations, however, the model rule r^* is too general to be included without inconvenience in the legal system. Often it must be specified in different respects, i.e., it must be equipped with some more requisites until one finally gets a rule, r', analogous to r and suitable as a candidate for membership in the legal system. By the term "rule separation" I refer to this step in the analogical use of legal rules.

Every stage in the specification which characterises the rule separation can be described by means of a model rule. An analogical use of rules can be schematically rendered in this way:

$$\begin{array}{ccc} r & \rightarrow & r^* \\ & & \downarrow \\ & & r^{**} \\ & & \downarrow \\ & & r' \end{array}$$

where r is the basic rule, r^* and r^{**} model rules, representing stages in the generalisation and separation processes, and r' the final result—the rule of application analogous to r.

It could now be objected that this is not the way lawyers make analogies. It is not an established technique that they hypothetically lay down a model rule and then separate a rule from that. Sometimes they do, but perhaps not generally. I suggest, however, that if we reconstruct their reasoning by analogy more closely, we would find that it fits well with the technique presented here.

Of course there are certain limits for the extent of the generalisation performed in analogical reasoning. Such limitations, which are natural for lawyers, can be regarded as the first step in the separation of a rule of application. Three principles of rule separation immediately suggest themselves.

(1) When an analogy is made topical for a judge, the given, concrete case fixes a natural boundary for the generalisation of a rule—it does not go further than including the given case with personal, spatial, temporal and similar indices excluded, and no more. Let us call this principle of separation *the principle of minimal generalisation.*
(2) With respect to institutional analogies it comes natural to separate a rule that is *isomorphic* to the basic rule (see Sect. 9.2.1 above), i.e., that between r and r' there is a correspondence such as, e.g.:

[40]Austin (1911), Vol. II, p. 579.

(*r*) If the seller is in serious delay delivering the goods, the buyer may cancel the contract; and

(*r′*) If the lessor is in serious delay having in readiness the goods, the lessee may cancel the contract.

(3) One further reasonable rule of separation is that the judge should not generalise to the extent that the model rule collides with existing rules in the legal system, thereby reducing them. This rule is not always observed (see Sect. 9.2.1 above).

However, sometimes judges go a bit further than what these rules of separation allow. It happens that they make the analogous rule more precise by adding to it a requisite having no counterpart in the basic rule. Let me give an example from the Swedish Supreme Court.[41]

A Swedish company, P, was obliged to pay a certain amount of money in Swedish kronor to a company in Venezuela, I, in commission of two vessels sold by P through the agency of I. The payment should take place in Venezuela. P paid the sum first after its duty to do so had been affirmed by a court decision. In the time between the claim and the court decision the Swedish krona had dropped in value compared to the US dollar, to which the Venezuelan currency was tied. The question was whether P had an obligation to compensate I for loss on exchange due to the delay or not.

The Swedish Promissory Notes Act says about a similar situation (for the sake of simplicity rendered in my words):

(*r*) If a promissory note is in a currency which is not current coin where the payment shall take place, and if the note has not been discharged in due time and if the rate of the foreign currency has fallen there, the creditor can claim payment in the currency of the place of payment according to the rate of the day when payment should have taken place.

Both the Court of Appeal and the Supreme Court enjoined P to compensate I for the loss on exchange. That an analogy was made from the provision in the Promissory Notes Act is particularly obvious in the opinion of the Court of Appeal. Let us assume that the Court of Appeal propounded the following model rule based on the provision

(*r**) If a debt is in a currency ... take place, and if the debt has not been discharged... has fallen there, the creditor ... should have taken place

and then, as a first step in the separation of an applicable rule, propounded

(*r***) If a claim of commission is in a currency... take place, and if it has not been discharged... has fallen there, the creditor ... should have taken place.

However, it was not *r*** that was applied by the Court of Appeal. For it added another requisite to *r*** which had no counterpart in the provision: a proximate cause requisite to the effect that the loss on exchange should have been predictable. The rule of application, then, can be formulated like this:

---

[41]NJA 1951, p. 444.

(r') If a claim of commission is in a currency... take place, and if it has not been discharged... has fallen there *and* if the loss on exchange was predictable, the creditor ... should have taken place.

9.4.3 The Ideology of Analogical Reasoning

There are two juridical principles indispensable for the understanding of the juridical technique of argumentation and, not least, for the understanding of the juridical reasoning by analogy—the loyalty principle and the prohibition of denial of justice. Taken together, these two principles create something like a dilemma for the law-applier.

(1) *The loyalty principle* says that the law-applying authorities shall be loyal to the legislator in their decision-making. More exactly, it says that the administration of law shall, on the whole, content itself with *applying* legal rules given by the legislator and that very strong reasons must be adduced if the law-appliers can be allowed to omit applying a rule to a clear case. In a strict form, the loyalty principle includes a claim of caution with reductive use of rules, and its principle of statutory interpretation *par préférence* is the subjective one—the intentions of the legislator shall be found out and given cases shall be decided in a manner as close to these intentions as possible.

A certain amount of adherence to the loyalty principle is of course inevitable in every society where legislative organs give general rules to be applied to individual cases by other organs ("the regime of general rules"). In democracies the loyalty principle is justified by general rules being produced, directly or indirectly, by popularly elected organs. The answer to the question whether the loyalty principle *ought to* be adhered to depends of course upon the nature of the society in which the principle is meant to operate. In a society whose legal order violates the most basic claims of humanity and civilisation, no one is more entitled to respect than the judge who sabotages that legal order.

But also in societies where the legislator's ambition it is to comply with the demands of the law-state ideas, it is obvious that some boundaries of the loyalty of the law-appliers must be drawn. Every society of some amount of complexity must have some kind of division of labour between legislator and law-applier. However well thought-out the general rules that the legislator issues are, it is not in the legislator's power to avoid that the application of some rule to a given case just in this special case leads to unfortunate consequences. When this is the situation, the law-applier must have the possibility to make a reduction. A radical principle of loyalty is not desirable. In this connection the importance of the possibility for the legislator to provide the legal system with "emergency exits" in the form of, e.g., general clauses must be emphasised. It is important that the drawbacks of the regime of general rules are taken care of in such ways. The alternative to that regime—the authorities' decision-making by means of ad hoc decisions ("the regime of mandarin justice")—is no realistic alternative in a society adhering to the law-state values.

The loyalty principle can be seen as one side of the principle of the division of power between the supreme political organs and the courts of law: the former shall create the law, the latter apply it. The other side of the principle of division of power, *the principle of the independence of the courts*, says that the political organs are not allowed to interfere in the decision-making of the courts in individual cases.

The loyalty principle can also be seen as a weak *legality principle*.[42] A decisive difference between the weak loyalty principle and the stricter legality principles, however, is the preference of the latter for an antithetic use of legal rules.

(2) *The prohibition of denial of justice* (*déni de justice, non liquet*) forbids judges to dismiss a claim of a legal character without reaching the merits, i.e., to refuse to decide it when the assessment of it is uncertain, or even where an applicable rule is lacking altogether. The principle expresses a duty to decide. It is codified in Art. 4 of the French Code Civil but as a general principle it is of course not confined to civil law—it operates over the whole legal system. The effect of the principle, however, will often turn out differently in criminal law and in civil law respectively. As for the former, the combination of the loyalty principle and the prohibition of denial of justice leads to an antithetic use of rules: a trial must take place also with respect to uncertain cases but *in dubio* the prosecution shall be *dismissed upon the merits.* In civil law, on the other hand, there is, generally speaking, no preference in that direction. Rather, institutional analogies within the area of the law of property can be regarded as valuable, or even as a commitment. Here the teleological justifications of solutions to problems concerning different types of contracts are highly similar, and from the viewpoint of legal certainty there are certain advantages if the same general principle prevails within the whole field of the law of contracts.

To sum up:

A. *Reductive use of legal rules* serves in the first place the function of mitigating the disadvantages of the regime of general rules.
B. *E contrario-use of legal rules* serves in the first place the function of warranting that the strict legality principles—and, as a consequence, the law-state values of legal certainty, legal equality, legal accessibility and legal security—are realised.
C. *Analogical use of legal rules* serves in the first place the purpose of offering a solution to the "dilemma" that the loyalty principle and the prohibition of denial of justice taken together create. This dilemma can be formulated: The prohibition

[42]On legality principles see Frändberg (2014), Section 4.1.

of denial of justice demands a decision also when the law is obscure or silent. Still the law-applier must be loyal to the legislator. A way out of this dilemma is to lean on the existing legal system in a mediate way, thereby making decisions "in the spirit of the law". Analogical use of existing rules is such a mediate way.

References

Alchourrón C (1965) Juristische Schlüsse a fortiori und a pari. In: Archiv für Rechts- und Sozialphilosophie, vol 1965, pp 5 ff
Austin J (1911) Excursus on analogy. In: Lectures on jurisprudence or the philosophy of positive law, vol I and II, 5th edn., revised and edited by R. Campbell. Cornell University Library
Bobbio N (1938) L'analogia nella logica del diritto. Giuffre, Milano
Bocheński JM (1948) On analogy. The Thomist 11:474–497
Brewer S (1966) Exemplary reasoning: semantics, pragmatics and the rational force of legal argument by analogy. Harv Law Rev 109:923–1028
Carnap R (1950) Logical foundations of probability. University of Chicago Press, Chicago
Carnap R (1969) The logical structure of the world & pseudoproblems in philosophy
Cross R, Harris JW (1991) Precedent in English law, 4th edn. Oxford University Press, Oxford
Dorolle M (1949) Le raisonnement par analogie. Presses Universitaires de France, Paris
Fabreguettes MP (1914) La logique judiciaire et l'art de juger. F. Pichon et Durand-Auzias, Paris
Frändberg Å (2014) From Rechtsstaat to universal law-state. Springer, Berlin
García Máynez E (1965) Die Argumente a simili ad simile, a maiore ad minus und a minore ad maius. In: Archiv für Rechts- und Sozialphilosophie, vol 1965, pp 115 ff
Hacking I (2001) An introduction to probability and inductive logic. Cambridge University Press, Cambridge
Hage J (2005) The logic of analogy in the law. Argumentation 19:401–415
Hart HLA (1994) The concept of law, 2nd edn. Clarendon Press, Wotton-under-Edge
Heller T (1961) Logik und Axiologie der analogen Rechtsanwendung. Walter de Gruyter, Berlin
Hilpinen R (1969) An analysis of relativised modalities. In: Davis JW et al (eds) Philosophical logic. Springer, Berlin, p 189
Karlgren H (1965) Passivitet (estoppel by laches). Norstedts, Stockholm
Klug U (1966) Juristische Logik, 3rd edn. Springer, Berlin
Kyburg HE Jr (1970) Probability and inductive logic. Macmillan, Basingstoke
Lindenbaum Hosiasson J (1941) Induction et analogie: Comparaison de leur fondement. Mind 50:351
Reidhav D (2007) Reasoning by analogy. A study on analogy-based arguments in law. Lund University, Lund
Rosenkrantz RD (1981) Foundations and applications of inductive probability. Ridgeview Pub Co, Atascadero
Ross A (1959) On law and justice. The Lawbook Exchange, Ltd, Clark
Schneider E (1965) Logik für Juristen. Verlag Franz Vahlen GmbH, München
Segerberg K (1971) Some logics of commitment and obligation. In: Hilpinen R (ed) Deontic logic: introductory and systematic readings. Springer, Berlin, p 150
Sundberg JWF (1966) Om ansvaret för fel i lejt gods (On the liability of faults in hired goods). P. A. Norstedt & Söners förlag, Stockholm
Suppes P (1967) Introduction to logic. Van Nostrand, New York
Tammelo I (1969) Outlines of modern legal logic. F. Steiner, Lima
von Wright GH (1951) A treatise on induction and probability. Routledge, Abingdon
von Wright GH (1957) The logical problem of induction. Blackwell, Oxford

Chapter 10
On Conflicts Between Legal Rules

10.1 Choices of Law

Some topological relations signify conflicts between legal rules when applied to cases. In this and the two subsequent chapters we shall investigate some practically important types of conflicts between legal rules owing to their relations to cases.

The law-appliers as well as the legislators, each from their own starting points, are often confronted with problems which, on a theoretical level, can be described as *choice-of-law situations.*

For instance, law-appliers are faced with such a choice in the very unusual situations when they find themselves at "the extreme limit of the legal system"—shall the present problem be solved by legal means at all, or shall it be dismissed, without reaching the merits, as a non-legal problem (e.g., a declaratory claim that the earth is round)? Such legal choices we can call *trial choices.*

Another kind of choice-of-law situation is present in the far more usual situations when the law-applier is faced with an interpretation problem. Such a problem can, to be sure, be described in terms of a choice between different solutions, i.e., legal rules. This kind of choices of law can be called *choice of interpretation.* (When we in the following talk about "choice of rule", however, we disregard the choice of interpretation. In Sect. 14.3 below we shall investigate some classic principles guiding the law-applier's statutory interpretation.)

In a highly comprehensive and complicated norm-system such as a modern state legal system it is inevitable that conflicts and tensions arise between rules within it—tensions that get their most striking expression in collision conflicts and competition conflicts. Such conflicts will here be treated under the term *choice of rule.*

But not only conflicts within state legal systems may appear. Also confrontations of various kinds *between* such systems can arise—as well as between state and non-state legal systems. This might happen even if there is no conflict between rules in different systems. A choice of rule within private international law (conflict of laws) shall in principle be made even if rules covering the actual case are lacking in

Å. Frändberg, *The Legal Order*, Law and Philosophy Library 123,
https://doi.org/10.1007/978-3-319-78858-6_10

lex causae, or if the rule in *lex causae* and the rule in *lex fori* have exactly the same content, in which situations no conflict between rules exists. In Chap. 11 we shall investigate such *inter-systemic choices of law.*

One further type of conflict that also might be called inter-systemic arises in connection with amendments of law, so-called inter-temporal problems (studied within the discipline transitional law). Chapter 12 is devoted to *inter-temporal choices of law.*

Finally, conflicts may arise making a choice necessary between a rule in the legal system and some extra-legal norm, e.g., a clause in a contract drawn up within the area of optional law or some kind of customary norm, when a case is connected to both.

Choice-of-law problems are often solved by existing rules in the legal system. Therefore we can imagine two classes of rules in modern legal systems: *first order rules* and *choice-of-law rules*. The latter are second order rules or higher, indicating either which rule shall be the applicable one in choice-of-rule situations or from which legal system the applicable rule shall be taken. There are different kinds of choice-of-law rules. Legal rules that are not choice-of-law rules are first order rules. We draw up the following classification (cf. Sect. 2.11 3 above):

I. First order rules
II. Choice-of-law rules:

   1. Coherence rules (solving collision and competition problems)
   2. International choice-of-law rules (so-called collision norms)
   3. Transitional rules
   4. Extra-state choice-of-law rules (letting private or customary norms take precedence over state law or vice versa).

This chapter deals with conflicts in the form of collision and competition between legal rules.[1]

10.2 Some General Remarks Concerning Collision and Competition

Collision and competition constitute choice-of-law situations where a choice between two or more rules within the same legal system must be made. Those two choice-of-law situations will be clarified within the framework of two different *choice-of-law types*. In order to formulate these two types we need some auxiliary concepts, viz., (a) "conditioned sphere of operative facts" ("*COF*"), (b) "conditioned

[1]In Lindahl and Reidhav (2015), pp. 49–95, definitions of different kinds of conflicts – including conflicts between competence (power-conferring) norms – are formulated within the framework of a formal language.

application relation" (c) "norm-relation", (d) "application situation", and (e) "choice-of-law situation".

(a) A conditioned sphere of operative facts, COF_r, relative to a rule r, is the set of cases to which r would always be applied, were it not for the fact that r collides or competes with another rule in the system.
(b) The relation between r and a member, c, of COF_r, ($c \in COF_r$), we call *a conditioned application relation.*
(c) "Norm-relation" covers the GT-relations (1)–(32) between F-sets and N-sets defined in Sects. 8.2 and 8.3 above. The relations were built on combinations of the more basic relations (i) identity ($F = F'$), (ii) specification ($F' \subset F$), (iii) expansion ($F \subset F'$), and (iv) disjunction ($F' \cap F = \phi$).

These four basic relations are fruitful not only for clarifying concepts such as "analogy", "*e contrario*" and "reduction" but also for clarifying "collision" and "competition". However, with respect to the latter, which interest us here, we must add a fifth, useful for clarifying in certain respects what competition between legal rules amounts to:

(v) *Overlapping* (lap): There are (1) cases belonging to COF' but not to COF, (2) cases belonging to COF but not to COF', and (3) cases belonging to both COF' and COF.

In Chap. 8 we made an important distinction between the spectrum (GT-relations 1–16) and the antithetic spectrum (GT-relations 17–32) of a legal rule. The latter are of special importance with respect to collisions between rules.

(d) Choices of law take place in *application situations.* An application situation with respect to a case, c, is, simply, an occasion where c is undergoing a trial at a court of law. One single application situation can, as is well known, include several cases, $c_1, c_2, \ldots, c_n$, (through consolidation of actions or joinder of causes of action), which, of course, is of interest with respect to competition between rules. We symbolise application situations with expressions such as "$AS(c)$" or $AS(c_1, c_2, \ldots, c_n)$.
(e) *A choice-of-law situation* is an application situation, where two or more conditioned application relations are brought to the fore.

Furthermore, there is a practically important type of application situations that could be called *iterative application situations.* What characterises an iterative application situation is that in a given application situation *another* application situation—already finished or occurring simultaneously with the former—is brought to the fore. One application situation—at least if we allow ourselves some generosity with respect to the use of the word "case"—can exist in another application situation. Let expressions of the type "$AS^*(c)$" symbolise application situations that are components of other application situations. "AS^*c" can be read "c has been legally decided in AS^*" or "c is object of adjudication in AS^*" respectively, ($AS \neq AS^*$).

Two kinds of iterative application situations are of special interest.

(1) $AS(c, c', AS^*(c''))$

Situation *AS* "contains" cases *c*, *c*′, and $AS^*(c'')$. Example: In *AS* person A is tried for theft (*c*) and for embezzlement (*c*′). In addition to this, A has in a previous trial been sentenced for fraud, but that sentence has not yet been executed (fully). Hence, in *AS* it can come into question to impose a joint penalty for all three crimes (a type of competition which we (below) call "multi-case competition").

Another type of iterative application situation is this:

(2) $AS(c, AS^*(c))$.

Here situation *AS* "contains" cases *c* and $AS^*(c)$. This situation exists when *res judicata* or pendency of an action (*lis pendens*) is brought to the fore. In situation *AS*, where *c* is to be tried, the court must take its stand on another, completed or ongoing, application situation, *AS**, where *c* has been tried or where trial concerning *c* is in progress. *Res judicata* and *lis pendens* situations have the same formal structure as, what will be called below, "one-case competition". (In order to express the distinction between the *res judicata* and the *lis pendens* situations, this can be done by enriching (2) with indices for different points of time.)

In the following we leave iterative application situations out of consideration.

As we all know, problems concerning competition are mainly treated within criminal law. However, competition problems do appear not only within this discipline, they can arise in other areas of law as well. The concept formation proposed here is aimed at being applicable to any part of a legal system alike.

Let us make a distinction between two *main types of choice of law*. The first consists of application situations that "contain" only one individual case, i.e., situations of type $AS(c)$. The other consists of application situations that "contain" two or more individual cases: $AS(c, c')$ or $AS(c_1, c_2, \ldots c_n)$. The two main types are constructed as combinations of application situations and conditioned application relations.

Main type I has the following structure:

$$\text{(MTI) } AS(c) : c \in COF_r \text{ and } c \in COF'_{r'}.$$

MTI means that rules *r* and *r*′ are both applicable to *c* in a given application situation, *AS*. MTI is the prototype of *one-case collision* and of *one-case competition* (to be treated below).

At this point a comment must be made that is of importance with respect to one-case competition. When we say that two rules, *r* and *r*′, are different rules we do not exclude that *r* and *r*′ have exactly the same content, i.e., that they are identical as regards their meaning. What we are talking of here is two different *systematic occurrences* of legal rules. A provision in one statute can have the same content as a provision in another statute. As regards one-case competition it is then appropriate to treat them as two different rules.

Main type II has the following structure ($c \neq c'$; we restrict ourselves to situations containing two cases, but the scheme can easily be extended to more than two):

$$\text{(MTII) } AS(c, c') : c \in COF_r \textit{ and } c' \in COF'_{r'}.$$

MTII is the prototype of multi-case collision and of multi-case competition.

Let me by way of introduction say a few words about the distinction between collision and competition. Here an example of each of them. (1) Z has shot a wild cat in his garden. This action is permitted according to national law but forbidden according to a municipal regulation (one-case collision). (2) X has without Y's consent and knowledge taken Y's cheque-book when it was in Y's possession. Suppose that according to the criminal law of the legal system this case complies with the requisites of both larceny and arbitrary conduct (one-case competition).

What is then the difference between competition and collision? The answer is this. With respect to competition the alternative rules belong to each other's spectrum (see Chap. 8 above), while, with respect to collision, they belong to each other's antithetic spectrum. From this it follows that in the case of competition both rules are logically possible to apply in a way that allows compliance—it is not impossible to be subjected to penalty for both larceny and arbitrary conduct. In the case of collision, on the other hand, it is logically impossible to comply with the alternative rules. You cannot suffer punishment for killing a wild cat and, at the same time, not suffer punishment for killing that cat. The problems related to competition do not consist in conflicts of a logical nature but in the fact that application of all alternative rules involved leads to different kinds of inconveniences (to be investigated later in this chapter).

That we use the phrase "possible to apply in a way that allows compliance" with respect to competition and do not talk about "application" *simpliciter* matters. Application is a linguistic act which is completed as soon as the judge has produced a sentence officially in writing or in speech. And even in a case where the judge has at the same time applied several rules, which are, for logical reasons, impossible to comply with taken together, he nevertheless has applied the rules. To pronounce a contradiction is also a linguistic act. Hence, the concept "competition" must be determined in terms of application in a way that allows compliance.

So, to the question "Which entities conflict in collision and competition situations?" we answer "legal rules". To the question "What are legal rules conflicting about in collision and competition situations?" we answer "to be applied in a way that allows, fully, compliance to any case to which the rule is applicable". If this actually is the case with respect to some rules there is neither any collision problem nor any completion problem between the rules involved. Competition problems are caused by circumstances of a factual or a legal nature, which can be looked upon as a kind of limits to competition. If you like, collision is a type of competition that is impossible from the very beginning. Collision is always problematic, while competition can be totally unproblematic. Competition problems arise when what can be called a collective inconvenience is the consequence of the application of all rules involved (to be treated below).

From a logical viewpoint the distinction between competition and collision is based on the more basic distinction between the spectrum and the antithetic spectrum of legal rules—just as is the case with respect to the distinctions between precisation and reduction, between analogy and *e contrario*, and between extensive and restrictive interpretation. For this reason the distinction between the spectrum and the antithetic spectrum of a rule seems to me to play a fundamental role for the study of legal norm-relations.

In Sect. 10.3 we investigate rule collision and in Sect. 10.4 rule competition.

10.3 Rule Collision

It follows from what has just been said that the law-applier *must* make a choice between colliding rules, while that is not the case with respect to competing rules. In the latter case a choice is motivated for reasons of expediency or of principle.

In order to meaningfully describe different collision situations we must as a point of reference use a certain action (or, by way of exception, a certain state of affairs) that is permitted, obligatory or forbidden according to the rules involved. If a given action, *a*, is permitted or obligatory according to a rule, *r*, and at the same time forbidden according to another rule, *r′*, under exactly the same circumstances, and both rules are brought to the fore in the same application situation, then *r* and *r′* collide.

One-case collision comes within the scope of main type I:

$$(\mathrm{MTI})\ AS(c) : c \in COF_r \ and \ c \in COF'_{r'}.$$

Let *a* be an action that falls under rules *r* (with the sphere of operative facts COF_r) and *r′* (with the sphere of operative facts $COF'_{r'}$). Further, let "*P//F a*" symbolise the antithetic situation where one of the rules permits or enjoins *a*, while the other forbids *a*.

We focus on the following three variations of one case-collision (the variation *COF′ dis COF* is, as is easily seen, logically impossible under MTI).

(1)	*COF′ id COF*	*P//F a*
(2)	*COF′ spec COF*	"
(3)	*COF′ lap COF*	"

Examples:

Of (1). X has shot Y's cat in his garden.

r: If anyone discovers a cat close by his dwelling house, he may kill it.
r′: If anyone discovers a cat close by his dwelling house, he may not kill it.

Of (2). X has shot a wild cat in his garden.

r: If anyone discovers a wild animal close by his dwelling house, he may not kill it.
r': If anyone discovers a wild cat close by his dwelling house, he may kill it.

Of (3). X has shot a wild cat in his garden.

r: If anyone discovers a wild animal close by his dwelling house, he may not kill it.
r': If anyone discovers a cat close by his dwelling house, he may kill it.

That these three situations are one-case collisions is determined by MTI and the antithetic relation between the modalities of the rules involved. The set-theoretical relations between the set of operative facts (constituting the norm-relations), on their part, are of particular interest when the task is to give solutions to collisions. Perhaps the most common of the conflict-solving principles, *lex specialis derogat legi generali*, is, for purely logical reasons, applicable only to situation (2), where the sphere of the operative facts of one rule is a proper subset of the sphere of the operative facts of the other. In situations (1) and (3) it is meaningless to say that one rule is more "special" than the other—in (1) the two spheres are identical and in (3) they overlap (in our example: there are wild animals which are not cats, there are cats which are not wild animals, and there are cats which are wild animals).

Multi-case collision comes within the scope of main type II:

$$\text{(MTII)}\ AS(c, c') : c \in COF_r \ and\ c' \in COF'_{r'}.$$

In this connection only the following norm-relation is of interest:

$$COF'\ dis\ COF \quad P//F\,a.$$

Example:

c: In a purchase relation the seller is in delay delivering the goods.
c': In the same purchase relation the buyer is in delay with a minor part of the purchase money.
r: If the seller is in delay delivering the goods and the buyer so claims, the seller shall immediately deliver the goods to the buyer.
r': If the buyer is in delay paying the purchase money, the seller may omit delivering the goods to the buyer.

The buyer's claim of delivery, as well as the seller's claim of payment and his refusal to deliver the goods until payment has been made, are tried in the same judicial process.

It is obvious that, if an injunction to the effect that the seller shall deliver the goods immediately is issued, and simultaneously a permission is given for the seller to abstain from doing so until he has received payment, the seller is on the horns of a dilemma if he wants to make use of the permission not to deliver immediately. Therefore, the judge must make a choice between the two conflicting rules.

The problem concerning multi-case collision has a nature distinct from the nature of the problem concerning one-case collision. (There is a corresponding difference between multi-case competition and one-case competition; see Sect. 10.4 below.)

The situation with respect to one-case collision is, schematically, this:

The case: *c*
The rules:

(r_1) if *c*, so permitted that *a*
(r_2) if *c*, so forbidden that *a*.

One-case collision always exists when the same (generic) operative fact falls under each rule involved—this type of collision is, so to speak, necessary, or permanent. It is a constant system problem.

The situation with respect to multi-case collision is, schematically, this:

The cases: c, c'
The rules:

(r_1) if *c*, so permitted that *a*
(r_2) if c', so forbidden that *a*.

Multi-case collision is not, as is one-case collision, necessary but only possible when a case, *c*, falling under one of the rules, *r*, is present. Multi-case collision arises only when *c* is present together with other circumstances, case c', which are irrelevant and accidental from the point of view of *r* solely. Multi-case collision is not a collision that arises every time a case falling under a certain rule is present; it is not permanent but accidental.

Hence, one-case collision between two rules is a problem that can only be solved by, *once and for all*, either abolishing one of the rules totally—variation (1)—or reducing (derogating) it partially—variations (2) and (3) (at p. 194 above). With respect to multi-case collision, on the other hand, it is not a matter of abolishing a colliding rule or reducing its sphere of operation once and for all, but only of laying down an order of preference for the application of the colliding rules. For these rules shall in the future be applicable to exactly the same cases as before. Had the two cases *c* and c' in our purchase example not appeared in the same application situation but only in one of them, *r* would of course have been applied to *c* or r' to c'—and in the future as well *r* shall be applied to *c* and r' to c'. Only when *c* and c' happen to appear in the same application situation must the judge, for the sake of logical consequence, omit to apply either *r* or r'. With respect to one-case collision, the judge must make *a confinement* of the sphere of application of a rule, while with respect to multi-case collision he must make *a momentary suspension* of the application of a rule.

It is an important task for the legislator to prevent collisions in his legislative products. Some aspects on how to achieve this will be presented in Chap. 15. Here we shall focus on collision from the point of view of the law-applier.

Let us begin with one-case collisions. When the legislator does not even notice that he has created such a collision, or when he notices it but does not care, he has laid a considerable responsibility on the law-applier. The latter is put in an awkward position, where he on his own shall, totally (desuetude) or partially (reduction), repudiate the legal system by eliminating one of its rules—even if this situation has come about through negligence on the part of the legislator.

Lawyers usually regard the solution of collision problems as a matter of interpretation of the rules involved, which at first might seem to be somewhat bewildering. However, the juridical technique of argumentation used in "ordinary" interpretation of statutes can also be mobilised when solving collision problems. Solutions to these kinds of problems can be found in precedents or in preparatory materials, systematic arguments can be relevant—for instance, one of the colliding rules can be conceived as an emanation of a general principle of law, which, for that reason, shall be given priority—and also teleological (consequentialist) balancing of interests can be a useful means in problem-solving of this kind.

Besides the ordinary principles of statutory interpretation, however, the so-called derogatory principles play an important role from the viewpoint of principle (whether and, if at all, to what extent they actually operate in the administration of law we know, I think, little or nothing about). These principles are, expressed in their traditional Latin formulation, the following:

(i) *lex specialis derogat legi generali* (a special law supersedes a more general one)
(ii) *lex superior derogat legi inferiori* (a higher law supersedes a lower one)
(iii) *lex posterior derogat legi priori* (a later law supersedes an earlier one)

And, as derogatory principles of a higher order (operating on a meta-meta level),

(iv) *lex superior prior derogat legi inferiori posteriori* (an earlier higher law supersedes a later lower one)
(v) *lex superior generalis derogat legi inferiori speciali* (a higher general law supersedes a lower more special one)
(vi) *lex prior specialis derogat legi posteriori generali* (an earlier special law supersedes a later more general one). This principle is sometimes expressed in a weaker formulation:
(vi′) *lex posterior generalis non derogat legi priori speciali* (a later, more general, law does not supersede an older, more special one).

As we see, principles (iv)–(vi) indicate an order of hierarchy between principles (i)–(iii): the *lex superior* principle supersedes the *lex specialis* and the *lex posterior* principles, and the *lex specialis* principle supersedes the *lex posterior* principle.

Let us pay some attention to the arguments behind these principles.

One argument for the *lex posterior principle* relates to the law-applier's attitude towards the actual legislator. If the loyalty of the former to the latter is strong, and there is a collision between a recently issued rule and a considerably older one, it probably takes a lot for the law-applier to choose the older one, and thereby in a way disavow the present legislator. Obviously the difference in time is important—if two recently issued rules collide with a small difference in time between them, the *lex posterior* principle is probably of little importance. The same is very likely the case when two very old rules collide, even if the difference in time between them is considerable. A more substantial argument compared to this loyalty argument, although close to it, is the idea that a more recent rule takes priority over an older one as far as it reflects changed, now adopted ideas of a moral, social or economic character. In this respect a useful aid for the law-applier might be a hypothetical test: Is it possible that the legislator, had he been more observant, would have changed or abolished the older rule when issuing the new one?

The most important derogatory principle in practice is probably the *lex specialis* principle. The main reason for this is that the law-applier, when using it, falls back on an important principle of legislative methodology: the ordering of statutory provisions according to the model "principal rule—exception", where the principal rule is a general one and the exception a more special one. The law-applier thereby acts as "the prolonged arm" of the legislator. This legislative principle becomes in the hands of the law-applier a derogatory principle. It is a commonplace that an exception shall have precedence over the principal rule when applicable to a clear case—otherwise the exception would be useless. (Another thing is the principle of statutory interpretation to the effect that *in dubio* exceptions shall be interpreted restrictively. The reason for this principle is to maintain the function of the principle rule exactly as a principal rule and not undermining that function.) Principle (vi) shows that "the system aspect" is regarded as more important than the time aspect.

Just as is the case with the *lex posterior* and the *lex specialis* principles, also *the lex superior principle* is best understood in the light of the law-applier's loyalty to the legislator. This principle is closely connected to the idea of legalism—the law-applier's adherence to the law. An understood necessary condition for the principle to function is that there exists a conception, shared by legislators and law-appliers alike, of a hierarchy of statutes on different levels over which the principle can operate. Collision problems must be solved and one important aspect in this connection is no doubt the provenance of the colliding rules.

The hierarchy in question is usually something similar to the following: (a) constitutional rules, (b) ordinary statutory provisions issued by the legislative assembly, (c) regulations issued by the government, (d) regulations issued by lower state authorities, (e) municipal ordinances.

There are good reasons to differentiate between, on the one hand, collisions between constitutional rules and lower rules, and, on the other, collisions between rules on different lower levels. The first relation has an importance far beyond the (technical) task of eliminating collisions, since the *lex superior* principle with respect to this relation is the basis of the institution of *judicial review*. The protection of the individual's fundamental rights is in focus here.

With respect to the second relation, it is rather the fact that the colliding rules emanate from different legislators that comes to the fore. Here the hierarchy mirrors a hierarchy of legal power. In democratic societies, the supreme legal power is in the hands of a popularly elected assembly, and any legislative competence apart from this supreme power is regarded as a kind of delegation from it.

It is important to emphasise that the derogatory principles (i)–(vi) are, precisely, principles—and, hence, at times must be balanced against other values or principles.

Finally, a few words about *multi-case collision.* With respect to them, the derogatory principles seem to be of little use. Why, one could ask, should higher law supersede lower or later law supersede older, when the two colliding rules are about totally different things (the proper subset relation that the applicability of the *lex specialis* principle presupposes is very unlikely to exist in multi-case collision situations)? When solving multi-case collisions, arguments pertaining to the branch of law in point must be decisive, the ordinary principles of statutory interpretation must be mobilised and a balancing of competing interests seems unavoidable.

10.4 Rule Competition

10.4.1 Introduction

In this section I shall start with some reflections on what causes competition between legal rules by formulating some, which I call general, conditions of competition (Sect. 10.4.2). Then I shall deal with one-case competition (Sect. 10.4.3) and multi-case competition (Sect. 10.4.4), respectively. (In Chap. 15—in connection with an investigation of principles of legislation—we shall investigate the legislator's attitude towards competition problems.)

10.4.2 Some General Conditions of Competition

Is it possible to discern and characterise some typical, juridically interesting general rule-competition situations (or competition conditions)? Let us make some reflections on this topic.

One could speak of different kinds of defects of legal rules. One such defect would be that a given rule is more or less *inexpedient* as a means: the social state of affairs intended to be achieved by the observance of the rule seldom or never comes about when the rule is complied with. Another defect would be that the rule is more or less *unsuitable*: the state of affairs brought about by the compliance with the rule is not a desirable social state of affairs at all.

Now, a rule might be expedient as well as suitable when taken in isolation but, nonetheless, inexpedient or unsuitable when applied together with one or more other rules. We can talk about collective inexpediency and collective unsuitability, respectively, or, using a common term, *collective disadvantage.*

With respect to collective unsuitability, the state of affairs brought about when more than one rule is applied simultaneously is not a desirable one, e.g., that a person for the same act is punished for both theft and gross theft. With respect to collective inexpediency—or, better, collective counteraction—it is the case that the application of one rule some way or another counteracts the application of another rule, as happens when it is physically difficult, or even impossible, to comply with both rules simultaneously. For example, a person is sentenced to prison for assault and, simultaneously, to pay damages to the victim, but the loss of income that is a result of the imprisonment makes it more difficult to pay these damages. Of course it is possible that both unsuitability and inexpediency prevail (which, if so, does not make things worse but rather the contrary, since the inexpediency, as it were, might prevent the unsuitability from coming about).

It is exactly when collective disadvantage prevails that choice-of-rule problems come to the fore.

It is of course possible to conceive of every situation where collective disadvantage prevails, and, hence, some kind of choice of rule must be made, as a competition situation. In that case we get a very broad concept of legal competition. On the other hand, there is no reason to confine the area of application of this concept to criminal law, although it often has been regarded as a special criminal law concept. Competition problems appear in all spheres of law. However, since competition problems have been investigated mainly in criminal law doctrine, it might be wise to take our point of departure there as a kind of model. Let us focus on three typical competition conditions, put forward with the use of the concept in criminal law doctrine in view.

(1) A first, rather obvious competition condition is that one or more cases are tried in the same application situation. That a person is on trial for drunken driving at court C_1 and simultaneously for fraud at court C_2 does not constitute a competition situation. Only if, at one of the courts, it is decided, at the meting out of punishment, to take into consideration the sentence of the other court does a concurrence situation arise. But then this takes place within the same application situation (cf. what was said about so-called iterative application situations, at pp. 191 f. above).

(2) When, within the criminal law doctrine, competition between two or more cases is discussed (Ger. *Realkonkurrenz*), it is, to all appearances, implied that the same parties are involved in all cases (multi-claim litigation). (In criminal cases and tax cases there is, to be sure, a "constant", always present party, "the State"—or whatever it is called in different legal systems.) Then the idea presents itself immediately that multi-claim litigation could be made a general competition condition. But then one must be clear about in so doing, one might exclude certain kinds of collective disadvantage from falling under the competition concept, although they prompt the law-applier to make a choice of rule. Such a choice can also come to the fore when he has to deal with a multi-party litigation.

A conspicuous feature of the legal process is what could be called "the isolation of the claim". In radical form this means that, within the framework of the legal process, a claim of a party shall be regarded as an isolated entity in the respect that, if his claim is based on proven circumstances and valid law, the claim shall be sustained without the judge's taking into consideration that third persons not involved in the process can suffer from that. Hence, a debtor shall settle his debt even if this leads to his going into bankruptcy to the disadvantage of other creditors and a sentence of imprisonment shall be executed even if the convicted is thereby unable to support his family. In this perspective there is some truth in the old saying *fiat justitia, pereat mundus*. To a certain extent the isolation of the claim is no doubt justified by the value of equality before the law. A party who has to compete with other persons' rights outside the scope of the process, e.g., other creditors, is not in a worse position *within the scope of the process* compared to a party in another process who does not have any such competitors.

If the principle of the isolation of the claim is strictly upheld, it would come natural to confine the juridical concept "competition" to multi-claim litigation situations. Possible repercussions on third persons would be irrelevant. However, the principle is not without exception (at least not in Swedish law). Let me give an example. In the Swedish Liability for Damages Act there is a general provision concerning apportionment of damages. In the preparatory materials of that provision the legislator suggests that damages caused by crime could be adjusted if paying it fully would counteract the social rehabilitation of the offender. If the criminal case and the tort case are tried in the same process, we have not a multi-claim but a multi-party litigation. But nevertheless there is a kind of competition here between criminal law and the law of torts. And the suggestion in the preparatory materials has the consequence that considerations of social rehabilitation "are taken out on" the injured person. She is in a worse position than an injured person in a trial where no such considerations arise—a dubious consequence from the viewpoint of the principle of equality before the law.

(3) A third competition condition might be that the legal consequences of the alternative rules—or, more exact, their norm-themes—are commensurable. This condition is most easily fulfilled when the norm-themes involved are measurable, and, moreover, measurable with the same measure, or with measures that can be mutually exchangeable with each other by following a certain scheme, e.g., imprisonment measured by time and pecuniary penalty measured by money. This explains to a certain extent why legal competition has come to be of certain interest to criminal law. But in other fields of law as well, norm-themes are commensurable in this way. Then, of course, it can be a matter of distributing unpleasantness, as in criminal law, or a matter of distributing advantages, as in social insurance law. In the latter case it might well happen that a person is simultaneously entitled to many different insurance amounts, in which case it would be unreasonable to allot them all to her. Further examples can be found in tax law and the law of torts.

10.4.3 One-Case Competition

One-case competition between legal rules has in common with one-case collision that both come within the scope of main type I:

$$(\text{MTI})\ AS(c) : c \in COF_r \ and\ c \in COF'_{r'}.$$

One-case competition appears in one of the following nine variations (variation "*COF′ dis COF*" is logically impossible under MTI and variation "*N′ lap N*" can be split up into its "components" identity and disjunction, respectively):

(1)	*COF′ id COF*	*N′ id N*
(2)	*COF′ id COF*	*N′ spec N*
(3)	*COF′ id COF*	*N′ dis N*
(4)	*COF′ spec COF*	*N′ id N*
(5)	*COF′ spec COF*	*N′ spec N*
(6)	*COF′ spec COF*	*N′ dis N*
(7)	*COF′ lap COF*	*N′ id N*
(8)	*COF′ lap COF*	*N′ spec N*
(9)	*COF′ lap COF*	*N′ dis N*

Comments:

Ad (1)–(3). (1) is a marginal case of one-case competition, which could be called "total rule redundancy". Two different rules—in the sense of different occurrences—constitute one single rule in the sense that both occurrences have the same content. Here it is logically possible (though, of course, practically absurd) to add the norm-themes of the two rules. From a material point of view it is irrelevant which one of the rules is applied, but there can be aspects of principle urging the law-applier to choose one of the rules before the other. (2) is probably uncommon in societies where the legislator is observant. When the legislator, as in situation (3), attaches different legal consequences to the same operative facts, this is usually no accident at work but use of an established technique of statutory drafting.

Ad (4)–(6). The difference between this group of situations and the group (1)–(3) is that, in (4)–(6), the sphere of operative facts of one of the rules is a proper subset of the operative sphere of the other, i.e., the former is more specialised, or made more precise, than the latter. Hence, the *lex specialis*-principle is applicable here. (4) can be chosen by the legislator when he in a separate rule wishes to emphasise a certain generic case that in itself falls under another rule with the same legal consequences. In (5) one of the rules is a precisation of the other, both with respect to the sphere of operative facts and the legal consequences—a technique not uncommon in criminal law. As for (6), what is said about (3) is applicable. Situations (4) and (5) can be characterised by the term "partial rule redundancy".

Ad (7)–(9). The crucial difference between (7)–(9) and (4)–(6) is that the *lex specialis*-principle does not operate on the former. With respect to overlapping spheres of operative facts it is not meaningful to characterise one rule as more specialised than the other. (7) and (8) are examples of partial rule redundancy.

10.4.4 Multi-Case Competition

Like multi-case collision, multi-case competition comes within the scope of main type II:

$$(\text{MTII})\ AS(c) : c \in COF_r \ and\ c' \in COF'_{r'}$$

where $c \neq c'$.

Examples: (1) A person is prosecuted in one and the same trial for theft, fraud and rape. (2) An official has to decide whether a person, who *prima facie* is entitled to several different social insurance amounts, shall receive all of them.

It has no practical purpose, with respect to multi-case competition, to construct a scheme for the norm-relations that can hold between r and r'. However, a marginal case of multi-case competition deserves mentioning, namely:

$$COF'\ id\ COF \qquad N'\ id\ N$$

i.e., that $r = r'$ (in practice usually one and the same occurrence), for example, when a person has committed several different thefts. This kind of multi-case competition is referred to in criminal law as "similar competition".

It might seem a bit strange to conceive of similar competition as a competition between rules—is it meaningful to say that a rule competes with itself? Is it not rather the situation that different cases, each of which standing in an application relation to r, compete for being actually applied to by r in a given application situation? That may be, but on the other hand there is no reason to complicate things because of this—it is not totally unreasonable to say that a rule competes with itself for being applied to many cases simultaneously. In other words, the question is: How many application relations can the rule "cope with" in one and the same application situation?

The difference between one-case collision and multi-case collision mentioned in Sect. 10.3 (at p. 196 above)—to the effect that, as for the former, we are faced with a confinement of the application of a rule, while, as for the latter, with a momentary suspension of application—exists also between one-case competition and multi-case competition. A difference, however, between collision and competition is that with respect to many-case competition momentary suspension is a possible but not necessary solution, while with respect to many-case collision it is a necessary solution. In criminal law, one-case competition is sometimes called "ideal competition" and multi-case competition "real competition". This distinction is of interest since the solutions of one-case-competition problems involve a more radical interference with the legal system than solutions of multi-case ones. It is only with respect to one-case competition that the result becomes a (total or partial) rule redundancy.

Reference

Lindahl L, Reidhav D (2015) Conflicts of legal norms: definitions and varieties. In: Araszkiewicz M, Pleszka K (eds) Logic in the theory and practice of lawmaking. Springer, Berlin, pp 49–95

Chapter 11
On Relations Between Legal Systems

11.1 Introduction

In the previous chapter we investigated conflicts between individual rules within the same legal system. In this and the next chapter we shall study different relations that can exist *between legal systems*—systems contained in state legal orders, temporally momentary legal systems contained in the same inter-temporal legal system, and extra-national systems (which, for the sake of convenience, I also refer to here as legal systems).

In Sect. 11.2 we shall investigate the claims to applicability that state legal systems can lay—let us call them their *range of adjudication*. This shall be done by means of an ideal-type construction (the maximum range of adjudication). After that I will take up some problems concerning the connections between legal systems and four main types of solutions to such problems (Sect. 11.3). Section 11.4 contains a clarification of the concept "connection" ("connecting factor"), which is of crucial importance to all inter-systematic problems. How shall we understand the relation "case *c* is connected to the legal system *S*"? Finally, in Sect. 11.5, we define four different "attitudes towards coexistence" that different state legal systems can have to each other.

11.2 On Ranges of Adjudication of State Legal Systems

11.2.1 Introduction

As a point of departure for a study of different relevant relations between legal systems I find it appropriate first to investigate what kind of claims modern state legal systems have with respect to the scope of their applicability in different respects—their range of adjudication.

Å. Frändberg, *The Legal Order*, Law and Philosophy Library 123,
https://doi.org/10.1007/978-3-319-78858-6_11

Such an investigation reveals very soon that a system's range of adjudication is a highly sophisticated, "multidimensional", phenomenon.

Let us begin with a definition. A legal system, *S*, is a *momentary legal system* existing between points of time t_0 and t_i ($t_0 < t_i$) if and only if an alteration (an addition of a rule, a change of some rule, or an elimination of any rule whatever in *S*) has taken place at t_0 and t_i but not between these two points of time. *An inter-temporal (non-momentary) legal system* is a sequence (discrete succession) of momentary legal systems (these concepts will be made more precise in Chap. 12).

The aim of our study is to investigate the extent of the state of affairs over which momentary state legal systems claim applicability. It concerns, among other things, their relations to other state legal systems, to extra-state law and to older law within the same inter-temporal system, and it concerns state legal systems' adaption to other legal systems and the limitations they impose upon themselves in their relation to other systems. The concept "range of adjudication" will in the following be used in order to clarify different kinds of conflicts and other relations between legal systems.

11.2.2 The Maximum Range of Adjudication

As a starting point for our investigation we shall contemplate an imaginary ideal-typical legal system (of an extremely repugnant kind). It is a legal system suffering from megalomania, claiming the most far-reaching totalitarianism and unlimited sovereignty—a Leviathan knowing no bounds for its self-assertion, but granting itself a totally unlimited range of adjudication. This legal system considers itself as having jurisdiction over any case whatsoever, even completely "internal" ones taking place on the other side of the earth, and naturally this system does not accept any derogation of the jurisdiction of its courts of law. Nor does the legal system respect any final judgments and there are no limits to the kinds of cases that can be tried by its courts. They can declare that every kind of abortion is illegal, that it is illicit to wear brown shoes with a tail-coat, or that God exists. The system does not pay heed to other legal systems, in every case with an international connection the *lex fori*-principle is applied, and the rules of the system are without any limitation retroactively applicable to cases having taken place before the momentary system in force came into existence. Public international law is not taken into account. Any concessions in favour of custom, e.g., commercial custom, is out of the question and all rules in the system are mandatory—not even the most modest degree of autonomy for contractual parties or litigants is allowed. In such a system there is no room for any collision norms "opening to" other systems.

Let us say that such a legal system has *a maximum range of adjudication*—which, of course, it has irrespective of whether it is effective or not (it is perhaps only a dream of grandeur in the brain of some crazy religious zealot).

In all respects just mentioned *actually valid* state legal systems to a higher or lower degree impose restraints on themselves, for example in the way that

(1) the claims to jurisdiction are limited
(2) earlier final judgments are respected
(3) certain "non-legal" situations are not tried by organs of the legal order to which the legal system belongs
(4) the legal order allows its organs to apply rules in other state legal systems or in public international law
(5) the legal order allows its organs to apply rules in older systems within the inter-temporal system to which it belongs
(6) the legal order allows its organs to apply rules in non-state legal systems (customs)
(7) the legal order allows its organs to apply rules created by private persons (contracts)
(8) certain rules in the system are adapted to rules in other legal systems of the kind mentioned in (4)–(7).

Each of (1)–(8) can be seen as "a dimension", the extreme point of which lies in the ideal-type called "the maximum range of adjudication". The dimensions are a kind of scales on which "real types" can be placed, indicating how far from the ideal type on each scale actually valid systems are situated, a device that facilitates comparisons between them.

Such restrictions are expressions of *an abandonment of monopoly* on the part of state legal systems (here of course not in the normative sense that state legal systems would have legitimate claims to monopoly, which they sometimes benevolently renounce). Such abandonments can be in favour of, for example

(a) other state legal systems or public international law
(b) older legal systems in the same inter-temporal system
(c) non-state legal systems
(d) rules created by private persons
(e) "the lawless space"
(f) legal status quo (due to *res judicata*).

11.2.3 The Concept "Range of Adjudication"

Let me clarify this concept in the following way. (We talk about the range of adjudication for legal systems but could as well have predicated the concept to legal orders.) In brief, the range of adjudication is the range outside which any case shall be dismissed (not tried upon the merits). Cases outside the range of adjudication are not covered by the prohibition of denial of justice.

Let *S* be a state legal system. Relative to *S* we can define (i) the jurisdiction sphere of *S*, (ii) the material sphere of *S*, and (iii) the formal sphere of *S*. By means of these three concepts the concept "range of adjudication" will be defined.

The jurisdiction sphere of S, J_S, is the set of cases such that, for each case, c_i, in J_S there is an organ constituted by *S* that, exclusively according to the international jurisdiction rules of *S*, is legally competent to decide c_i.

In other words, the jurisdiction sphere of *S* is the set of cases with respect to which there is some organ constituted by *S* that has jurisdiction competence (international procedural competence). The clause "exclusively according to the international jurisdiction rules of *S*" in the definition is important. It is a sufficient condition for a case, c_i, to belong to J_S that some organ constituted by *S* has jurisdiction over c_i even if trial upon the merits is excluded due to *other rules* in *S*, e.g., that c_i cannot be tried due to *res judicata.* Our definition covers also cases which are directed by means of jurisdiction agreements to some organ constituted by *S*, when the rules about choice-of-law agreements in *S* allow it.

In order to define the concepts "material" and "formal sphere of *S*", we must first define two auxiliary concepts "material dismissal rule" and "formal dismissal rule", respectively, i.e., dismissal without reaching the merits.

A material dismissal rule in *S* is a rule saying that a case, c_i, shall be dismissed without reaching the merits due to the material character of the problem actualised by c_i.

Examples: Suppose that someone at a court of law constituted by *S* wants a declaratory judgment that God exists. If such a claim, according to a rule, r_1, in *S* shall be dismissed without reaching the merits, then r_1 is a material dismissal rule. Or suppose that claims based on *pacta turpia* shall be dismissed in the same way by rule r_2 in *S*. Then also r_2 is a material dismissal rule.

A formal dismissal rule in *S* is a rule saying that c_i shall be dismissed without reaching the merits, and which rule is neither an international jurisdiction rule nor a material dismissal rule.

Example: A buyer has not paid the purchase money and the seller claims performance of the contract. If this claim according to rule r_3 shall be dismissed without reaching the merits due to *res judicata*, then r_3 is a formal dismissal rule—problems concerning payment of purchase money are in themselves of the kind that shall be tried by rules in *S*.

By means of the concepts "material dismissal rule" and "formal dismissal rule" the concepts "material" and "formal sphere of *S*" can be defined:

The material sphere of S, M_S, is the set of cases such that, for each case c_i in M_S, there is some organ constituted by *S* which, exclusively according to the material dismissal rules of *S*, has the competence to decide c_i.

The formal sphere of S, F_S, is the set of cases such that, for each case c_j in F_S, there is some organ constituted by *S* which, exclusively according to the formal dismissal rules of *S*, has the competence to decide c_j.

It follows from the definitions of J_S, M_S and F_S that any case, c_k, is allowed to be tried on its merits if and only if c_k belongs to each of J_S, M_S and F_S. The range of adjudication, RA_S, of a legal system *S* can then be defined as the intersection of J_S, M_S and F_S:

$$RA_S = J_S \cap M_S \cap F_S.$$

The outer limit of RA_S is the dismissal limit: every case outside RA_S shall be dismissed without reaching the merits.

11.3 On Connection Problems Between Legal Systems

Let us take up (1) *international*, (2) *inter-temporal*, and (3) *extra-national connection problems*, i.e., problems concerning connections between state legal systems, connections between different momentary systems within the same inter-temporal legal system, and connections between state and non-state (extra-national) legal systems.

There are four common techniques for solving connection problems between legal systems, let us call them (a) *competence-regulating solutions*, (b) *harmonising solutions*, (c) *division solutions*, and (d) *system-choice solutions*. Competence-regulating solutions aim at solving connection problems by issuing rules for the (external) competence of organs constituted by *S*. Harmonising solutions aim at solving such problems by standardising the content of rules belonging to different legal systems. Division solutions mean that claims that different nation-states compete for are split up into parts that are distributed over the states involved. The system-choice solutions, finally, make it possible for organs constituted by a state legal system to apply rules in other legal systems by means of so-called collision norms. These techniques can, of course, be used in combination, and there might also exist other techniques besides these four.

A. *Competence-regulation* is a common technique for solving international connection problems. Competence-regulation can be unilateral or multilateral. In the latter case we can talk about division of competence between legal systems (or orders). This is usually achieved by assenting to international conventions. Competence regulation is neither a question of standardising *the content* of legal rules, nor of *splitting up* claims, nor of *applying rules belonging to other legal systems*.

- Competence-regulation can be *positive*, i.e., competence is conferred on organs constituted by some legal system, or *negative*, i.e., that such organs are deprived of competence ("to the advantage of" some organ constituted by another legal system).
- Usually competence-regulation is brought up in connection with questions concerning international jurisdiction. Competence conflicts arising here are of two kinds, which also can be called positive and negative. The former exists when proceedings concerning the same issue between the same parties take place in two (or more) states. The opposite, that there is no competent organ in either state—in which case the parties are lawless—is a negative-competence conflict.

- The remedy of positive-competence conflict is negative-competence regulation, i.e., that courts of law of one legal order dismiss cases without reaching the merits "in favour of" courts of another legal order (usually by means of conventions). A weaker variation is that foreign law is respected in so far as an on-going trial in one state entails *lis pendens* in another state. The remedy of negative-competence conflict is positive-competence regulation.
- Other examples of competence regulation within the fields of international procedural and criminal law are rules to the effect that states recognise legal force (*res judicata*) with respect to each other's judgments, that they execute each other's judgments, and that they allow derogation of their jurisdiction to other legal orders as a consequence of private choice of court agreements. Further examples are rules about extradition, international legal aid in criminal cases, transfer of legal proceedings, etc.

B. As for *harmonising solutions* we can specify two extremes on a scale indicating the degree of harmonisation of one legal system to another. The one, *minimum harmonisation*, is situated in the ideal-type "the maximum range of adjudication" (Sect. 11.2.2)—in other words, there is no harmonisation at all. With respect to the opposite extreme, *maximum harmonisation*, two state legal systems, or parts of such, are identical, i.e., they contain the same set of rules. This is the case when *reception* (incorporation) has taken place (as happened in 1929, when Turkey incorporated the Swiss Civil Code *in toto* in its own legal system) or in the case of *unification*. (However, with respect to reception and unification we must always be observant of the phenomenon of *law-gliding*, i.e., that an incorporated statute undergoes a shift of meaning due to developments in legal usage.) Between the two extremes different degrees of harmonisation may occur.

- In an inter-temporal perspective corresponding extremes can be specified: On the one hand that a new statute is issued without any consideration whatsoever of the older, repealed one, or, on the other hand, that older law is not changed at all but only re-edited. Between these two extremes different kinds of harmonisation may occur. (Ideas and technical devices that can come to the fore in this connection will be dealt with in Chaps. 12 and 16.)
- Also with respect to adaption of state legal systems to extra-national ones (customs, contracts) it is possible, from the viewpoint of principle, to specify analogous extremes. Legalisation of extra-legal practice is no unknown phenomenon. For instance, when the Swedish Sale of Goods Act of 1905 (no longer in force) was prepared, norms developed in commercial life exerted a great influence on the content of the statute.
- An often used technical device by means of which harmonisation of a state legal system with extra-national systems can be performed is the creation of so-called *standards*, functioning as a kind of "sluices" between a state system and a non-state one. Standards are a type of rule including a blank requisite (standard requisite), e.g., "sound commercial practice" and "good advocate conduct", that refers to non-state norms (becoming law just due to the authority of the blank rule). A standard is a kind of machine that can always be re-programmed (e.g., as a consequence of changes in what is regarded as

sound commercial practice) without the machine itself needing re-building. By means of standards privately created law is, in a way, allowed to penetrate into the state legal system in a more radical way than optional provisions, since, with respect to standards, extra-national law is master over the content of requisites in *mandatory* rules in the state system.

C. As was just said, *division solutions* mean that claims that different national legal systems compete for are split up into parts that are distributed over the states involved. The term "claim" is here used in a very wide sense, including claims to perform a duty or claims to submission, e.g., serving a prison sentence. In international tax law we find many examples of division solutions. There are rules about the right to deduct foreign tax when determining income tax and there are rules contained in tax agreements among states for the avoidance of double taxation. From the field of international criminal law can be mentioned rules allowing a prison sentence served in country A to be taken into consideration when the same crime is tried in country B.
D. As for *the system-choice solutions,* I refer to the standard literature in the field of private international law (conflict of laws). However, we shall (in the next section) investigate a basic concept of private (criminal, procedural) international law, namely the concept "connection". Let me also, in passing, draw our attention to the fact that also international collision norms can be harmonised, to the effect that the same *lex causae* is indicated with respect to a certain case irrespective of where the case is tried.

11.4 The Concept "Connection"

System-choice problems between legal systems arise when a court of law is met with a case that, some way or another, has connection to at least two different legal systems. Connection, then, is a relation of the type

(C) Case c has connection to legal system S

or

(C′) c has connection to legal systems $S_1, \ldots, S_n$.

Here, as before, legal systems can be different national legal systems, different momentary systems within the same inter-temporal system or extra-national legal systems. Our concept "connection" is wider than that of international private law.

Such connections, or connecting factors, can, of course, be of greatly differing kinds. Yet, some typical ones are discernible. It is among such connecting factors that legislators, when constructing international jurisdiction rules as well as international collision rules, choose those that shall be decisive as far as allocating procedural competence and pointing out *lex causae* are concerned.

A condition for a clarification of inter-systematic choices of rules is that we have some understanding of what it means that a case has connection to a legal system. How is the relation C to be understood?

Let k_c be some component of a case, *c*. We take the term "component" in a very wide sense: it covers actions, legal positions, states of affairs, persons, or things. Let, further, *L* be some statute, the rules of which belong to legal system *S*.

The relation C can now be made more precise in different directions, such as:

(C_1) *L* is the law of the geographical place of k_c.

Examples: *L* is the law of the place where a crime has been committed (*lex loci delicti commissi*), where a contract has been entered into (*lex loci contractus*), where an obligation shall be fulfilled (*lex loci solutionis*), where a person has her habitual domicile (*lex domicilii*), where a thing or a real estate is situated (*lex rei sitae*), or where a wedding has taken place (*lex loci celebrantionis*).

(C_2) *L* is the status-conferring law of k_c.

Examples: Two persons are married according to *L*, a person's nationality is given to her by *L* (*lex patriae*), a limited company is established by *L*, or an adoption has come about by *L*.

(C_3) *L* is the law at the time of k_c.

This relation is restricted to pertain to momentary legal systems belonging to the same inter-temporal system.

Examples: When a certain crime is committed, *L* is the law in force concerning that *kind* of crime. When a certain contract has been entered into, *L* is the law in force for that *kind* of contract. When a certain breach of contract has taken place, *L* is the law in force for that *kind* of breach of contract.

The relations C_1–C_3 are examples of what could be called *material connection*: *c* has material connection to *L*. By this I mean, roughly, that the connection is a relation between k_c and a component (rule, requisite), l_L, in *L* such that l_L "describes" k_c. But there is also another kind of connection between *c* and *L*, which could be called *formal connection*.

Let us by the term *actualisor* refer to any procedural act-in-the-law by means of which a trial before a court of law is started, e.g., a summons application—in other words, a correct procedural opening gambit. Let further $(a_f)c$ be such an actualisor with respect to case *c* and court (forum) *f*. Relation C can now be made more precise in two further directions:

(C_4) *L* is the law of the geographical place of $(a_f)c$
or, in other words, *L* is *lex fori* with respect to *f*.

(C_5) *L* is the law at the time of $(a_f)c$.

Also this relation is restricted to pertain to momentary systems belonging to the same inter-temporal one.

Examples: When a certain crime is prosecuted, *L* is the law in force for that *kind* of crime. When an action is commenced concerning the content of a certain contract, *L* is the law in force for that *kind* of contract. In such cases we can say that *L* is *lex nunc* with respect to *c*.

Usually, of course, *c* has both material and formal connection to *L*. But it is theoretically and also practically possible that only formal connection exists. One example is the situation where, although *c* lacks any material connection to the legal system *S* to which *L* belongs, there is a choice of court agreement that *c* shall come under the jurisdiction of a court constituted by *S* and that an action also has been commenced at such a court (thereby giving *c* formal connection to *S*). Another example could be that *c* has taken place completely "under" older law (*lex tunc*) but that it is actualised first when that law has been succeeded by another. This shows that a distinction of the type material-formal connection is necessary to make.

We can look upon *will of the parties connection* as a third kind of connection besides the material and formal ones:

(C_6) *L* is the law pointed out by *(wp)c*

where "*(wp)c*" is an expression of parties (usually in so-called "overriding clauses") declaring that it is the will of the parties either that the law of a certain country shall be applied in case of dispute (material will of the parties connection) or that a certain court shall try it (formal will of the parties connection).

It goes without saying that the material connection of a case to *lex fori* in international choice-of-law situations, as well as the material connection of a case to *lex nunc* in inter-temporal ones, can include many or few components of the case and also that such components can be more or less legally relevant.

What we have said about connection so far has mainly had international and inter-temporal choice-of-law problems in view. But what about the connection of a case to extra-national law? Is it even meaningful to say that a case has a connection to, e.g., the content of a contract?

To start with, what could it mean that a case has a connection to local custom? The answer immediately suggests itself—it must be a connection of type C_1. Formal connection is hardly relevant in practice here although local organs, similar to courts of law, are imaginable.

That a case has connection to commercial customs and the like is chiefly to be analysed in terms of C_2—there are more or less explicit rules indicating which persons shall count as (have status as) "addressees" for those customary rules, for example, members of a certain professional category. Also here formal connection is imaginable, namely to private organs such as committees of review, councils on business practices, etc.

Agreements can be regarded as—more or less extensive—legal systems and this aspect of them is *par préférence* that of the judge. Three characteristic features distinguish this kind of private law-creation, although in different degrees and not without exception.

(1) It is a matter of *law-creation ad hoc*, i.e., the purpose of the agreement is to carry out a certain specified project by regulating the forms of its accomplishment. The agreement "is consumed" when accomplished. Sometimes such projects are the work of an instant, but often they have a very long duration, which means a permanent legal relation between the parties.
(2) It is a matter of *law-creation of their* (the parties') *own*, i.e., the rules of the agreement are applicable exclusively to the parties *who have entered into it* (the parties and the addressees of the agreement are usually the same persons).

However, this is not always the case. Collective agreements in the field of labour law are usually binding not only for the contracting organisations but also for their members and, in some cases, even former members.

(3) It is a matter of *self-law-creation*, i.e., the rules of the agreement are applicable only to the parties *who have formulated the rules* (the parties and "the legislators" are usually the same persons). But this is not without exception either—suffice it to refer to the frequent use of standard contracts, e.g., in the insurance business.

Agreements can, of course, be limited both locally and temporally. Collective agreements are usually limited in time and, by means of recurrent collective bargaining, momentary systems based on collective agreements succeed each other in time in a way that reminds one of momentary state systems. To agreements could also be connected "a legal organisation" ("courts"), for example by means of clauses referring to private arbitration proceedings.

The connection of a case to a system of rules based on agreements is, of course, chiefly of a status character (C_2). Cases have connection to such systems when persons involved in a case regulated by the agreement have the status of party of that agreement (or stand in some fixed relation to a party).

11.5 On Attitudes Towards Coexistence Between State Legal Systems

First of all it must be emphasised that I am speaking somewhat metaphorically here. Men can have attitudes, legal systems cannot. However, bearing that in mind, I do not see any inconvenience here to use the word "attitude" also for products of human culture such as legal systems.

That a legal system has a monopolistic attitude means that, in an ideal-typical form, it does not take into consideration foreign law at all. The less a system is informed by a monopolistic attitude, the more it is informed by an open attitude. A system can be open in two respects: (1) the system allows foreign rules, pointed out by its collision norms, to appear as guests and (2) it is open to adaption, for example by harmonisation, of its own rules to foreign rules.

It is a well-known fact that some areas of law traditionally present a rather strong monopolistic attitude (e.g., land law and real estate law), others a more open one (e.g., patent law and freight law).

The monopolistic attitude can appear in a stronger and a weaker form. According to the stronger one *lex causae* is always *lex fori.* According to the weaker one a room for guests is offered by means of collision norms but the system reserves the right to make selections (reprobation) with respect to which guests it will welcome. The so-called *ordre public* (public policy) mechanism functions as a Cerberus in these situations.

Let us by means of this simple conceptual framework schematically characterise four different *attitudes towards coexistence* between state legal systems. (The scheme might perhaps be of some interest in discussions on comparative matters.) Of course, a system can have one attitude to some foreign systems and another attitude to others. The cause of that being the case can be that the state in question belongs to a supranational organisation such as the EU or that a special solidarity informs the relation within a group of states, as is the case between the Nordic countries.

The attitudes are the following.

I. *The self-assertive attitude* is characterised by (i) a wide jurisdiction sphere and (ii) a strong monopolistic attitude.

   Examples: French law can be said to have had this attitude to a certain degree before France joined the European project. The USA of today shows signs of it. Perhaps this attitude can be regarded as a "great power attitude".

II. *The self-sufficient attitude* is characterised by (i) a narrow jurisdiction sphere and (ii) a strong monopolistic attitude.

   Example: Swedish law up to, say, 1800.

   Between two systems both informed by the self-sufficient attitude there is an obvious risk of negative jurisdiction conflicts, i.e., that neither system is applicable and the litigants are left in a law-less state of affairs.

III. *The submissive attitude* is characterised by (i) a narrow jurisdiction sphere and (ii) a weak monopolistic attitude (= a strong open attitude).

   Example: In the Soviet Union the law of the federation states had to no small degree a submissive attitude towards the federal Soviet law.

IV. *The service attitude* is characterised by (i) a wide jurisdiction sphere and (ii) a strong open attitude (a weak monopolistic attitude).

   Examples: The European legal systems during, say, the last 50 years have no doubt developed in the direction of the service attitude, of course in the first place due to the rise of the European Union. In many respects and over a long period of time the Nordic countries have had a service attitude towards each other.

Chapter 12
Retroactivity, Simulactivity and Infraactivity

12.1 Transitional Law

Characteristic of legal dogmatics—as well as of many other scientific branches—is that names signifying certain special legal sciences also are names of the subject of those sciences. Thus the term "civil law" signifies a certain part of the legal system but also the branch of legal dogmatics that studies that part of the system.

In the same manner we can use the term "transitional law" to designate that part of a state legal system which regulates certain matters connected with changes of the system ("transitional problems"). And the branch of legal science whose task it is to study transitional law in this sense we can call "transitional law" as well. The main task of transitional law is the investigation of problems concerning the legal regulation of the applicability of legal rules in a temporal perspective, which problems in the first place are due to changes within the legal system.

Transitional problems can be traced back to two, in principle distinct questions:

I. During which period of time is a given legal rule applicable?
II. During which period of time shall cases have taken place in order that the rule is applicable to them?

Our investigation is exclusively concerned with changes in statutory law.

Logically, transitional law is situated on the same level as private international law (conflict of laws). Indeed, the German term "*intertemporales Privatrecht*" is constructed by analogy with the term "*internationales Privatrecht*".[1] Just as the collisions rules of private international law are a kind of second order rules (meta-rules)—i.e., rules not solving problematic social situations but deciding the choice between two or more in different respects conflicting state legal systems—so the

[1]Level (1959). The German term is used for the first time by Affolter (1902). However, also the term "*Übergangsrecht*" is used (Affolter (1903)). In France and Italy the terms "*droit transitoire*" and "*diritto transitorio*" are usually used (Cavaglieri (1904)).

Å. Frändberg, *The Legal Order*, Law and Philosophy Library 123,
https://doi.org/10.1007/978-3-319-78858-6_12

rules of transitional law decide choices between different momentary systems within the same inter-temporal legal system. Transitional law is usually expressed in special transitional regulations and promulgation acts. The rules of transitional law we call *transitional rules.*

Transitional law has a long history.[2] The focus has, not surprisingly, been on problems related to retroactive legislation. Cicero (in *Contra Verres*) vehemently attacks this bigwig, having retroactively cancelled the legal consequences of testaments made earlier. Transitional problems are articulated by Roman lawyers such as Paulus and Ulpianus, and are thoroughly treated in *Corpus juris.* The tradition is conveyed by the glossators and the commentators. In many of the grand codes from the eighteenth and nineteenth centuries prohibitions of retroactive legislation are inserted as a consequence of the efforts of the Enlightenment to counteract abuse of power by those in authority. Thus, for example, in the constitution of the United States (1787), in the declaration of human rights that constitutes the introduction to the French constitution of 1793 ("*la loi qui punirait des délits commis avant qu'elle existât, serait une tyrannie; l'effet retroactif donné à la loi serait un crime*"), in *Allgemeines Landrecht für die preussischen Staaten* (1794), in *Code Civil* (1804, Article 2), and in the Norwegian constitution of 1814 (Article 97). (On the other hand, no prohibition of retroactive legislation is inserted in the German *Bürgerliches Gesetzbuch* about a century later). For the French revolutionaries, however, the confession to the prohibition of retroactivity was to a high degree a lip service—as a matter of fact, a number of statutes with radically retroactive effect were issued during the revolutionary days (I shall come back to this below). The nineteenth century saw a considerable advance of the study of transitional law in Western legal science. A special interest was devoted to the doctrine of so-called vested (or acquired) rights, which, by their very nature, were regarded as immune to changes of the law (see further Chap. 16).

Analogies between international private law and transitional law play an important role in nineteenth century legal writing. Transitional problems are regarded as a matter of conflicts between legal systems.[3] Such a conflict can be present when a given case has a connection to two or more different national legal systems. But more or less analogous problems arise, it would seem, when a case has a connection to two different momentary systems, S_1 and S_2, where S_2 succeeds S_1 within the same trans-temporal legal system. In the former case the conflict is solved by means of rules in international private law, in the latter of rules in transitional law. In both cases there is a *conflit de lois*—in the former case a *conflit de lois dans l'espace*, in the latter a *conflit de lois dans le temps.* In both cases the conflict is resolved by some *jus supra jura.* The result might very well be that foreign law supersedes domestic law and that older law supersedes newer.

But, as Roubier rightly argues, the reasons for giving foreign law preference to domestic law have quite another character than the reasons for giving older law

[2]See further Roubier (1960), p. 30 ff., from which I have borrowed here.

[3]Roubier (1960), p. 3 ff.

preference to newer.[4] In the former case the motivation has a flavour of foreign policy, the concern being what attitude one is to take with respect to the surrounding world, while in the latter the motivation is of a downright domestic nature; for instance, that the social order would be unduly disturbed by legislative interferences in established legal relations. In addition to this, transitional rules are by their very nature provisional—after a certain, shorter or longer, period of time no transitory problems arise and the validity of the transitional rules is self-effacing. With these conclusive differences in mind we can safely conclude that the analogy between international and inter-temporal law must not be forced as far as advancing the same or similar principles for solving problems within the two areas of law.

Let us—briefly—say a few words about factors that create transitional problems within different areas of the law.

In the law of contract and property we meet problems caused by legislative interference in established legal relations. In particular, interference in relations of long standing and relations in institutionalised forms, such as limited companies, are often the cause of difficult transitional problems. Also family law regulates long standing relations between human beings. Here we are faced with questions concerning purely personal, often intimate, relations. This is an area of law where changes in moral conceptions play an important role, which can have transitional relevance. In criminal law (deprivation of liberty or property), some parts of procedural law (e.g., rules about detention and search of premises), administrative law (e.g., deprivation of liberty for medical reasons), and tax law (deprivation of property) the law-state protection of individuals' legal security against the state comes to the fore. But in tax law, as well as in financial political legislation (e.g., currency regulations and price-freeze) the very purpose, in some extraordinary situations, of the regulations cannot be realised if they do not come into force promptly, perhaps even surprisingly. Here the balancing of the economic values and the value of legal certainty are brought to a head. As for procedural law, litigation—or, in the case of appeal, a sequence of litigations—is a course of events that often extends over a long period of time, and during such a period changes of the procedural law may occur. As a consequence, part of a judicial process might fall under an older law and part of it under a new one. These consequences might turn out to be unfortunate, taking into consideration that the different parts of a process form a whole. With respect to private international law, finally, we are faced with transitional problems on two different levels. The first concerns the time during which the collision norms themselves are in force. The other is that there might have been changes in the *lex causae*. An example of the latter is the case where a court of country A shall decide whether a gift shall be considered as an advance on inheritance, where *lex causae* is the law of country B. Then the question arises: Shall the law of B at the time of the gift or the law of B at the time of the court proceedings be applied, if the law of B has changed between these two events?

---

[4]Roubier (1960), p. 9.

Although transitional law has a long history, it is rather undeveloped from a conceptual and systematic viewpoint. Roubier characterises it in the following straightforward way: "*Au droit transitoire manquent encore certains des éléments indispensables à une science bien faite: il n'a pas une terminologie assez riche pour fixer toutes les idées; le sujet n'a pas été ordonné sur un plan rigoureux; les distinctions élémentaires ont été à peine entrevues*".[5] This chapter is an attempt to put some order in the foundations of transitional law and to do so within the framework of a general juridical topology.

At this point I want to draw our attention to a risk of a general kind which confronts jurisprudents and philosophers trying to clarify concepts of a certain type. There is a widespread temptation to what I am inclined to call *normative isolation of evaluatively charged concepts*, a phenomenon not uncommon in juridical concept formation and a cause of much confusion in juridical thinking.[6] Let me explain what I have in mind by means of some examples. Take the concept "retroactivity". Retroactivity is usually regarded as something bad. This might prompt jurists to define the concept in such a way that it denotes only "bad" instances of retroactivity by the exclusion of other, "good" ones. Or take the concept "discrimination". Here it can be tempting to include only the bad kinds of discrimination, leaving other forms of it outside the scope of the concept. When I investigated the concept "analogy" as a juridical concept I noticed in the literature the tendency in the "opposite" direction. Good analogies were included while bad ones, e.g., analogies within criminal law, were not, which in some cases led to untenable distinctions between analogy and extension. A prime example is, of course, the natural law tenet that the concepts "law" and "legal rule" only cover good or decent law (legal rules), while bad law is excluded from being called "law". What is usually regarded as something bad *is defined as* bad, and what is usually regarded as something good *is defined as* good. Concepts that stand out as based on intellectually objective considerations are in fact crypto-normative. What is wrong with normative isolation of an evaluatively charged concept is, of course, that the conceptual analysis is distorted from the very beginning.

An intellectually acceptable investigation of problems related to concepts of this kind must counteract such normative isolation. Concepts like "retroactivity", "discrimination", "analogy" and "legal rule" must be defined in a way devoid of value judgments. Only then is one in a position to classify, from an evaluative viewpoint, some kinds of, e.g., retroactivity, discrimination, analogy, and legal rules as good and others as indifferent or bad.

A natural way of looking at transitional law would be to conceive of its rules as operating completely within one single national legal system: a transitional rule can never, as a rule of private international law can, point out as applicable any legal system other than the one to which the transitional rule itself belongs. But on the other hand, the transitional rule is a choice-of-law rule and the choice, no doubt, is a choice

[5] Roubier (1960), p. 165.

[6] Such concepts can, but need not be, essentially contested concepts in Gallie's sense (Gallie (1956), pp. 167–198).

between elementary rules belonging to different legal systems, to which the case in question is connected. This observation emphasises a quality of indistinctness as regards the concept "legal system" in the inter-temporal perspective, and when constructing a foundation of transitional law this indistinctness must be removed.

One use of the term "legal system" permits us to speak of, e.g., "Swedish law 2016" and "Swedish law 1916" having in mind the same legal system "Swedish law"—although few of the rules that belonged to the system in 1916 do so in 2016. In other words, such a system can change but still preserve its identity. And when we say that transitional law operates within a legal system, what we have in mind are legal systems of this kind, for which we can use the term *inter-temporal legal systems.*

In connection with transitional law, however, it is appropriate to use one further concept "legal system" such that a given system, S_1, does not preserve its identity but instead transforms into another system, S_2, as soon as any rule is added, altered or repealed. That S_1 "changes" means here that it is replaced by S_2.[7] Raz has coined the term *momentary legal system* for these kinds of systems, and I shall use this well-chosen term here.[8] When we say that transitional rules are choice-of-law rules we mean that they decide choices between different momentary systems.

The relation between momentary and inter-temporal legal systems can be described in the following manner.

(1) A momentary legal system is a system of rules which exists at a given point of time.[9]
(2) An inter-temporal legal system is "a temporary and discrete succession of [momentary] legal orders".[10]

I leave aside the problem of stating conditions for the coming into existence and the expiry of inter-temporal systems. This problem is closely connected to the concept "continuity of law" and leads us straight into Kelsenian problems of no small degree of difficulty.[11]

Let us examine a bit more closely the structure of inter-temporal national legal systems based on statutory law.

By *a sequence of statutes* we refer to a series of statutes which succeed each other immediately.

[7] Cf. Alchourrón and Bulygin (1971), p. 88.

[8] Raz (1980), p. 34.

[9] Raz (1980), p. 34 and Alchourrón and Bulygin (1971), p. 89.

[10] Alchourrón and Bulygin (1971), p. 89. The term "inter-temporal legal system" is mine.

[11] Cf. Finnis (1973), p. 44 ff.

L_1, L_2 and L_3 are statutes succeeding each other temporally in order $L_1 \rightarrow L_2 \rightarrow L_3$. Here and in the following arrows symbolise the flow of time. The ordered set $<L_1, L_2, L_3>$ is a sequence of statutes.

Let S_1 be the system of rules based on L_1, S_2 on L_2, and S_3 on L_3. The ordered set $<S_1, S_2, S_3>$ is *a system sequence*. Between S_1, S_2, and S_3 there is legal continuity.

An inter-temporal national legal system, *IS*, can be seen as a set of system sequences:

$$SS = <S_1, S_2, \ldots, S_k> \in IS$$
$$SS' = <S'_1, S'_2, \ldots, S'_m> \in IS$$
$$SS'' = <S''_1, S''_2, \ldots, S''_n> \in IS$$

etc., where *SS*, *SS'*, and *SS''* are system sequences. Hence

$$IS = \left\{SS, SS', SS'', \ldots\right\}.$$

Through an inter-temporal legal system a "cross-section" at a given point of time can be made. Such a cross-section through *IS* at time *t* is the set, *M*, of all rules in *IS* at *t*. Hence, *M* is a momentary legal system in the succession of momentary systems which together make up *IS* – *M* is "the manifestation of *IS* at *t*".

Out of an inter-temporal system we can cut slices, partial sequences, delimited by two distinct points of time (t_1 and t_n) according to the following schema (S_1–S_6 are system sequences; $IS = S_1, \ldots, S_6$).

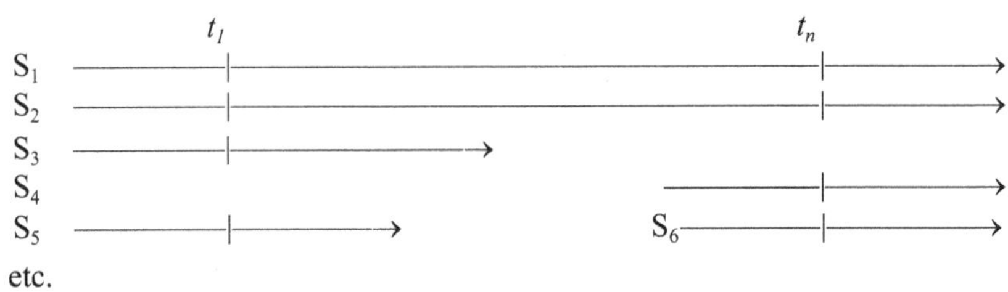

S_1 and S_2 are system sequences extending over the whole period t_1–t_n. S_3 is a sequence that expires during that period, while S_4 is a sequence that begins during the period. S_5 and S_6 illustrate the situation that a sequence, S_5, expires during the period, only to "revive" as a new sequence, S_6, after a period of "legal rest".

Suppose that we have two systems, S_1 and S_2, and that S_2 succeeds S_1. Then S_2 is the successor of S_1 and S_1 the predecessor of S_2.

In Sect. 12.2 we shall present some basic concepts of transitional law and in Sect. 12.3 we formulate the problems of transitional law and their solutions from the viewpoint of principle.

12.2 Basic Concepts of Transitional Law

All transitional law involves three different kinds of phenomena and the relations between such phenomena:

(1) time components: points of time, spaces of time (time intervals between occurrences)
(2) states of affairs (factual or imagined; individual or generic): cases, occurrences, situations, actions, etc.
(3) normative legal components: legal rules.

We take our point of departure in a conventional concept of time, sufficient for our purposes, based on the following conditions:

(a) We use an objective concept of time, not a concept of subjectively experienced time.
(b) Time is regarded as a linear order of discrete points of time, not as a continuum.
(c) Time has a direction; it "flows" from the past to the future (in our representation from left to right). The point of time where the past conquers the future is the now. This enables us to talk about an occurrence as existing before, simultaneously with, and after another one.
(d) Time is measurable.

Our simple model of representation, based on these conditions, has the following structure.

(i) t, t' or $t_1, \ldots, t_n$ are variables for points of time.
(ii) $\longrightarrow$ is a linear order of discrete points of time where, for any arbitrary points of time, t_i and t_j, t_j occurs later than t_i if and only if t_j is situated on the right of t_i on the arrow.
(iii) $<$ is a point of time that is a *terminus a quo* (the starting point of some occurrence) and $>$ a point of time that is a *terminus ad quem* (the point of time where an occurrence ceases to exist). All other points of time are symbolised by |.

Example:

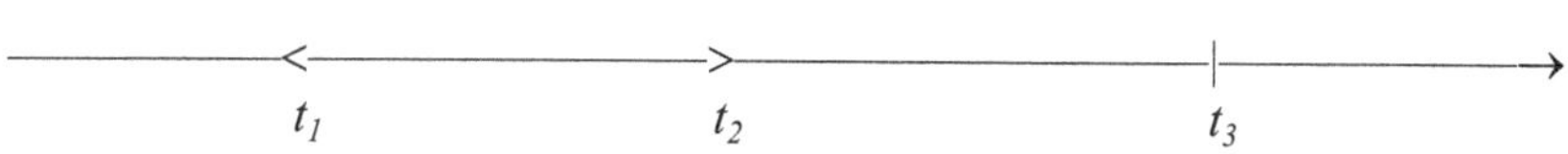

where t_1 is a *terminus a quo* and t_2 a *terminus ad quem* for some occurrence, and t_3 is a point of time not indicating any time limit.

We can now construct a model of representation in, for example, the following manner

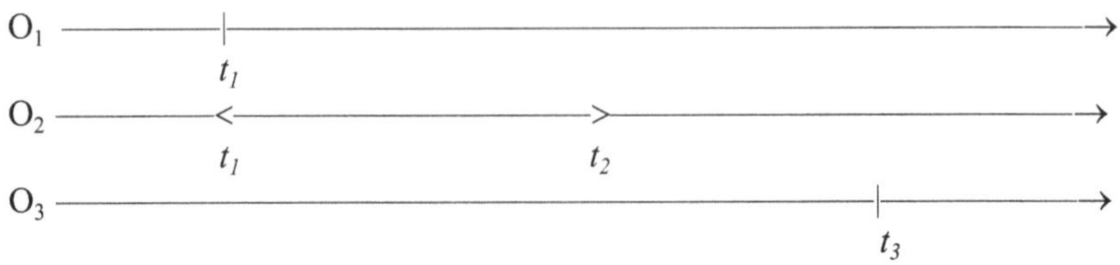

in order to indicate that an occurrence, O_1 takes place simultaneously with the beginning of another occurrence, O_2, but before O_2 ends, and that still another occurrence, O_3, takes place after O_2 has ended.

As appears from this, our model of representation is inspired by the standard Western musical notation. Also the musical notation, as we all know, makes use of parallel lines where the direction of time goes from left to right and where different musical occurrences are indicated on (and between) the lines.

By means of this model of representation we shall define some basic concepts of transitional law. These concepts can be divided into two different conceptual families.

The first family consists of concepts predicated on legal rules, and all of them designate some kind of rules *being in force.* If "x-force" is a variable for these kinds of being in force, then the concepts belonging to this family all have the structure "rule r has x-force (is in x-force) during t_1–t_n".

The second family consists of topological concepts predicated on cases and all of them describe some temporal relation between cases and rules in force, e.g., the concepts *factum praeteritum*, *factum pendens* and *factum futurum* (to be explained below). Relatives in this family are also some concepts of a procedural nature closely related to the former, *causa finita* and *causa pendens.*

Statutory rules are symbolised by r, r' etc. or by $r_1, \ldots, r_n$,. We use r' to symbolise the immediate successor of r. Cases are symbolised by c, c' etc.

When in the following we discuss transitional relations between rules and cases we of course take it for granted that the rules by virtue of their content are applicable to the cases.

A. Let us begin with concepts belonging to the first family, *the being-in-force concepts.*

In order to ascertain whether a rule is in force at a time t or not we need, on the one hand, criteria stating the conditions for a rule coming into force and, on the other hand, criteria for a rule to be annulled. Then we can say that r is in force at t if and only if the coming-into-force criteria are fulfilled with regard to r but not the being-annulled criteria at t.

Here I deliberately refrain from a discussion about these two sets of criteria. They are to a high degree system-dependent: they vary from one legal system to another. It is, however, not logically impossible to formulate general, system-independent criteria of this kind, although they of necessity must be rather abstract. (One suggestion could be the following coming-into-force criteria: *r* comes into force at *t* if *r* has come about in a constitutionally correct way, *r* has been stated in a legally correct manner to come into force at *t* and *t* is now—and the following being-annulled criteria: *r* is annulled at t' if *r* has come into force, has not previously been annulled, has been stated to be annulled at t', and t' is now.)

For reasons that I shall now present, this kind of being-in-force can be characterised as *unspecified.* There is, namely, a certain complication connected with the term "being in force".[12] Suppose that we have a rule, *r*, criminalising certain types of actions, *A*. *r* is explicitly, according to a transitional provision, coming into force January 1, 1995, and is annulled December 31, 2014. Suppose further that an action, *a*, of type *A*, committed in November 2014, is not tried before a court of law until May 2015. So, in spite of the fact that *r* then is no longer in (unspecified) force, it might well happen—and does, in fact, often happen for certain types of cases—that *a* shall be decided according to *r*. Then we are faced with something that has a certain resemblance to a paradox: *r* seems to be in force although it is not in force.

This is, of course, not a genuine paradox but a default of our juridical language, which is not rich enough to cope with apparent paradoxes of this kind. A simple distinction can take care of that.

Let us, for this purpose, make a distinction between *case-related force* (*C-force*, for short) and *decision-related force* (*D-force*, for short).

r has C-force during the space of time when cases covered by the requisites of *r* must occur, according to transitional law, in order to be lawfully decided by the use of *r*.

r has D-force during the space of time when decisions given according to *r* are lawful, i.e., during the space of time when the legal consequences of *r* are lawfully attached to cases falling under *r* according to transitional law—i.e., cases that have occurred when *r* had C-force.

So in our example above *r* has C-force between January 1, 1995, and December 31, 2014—and D-force as from January 1, 1995, up to that point of time when every possible crime of type *A* committed between January 1, 1995, and December 31, 2014, falls under the statute of limitations, i.e., from that point of time at which we arrive when the period of limitation is counted from the point of time when the C-force of *r* expires.

By means of our distinction between C-force and D-force we are now able to define three different kinds of being in force as predicated on (statutory) legal rules: being in force *retroactively*, *simulactively*, and *infraactively*. The term "retroactivity" is a classical one; the other two are inventions of mine.

When we talk, in juridical discourse, about rules being in force, we do that on two separate levels, one where we relate "being-in-force" to some given case, *c*,—*r* is in

[12]Clearly pointed out by Strömberg (1972), p. 668.

force with respect to *c*—and one where we do not relate a case and a rule in this way but speak more generally.

Case-related being-in-force can be represented like this:

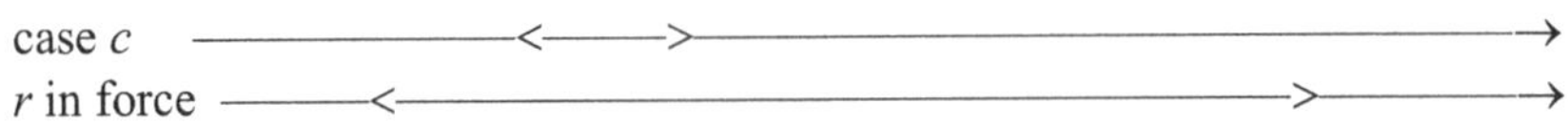

and generally being in force (*r* is in force during t_1–t_n):

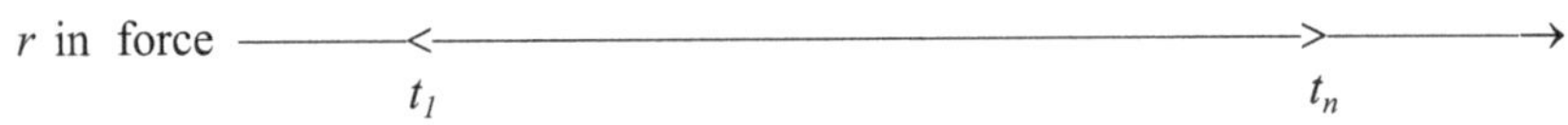

This distinction also applies to *retroactivity*, *simulactivity* and *infraactivity*. Let us first define these concepts on a general level.

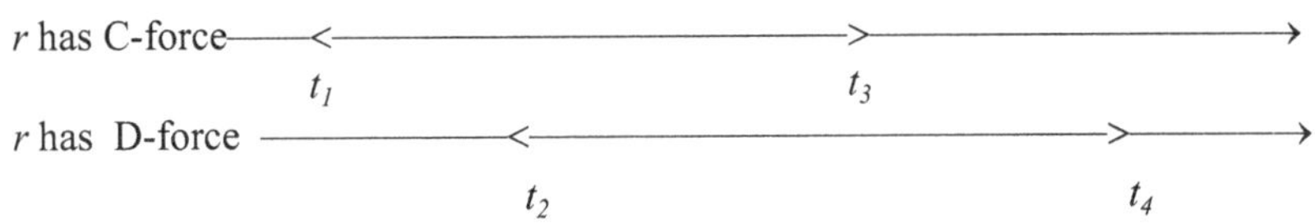

We say that

(i) *r* is in force retroactively during the period t_1–t_2
(ii) *r* is in force simulactively during the period t_2–t_3
(iii) *r* is in force infraactively during the period t_3–t_4

Or, in other words,

(i′) *r* is in force retroactively during the period when *r* has C-force but not D-force
(ii′) *r* is in force simulactively during the period when *r* has both C-force and D-force
(iii′) *r* is in force infraactively when *r* has D-force but not C-force.

Then we define case-related retroactivity, simulactivity and infraactivity.

(a) Case-related retroactivity (*r* is retroactively applied to *c*):

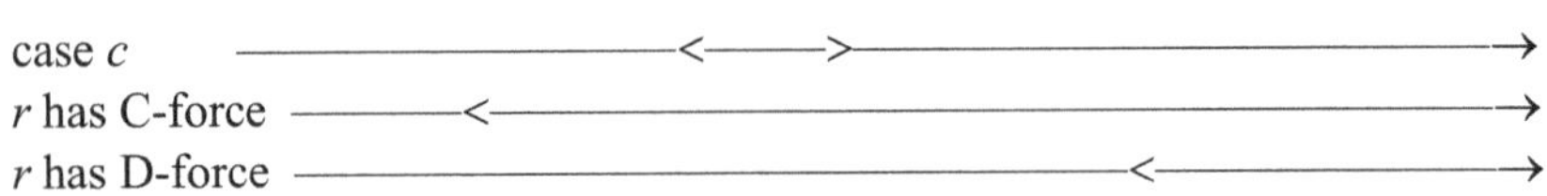

(b) Case-related simulactivity:

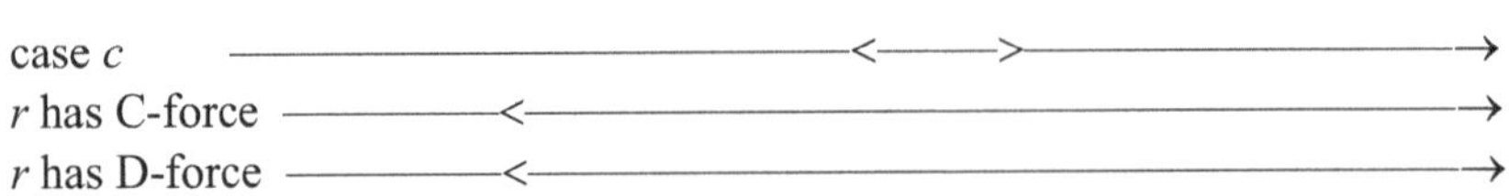

(c) Case-related infraactivity:

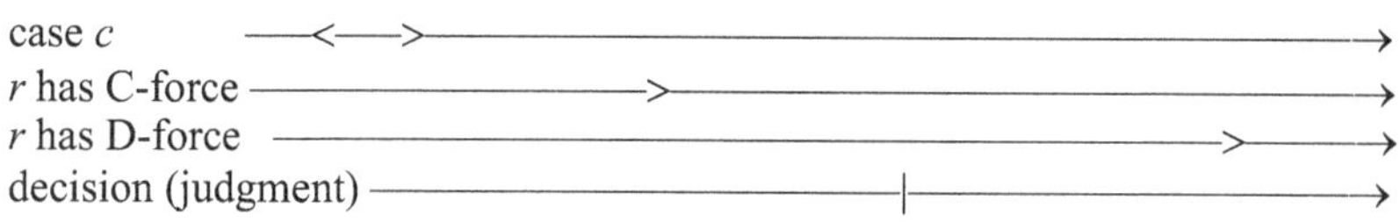

B. We now turn to the second family of temporal juridical concepts, viz., *concepts predicated on cases.*

Cases (operative facts) can, with respect to their temporal relation to the being-in-force of rules, be divided into three kinds, known already in Roman times[13]: *facta praeterita* (sing. *factum praeteritum*), *facta pendentia* (sing. *factum pendens*), and *facta futura* (sing. *factum futurum*). We define them in the following way.

(1) *Factum praeteritum* (*c* is a *factum praeteritum*)

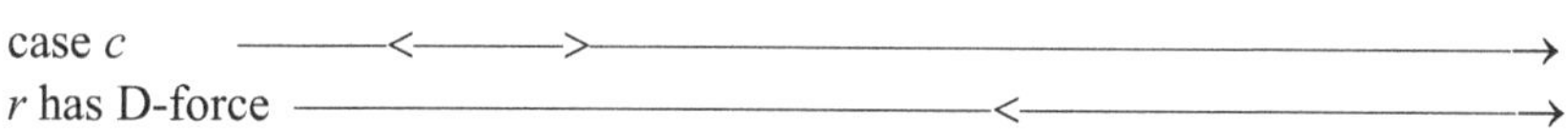

(2) *Factum pendens* (*c* is a *factum pendens*)

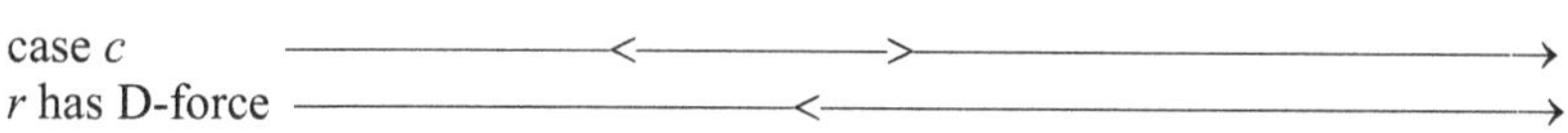

(3) *Factum futurum* (*c* is a *factum futurum*)

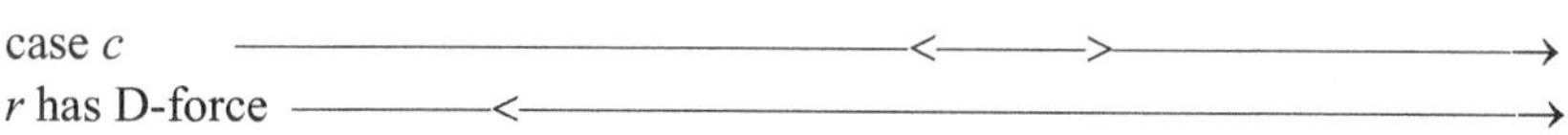

Moreover, to this family belong two concepts with a distinct procedural flavour, *causa finita* and *causa pendens*. Also these concepts have a Roman origin.[14] The ambiguous term "*causa*" is here used in the sense of "litigation". A *causa finita* is a litigation that is ended before a certain legal rule comes into D-force and a *causa pendens* a litigation that is going on when a certain rule comes into D-force. In our notation:

[13]Roubier (1960), pp. 33 ff.

[14]They are used by *inter alia* Paulus and Ulpianus. Roubier (1960), p. 32.

(4) *Causa finita* (the litigation is a *causa finita*)

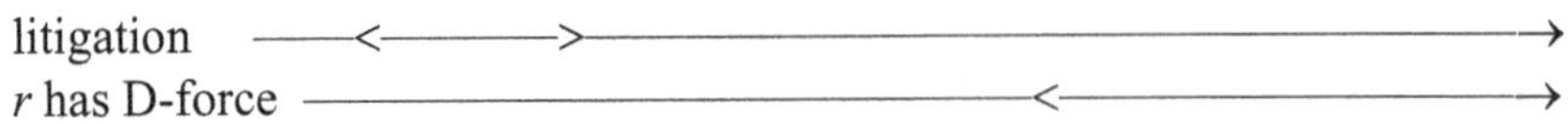

(5) *Causa pendens* (the litigation is a *causa pendens*):

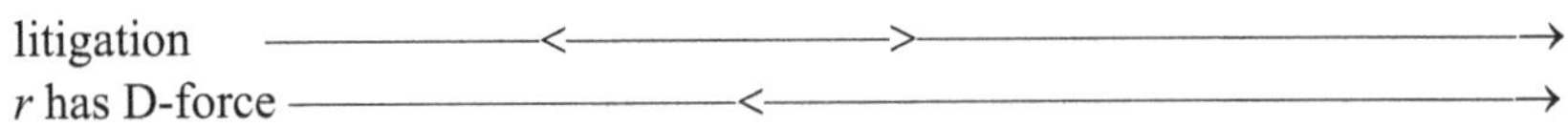

Finally, we have to make use of the concept of *trigger*. A trigger is an action by means of which some legal procedure is initiated, e.g., the action of commencing a prosecution. The point of time when a trigger is used can be seen as the *terminus a quo* for the litigation (while its *terminus ad quem* is the point of time for the judgment or, for some purposes, the point of time when the judgment acquires legal force, i.e., when the case becomes a *res judicata*).

After this exposition about legal rules being in force it might be objected: But we have not yet learnt what it in fact means that a legal rule is in force. What does the legislator have in mind when he, through some transitional statutory provision, declares that some statute enters into force at a certain point of time?

The answer to that question seems to me to be a simple one. What the legislator wants to achieve by a transitional rule of the type

(*tr*) This statute comes into force at *t*

is, of course, that the statute is complied with from *t*, i.e., that the citizens follow it in adequate circumstances and the relevant authorities apply it when it is brought to the fore in adequate circumstances. Thus it presents itself immediately to conceive of *tr* as a norm obliging citizens and authorities to comply with it from *t*:

(tr_n) This statute shall be complied with from *t*

But the fact that *r* is in force is, of course, not equivalent to—and does not imply—that *r* is valid. tr_n does not say that *r* is valid, it says that *r* shall be valid. From this "self-assumed validity" it does not follow that *r* is in fact valid.

In Chap. 13 we shall come back to the concept "validity". Suffice it to say here that a rule is valid if it is in relevant situations in fact applied by and large by the relevant authorities.

Let us have a look at the following situations:

(1)

Here *r* has total validity: *r* is valid during exactly the same period of time as it has D-force. Total validity is a legislative ideal, based on (i) the idea that individuals are in a state of legal uncertainty if rules in force are not applied and (ii) the idea that rules no longer desirable shall be rejected from the legal system.

But total validity is not always the case.

(2)

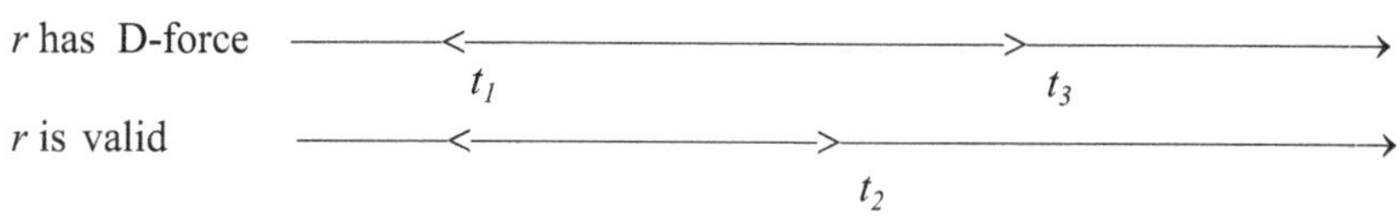

During the period t_2–t_3 *r* is *obsolete* (it has fallen into desuetude).

(3) Also this situation is possible:

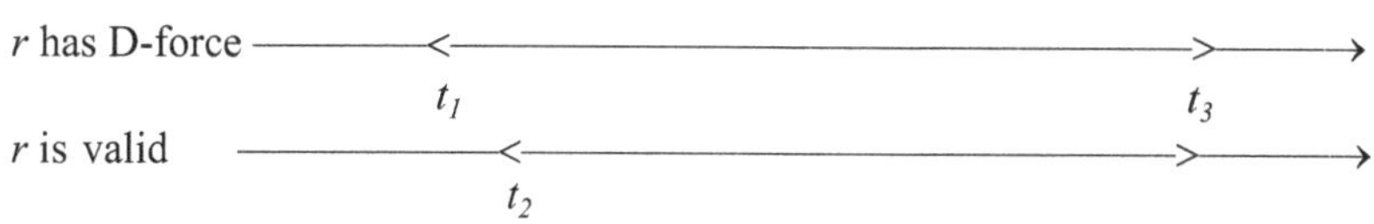

Also this situation can be regarded as a kind of desuetude. *r* is obsolete during the period t_1–t_2. Example: Suppose that a statute to the effect that it is obligatory to use seat belts has D-force from January 1 a certain year. Suppose further that the police want people to get used to the new regulation and therefore abstain from fining people breaking the law during the period January 1 to January 31. During this period the statute is, in a sense, obsolete.

(4)

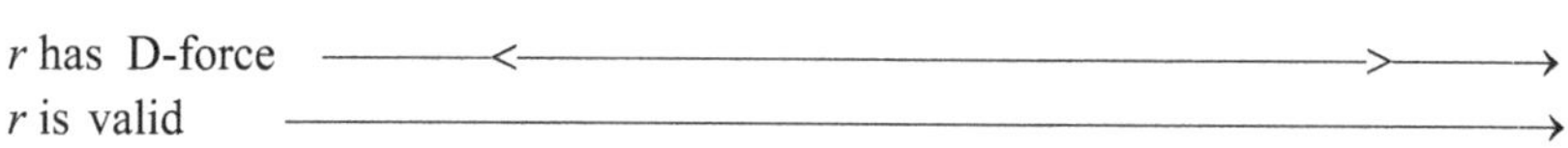

The strange situation is illustrated here where a rule is in force but never applied when brought to the fore. The rule is, as it were, obsolete already from the start. The situation can be described as pathological, or perverted. It may well happen that this situation is in fact wanted by the legislator, whose aim with the statute in question might be, e.g., to exhibit a false front of "law-stateness" to the surrounding world.

We have now constructed a piece of conceptual machinery, subtle enough, I think, to allow us to formulate transitional problems and their solutions from the viewpoint of principle in a more precise manner than is usually the case. In the next section we shall put the machinery to work.

12.3 Problems and Solutions in Transitional Law

12.3.1 Introduction

Let us adopt the position of the legislator. Suppose that we are about to substitute a rule r' for another one in force, r. The transitional problems can, on a general level, be stated like this:

(1) When shall the C-force of r expire?
(2) When shall the D-force of r expire?
(3) When shall the C-force of r' begin?
(4) When shall the D-force of r' begin?

Sometimes also the following questions are relevant already at the moment of issuing r':

(5) When shall the C-force of r' expire?
(6) When shall the D-force of r' expire?

The answers to these questions are, of course, dependent on considerations of a legal-political nature. But there is also a purely technical aspect involved, viz., to map out the spectrum of possible solutions available to the legislator.

In Sects. 12.3.2, 12.3.3, 12.3.4, 12.3.5, 12.3.6 we investigate problems pertaining to questions (1)–(4) and in Sect. 12.3.7 problems pertaining to questions (5)–(6). Problems pertaining to questions (1)–(4) can be of different kinds. Let us look a bit more closely at the following main problems (A–E).

A. Let us begin with question (4): *When shall the D-force of* r' *begin?*

   An extreme solution is to let r' come into force already simultaneously with its promulgation. We call that solution *immediate coming into D-force.* From this extreme solution the legislator can digress; the more so, the longer the time he allows to pass between promulgation and coming into D-force.

   This question will be dealt with in Sect. 12.3.2.

B. Another question is: *Shall r be in force infraactively after* r' *has come into (C- and D-) force?* This question is a reformulation of question (2).

   An extreme solution is to let the (C- and D-) force of r expire when r' comes into force, i.e., not to give r any infraactivity at all. Let us call that solution *minimum infraactivity.* From this extreme the legislator can digress; the more so, the longer time he allows infraactive force to r.

   This question will be dealt with in Sect. 12.3.3.

C. Still another question is: *Shall* r' *be applicable to facta pendentia?* The answer to this question is a component of the answer to question (3)—and, hence, also to question (1).

An extreme solution is to let r' be applicable to all *facta pendentia*. Let us call this solution *maximum pendens-retroactivity*. From this extreme solution legislators can digress; the more so, the fewer kinds of *facta pendentia* he allows r' to be applicable to. In the following we us the terms *retropendency* as short for "pendens-retroacticity" (the retropendency of r') and *infrapendency* for "pendens-infraactivity" (the infrapendency of r)—regardless of any linguistic inadequacy I might be guilty of in so doing.

This question will be dealt with in Sect. 12.3.4.

D. A fourth question is: *Shall r' be applicable retroactively*, i.e., Shall r' be applicable to *facta praeterita*? The answer also to this question is a component of the answers to questions (3) and (1).

An extreme solution is to let r' be applicable to all *facta praeterita*. We call that solution *maximum retroactivity*. From this extreme solution the legislator can digress; the more so, the fewer kinds of *facta praeterita* he allows r' to be applicable to.

This question will be dealt with in Sect. 12.3.5.

E. A sub-question to D is: *Shall r' be applicable to facta praeterita with restitutive retroactivity*, i.e., Shall r' be applicable to *causae finitae*?

By "restitutive retroactivity" we mean that also *facta praeterita* that have already been legally decided by courts of law or other law-applying bodies (*causae finitae*) are repealed and subject to re-examination according to a later law (we leave aside problems connected with *causae pendentes*). Of course, restitutive retroactivity is a most extraordinary measure. However, it is, as we shall see, not unknown in Western legal history.

An extreme solution is to let r' be applicable to all *causae finitae*. We call that solution *maximum restitutive retroactivity*. From this extreme solution the legislator can digress; the more so, the fewer *causae finitae* he allows r' to be applicable to.

This question will be dealt with in Sect. 12.3.6.

We have now defined "extreme solutions" to five types of transitional problems. These are (i) immediate coming into D-force, (ii) minimum infraactivity (of r), (iii) maximum retropendency, (iv) maximum retroactivity, and (v) maximum restitutive retroactivity. From each of these extreme solutions the legislator can digress in the directions mentioned.

Every extreme solution implies that r' is given *maximum impact* in its competition with the older rule r—or, in other words, that r' with the highest degree of effectiveness eliminates r when transitional problems are solved.

But the five extreme solutions, in their mutual relationships, also indicate different degrees of the impact of r' in its relation to r. The series (i)–(v) of solutions indicates an intensification of the impact of r' relative to r. If the legislator were to choose all these solutions, he would give *r' a total maximum impact relative to r*. This situation is an ideal-type situation and real-type situations are digressions from it. (I take it to be obvious that "ideal-type" is used here in the Weberian, non-normative sense.) This conceptualisation allows us to say that a given solution, S_1, gives r' a greater (or smaller) impact relative to r than another solution, S_2.

12.3.2 Rule r' Coming into D-Force

The legislator can let a shorter or longer period of time pass between the point of time when r' is promulgated and the point of time when r' comes into force.

The standard solution looks like this:

r has C-force————————>————————————→
r has D-force——————————>——————————→
r' is promulgated ——|————————————————→
r' has C-force ————————<————————————→
r' has D-force ————————<————————————→

The Swedish Code of Judicial Procedure now in force was promulgated in 1942 but did not come into (C- and D-) force until 1948. Such a long interval may be justified when the new order involves a radical change and the legislator for that reason wants the authorities and the public to have ample time to adjust themselves to the new law and its consequences. During that period information can be distributed, new institutions established, professional routines changed or implemented, training of officials performed, etc. Circumstances of these kinds were to a great extent present with respect to the replacement of the Swedish Code of Judicial Procedure.

On the other hand a short, or even non-existent, interval might be justified when the effect of the new law would be weakened if the public had the opportunity to take measures in order to evade these effects—i.e., situations where the very point of the new law is to take the public by surprise, e.g., statutes concerning price-freeze, drain of foreign exchange and certain taxes. It must be emphasised, however, that immediate coming-into-force borders on retroactivity and, hence, must be used only for very good reasons.

12.3.3 Infraactivity

To let the C-force and the D-force of r be annulled simultaneously is in a way to let its successor r' come into force retroactively. For if a case, which took place while r had C-force, is brought to the fore after r has been annulled simultaneously, the case will be decided according to r':

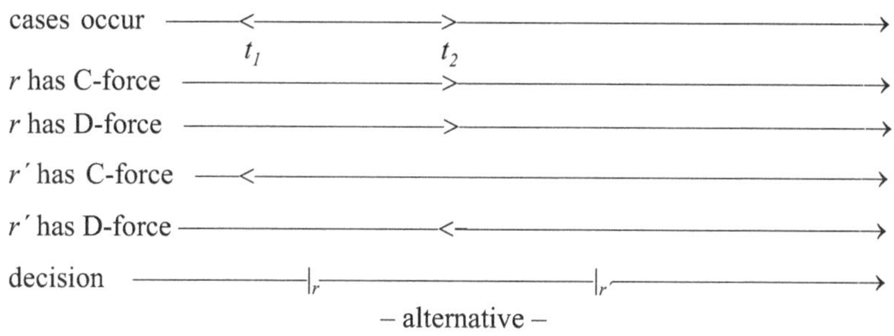

Hence, cases occurring during the period t_1–t_2 will be decided according to *r* if decided before the D-force of *r* is annulled and according to *r*′ if they are decided after that point of time. In this sense *r*′ is in force retroactively if the C-force and D-force of *r* are annulled simultaneously. During the interval t_1–t_2 there is "a divided C-force": *r* has C-force with respect to some cases and *r*′ with respect to other cases. Before t_1 *r* has *complete* C-force and so has *r*′ from t_2.

The situation now described is a "borderline case" of the infraactivity of *r*: minimum infraactivity (i.e., no infraactivity at all). Minimum infraactivity is the one end of a possible space of time, whose opposite end—maximum infraactivity—is the point of time when any bringing to the fore of cases that have taken place when *r* had C-force becomes impossible. This might be the case due to physical necessity or factors of a legal character, such as limitations.

In criminal law strong reasons based on the ideal of legal certainty speak in favour of a maximum infraactivity *in mitius*, i.e., if *r* allows for a more lenient sanction than *r*′, *r* shall be applicable to all cases which have occurred during the period when *r* had C-force, however long after the end of that period a case is brought to the fore.

12.3.4 Retropendency and Infrapendency

There are *facta pendentia* of many different kinds, and often a very long time can pass between the beginning of a pendency case and its consummation. Let us, in order to illuminate some problems connected with *facta pendentia*, take our starting point in a special case of this kind.

In 1970 Swedish law gave illegitimate children a right of inheritance after their biological father and his relatives. Of course the new law should be applicable to illegitimate children born after the coming into D-force of the provisions to this effect. But what about the pendency cases where the paternity had been established before that point of time—perhaps decades earlier—but the death of the father occurs after it?

Let c be a case of this kind and let us regard the birth of the child as its *terminus a quo* and the death of the father as its *terminus ad quem*.

The legislator has three possible solutions here:

1. c is comprised by the C-force of r'
2. c is comprised by the C-force of r
3. c is comprised by the C-force of r if its *terminus a quo* occurs before some stipulated point of time, t^*, and comprised by the C-force of r' if its *terminus a quo* occurs after t^*.

Expressed in our model of representation:

Solution 1.

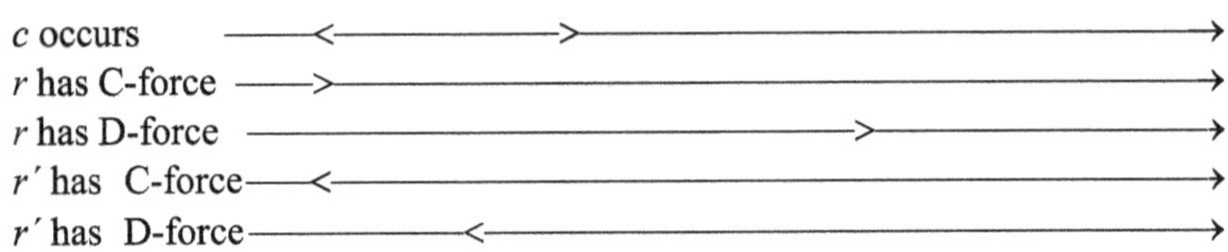

This solution (maximum retropendency) was in fact chosen by the legislator.

Solution 2.

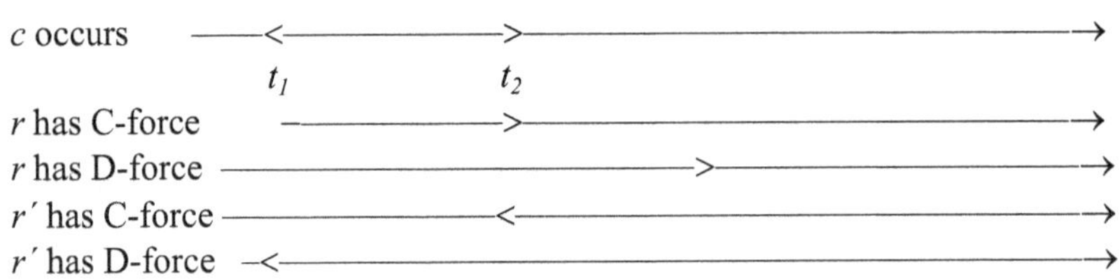

Although r' formally has D-force from t_1, it cannot be applied until t_2. t_1 is the time for an unspecified coming-into-force according to the statutory text.

Solution 3.

Let t_i be the *terminus a quo* of c.

(a) if $t_i \geq t^*$: solution 1
(b) if $t_i < t^*$: solution 2
("≥" signifies "earliest at" and "<" signifies "before". ">" below will signify "after".)

Solution 1 gives maximum retropendency to r' (and minimum infrapendency to r) and solution 2 minimum retropendency to r' (and maximum infrapendency to r). Solution 3 is an intermediate position between solutions 1 and 2.

In the example chosen, what speaks in favour of solution 1 is that the new regulation has a stronger impact from the start and that the system of rules regulating the matters in question is less complicated. In favour of solution 2 would be the argument that inheritance rights do not risk being founded on an old, from a scientific viewpoint dubious, establishment of paternity and that such rights are not extended to cases where father and child are complete strangers to one another and the father has a family life perhaps someplace else in the world. On the other hand, a weighty argument against solution 2 is that, if chosen, the new regulation will not acquire full impact until many decades have passed. Solution 3 might seem like a good compromise, but has a touch of arbitrariness.

Generally speaking, we have two possible solutions to pendency problems. Either the old or the new law is applicable. The principle that the old law shall prevail we call *the infrapendency principle* and the principle that the new law shall prevail we call *the retropendency principle.*

A spectacular example of the use of the infrapendency principle in Swedish law is the old marriage code, which was succeeded in 1920 by a new one, which, in turn, was replaced by another in 1987. But with respect to matters of property the old marriage code, whose unspecified force expired in 1920, continued to be applicable to marriages entered into before 1921 until the last of these venerable marriages became extinct in the 1990s.

In favour of *the retropendency principle* the following arguments are important. (a) If the legislator has substituted the new regulation for the old one he must, in all likelihood, regard the new one as better than the old one. Therefore it should be applicable as soon as possible. This argument, however, requires some substantial qualifications. (b) The same kind of argument is relevant *a fortiori* when the new law is intended to eliminate considerable social evils. (c) If the new law gives expression to new ideas of a moral or social character, these ideas should gain impact as soon as possible. This argument is often of great importance in family law. (d) Retropendency might, as has already been pointed out, be justified with respect to legislation concerning financial policy in times of economic crisis, where the effects of the law depend upon surprise in order to avoid circumvention of the law. (e) If the infrapendency principle is used, we have double systems of rules which exist parallel to each other for, perhaps, a long period of time. This makes the total legal system more complicated, which can threaten legal certainty. (f) If the infrapendency principle is used, it might take a very long time before the new law has a full effect. (g) If the most important (weightiest) of the components that together constitute the case (the *factum pendens*) have occurred after the new law has acquired D-force, then the new law should prevail since the case has a greater connection to that law (compare international private law).

In favour of *the infrapendency principle* the following arguments are important. (a) This principle has its greatest importance with respect to legislative interference with lasting legal relations, especially contractual ones. Such relations often extend over a considerable span of time. The contractual mechanism would function in a less effective manner if the parties could not foresee the legal effects of their contract when entering into it. It has little meaning to enter into a contract if one cannot rely on the legal consequences agreed upon to hold good. (b) Retropendency is a marginal case of retroactivity. Hence, the arguments against retroactivity can be launched against retropendency as well. Also this argument, however, requires important qualifications. (c) If the most important (weightiest) of the components that together constitute the case have occurred before the new law has acquired D-force, then the old law should prevail since the case has a greater connection to that law.

12.3.5 *Retroactivity*

That r' is applicable retroactively means

(1) either that r' shall be applied to *facta praeterita* brought to the fore (by some procedural trigger) at a point of time not earlier than the point of time when r' comes into D-force:

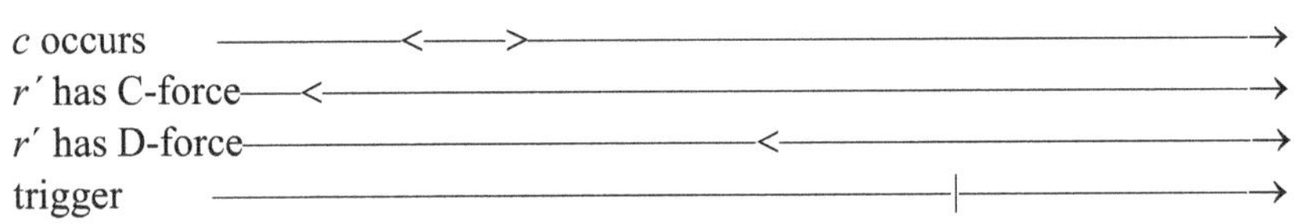

(2) or that r' shall be applied to *facta praeterita* brought to the fore at a point of time earlier than the point of time when r' comes into D-force but where the decision (judgment) is given after that point of time (*causa pendens*-retroactivity):

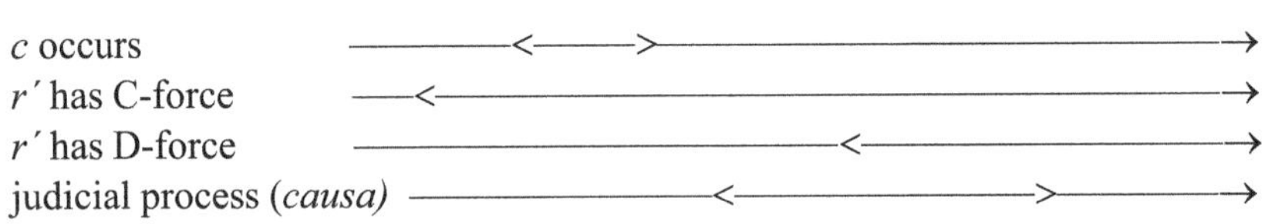

r' has the more impact, the longer back in the past it is allowed to have retroactive effect. If no time limit is stipulated, r' has *maximum retroactivity.*

An extreme variant of retroactivity is *exclusive retroactivity*:

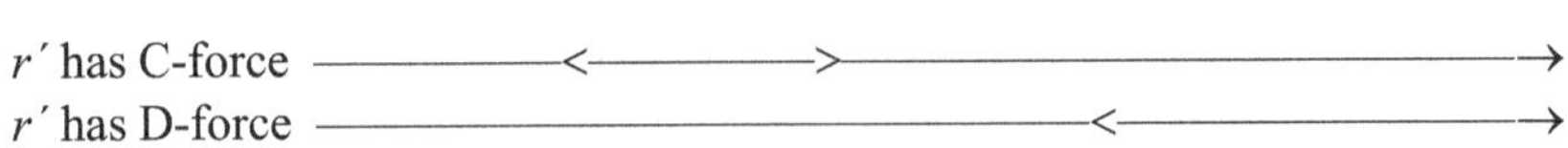

Exclusive retroactivity means that the rule in question cannot be applied to any other cases than cases already consummated before the rule comes into D-force. This is, of course, an extraordinary phenomenon, although not completely unknown.

Thus, in 1952 a so-called "state of the market tax" to that effect was imposed in Sweden, and the only purpose of the statute was to absorb trade profits earned in the years before.

The main reasons *against* retroactive legislation are the following.

1. Retroactive legislation violates the value of legal certainty[15] and the reason for that is the following. A rational person who at time t is thinking about performing one of many alternative actions bases his decision on the weighing of the pros and cons of the various alternatives. Some of these pros and cons are legal effects that the legal system connects with actions of the kind under consideration—or that the legal system in a foreseeable future is likely to connect with them. In both cases our agent has to make his decision on the basis of the information on legal and factual matters available to him at t.

   But suppose that the legislator at a time t' ($t' > t$) retroactively changes the legal system in such a way that the action a that our agent chose to perform at t has other legal consequences tied to it than it had at t, that these legal consequences are such that a becomes a worse alternative for him than at least one of the other alternatives he considered at t and that he could not, at t, predict the change of the law. This means that he is subjected to an inconvenience by having performed an action he would not have performed had he known about the coming change of the law. The first main argument against retroactive legislation is that one should not put people in situations like this. Legal consequences of an action *already performed* must not, according to this argument, be changed *after the action has been performed.*

   So what is dubious with retroactive legislation from the viewpoint of legal certainty is (1) that the agent is subjected to legal consequences that he had no reason to expect as effects of his action—since these effects were not the legal consequences of his action at the time of its performance and (2) that he is not affected by the legal consequences he had reason to expect as effects of his action—although these effects were the legal consequences of the action at the time of its performance. And what is more: he can do nothing about it, since the consequences he is in fact subjected to are completely determined by an action already performed. With respect to the past we are all, I guess, fatalists.

   As we all know, legal certainty is of particular importance within the areas of law where the state can deprive the individual of freedom and property, or even her life—i.e., within criminal law, tax law, and medical care (treatment against one's own will). But legal certainty is, of course, of the utmost importance in all areas of law.
2. Retroactive legislation can also violate the value of equality in the law. If two persons, A and B, are placed in exactly the same kind of legal position at a given point of time, and A performs an action which—later—has a negative consequence for A because of a retroactive law, while B does not perform an action of

[15]Cf. Frändberg (2014), Ch. 6, esp. at pp. 123 f.

that kind, then B's position is better than A's and that due to circumstances beyond both A's and B's control.

3. As for *causa pendens*-retroactivity, there is also an argument of a procedural-strategic nature. Suppose that a person has brought an action believing that the case will be decided according to the law in force then, but a new law becomes applicable to the case retroactively during the trial. Perhaps that person, had she known this, would have chosen a completely different procedural strategy, or not even brought the action at all.

There are two main reasons *for* retroactive legislation.

1. If the new law instead of increasing penalties, taxes or other burdens on the contrary reduces them, the hesitation regarding retroactive law is, of course, less. It might even be the case that the new law *shall* be applied retroactively. This is the case in the criminal law of many countries when the new law attaches a less severe punishment to the crime than the old law, or if crimes are decriminalised by the new law (retroactivity *in mitius*, according to the principle of *lex mitior*) This exception from the prohibition of retroactive legislation in criminal law is justified by the value of legal certainty as well as by considerations pertaining to criminal policy.
2. There are extraordinary situations where the task is to radically and resolutely disarm an older legal system. This is the case when tidying up after, e.g., a dictatorship that has violated the most basic values of humanity and law-state thinking, such as Nazi Germany. In order to quickly and efficiently remove the "pathological" parts of the system retroactive legislation might be a powerful instrument. Even restitutive retroactive legislation might then be appropriate, e.g., in order to restore confiscated property to the deprived—Jews or class enemies or whatever kind of persons the power-holders in their arrogance had taken the liberty to regard as less human, or even non-human. Such a step can be compared to that of a doctor curing a sick person with a medicine that would make a healthy person sick.

12.3.6 Restitutive Retroactivity

A rule, r', applies with restitutive retroactivity when r' applies to *causae finitae*, i.e., to *facta praeterita* already decided by courts of law or other law-applying bodies. This means that old decisions are repealed and decided according to the new law:

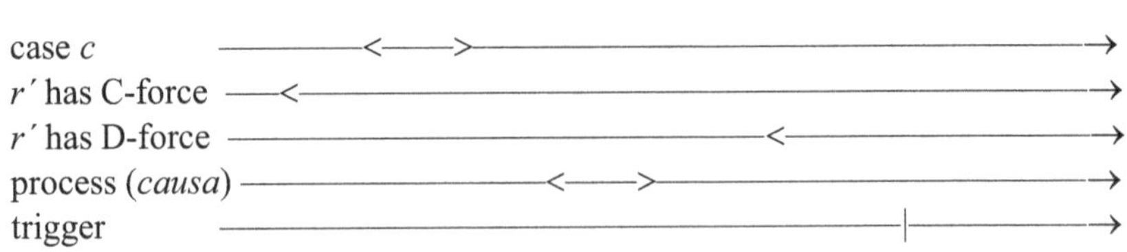

To use restitutive retroactivity is, of course, a most extraordinary legislative measure. However, it is not unknown in Western legal history. The inheritance act passed by the French revolutionary legislators in the month of *Nivôse* in year II had retroactive force from the 14th of July 1789 (a date surely not chosen by chance) and all decisions made according to older law were repealed.[16]

The main reason against restitutive retroactivity is that it collides with the principle *ne bis in idem*, i.e., that a decided case is a *res judicata* and as such immune from new trials. This principle is an important part of law-state thinking, for without it legal certainty in the respect that you can trustfully act according to the content of the law is, indeed, precarious.

12.3.7 Imposing Time Limits on Rules' Being-in-Force

When statutes are promulgated they are usually intended to be in force during an indeterminate period of time in the future. But it happens now and then that the legislator, already when issuing a new statute, stipulates that its being-in-force shall be annulled at a certain future point of time. He then answers the questions raised in Sect. 12.3.1:

(5) When shall the C-force of r' expire?
(6) When shall the D-force of r' expire?

The stipulated (unspecified) point of time here shall usually be regarded as the time for the annulment of the C-force, whereupon the D-force abates in the usual way. Reasons for imposing a time limit on statutes are, e.g., (i) that there is need for a rapid intervention against some acute evil in society and the legislator wants to act quickly with perhaps a not too well worked-out piece of legislation, (ii) that the statute gives the authorities a far-reaching power to violate the personal integrity of individuals, for instance the authority to use telephone tapping when investigating serious crimes, and the legislator wants to review these powers at certain intervals—and then, of course, it is of importance that the legislator does not yield to routine-like prolongation—or (iii) that the legislator wants to experiment in order to test certain legislative measures—in which case it is of great importance that such an experiment does not affect some group of people ("the guinea pigs") in an unduly discriminatory way.

[16] Roubier (1960), p. 286.

References

Affolter F (1902) Geschichte des intertemporalen Privatrechts
Affolter F (1903) System des deutschen bürgerlichen Übergangsrechts
Alchourrón C, Bulygin E (1971) Normative systems. Springer, Berlin
Cavaglieri A (1904) Diritto internazionale privato e diritto transitorio. Fratelli Drucker, Padua
Finnis JM (1973) Revolutions and continuity of law. In: Simpson AWB (ed) Oxford essays in jurisprudence, second series. Oxford University Press, Oxford, pp 44 ff
Frändberg Å (2014) From Rechtsstaat to universal law-state. Springer, Berlin
Gallie WB (1956) Essentially contested concepts. In: Proceedings of the Aristotelian Society, vol 56. pp 167–198
Level P (1959) Essai de systématisation du conflit de lois dans le temps, La Librairie générale de droit et de jurisprudence
Raz J (1980) The concept of a legal system, 2nd edn. Oxford University Press, Oxford
Roubier P (1960) Le droit transitoire, 2nd edn. Dalloz et Sirey, Paris
Strömberg T (1972) Om retroaktivitet, in Festskrift till Per Olof Ekelöf

Chapter 13
Some Basic Praxeological Concepts: Application of Law and Validity of Law

13.1 Introduction: Some Remarks on General Praxeology

Praxeological concepts are concepts signifying actions and phenomena logically (conceptually, necessarily) related to actions. The philosophical investigation of praxeological concepts we call, following von Wright, *praxeology*.[1]

The key concept is, of course, the concept *action* (act, acting, activity) itself. I do not have the intention here to offer an investigation of this concept itself. My purpose is much more modest. It is only to formulate a conception sufficient to give sense to what I have to say about juridical praxeology.

An action is an intervention of a certain kind by a human being or some other animal in the course of nature (the world).[2] In order to clarify this idea we need some "pre-praxeological" concepts. First of all, the concept *state of affairs* is crucial for that purpose. Let us say, very roughly, that a state of affairs is an—imagined or actual—part ("feature") of the world. If a state of affairs is an actual part of the world it is *a fact*. A proposition to the effect that this part of the world exists is true. "The planet Earth has two moons" is a state of affairs that is logically possible but not a fact. The proposition to this effect is false.

An action results in a change in the world (the course of nature). But how shall we understand the concept *change*, which is indeed crucial here. In Sect. 6.2 we presented the basic ideas of von Wright's logic of change, which, no doubt, is a most fruitful tool also for clarifying the concept *action*. Change is a succession in time. This logic introduces four types of events: pTp (p obtains at two successive points of time, t_1 and t_2; p is unchanged), $pT{\sim}p$ (p obtains at t_1 but not at t_2; a change has taken place), ${\sim}pTp$ (${\sim}p$ obtains at t_1 but not at t_2), and ${\sim}pT{\sim}p$ (${\sim}p$ obtains at both

[1] See von Wright (1968), p. 12 f. As signifying a key concept in economics the term "praxeology" was introduced by von Mises (1949), a prominent member of the Austrian school of economics.

[2] See von Wright (1963), p. 36. The concept "action" formulated here is in all essentials based on von Wright.

Å. Frändberg, *The Legal Order*, Law and Philosophy Library 123,
https://doi.org/10.1007/978-3-319-78858-6_13

t_1 and t_2). Changes can be brought about by an agent, *x*, or by "nature" (sometimes including other agents than *x*).

By means of an action, a certain state of affairs, the initial state, can change into another certain state of affairs, the end-state. Also the relation between an initial state and an end-state is a state of affairs (e.g., the door is open, the agent closes it, the door is closed). To the four types of events just mentioned, we get four corresponding types of elementary acts (*d* is a symbol for acting; *p* represents, as an example, the sentence "The door is open").[3]

(i) *d(~pTp)*: "the doing of *p*", "*p* is done" ("the door is being opened")
(ii) *d(pT~p)*: "the destroying of *p*" ("the door is being closed")
(iii) *d(pTp)*: "the preserving of *p*" ("the door is open and remains so").

It is important to realise that *pTp* can be the result of an action. This is the case if the door would be closed, perhaps by a gust of wind, were it not for the intervention of the agent keeping it open with his hand.

(iv) *d(~pT~p)*: "the suppression of *p*" ("the door is closed and remains so").

Also *~pT~p* can be the result of an action. This is the case when a door would be opened by a person, were it not for the intervention of the agent hindering that person from opening the door.

Omission (forbearance) is a "correlate" to action. Omission is either the agent's *leaving* something unchanged or his *letting* a change take place.[4] Depending on what we put into the terms "leave" and "let", we can formulate more precise and stronger concepts of omission. As we see, every description of an action or an omission contains implicitly a counterfactual element.

So far we have relied heavily on von Wright. Now we shall focus on two other important aspects of actions, not treated by him. The first concerns the distinction between what I shall call *pure actions* and *extended actions.* Among the latter we shall distinguish between *consequential actions* and *qualified actions,* respectively. These distinctions are of the utmost importance from the viewpoint of law.

Let us start with an example. A person *moves his fingers* (a pure action). By doing so he *kills* another person by discharging a pistol (a consequential action). Or he moves his fingers and by doing so he *plays The Funeral March* by Chopin on the piano (a qualified action). Moving one's fingers, killing and playing the Funeral March are all actions in ordinary parlance. But how do they differ—which they obviously do? Five questions could be asked in this connection:

(1) How shall we characterise a pure action? (What is a pure action?)
(2) How shall we characterise an extended action? (What is an extended action?)
(3) How shall we characterise a consequential action? (What is a consequential action?)

[3]See von Wright (1963), p. 42 ff.

[4]See von Wright (1968), p. 38.

(4) How shall we characterise a qualified action? (What is a qualified action?)
(5) What is the relation between a pure action and a "corresponding" extended action?

A pure action is, broadly speaking, a bodily movement initiated by some mental occurrence. (The role of mental components of actions will be treated below.) Examples are running, lifting an arm, or shaking one's head. Absence of the mental component rules out as actions phenomena like breathing, sleeping, reflexes like blinking, and knowing. Nor are extended actions, strictly speaking, any actions at all, although we, for the sake of convenience, call them that. An extended action is a pure action to which a certain complement, not itself a pure action, is added. With respect to consequential actions this complement to a pure action, *pa*, is a "brute fact" (a pure state of affairs), *b*, such that *pa* causes *b*. The consequential action includes the consequences of a pure action.[5] Examples: The agent moves his fingers, a shot is fired, a person dies. The agent moves a foot, the foot touches a football, the football is set in motion and smashes a windowpane. Consequential actions are of crucial importance in criminal law and the law of torts.

As for qualified actions, the relation between a pure action and its complement has another character. The complement is not a consequence, but *an interpretation of* the pure action. To interpret can be seen as creating an idea about the thing interpreted. Qualified actions could for that reason also be called "cultural actions". The qualified action includes the interpretation of a pure action. Examples: The agent moves his fingers. This is qualified (interpreted) as his playing The Funeral March by Chopin. The agent moves a foot, the foot touches a football, the ball is set in motion and ends up between two posts. This is interpreted as the agent's scoring a goal.

For this reason it is misleading to formulate this relation, as is often done, as "by doing action *a* (e.g., moving his fingers) the agent does action *a′* (e.g., playing The Funeral March)". This formulation not only blurs the distinction between causality and interpretation, it is misleading also in that it conceives of the relation between a pure action and a corresponding extended action as a relation between two actions. But this is not the case. That a person dies, that a windowpane is smashed, that it is The Funeral March by Chopin that is played, and that a goal is scored are no actions, they are (another kind of) state of affairs.

We see that the distinction between pure actions and qualified actions is a special variation of the well-known distinction between brute facts and institutional facts.[6] The importance of qualified actions in the realm of law is evident.

As far as I can see, the theory of action now presented is totally compatible with the standpoint that speech acts (including performatives) are actions.

Actions can be qualified (interpreted) on the basis of legal, moral, aesthetic, religious, metaphysical ideas, etc., or on scientific theories. Such ideas are often value ideas or normative ideas (e.g., legal rules). In law, the distinction between

[5]Cf. Austin (1911), p. 415: "Most of the names which seem to be names of acts, are names of acts, *coupled with* certain of their consequences" [my italics].

[6]On this distinction see Subsection 2.3 above.

natural and legal persons is of interest here. Legal persons as such cannot perform pure actions. Pure actions performed by natural persons (human beings) are attributed to a legal person. In the case of legal persons we have in fact "a double qualification": (i) Some positions created by the law are qualified as a legal person and (ii) certain actions (pure or qualified) are qualified as performed by that legal person.

The other important aspect of actions is their conceptual relation to some mental phenomena. It is often said that what distinguishes actions from occurrences like coughing or breathing is that the former happen "intentionally", i.e., by some kind of interference of the will. That this is the case seems to me to be inevitable. However, I also find it proper to assume that the intervention of the will with respect to pure actions, consequential actions and qualified actions, respectively, differs between them.

As for pure actions, what triggers the action is probably a rather quick and momentary impulse of volition (although this impulse can be extremely strong all the same). A person moves her fingers on a mere impulse or for letting her nail varnish dry quicker. In the latter case the pure action is contained in a consequential one. In both cases the impulse of volition triggering them is probably instantaneous and almost unconscious. Even more impulsive, probably, are pure actions committed by animals. But consequential actions performed by human beings are often much more conscious in that the pure action is *a means* to obtain a certain consequence (result) as a goal and, if so, it is important to distinguish between the mental occurrence that triggers the pure act and the mental occurrence that urges the agent to obtain that goal. In such cases it is adequate to talk about the agents' *intentions*. Suppose, e. g., that religious zealot A wants and intends to kill B because B is an abortion doctor and A does so by means of a golf-club. With respect to the total consequential action, the mental state of affairs which—together with other occurrences—can be said to cause the killing of B is a most complicated phenomenon including certain feelings, values, prejudices, knowledge of certain states of affairs, and volition. But that notwithstanding, the mental state of affairs triggering him to swing the club (the pure action) can be a very quick and momentary thing—B turns suddenly up on the green and there is A, club in hand.

Capable of being qualified are pure actions, consequential actions, and also qualified actions. When is an action, *a*, qualified? The simple answer must be: When someone qualifies (interprets) it—i.e., labels it legally (*a* is accepting an offer or committing a burglary), morally (*a* is violating a person's dignity), aesthetically (*a* is creating a work of art), religiously (*a* is worshipping some god), etc. The mental processes involved here can be summarised under the term "interpretation".

Are the mental processes involved here—whatever they are—components of the actions? Perhaps it is not of the utmost importance to take a stand on this question. Personally, I am inclined to regard them as phenomena outside the actions themselves, triggering the actions to happen.

Now, however, we must differentiate between the situation where the agent himself (the person performing the pure action) makes the qualification and the situation where somebody else does so. In the first case—e.g., the agent intends to make an agreement by signing a paper or the agent knows that he is committing a burglary by breaking into Smith's house—it comes natural to call the pure action-cum-qualification an action. But suppose that somebody else makes the qualification, e.g., a judge? What kind of action, if any, is this?

Is interpretation an action? It follows from what I have already said that I think it is not. A pure action cannot be a component of interpretation as such. Interpretation is a purely mental process.[7] And it is, moreover, an ordered, "institutionalised" thought process. It is a mental process which is qualified as "interpretation".

As "omission" is defined here, also omitting—letting something happen or leaving something as it is—is triggered by a volitional impulse.

Even if I choose not to regard juridical phenomena such as "interpretation", "evaluation of evidence", and "application of law" as actions, but as intellectual, mental processes, I assign also such phenomena to the realm of praxeology.[8] The reason for doing so is that these concepts are inextricably connected to the action concepts. Juridical interpretation is in general interpretation concerning actions. Valuation of evidence generally involves ascertaining whether an alleged action has actually been performed or not. Application of law includes interpretation and evaluation of evidence, and generally results in the performance of an action, the pronouncement of a judgment.

13.2 Juridical Praxeology

The crucial role of praxeological concepts in juridical thinking cannot be exaggerated.

The intimate interplay between morphological, topological, and praxeological juridical concepts is obvious. Praxeology focuses on how lawyers handle the normative ideas we call "legal rules"—whose closer structure is examined by the morphology of law—when these ideas are confronted with topological phenomena (cases). And very close to juridical praxeology is juridical methodology, the branch of juridical thinking dealing with how lawyers *shall* handle the legal rules.

So the most fundamental pre-juridical concepts, on which the whole of juridical thinking is based, are *norm* and *action*. And this is no wonder, since "norm" and "action" are also the most fundamental *pre-legal* concepts. The whole of legal life revolves round actions that are in different ways regarded in the light of norms, be it to marry, to make an agreement, to pay a debt, to deliver a judgment, or to commit a crime. This prompts us to make a simple classification within the sphere of legally and juridically qualified acts (or actions).

---

[7]According to Geach (1957), pp. 1 ff., mental processes like thinking, feeling, seeing and hearing are acts – mental acts.

[8]Von Wright (1968), p. 12, regards concepts such as "choice", "decision", "desire", "freedom", and "will" as praxeological concepts.

A. *Legally qualified acts*

  I. Primary acts

    1. Acts-in-the-law
    2. Delicts

  II. Juridical, legally qualified acts

B. *Juridical, juridically but not legally qualified acts*

Primary acts are such acts that the legal system claims or promotes (acts-in-the-law) or counteracts (delicts). Primary acts have a closer connection to what I in Chap. 1 called the Fundamental Idea of Law.[9] Juridical acts play an instrumental role in the realisation of this idea. Examples of acts-in-the-law are making an agreement (offer, acceptance), paying of a debt, making a tradition of a thing, and answering "yes" at the marriage ceremony. Examples of delicts are crimes and negligent acts. Examples of juridical, legally qualified acts are adjudicating, interpreting statutes, valuating evidence and applying legal rules *as far as such actions are qualified by legal rules—and then the concepts signifying these actions are L-concepts as well as J-concepts* (and expressed by JL-terms).[10] But actions of the kind just exemplified can also be system-independent—and then the concepts signifying them are "pure" *J-concepts* (jurisprudential, technical concepts). Our concern here is mainly juridical acts in the latter sense.

From the viewpoint of juridical praxeology, primary acts (belonging to the sphere of legal praxeology) are topological phenomena. Acts are (parts of) "cases" interpreted by the lawyers in the light of legal rules, which they also apply to the cases.

Let us now focus on some fundamental juridical-praxeological concepts. Central are, of course, the concepts "follow" ("comply with", "conform to", "obey", "observe", "adhere to") and "break" ("violate") a legal rule.

One can follow a rule in a weak and in a strong sense. In the weak sense person *x* follows an obligation to do *a*, if *x* actually performs *a*, and breaks the obligation if she in fact does not perform *a*; and follows a prohibition to do *a* when she in fact does not perform *a*, and breaks it when she in fact performs *a*—in all cases irrespective of her reasons for doing or not doing it, and even if she does not have any reasons at all or does not even know that she is following or breaking it. Weak following or breaking can be pure actions exclusively.

In the strong sense (and the "strength" can be of a lower or higher degree) "following" and "breaking" imply knowledge of the fact that the agent is following or breaking a legal rule or, at least, a hunch that this is the case, and that some kind of reflection, or deliberation, has preceded taking the step to follow or break the rule. Legislators especially appreciate it, of course, if their rules are followed by the

---

[9]Subsection 1.6 above.

[10]See Subsection 1.2.3 above.

citizens in a strong sense—in a mood of respect for the legal order. For following in the strong sense the terms "obey" or "comply with" could be appropriate and the term "violate" for breaking in a strong sense. In the following, however, we take all these terms in the weak sense.

It is important for judges and other law-applying officials to know when legal rules are broken—in order to be able to ascertain whether this is the case with respect to individual cases. In Chap. 2 (Sect. 2.9.3) I argued that all legal rules are norms and that all legal rules except genuinely permissive rules are different kinds of mandatory rules, i.e., either obligations or prohibitions (which are inter-definable).

Let me be a little more precise about what it means to break a legal rule. I have already done that in Sect. 2.9.3 in connection with my presentation of different kinds of legal rules, since I found it appropriate to deal with what breaking a legal rule amounts to together with the standard forms of different rule types and the conditions of their being broken. However, I will repeat briefly these conditions here because of their genuinely praxeological character.

What it means to break an elementary rule in the weak sense I have just mentioned. As for the elliptical should-rules, they are ordinary elementary obligations when the implicit complementary requisite or norm theme is explicitly added to the rule. As for validity rules (competence rules and form-prescribing rules), they are followed if used correctly by the addressees and broken if not, i.e., when an addressee acts *ultra vires* or does not bother about prescribed forms (in other words, acts incorrectly). Statutory manifestos, as well as statutory guidelines, are broken when the circumstance that shall be taken into consideration is not taken into consideration. Genuine permissions (options) cannot be broken, but in statutory texts permissions are usually exceptions from elementary rules and shall be regarded as such. Qualificatory rules (statutory definitions) shall be used by their addressees and are, hence, broken if not, i.e., if they do not substitute the definiens for the definiendum. A goal-directive, finally, is broken when (i) the addressee is not creating and using some device which he in all honesty believes will attain the goal, or (ii) when the device is against the law.

Another important praxeological concept is *expediency* (rule *r* is expedient with respect to its purpose (goal), *g*). This concept is praxeological, since it must be defined in terms of actions. Of course, when we say that a rule is expedient (well adapted for its purpose) we speak in an elliptical manner about certain states of affairs, which I shall try to clarify a bit here.

It is meaningful to talk about the expediency of legal rules only if one has a teleological (finalistic, instrumental) view of legal rules. They are the means of achieving desired social states of affairs. Hence it comes natural to think in terms of praxeological statements such as (*s* is a desired social state of affairs):

(i) *r* is intended to achieve *s*
(ii) if *r* is followed, *s* comes about
(iii) if *r* is applied, *s* comes about
(iv) if *r* is followed, *s* probably comes about
(v) if *r* is followed on the whole, *s* (probably) comes about

and the like. Such statements are statements about legal bases. The concept *legal basis* (itself a praxeological concept) was dealt with in Sect. 9.3.4 above, due to its close connection to the concept "analogy" investigated there.

Let us define "expediency" in the following manner

(E1) The rule "If circumstances *F*, then *x* shall perform action *a*" is expedient with respect to achieving *s* if and only if it is the case that, if *x* performs *a* when *F*, then *s* will, with a high degree of probability, come about or be maintained.

(E2) The rule "If *F*, then *x* may not perform *a*" is expedient with respect to achieving *s* if and only if it is the case that, if *x* does not perform *a* when *F*, then *s* will, with a high degree of probability, be maintained or come about.

E1 and E2 boil down to

(E3) *r* is expedient with regard to *s* if and only if it is the case that, if *r* is followed (applied), *s* will, with a high degree of probability, come about or be maintained.

As for a permissive rule, *pr*, that is an exception from an obligation or a prohibition, *r*, it could be said that *r* is not expedient (but perhaps even the opposite) with respect to the (generic) case regulated by *pr* although that case is subsumable under *r*, which, things being so, justifies the exception. As for genuine permission (options) it could be said that they are neither expedient nor not expedient. However, it might be that *the very case that an agent has freedom of choice* is a desirable social state of affairs in the relevant circumstances.

The elliptic should-rule is expedient if the corresponding spelled-out mandatory rule is expedient. A validity rule is expedient if the desired social state of affairs comes about when the rule is followed. A qualificatory rule (statutory definition) with the structure *Shall:* $t =_{def.} u$ is expedient if, for any rule, *r*, within the set of rules to which the definition is applicable, *r* is expedient if *u* is substituted for *t* in *r*. Statutory manifestos and statutory guidelines are expedient in a much more indirect way. Perhaps they can be said to be expedient only in the sense that, if they are used for the purpose of interpreting requisites in the rules to which they are applicable, the probability that those rules will become more expedient increases. Goal-directives, finally, are expedient in an even more indirect, or mediate, way. Their expediency is dependent on the expediency of the supplementary rules (created by the addressees of the goal-directive) as a means to achieve the goal expressed in the goal-directive.

Closely associated with the concept "expediency" is the concept *effectiveness*. "Effectiveness" is also a praxeological concept. A rule, *r*, cannot be said to be effective, however expedient, if it is not followed by and large by its addressees. On the other hand, *r* cannot be said to be effective, however slavishly followed, if it is not expedient. Hence, *r* is effective if and only if it is (i) expedient and (ii) followed by and large by its addressees.

The rest of this chapter will be devoted to two crucial juridical-praxeological concepts, viz., *application of legal rules* (Sect. 13.3) and *validity of legal rules* (Sect. 13.4).

13.3 Application of Legal Rules

13.3.1 Introduction

What do we reasonably mean when we say that a certain legal rule is applied to a certain case?

First of all, can anybody apply a legal rule? My answer is no. It seems to be a more or less understood consensus among lawyers that only persons in authority, notably judges, can apply legal rules. If so, it is no application of law when private persons follow rules or, some way or another, adapt their behaviour to them. Neither is it an application of law when an advocate gives advice to a client of his. For that reason, I lay this restriction on the concept here. In so doing I do not claim that there should exist a gulf between application of law and other uses of law. On the contrary, the former is for many reasons a kind of model for juridical argumentation on the whole.

From this follows, that we must take the distinction between citizen-addressed and judge-addressed rules into consideration.[11] That a judge applies a judge-addressed rule in his exercise of authority cannot mean anything else but his following the rule—where "follow" has the same meaning as that defined in the previous subsection. Hence, a judge applies the rule "If somebody has stolen something, he shall be sentenced to at most two years of imprisonment" by his sentencing a thief to, e.g., 1 year of imprisonment.

But what about a citizen-addressed rule? Can such a rule be applied? The answer is strictly speaking: No. What is applied is a judge-addressed rule, constructed (usually more or less unconsciously) through transformation of a citizen-addressed rule.[12]

Application is a special kind of following a rule. The reason why this kind of following is signified by a special concept, "application", is that it draws attention to the fact that (i) there are legal rules that can only be followed by persons in authority, (ii) the following of these rules has another social function than the following of citizen-addressed rules (the following of the latter rules are intended, in a more direct way, to result in desired social states of affairs, while the following of the former are intended to guarantee the following of the former), and (iii) that it is to a high degree called for to have a unifying concept for the different intellectual operations that together make up the judges' observance of the law (its application).

[11]See Subsection 4.4.

[12]Ibid.

The legal source material is a kind of raw material, or semi-product, that is worked up in different ways by juridical thought processes. The most important of those processes are inescapable components of rule application. That the core of administration of justice is *application of legal rules* I take for granted. In the following I shall present what I call *direct application* (Sect. 13.3.2), *rejection of application* (Sect. 13.3.3), and *iterative application* (Sect. 13.3.4).

13.3.2 Direct Application

Let me, by means of an example, explain what I have in mind with this kind of application.

The facts (of the case) are the following. Person A gets into his car and starts the engine. Then he leaves his car in order to scrape off ice from the windscreen. In so doing he slips on the ice-covered ground and injures his neck. A claims 30.000 kronor in damages from his insurance company B. The court decides in favour of the plaintiff.[13]

Let us reconstruct this piece of law-applicative reasoning as a line of arguments[14]:

(1) For bodily injury or property damage as a consequence of motor traffic, motor traffic insurance shall be paid.
(2) If a person has suffered bodily injury or property damage as a consequence of motor traffic [and she claims damages and . . .], then the judge shall order the person's insurance company [as defendant] to pay motor traffic insurance.
(3) If a person has suffered bodily injury by slipping when clearing the windscreen of her car [and has claimed damages and . . .], then the judge shall order the person's insurance company to pay motor traffic insurance to this person.
(4) A has suffered bodily injury by slipping when clearing the windscreen of her car.
(5) A has claimed damages and . . .
(6) The judge shall order B to pay motor traffic insurance to A.
(7) B shall pay 30.000 kronor to A.

(1), (2), and (3) are legal rules. The starting point of every application of law is a rule, here represented by (1), which the judge has found *prima facie* to be relevant for the case before him. In the following, application of legal rules shall be clarified in terms of relations between sentences of the type (1)–(7). I shall proceed in the following manner. First I give a short characterisation of the sentence types involved. Then I define *the components of a* (full-fledged) *application of legal rules* in terms of these relations.

Rules of type (1) we call *basic legal rules*. Such rules can be expressed in statutory provisions or be embedded in precedents. Rules of type (2) we call

[13]The Swedish Supreme Court case NJA 2007, pp. 997 ff.

[14]Cf. Subsection 6.6 above.

molecular legal rules. A molecular rule is—for the purpose of deciding the case—a complete specification of basic (fragmentary) rules. Such a specification includes, when needed, transformation of citizen-addressed to judge-addressed rules.[15] Rules of type (3) we call *atomic legal rules* (or *subsumption rules*). An atomic rule is a—for the purpose of deciding the case—completely interpreted rule, i.e., it can be immediately applied to the case.

A direct application of a basic rule has taken place when the relation between the basic rule and its corresponding atomic subsumption rule is either an application proper, a precisation, a restrictive interpretation, or an extensive interpretation.[16]

Propositions of type (4) we call *evidentiary sentences*. Such sentences signify states of affairs submitted as evidence.

However, a first step in order to arrive at a legally correct decision is that requisites in a lot of other rules than (1)–(3) are fulfilled—and it is the duty of the judge to ascertain that they are, since, if they are not, the case shall not be tried at all but dismissed without trial. First of all, of course, a claim must have been made by a plaintiff. Furthermore, the court must be a competent one, the judge must be competent with respect to the case in question, the case must not be a *res judicata*, there must not be pendency of the action, etc. Sentences signifying such legal positions we call *pre-applicatory sentences*, since questions concerning them must be answered before the "real" application takes place. (5) is an example of such a sentence. (6) can be logically deduced from (3), (4), and (5). Such deduction is the backbone of every application of law. Sentences of type (6) are logical conclusions. With Kelsen, we refer to them as *individual legal norms*.[17] It is of importance to realise that individual legal norms in this sense are not identical to sentences expressing the judgment, i.e., sentences of type (7), which we can call *judgment sentences*. Examples of individual norms are "C shall be sentenced to between two and six years imprisonment for theft", "D shall pay damages to E", and "The plaintiff's claim shall be dismissed". The judge *follows* the individual norm by issuing the judgment sentence. The deduction of an individual norm can be called *application in the weak sense* and the further addition of a judgment sentence *application in the strong sense*.

In terms of sentences of types (1)–(7) we can make a rational reconstruction of the juridical activity "application of law". This activity comprises in its more developed form seven components:

A. Pre-applicatory decisions
B. Qualification

    1. Choice of law and finding of prima facie applicable rule(s)
    2. Specification
    3. Interpretation

---

[15]We investigated such transformations in Chapter 4 above.

[16]See Chapter 8 above.

[17]Kelsen (1996), p. 12.

C. Evaluation of evidence
D. Applicative deduction
E. Choice of individual legal consequence.

It must be clearly emphasised from the beginning that this is a logical reconstruction of law-application. Hence, I do not argue that judges in their decision-making actually proceed step by step according to our schema. Neither do I argue that judges are constantly aware of the different elements when judging. More often than not the decision is probably made more or less "intuitively", whereupon the opinion is formulated afterwards.

Pre-applicatory Decisions

Decisions of this kind usually belong to the sphere of procedural law (including international procedural law). I have mentioned as examples the establishing that the court is competent with respect to the present case and that the case is no *res judicata.* Some other examples are that the plaintiff has standing to litigate and that no disqualification of a judge exists.

It might be objected that establishing such things do not belong to the application of legal rules *to the present case* at all (as also the term "pre-applicatory" suggests). However, as I shall argue below (in Sect. 13.3.4), application of law in the widest sense of the term is a cluster of iterative applications, of which the pre-applicatory decisions form a part.

Qualification

By "qualification" I mean the establishing of a legal rule whose function it is to be a premise in the logical deduction, the conclusion of which is an individual legal norm. In other words, the result of the qualification is the establishing of a subsumption rule—a rule of type (3)—which is always an atomic rule. Usually the subsumption rule is constructed by means of another legal rule, the basic rule. Qualification is, as it were, the legal labelling of states of affairs.

One of the genetic-topological norm-relations (1)–(32) presented in Chap. 8 holds between a basic rule and its corresponding subsumption rule, if we take both direct and indirect application into consideration (the latter to be dealt with in Sect. 13.3.3). Qualification consists of three elements: (i) choice of law and finding of *prima facie* relevant rule(s), (ii) specification, and (iii) interpretation.

Our reconstruction makes use of two aspects of rules which are relevant for the law-applier: the *ex ante*-aspect and the *ex post*-aspect. We say that a rule, *r*, lies under an *ex ante*-aspect for the law-applier if *r* is *the starting point* for him at a given stage of the law-applying process, while *r* lies under an *ex post*-aspect for him if *r* is *the result* of a given stage in this process. A rule that, at a given stage, lies under an *ex ante*-aspect, lies under an *ex post*-aspect at the immediately following stage.

Choice of Law and Finding of Prima Facie Relevant Rule(s)

In situations where two (or more) legal rules within the same legal system, or two (or more) rules belonging to two (or more) different legal systems, are candidates for application to the present case, a choice of applicable system and applicable rule must be performed. The choice can concern colliding or competing rules (investigated in Chap. 10), between state law and law created by private persons (by means of contracts), between different state legal systems (Chap. 11), and between rules belonging to different momentary legal systems within the same non-momentary legal system (Chap. 12).

But whether or not a choice of law must be performed, the judge must always pick some rule or rules as being *prima facie* relevant as candidates for application.

Specification

By "specification of law" relative to a certain case, *c*, I mean the putting together of basic fragmentary rules necessary for the legal qualification of *c*. For that purpose the systematisation of different types of rules and relations between them (made in Chap. 2) is helpful.

The starting point of the specification is the given case, *c*, and the law (ordered as a legal system). The conventional units (which we, in the first place, find in statutory law)—articles, paragraphs, etc. are *fragmentary rules.* In the first step of specification such rules lie under an *ex ante*-aspect for the law-applier. The result of the specification is *a well-developed legal rule.* Well-developed legal rules can be expressed in standard forms for legal rules (see Chap. 2).

A well-developed legal rule can be more or less specified. A well-developed rule that is *completely specified* relative to *c*, i.e., a rule that is composed of all fragmentary rules necessary, and together sufficient, for a complete qualification of *c* with respect to the whole legal system, we call *a molecular legal rule* relative to *c*. Under the process of specification fragmentary rules lie under an *ex ante*-aspect for the judge and a molecular rule under an *ex post*-aspect.

Let us illustrate this by means of an example. A bleak Thursday in November at 11 o'clock a waiter at a restaurant serves a chilly guest a big glass of port. An overzealous prosecutor ponders over whether he should prosecute the owner of the restaurant for having violated the Regulation concerning Sale of Intoxicating Liquors. In those gruesome regulations he finds the following provisions (fragmentary rules).

(1) Intoxicating liquors may not be served before 12 o'clock on weekdays and not before 1 o'clock on Sundays and holidays.
(2) A restaurant owner is responsible for crimes committed by an employee of his as if the crime had been committed by himself.
(3) Anyone who sells intoxicating liquors without permission to do so or exceeds such a permission shall be imposed fines.
(4) To intoxicating liquor is in these regulations assigned spirits, wine and strong beer. By wine is understood every beverage produced by alcoholic fermentation of juice from grapes, berries or fruit containing more than two and a quarter but not more than 22% by volume ethyl alcohol.

Rule (1) is an example of what can be called *a core rule*, i.e., a fragmentary rule being the natural starting point for the legal qualification of a case. Rules (2)–(4) are examples of *subsidiary rules* relative to (1), either in the sense that they add some requisite to (1)—a *supplementary rule*—(of which (2) is an example), or in the sense that they attach a legal sanction to violations of (1)—*a sanction rule*—(of which (3) is an example), or in the sense that terms and expressions in rules of type (4)—*substitution rules*—shall be substituted for terms and expressions in rules of type (1)–(3). Substitution rules are qualificatory rules (statutory definitions).

The fragmentary rules (1)–(4) can now be put together in a well-developed rule, *vr*, which, in this first step in the specification process lies in an *ex post*-aspect for the law-applier.

(*vr*) If an employee in the service of a restaurant owner provides a guest with a beverage before 12 o'clock on a weekday, which beverage is produced by alcoholic fermentation of juice from grapes containing more than two and a quarter but not more than 22% by volume ethyl alcohol, the judge shall impose fines on the restaurant owner.

vr can, as we see, easily be expressed in a standard form for legal rules.

However, *vr* is of course far from being a complete specification of a rule minimally necessary for solving the prosecutor's problem. A lot of other subsidiary rules must be taken into consideration. (In practice, most requisites in such rules are usually so obviously fulfilled or not that the law-applier hardly is aware of it. His attention is focused on the problematic requisites, towards which he turns the searchlights, leaving the rest of the stage in obscurity.) Consequently, the restaurant owner must be of age, there must not exist any rule of exception from punishment, he must actually be the owner, and many other things as well. Admittedly, the borderline between the procedural pre-applicatory decisions and decisions of the kind just mentioned can sometimes be vague.

It is, at least theoretically, possible to put together all these rules in one single (and rather horrid) rule—a molecular rule—comprising all rules minimally necessary to decide the case.

A most important element in the specification process is the transformation of citizen-addressed rules into judge-addressed ones. Well-developed rules (including molecular ones) are always judge-addressed. From this follows that, at this stage, classifications of legal rules of the kind made in Chap. 2 lose their interest. All well-developed rules are ordinary regulative rules, and competence rules, qualificatory rules, etc., i.e., all fragmentary rules, have "changed into" requisites in the molecular ones. When the specification is completed, the molecular rules lie in an *ex post*-aspect from the viewpoint of the law-applier.

Let me elaborate a bit more on specification of legal rules. As far as I can see, there is a hidden performative element in every molecular (judge-addressed) rule, which deserves to be brought to light.[18]

It happens in human life that a person orders another person to order a third person to perform a certain action. Such an order can be expressed by the first-mentioned person like this: "*I* order *you* to order *her* that . . .". Something similar is

[18]The "detection" of performatives is attributed to J. L. Austin. See his *How to do Things by Words*, 2nd ed., 1976, *passim*.

the case with judge-addressed rules—a characteristic feature of such rules is that they are "orders" given by the legislator to the judge to the effect that the judge shall "order" some other person to do something, which can be expressed in sentences where the legislator is mentioned in the first person, the judge in the second person, and the individual to which the judgment is addressed in the third person. Closely connected with this is that judge-addressed (molecular) rules contain a performative element. By means of speech acts (judgments, decisions) the judges issue norms and the complying with these norms is intended to cause the legal consequences of the general rules to be realised.

Consider the following sentences:

(1) I promise to visit you tomorrow.
(2) He promises to visit you tomorrow.
(3) I promised to visit you tomorrow.
(4) I play the harp.

Of these four sentences (1) differs in an interesting way from the other three. The person who utters (1) actually performs exactly the action about which (1) makes a statement—the action to promise to visit "you" tomorrow—precisely by uttering (1). The promise is created by his words. The same applies to sentences like

(5) We welcome you all.
(6) I christen you Sophia Albertina.
(7) I invite you to dinner.

Sentences (1) and (5)–(7) are examples of *performatives*. What characterises them is that they give an impression of describing an action when in fact they are (a part of) this action itself. By saying "I invite you to dinner" I invite you to dinner (given that the utterance is made under certain adequate circumstances). On the other hand I do not play the harp only by uttering sentence (4). Typical performatives appear in the first person the present tense indicative (singular or plural)—or are equivalent to sentences in such a form. (1) is a performative but not (2) and (3).

Many sentences of a legal character are performatives, e.g.:

(8) You are hereby offered a lot of first-class pears.
(9) I now declare you man and wife.

Among performative sentences of or about the law, sentences appearing in judgments and similar legal decisions are of special interest for us here, e.g.:

(10) With approval of the claim, A is under an obligation to pay 10.000 kronor in damages to B.
(11) The claim of payment is dismissed.
(12) The court of appeal sentences E for careless driving to 40 day-fines, each day-fine to the amount of 200 kronor.

Precisely by uttering these sentences (under adequate circumstances) the judge obligates A to pay 10.000 kronor to B, dismisses the claim of payment, and sentences C to 40 day-fines. In this lies their performative nature.

From our viewpoint it is of importance to bear in mind that some performatives have a, let us call it, norm-promulgating effect. The person who utters (1) under adequate circumstances issues a norm (addressed to himself): "I have a duty to visit 'you' tomorrow". All performatives of type (10)–(12) also have such an effect. By uttering these sentences the judge issues the following norms:

(10*) A shall pay 10.000 kronor to B.
(11*) C may omit payment to D [where C and D are the parties of the litigation].
(12*) E shall pay 40 day-fines, each day-fine 200 kronor.

With respect to declaratory judgments I find it proper to regard them as issuing *hypothetical norms*. For example, to the declaratory judgment given at time *t*

(13) The district court finds that F on the date of maturity is under an obligation to pay 50.000 kronor to G in accordance with the promissory note presented by G

corresponds the norm

(13*) If . . ., then F shall pay 50.000 kronor to G on the date of maturity

where ". . ." signifies operative facts that may occur between *t* and the date of maturity.

The performative expressions in (10)–(13)—"be under an obligation", "is dismissed", "sentences" (= as a verb synonymous with "pronouncing a judgment") can all, I argue, be traced back to the concept *decide*, conceived as a performative. Hence we regard the following sentences as equivalent to (10)–(13):

(10′) *The court decides that* A *shall* pay 10.000 kronor to B.
(11′) *The court decides that* C *may* omit the payment to D.
(12′) *The court of appeal decides that* E *shall* pay 40 day-fines, each day-fine 200 kronor.
(13′) *The district court decides that* F *shall* pay 50.000 kronor on the date of maturity, if . . ..

I said above that the molecular rule can be seen as an order to the law-applier to order someone to do something. The latter order consists in issuing a performative with a norm-creating effect, i.e., to *decide that* someone *shall*, *may not* or *may* do something. The molecular rules regulate the law-appliers' decision-making. They can be conceived as an imposition on the judges to issue, by means of norm-promulgating performatives, legal norms of the type judgments. And if so is the case, the performative element must be represented in its standard form. Such a standard form for a molecular rule can be formulated like this ("*j*" is a variable over judges and "*x*" a variable over persons to whom judgments are addressed):

(SMR) If . . ., then shall (may not, may): *j* decides: *x* shall (may not), may) . . . .

The performative component of a legal rule we call *the performative factor.*[19]

[19]Cf. Subsection 4.4 above.

Interpretation

As we all know, the juridical qualification often is not accomplished when a molecular rule has (more or less unconsciously) been formulated. Terms and expressions in such a rule may be vague, obscure or ambiguous with respect to the rule's applicability to the case and, hence, in need of interpretation.

Every interpretation of a rule we regard as a rule as well.

In our reconstruction of the juridical qualification a molecular rule lies in the beginning of the interpretative phase in an *ex ante*-aspect for the law-applier. (This, of course, does not mean that I argue that the qualification in practice comes about by first specifying and then interpreting rules. The only purpose of our reconstruction is to discern and separate these two components of the qualification.)

An interpretative process can proceed in different steps, where the rule under interpretation becomes more and more precise. An interpreted rule (an interpretation) that at a certain step lies under an *ex post*-aspect lies in the immediately following step in an *ex ante*-aspect for the law-applier.

A molecular rule is an *atomic rule* relative to a given case if and only if the rule is as precise (completely interpreted) as is minimally necessary in order for the applier to apply it to the case. Atomic rules lie under an *ex post*-aspect with regard to both specification and interpretation. They are the result of the whole qualificatory process. Let us for an example return to the case of the driver who slipped.[20] There (1) is a basic rule, (2) a molecular rule, and (3) an atomic rule. To sum up, we have used the following types of rules in our reconstruction of the juridical qualification of cases:

A. *Basic (fragmentary) rules*

   1. Core rules
   2. Subsidiary rules

      a. Supplementary rules
      b. Sanction rules
      c. Substitution rules

B. *Well-developed rules*

   1. More or less specified rules
   2. Molecular rules (completely specified rules)

      a. More or less interpreted rules
      b. Atomic rules (completely interpreted rules).

The essential types of rules in this classification are *the basic (fragmentary) rules*, *the molecular rules*, and *the atomic rules.*

Atomic rules are subsumption rules, i.e., premises in applicative deductions.

[20]Introduced in the beginning of Subsection 13.3.2.

Interpretation of legal rules will be investigated more closely in Chap. 14.

Evaluation of Evidence
Evaluation of evidence consists, as we all know, of an examination of the truth value of sentences describing states of affairs advanced as evidence. We call such sentences *evidentiary sentences.*

Applicative Deduction
The law-applicative process can now be reconstructed as a logical deduction with a set of premises consisting of an atomic subsumption rule (or a conjunction of such rules), and an evidentiary sentence (or a conjunction of such sentences)—and an individual legal norm as the conclusion. The performance of such a deduction we call *an applicative deduction.* In the example of the driver who slipped,[21] to draw the conclusion (6) from premises (3), (4), and (5) is to make an applicative deduction.

An applicative deduction is an inference combining the logical rules *modus ponens* (if p then q, and p; hence q) and universal specification as this term is used in the predicate calculus.

The rule of universal specification means that a statement true of everything in a certain set is true of any arbitrary member of that set. From "All knights are brave" we are allowed to infer "If Roland is a knight, Roland is brave". If all that have committed burglary shall be punished, then A, who has committed burglary, shall be punished. To put it simply: The rule of universal specification means that it is admitted to infer from $(x)(Fx \rightarrow Gx)$ (reads: "for every x: if x has quality F, then x has quality G) to $Fa \rightarrow Ga$, where a is an individual.[22] Thus, the logical schema for the applicative deduction is the following:

(1) $(x)(Fx \rightarrow Gx)$
(2) Fa

---

(3) Ga

Choice of Individual Legal Consequence
The judge-addressed individual legal norms that are conclusions of applicative deductions express norms to the effect that, e.g., the judge shall sentence A to imprisonment, rescind the contract between B and C, order D to pay damages to E, and dismiss the claim against F. The next, and final, component in the applicative process must then be that judges comply with the individual norms addressed to them. They do so by issuing judgment sentences ("sentence" in the linguistic sense, of course) of the type "A is sentenced to 2 years imprisonment for theft", "The agreement between B and C concerning the purchase of the excavator is void", "D shall pay 10.000 kronor in damages to E", and "The claim of F concerning the custody of child G is dismissed". This final component of the applicative process we call *choice of individual legal consequence.*

---

[21] Ibid.

[22] Suppes (1967), p. 59 f.

13.3.3 Rejection of Application

Suppose that the judge finds that, within the legal system, no reasonable rule candidate is in fact applicable to the case before him. Since, by virtue of the denial of justice prohibition, he is not allowed to leave the case undecided, he must create a rule within the spirit of the law in its totality.

In such situations the case lies either clearly outside even a most doubtful linguistic borderline (*e contrario* and analogy relations) or clearly inside even a most doubtful linguistic borderline—it belongs to the set of "clear" cases—but, that notwithstanding, it is not reasonable to apply the basic rule to the case (reduction). Whether the atomic rule is created *e contrario,* analogously or reductively by means of the basic rule, by laying it down the judge *rejects* a direct application of the basic rule to the case.

Let me give an example of a rejection *e contrario:*

- (Basic rule) For bodily injury or property damage as a consequence of motor traffic, motor traffic insurance shall be paid.
- (Subsumption rule) If a person has suffered bodily injury by slipping when running to catch a bus, payment of motor traffic insurance may be refused.

The use *e contrario* of legal rules is more important than, perhaps, usually is realised. This is due to the fact that an *e contrario* relation is always established when a judge *dismisses a claim upon its merits*, as in the example given. The close connection between the *e contrario* relation and the idea of legalism is here clearly brought to the light.

Next an example of a rejection by means of analogy:

- (Basic rule) If someone spreads poison by gross negligence, he shall be sentenced to prison or fines.
- (Subsumption rule) If somebody by carrying with him a radioactive iridium isotope shows gross negligence, he shall be sentenced to prison or fines.[23]

Finally an example of rejection by means of reduction:

- (Basic rule) If the same goods are sold to two buyers, the first buyer may keep the goods.
- (Subsumption rule) If the same goods are sold to two buyers and the second buyer has acquired possession of the goods in good faith, he may keep the goods.

How do the components of the direct application relate to the components which come to the fore when application is indirect (rejection)?

First of all, the judge must *establish* the fact that, with regard to *e contrario* and analogical use, the basic rule is not applicable to the case and, with respect to reduction, that the rule is applicable. Therefore, the rejection must be preceded by a qualification of the basic rule. Then, when a subsumption rule is formulated *e*

[23]The Swedish Supreme Court case NJA 1959, p. 254.

contrario, analogously, or reductively, a further interpretation of this rule is probably necessary. The interpretation conflates, as it were, in such situations with the creation of the subsumption rule.

13.3.4 Iterative Application

Within the frame of each component of the application of law "an additional" process of application of law can take place—an "application within an application". Let us call this phenomenon *iterative application.*

Take, to begin with, the pre-applicatory decisions. Suppose that the question arises of a disqualification of a judge. Then factual circumstances allegedly being grounds for disqualification must be examined (examination of evidence) and the relevant rules specified and interpreted (qualification). Furthermore, that choice-of-law rules need interpretation, and evaluation of evidence is needed with respect to the connecting factors referred to, is obvious.

Or take specification. There might be implicitly or explicitly formulated legal rules, regulating the coupling together of fragmentary (basic) rules, themselves needing qualification. And with respect to interpretation, some legal systems have rather elaborate rules regulating interpretation of statutory provisions (e.g., that of the U.S.), which rules in turn might be in need of interpretation.

Evaluation of evidence is heavily guided by different kinds of rules concerning things like burden of proof, production of evidence, non-accepted kinds of evidence, etc.—which rules often are vague or obscure and, hence, in need of interpretation. Also evaluation of evidence within evaluation of evidence is possible, e.g., the establishment whether a testimony is hearsay or built on the witness's own experience.

Finally, the choice of individual legal consequence often brings to the fore all the components of a full-fledged application of law. If, for example, probation seems *prima facie* to be the appropriate sanction in a criminal case, the judge must qualify the rules concerning this sanction and evaluate evidence about the culprit's personal development, etc. Another example is determining the amount of damages to be paid, when such an estimation is required by legal rules.

Application of law in international conflict of law cases is a cluster of—sometimes very complicated—iterative applications. With respect to the choice of law, the judge has to decide (i) the choice of collision rule, (ii) the choice of *lex causae*, and (iii) the choice of applicable rules in *lex causae*. In all three situations iterative application might occur.

13.4 Validity of Law

13.4.1 Introduction

If a person says, in an unqualified way, that a legal rule is valid, i.e., that it is "objectively", in so many words, valid, she says something the meaning of which is very difficult to form a conception of.

However, the idea of validity with respect to legal rules is usually qualified in ways like (i) *r* is valid according to the moral doctrine *M*, (ii) *r* is valid according to the natural law doctrine *N*, (iii) *r* is valid relative to the practice of the courts of law belonging to the legal order *LO*, and (iv) *r* is valid relative to the doctrine of legal sources *DL*. With respect to (i) we can talk about *moral validity*, with respect to (ii) about *natural law validity*, and with respect to (iii) and (iv) about two different kinds of *positive law validity*. The questions arise: What use do lawyers have for a concept of "validity"? What does the addition of the term "valid" add to the term "law"? In a monograph about juridical thinking it comes natural to restrict oneself to positive law validity.

The concept "positive law validity" that I find most useful for practical as well as academic lawyers is a praxeological concept, and, more exactly, a concept of type (iii), i.e., validity relative to the practice of the courts of law.

As we all know, legal philosophers differ profoundly about the meaning of "validity".[24] There is a consensus, I believe, that validity can be correctly predicated on legal rules ("*r* is valid in society *S* at time *t*") and also on legal systems (as when we talk about "English, (French), . . ., law"). We also attribute validity to individual legal norms, acts-in-the-law, and legal instruments (such as contracts, wills, mortgages, etc.). With respect to legal systems, however, it is not altogether clear if all rules in a valid legal system are, themselves, valid or if one can talk about valid legal systems without implying that *every* rule in the system is valid. As I see it, there is nothing against predicating validity also to legal orders (in the sense that the term is used in this book).

There is a vigorous way of thinking in legal philosophy, especially within the so-called realistic movements, tending to blur the borderline between "legal rule" and "valid legal rule" (or between "law" and "valid law")—a norm, *n*, cannot be a legal rule at *t* unless *n* is functioning (is actually applied) at *t*. A norm that, if brought to the fore, is applied during the period t_1–t_n *is* a legal rule during that period, but if *n* ceases to be applied at t_n we cannot say that it is a legal rule but that it *was* such a

[24]A most illuminating investigation of positive law validity is Munzer (1972). Munzer offers a penetrating critique of the theories of Hart, Kelsen, and Ross. Particularly convincing is his refutation of Kelsen's and Hart's idea that validity is warranted by one single, ultimate master rule (Kelsen: the basic norm, Hart: the rule of recognition). Munzer argues that validity is better explained by substituting "rules of smaller scope" for such master rules. His own definition of validity is that it is "legal strength or adequacy" (pp. 3 and 37), meaning that "if something is strong or adequate in law, this means that it cannot be ignored or overthrown" (p. 39). My objection to his elaboration of this idea is that it is not precise enough to be useful for lawyers.

rule. And as for a norm appearing at *t* in a bill, one can only say at *t* that it *can become* a legal rule. With this approach, legal rules are a kind of sociological states of affairs and a tautology arises, if we predicate a concept "validity" to them, which concept, too, is defined in application of norms (although, of course, other concepts of validity can be predicated to them). This is, for example, characteristic of the so-called prediction theory put forward by O. W. Holmes.[25]

However, there is another linguistic usage permitting us to say about a no longer applied norm that it *is* a legal rule, and also that a norm merely existing in a bill *is* a legal rule. Both approaches are made possible by an ambiguity in the word "is". Suppose that someone at some point of time in 2016 pronounces the sentence "Socrates is a man", having in mind the Greek philosopher who died in 399 BCE. Well, in one sense this sentence is false—the physical human being Socrates does not exist in 2016. But in another sense the sentence is true—Socrates belongs in 2016, as well as always, to the set of human beings (dead, alive, or unborn)—he does not belong to the set of, e.g., gods or birds.

In my opinion it has certain advantages to be able to make, within the set of legal rules, a distinction between such rules that are actually applied and such rules that are not. For that reason, a more abstract, timeless concept—like the just-mentioned concept "human being"—is preferable. Such a linguistic usage is also more in accordance with ordinary juridical linguistic usage. For instance, also a norm expressed *de lege ferenda* by a legal scientist is, I think, regarded as a legal rule although by definition it is not applied. Or suppose that the two parties in a litigation refer to two incompatible norms which they claim shall be applied by the judge. Given that the two norms have such a formal (morphological) structure that they, as far as structure is concerned, could have been applicable legal rules, it seems appropriate to call both norms legal rules, in spite of the fact that perhaps only one of them, or none, is actually applied by courts of law (there and then)—or where there is doubt whether this is the case.[26]

Seeing things that way, the actual application must instead be expressed by means of an accessory qualification of the concept "legal rule".[27] A very good candidate for that purpose is the concept "validity". One reason for this is that one seems to say something absurd when stating that a rule is valid although it is not applied (by and large) by the courts.

This argument is also applicable to the terms "legal system" and "legal order". One should not deprive oneself of the possibility to talk about non-functioning, not "applied" legal systems and orders—whether they once were functioning or are only projects for the future.

In Sect. 13.4.2 the concept of validity with respect to legal rules, systems, and orders will be clarified. In Sect. 13.4.3 we turn to the validity of individual legal norms, acts-in-the-law, and legal instruments, i.e., to the validity of products of legal

[25]Holmes (1897).

[26]Cf. my distinction between legal rules in a stricter and in a wider sense in Subsection 3.2 above.

[27]Ibid.

systems. Finally, in Sect. 13.4.4, I shall say a few words about validity from the viewpoint of the legal dogmatist.

13.4.2 Validity of Legal Rules, Systems, and Orders Clarified

In this subsection I shall begin by giving more precise formulations of the two kinds of positive law validity presented in the beginning of Sect. 13.4.1: (1) *r* is valid relative to the practice of courts of law and (2) *r* is valid according to a legal source doctrine. Then I give reasons for preferring (1) to (2). After that I present some objections to (1), in the first place the so-called circularity objection. I refute that objection, which leads me to my theory of the validity of legal orders.

Let us preliminarily define "valid legal rule" in sense (1) as follows (*F* is some state of affairs). We assume that *r* is a judge-addressed rule (if needed created by means of the transformation of a citizen-addressed rule).

(D1) *r* is valid in *S* at *t* if and only if *r* is on the whole applied by the law-applying authorities (notably courts of law) in *S* at *t* provided that *F*

Let me make some commentaries to D1.

(a) It must be emphatically underlined that "practice of courts of law" is *not* the same as case law (law created by precedents), but something much more general. It covers all rules, be they statutory provisions or rules embedded in precedents. "The practice of the courts of law" signifies a social phenomenon and must not be conceived of as the name of a legal source.
(b) D1 does not express a prediction theory. It is not a prophecy of what the court might do in some future point of time but an assertion of what the courts would do just now, i.e., at *t*, if *F*. D1 expresses a hypothetical fact.
(c) An assertion that *r* is valid according to D1 is not invalidated by the fact that the law-applying authorities in some cases do not apply *r* if *F*. Like many other statements about social regularities, statements of this kind are always approximate.
(d) Morality and natural law claim universal validity. But positive validity is, as we all know, attached to national legal systems—we talk, e.g., about valid Swedish or German law. One cannot object to this that, e.g., a German rule shall be applied by a Swedish court when the Swedish choice-of-law rules point out German law as *lex causae* and, since these rules are valid according to D1, the applicable German rule thereby becomes a valid Swedish rule as well. That would not be a satisfactory rendering of what has taken place. It is better to differentiate, within the realm of valid rules relative to the practice of the courts of *S*, between (i) valid *S:ish* (e.g., Swedish) legal rule and (ii) valid guest rule according to *S:ish* law.

It is often objected to praxeological (or realistic) definitions of type D1 that such a concept of "validity" is not of any help to judges, since, it is said, the judge shall decide, not in accordance with how judges usually decide, but in accordance with what is valid according to the established doctrine of legal sources. The catchword is: A rule is not valid because it is applied, but it is applied because it is valid.

This objection is so common in the literature that one gets the impression that many think it devastating for D1. For my part, I do not find it particularly serious.

Strictly speaking, the "objection" does not contain any immanent criticism against D1 at all. It is better seen as an apology for an alternative validity concept, a concept of type (iv), where validity is defined with reference to some doctrine of legal sources.[28] Such a validity concept could be defined like this (*DS* is some established doctrine of legal sources and *a* some law-applying authority):

(D2) *r* is valid according to *DS* for *a* at *t* if and only if *r* according to *DS* may (should, shall) be applied by *a* at *t* provided that *F*.

"May", "should", and "shall" indicate a scale from a weaker to a stronger validity concept.

At first sight it might seem as if D2 comes closer to the way lawyers actually think of validity than D1 does. However, as I shall argue below, there are some shortcomings of the former, making it less suitable as a workable juridical concept.

As a matter of fact, the situation is such that there is, on the one hand, a set of rules, *M1*, such that they are actually applied in *S* at *t* and, on the other, a set of rules, *M2*, such that they can be stated by means of the established doctrine of legal sources in *S* at *t*. The juridical language needs names for both *M1* and *M2*.

It is not my intention to exaggerate the difference between D1 and D2. Although having different connotations they have to a high degree the same denotations—there is extensional but not intentional equivalence between the two definitions. *M1* and *M2* tend to conflate and it is a legalistic ideal that they do. Furthermore, in order to ascertain whether a rule is valid in sense D1 it is usually necessary (but not sufficient) to make sure that it is valid in sense D2.

In two important respects, though, D1 and D2 differ. Let me give an example. In a Swedish Supreme Court case[29] the problem was the following. In a provision in the Bankruptcy Act there was a requisite to the effect that a person "had paid a due debt". (The case was about reclamation by the bankruptcy estate.) In the case a person had delivered goods for which he had been paid in advance. Had he by so doing "paid a due debt"? Expert opinions of two civil law professors were presented. One argued that the person had paid due debt, the other that he had not. Each opinion can be expressed as a legal rule and these two rules, say r_1 and r_2, are mutually incompatible. The difference between D1 and D2 is evident from the example in two ways.

(i) r_1 and r_2 are without any doubt whatsoever both established according to the Swedish doctrine of legal sources at the time. Although incompatible, they both belong to *M2* vintage 1950. Generally speaking, it must be very common that

[28] See Subsection 13.4.1 above.

[29] NJA 1950, pp. 417 ff.

rules in *M2* are mutually incompatible. Every problematic interpretation situation (situations concerning so-called hard cases) is characterised by the fact that it is possible to formulate arguments, based on the legal sources, in favour of both standpoints in a litigation. This consequence of D2 must be accepted (unless one tries to conjure away existing incompatibilities by the strange notion we thought definitely out of date after the demise of the Franco-Belgian exegetical school in the nineteenth century to the effect that the legal system is complete, but, somewhat ghost-like, reappears in the form of Dworkin's thesis that in theory there always exists a right answer[30]). On the other hand, it is impossible that two incompatible rules can both belong to *M1*, for both cannot be applied on the whole at the same time. For example, r_1 and r_2 cannot simultaneously belong to *M2* (of Sweden 1950).

(ii) Before the judgment was pronounced in our example, both r_1 and r_2 belonged to *M2* but neither belonged to *M1*. At that time there was no valid Swedish law (according to D1) concerning the matter in dispute. And this is exactly what we expect from an advocate to answer the client asking him what was valid law with respect to this specific situation before the judgment had been pronounced.

Let me now formulate my objection to D2. The difference between D1 and D2 is this. No in-depth investigation of the doctrines of legal sources in different countries and at different times is needed in order to ascertain that such doctrines are fundamentally undetermined. Already modest juridical studies show that an established doctrine of legal sources can supply us with arguments for many different, and also mutually incompatible, solutions. Law students fresh out of school are often surprised that, in some cases, the district court decides in one way, the court of appeal in the opposite way, while the Supreme Court agrees with the district court, but with another justification. Pretty soon the astonishment evaporates and the insight becomes a triviality, but the very discovery of the phenomenon can be compared to the child's in H. C. Andersen's story about the emperor's new clothes. The insight illuminates a fundamental quality of law and must for that reason be taken seriously. Even with respect to the most specific and precise legal source, statutory law, it is a fact that, when reality presents its unpredictable and bewildering constellations of circumstances to the courts of law, the law is often inadequate, or even unsuitable—and as for the juridical technique of argumentation that is mobilised as a further resource, this technique is often of the kind that rules (solutions, interpretations) can be put forward, which rules are mutually incompatible (although all of them are based on arguments permitted by the doctrine of legal sources and, hence, each of them, is valid in sense D2). It is futile to believe that even the most sophisticated doctrine of legal sources can compensate for the imperfections of statutory provisions and other legal rules. For better or for worse we have to live with *the inescapable uncertainty of law*, and any theory of law that disregards this conveys in fact a false picture of the law.

[30]Dworkin (1977), pp. 279 ff. and 331 ff.

But the kind of inconsistency tormenting *M2* (the rules valid according to D2) does not affect *M1*, (the rules valid according to D1). As a consequence, *M1* has much fewer members than *M2*. That fact has its consequences both for practicing lawyers as well as for legal scholars.

It is a well-known fact that the terms of lawyers (often in a more or less distorted way) also belong to common parlance. This also applies to the term "validity". For a layman, e.g., an advocate's client, information to the effect that, in his situation, certain rules are *valid* certainly means that those rules are the ones he shall comply with and adjust himself to. But if the advocate only had in mind rules that are acceptable arguments according to the established doctrine of legal sources, the client might sustain heavy losses if he relies on the information and acts accordingly. The same goes for the legal scholar who, in a constructive manner, expounds some area of the law and brings forward his expositions as valid law. To use of the term "validity" in sense D1 can, with a certain overstatement, be said to be a point of honour. And, as I have mentioned before, it no doubt seems a bit strange to say that a rule is valid although it is not on the whole applied by the law-applying authorities.

Since we need a juridical term also for validity in sense D2, I suggest the terms "possibly valid (source-based) legal rule" and "probably valid (source-based) legal rule", the latter intended to signify that there is a strong probability that the rule actually is valid (in sense D1).

It may now be objected that *M1*—the set of valid rules—is far too small, since more often than not it is not possible to ascertain with a high degree of probability that a certain rule actually is valid. And so it is, indeed. And this is in fact the very reason why I prefer D1 to D2. The public, that the law is meant to serve, has an interest, which is as vital as it is legitimate, to know which rules are actually applied. This is the public's principal interest in information. As for the lawyer, on the other hand, the task is—after the validity or non-validity has been ascertained—to *argue* in favour of interpretations, amplifications, or even limitations of the valid law. In incisive words: Juridical thinking proper begins after the question of validity has been answered. Juridical thinking, over and above the thinking that moves on the level of pure knowledge of the legal sources, is argumentation.

Let us now pay attention to a serious objection to realistic definitions of type D1, the so-called *circularity objection*, put forward by, among others, Kelsen, who argued that this objection is devastating for such definitions.

According to the circularity objection the concept "authorities" in D1 is its weak point. For this concept in fact presupposes the validity concept, since the latter concept is necessarily a part of the definition of "authority". So, if we let "authority" be a part of the definition of "validity", the latter has been defined by means of a circular definition, which is not acceptable. Hence, D1 must be rejected.

The main point of the circularity objection—that "validity" is necessarily a part of the definition of "authority"—is based on the following reasoning. The creation of an authority, its forms of activities, and its cessation are regulated by valid legal rules and the same is the case with what qualifications persons must have in order to be persons in authority as well as the legal competence tied to different offices. And since all these things are decided by valid legal rules, a circular definition arises, if we define "valid legal rule" in terms of the concept "authority".

Now, does the circularity objection have such weight that D1 must thereby be refuted?

One way to avoid this objection is of course to deny that "authority" necessarily must be defined in terms of valid legal rules. If one succeeds in defining "authority" in a purely sociological, "non-legal", way the objection fails. However, I have strong doubts about the possibility of such a definition.

Kelsen's mobilisation of the circularity objection for the purpose of confuting the so-called court realism has been brilliantly demolished by Anders Wedberg in 1945.[31] He says:

> [. . .] But how shall we save ourselves from the circle that Kelsen thinks inevitable . . . ? The logic of relations is our resort. A circle completely analogous to the Kelsenian one arises if we first define husband as a man who has a wife and then define a wife as a woman who has a husband. In this case it is obvious how to avoid circularity. The fundamental concept is the relation of marriage: a man belonging to the domain of the relation we call a husband; a woman belonging to its converse domain we call a wife. Kelsen's circle can be solved in exactly the same way. There is a certain [. . .] relation – for which everyday language has no direct designation – and what belongs to one of its domains we call "valid legal rules", what belongs to another of its domains we call authorities [my transl.]

This does not contain any elaborate argumentation for the refutation of the circularity objection (and was not meant to; Wedberg's intention was only to show the usefulness of a knowledge of logic). It is rather a recipe for such a refutation. In the following I shall make use of that recipe. By means of it I shall in a more precise manner refute the circularity objection and hopefully give a helpful clarification of what it means that a *legal order* is valid.

Let us take as our starting point Wedberg's marriage analogy. Together the definitions

(D3) x is a husband $=_{\text{def}}$ x has a wife

(D4) y is a wife $=_{\text{def}}$ y has a husband

are obviously circular. The circle is solved by proceeding from the marriage relation and defining that:

(D5) A marriage is a relation between one (or more) men and one (or more) women such that . . .

where ". . ." indicates the more specific nature of marriage. (For the sake of simplicity we exclude homosexual marriages here.) Husbands are a proper subset of men and wives are a proper subset of women, and the marriage relation holds between members of these two subsets.

Men	Women
Husbands	Wives

[31] Wedberg (1945), pp. 10–13. Unfortunately this work is only available in Swedish.

By means of D5 we then define "husband" and "wife":

(D6) A husband is a man standing in a relation of marriage to one (or more) women

(D7) A wife is a woman standing in a relation of marriage to one (or more) men.

Unlike D3 and D4, D6 and D7 are not circular taken together. From D5 –D7 follows

(T1) If *x* is a husband, *x* has a wife

(T2) If *y* is a wife, *y* has a husband.

T1 and T2 taken together are not circular definitions but logical tautologies following from D5–D7.

Let us now in an analogous way follow this line of reasoning with respect to "valid legal rule". Together the definitions

(D8) r is a valid legal rule $=_{\text{def}}$ r is applied by the authorities

(D9) a is an authority $=_{\text{def}}$ a is constituted by valid legal rules

are obviously circular.

In order to solve this circle we need a relation, *R**, analogous to the marriage relation defined in D5 and such that it holds between valid legal rules and authorities according to the schema

(S) *R** is a relation between *X* and *Y* such that . . .

where *R** corresponds to the marriage relation, *X* to the set of men, and *Y* the set of women. *R** is the relation which, according to Wedberg, lacks a name in everyday language. But what is *X* and *Y*? These two sets must reasonably fulfil the following conditions:

(i) *X* is a set such that legal rules are a subset of *X* (*X* is *genus proximum* of legal rules, cf. "men" in D5).
(ii) *Y* is a set such that authorities are a subset of *Y*.
(iii) *X* and *Y* must not be defined in terms of *R**.

But what is *R** more exactly?

I argue that *this relation*, *R**, between legal rules and authorities is what can reasonably be called *a legal order*. And it is also in this way that we defined the concept in Chap. 2[32]:

(D10) *A legal order* is a relation between a set of legal rules (a legal system), *LS*, and a system of organisations (a legal organisation), *Lorg*, such that

(i) rules in *LS* constitute *Lorg*

[32]Subsection 2.12.

(ii) the function of *Lorg* is to handle (create, apply, etc.) rules of *LS*
and, in addition to that
(iii) the function of *LS*, in its totality, is to regulate social life in its fundamental parts and in a comprehensive way
(iv) one part of *Lorg* has the function to settle disputes among persons in accordance with rules in *LS* and to take a standpoint on alleged non-compliance with obligations or prohibitions of *LS* (i.e., courts of law)
(v) another part of *Lorg* has the function to impose and execute sanctions (punishment, damages, etc.) on persons under certain conditions stated by *LS* as the ultimate resource for obtaining the goals of the rules of *LS*.

Some might object to D10 that this definition is circular, too. For how can we define "organisation" without doing so in terms of the concept "rule"? Characteristic of a human organisation is, no doubt, that it is a kind of human co-operation following certain rules.

And so it is. But that does not necessarily mean that D10 is circular. For we can conceive of legal orders as a proper subset of something we might call "social orders", which can be defined like this:

(D11) *A social order* is a relation between a system of norms, *N*, and some human co-operation, *C*, such that

(i) norms in *N* regulate the activities within *C*
(ii) *C* consists in following the norms of *N*.

As examples of social orders we can, apart from legal orders, mention co-operation at a place of work, in a family, or in a fraternal order.

By means of D11—which itself is not circular since it is logically, and even empirically, possible that there exists human co-operation that is not regulated by norms (e.g., a sudden co-operation on a ship in distress)—we can reformulate D10 without changing its meaning, but in a way that clearly shows that it is not circular:

(D10*) *A legal order* is a social order such that conditions (iii)–(v) in D10 are fulfilled.

social rules	↔	SOCIAL ORDER	↔	human co-operation
official legal rules	↔	LEGAL ORDER	↔	authorities

By means of D10 we can now define "official legal rule" and "authority" like this (cf. D6 and D7):

(D12) *An official legal rule* is a rule, *r*, standing in a relation to some human co-operation, *C*, such that *r* and *C* together belong to the same legal order.

(D13) *An authority* is a human co-operation, *c*, standing in a relation to a system of rules, *R*, such that (i) *c* and *R* together belong to the same legal order and (ii) *c* is obligatory according to *R*.

D12 and D13 taken together are not circular.

Notice that "official legal rules" is not the same as "legal rules". The set of official legal rules is a proper subset of legal rules, for there are legal rules that are not official ones, e.g., a rule put forward *de lege ferenda* or a proposed interpretation rejected by a supreme court.

That an organisation (a human co-operation) is obligatory means that it, according (explicitly or implicitly) to the system of rules, shall exist. This condition is motivated by the fact that there can also exist non-obligatory, private organisations, constituted by legal rules, such as limited companies.

From D10, D12, and D13 follows (cf. T1 and T2):

(T3) If *r* is an official legal rule, it is the function of the authorities to handle *r*.

(T4) If *a* is an authority, *a* is constituted by official legal rules.

T3 and T4 taken together are not circular definitions but logical tautologies following from D10, D12, and D13.

Let us further formulate the following definitions:

(D14) *An official legal system* is the set of all rules belonging to a legal order.

(D15) *A legal organisation* is the set of all authorities constituted by a legal order.

Just as we can separate between valid and non-valid legal rules we can also do so between valid and non-valid legal systems and legal orders. As an example of a non-valid legal order can be mentioned the classical Roman one: its rules are no longer applied and its authorities, e.g., the praetor, are no longer in operation.

We define "valid legal order" in the following way:

(D16) *A valid legal order* at *t* is a legal order, {<*LS, Lorg*>}, such that the rules in *LS* are actually applied by and large by the authorities in *Lorg* at *t* and such that the authorities in *Lorg* actually operate at *t*.

social rules	↔	SOCIAL ORDER	↔	organisations
official legal rules	↔	LEGAL ORDER	↔	authorities
valid legal rules	↔	VALID LEGAL ORDER	↔	authorities in operation

By means of D16 we can now define "valid legal rule" and "authority in operation" (cf. D6 and D12, and D7 and D13).

(D17) *A valid legal rule* is an official legal rule, *r*, that stands in a relation to a legal organisation, *Lorg*, such that *r* and *Lorg* together belong to the same valid legal order.

(D18) *An authority in operation* is an authority, *a*, that stands in a relation to an official legal system, *LS*, such that *a* and *LS* together belong to the same valid legal order.

D17 and D18 taken together are not circular. From D16 to D18 follows (cf. T1 and T3, and T2 and T4)

(T5) If *r* is a valid legal rule at *t*, then *r* is actually applied by operative authorities at *t*.

(T6) If *a* is an operative authority at *t*, then *a* operates according to valid legal rules at *t*.

T5 and T6 taken together are no circular definitions but logical tautologies following from D16 to D18.

Notice the striking similarity between D1 and T5. When I argue that the circularity objection has been refuted, this is not due to the fact that I argue that D1 is a non-circular definition but that I argue that it is not a definition at all. The fundamental definition of the concept "validity" is expressed in D16. D1 is only a logical consequence of D16 and D17—it is, like T5, a tautology (T5 is only a weaker formulation of D1). And none of D10, D11or D16 is circular.

Our theory exposes to view that *the concept "(valid) legal order" is logically more fundamental than the concept "(valid) legal rule" in juridical thinking.*

Finally, we formulate the following definitions:

(D19) *A valid legal system* is the set of all legal rules belonging to a valid legal order.

(D20) *An operative legal organisation* is the set of all authorities belonging to a valid legal order.

13.4.3 Validity of Products of Legal Systems (Individual Legal Norms, Judgments, Positions, Acts-in-the-Law, and Legal Instruments) Clarified

A merit of Munzer's work on validity[33] is that he investigates not only the validity of legal rules and systems but also the validity of acts-in-the-law and legal instruments. He argues, if I have understood him correctly, that the same concept "validity" is applicable to both types,[34] and it might well be so if his rather weak concept of "validity" is used.

Here I shall take the stand that we mean different things by "validity" when it is predicated to legal rules, systems, and orders on the one hand, and individual legal norms, legal positions, acts-in the-law, and legal instruments on the other.

My reason for this is the following. In Sect. 2.13 above I made a distinction between legal phenomena belonging to the legal order (LO-elements) and legal

[33]See note 24 above.

[34]Munzer (1972), pp. 27 and 40 f.

phenomena outside the legal order. To phenomena of the latter kind I assigned what I called products of legal orders. These are individual legal norms, judgment sentences, legal positions that are not LO-elements (i.e., do not belong to the legal order), acts-in-the-law, and legal instruments.

That LO-elements, such as legal rules, are valid means that they *belong to* a valid legal order, as "valid legal order" has been defined in the previous subsection (let us say that they are "valid" in sense 1). That a product of a legal order is valid means that it *is in accordance with* that legal order. Then, what does "being in accordance" mean in this connection?

In fact, the validity of legal products must be ascertained in two steps. First, we must ascertain the validity of the set of legal rules, *L*, that a legal product, *lpr*, is a product of. Next, we must ascertain that *lpr* has been correctly established by means of *L*. Both these conditions must be fulfilled in order for us to state that *lpr* is valid. If they are fulfilled, *lpr* is in accordance with the legal order in question.

Hence, e.g., *the individual norm*

(*n*) The judge shall order B to pay motor traffic insurance to A

is valid (in sense 2) if and only if (i) the legal rule(s) on which *n* is based, e.g.,

(*r*) For bodily injury as a consequence of motor traffic, motor traffic insurance shall be paid

is valid in sense 1 at the time when *n* is made topical and (ii) *n* has been correctly established by means of *r*.

The corresponding judgment

(*j*) B shall pay 30.000 kronor to A

is valid (in sense 2) if and only if *n* is valid (in sense 2) at the time when *j* is issued and *j* has been correctly established by means of *n*.

An individual legal position (or sets of such), *lp*, e.g., the marriage between C and D or the limited company Volvo, is legally valid (in sense 2) at time *t* if and only if the legal rules *R* on which *lp* is based are valid in sense 1 at the time when *lp* has come about and *lp* has been correctly established by means of *R* (and has not been cancelled before *t*).

An act-in-the-law, e.g.,

(*a*) D offers E to buy D's car

is valid if and only if the rules of contract-making according to which the offer is made are valid in sense 1 at the time when the offer is made and *a* is performed by complying with these rules.

As for *legal instruments* the situation is bit more complicated. Legal instruments are legal documents in writing, such as wills, contracts and mortgages. In what sense can such phenomena be valid? They are, after all, only scraps of paper. A far as I can see, legal instruments are valid in the same sense as positions and acts-in-the-law. What is added is either nothing or just a requirement, a written form, which is included in the conditions for certain kinds of contracts or wills to be correctly established. Legal instruments do not constitute a special category such as individual legal norms, positions, and acts-in-the-law.

Crucial here is, of course, the notion "correctly established". That a legal product is correctly established cannot, as far as I can see, mean anything else but its having been established by the complying with valid legal rules. That means that validity is assigned to legal products by what Munzer calls rules of smaller scope,[35] varying from one legal system to another (just as doctrines of legal sources can vary from one system to another).

13.4.4 Validity and Legal Dogmatics

Of course, the theory of legal validity proposed here has its consequences for our view on juridical science, or legal dogmatics. What is the relation between legal science and valid law—and what should the character of that relation be?

Valid law is not "the object" of legal dogmatics in the sense that "the object" of a science usually is understood, namely as a phenomenon that science tries to explain and which phenomenon the scientist, when investigating it, must not exert an influence on. Admittedly, in practice such an influence is hard to avoid, something of which, e.g., physicists, psychologists and economists can give examples. But such an influence on the object of study is for the scientist an inconvenience that he tries to eliminate. This is not the case with respect to the legal dogmatist. His attitude to his object, the valid law, is not that of the astronomer to the celestial bodies but that of the potter to the clay—or, for the sake of not doing an injustice to legislators or judges—that of the refiner to the semi-product. Valid law is to the dogmatist not only an object of analysis but also an object to work up, to make more precise and, not least, an object of rational criticism. Valid law is only the natural starting point of legal dogmatics. Legal dogmatics is, in other words, a *constructive* intellectual activity and resembles in that respect, e.g., mathematics, philosophy, and the science of engineering. If one choses to call this intellectual activity "a science" or not is perhaps less interesting. The main thing is that it is performed in a rational and uncorrupted way.

From this it follows that the finished product of legal dogmatics is not valid law but an adaption and elaboration of it. The essential legal dogmatics begins after the question of the validity of the rules under investigation has been answered—legal dogmatics is, as juridical thinking as a whole, in the first place argumentation. Due to the inescapable uncertainty of the law a legal dogmatics that restricts itself to just reproducing valid law must be of limited value to law-appliers and legislators. If such a restricted legal dogmatics is seen as one pole of the scale, we find at the opposite pole the great classical legal doctrine: the commentators' legal concept formation that proved to be extremely important for the future development of the

[35] Munzer (1972), p. 63.

law, as well as the natural law doctrine of the seventeenth and eighteenth centuries, without which the grand European codifications could hardly have seen the light of day.

That the purpose of legal dogmatics should be restricted to reproducing valid law would, in my opinion, result in the abandoning of its most important task: the constructive guidance of the administration of justice and legislation. The main task of legal dogmatics is to offer logically, conceptually, technologically, and teleologically *better versions* of the valid law. (A deeper elaboration of this topic—however important—falls outside the scope of this book.[36])

References

Austin J (1911) Lectures on jurisprudence or the philosophy of positive law, vol I, 5th edn. (revised and edited by R. Campbell), J. Murray, London
Austin JL (1976) How to do things by words, 2nd edn. Harvard University Press, Cambridge
Dworkin R (1977) Taking rights seriously. Harvard University Press, Cambridge
Geach P (1957) Mental acts: their content and objects. Humanities Press, London
Holmes OW (1897) The path of law. Harv Law Rev 10:457–478
Kelsen H (1996) Introduction to the problems of legal theory (transl. by B. Litschewski Paulson and S. L. Paulson). Clarendon Press, Wotton-under-Edge
Munzer S (1972) Legal validity. Springer, Berlin
Suppes P (1967) Introduction to logic. van Nostrand, New York
von Mises L (1949) Human action, Irvington-on-Hudson: foundation for economic education
von Wright GH (1963) Norm and action. Springer, Berlin
von Wright GH (1968) An essay in deontic logic and the general theory of action. North-Holland Pub. Co, Amsterdam
Wedberg A (1945) Den nya logiken (The new logic), part II. Albert Bonniers Förlag, Stockholm

[36]See however Subsection 1.1 (The lawyer as jurist (legal scholar)) above.

Chapter 14
Statutory Interpretation Against the Background of a General Typology of Interpretation

14.1 Introduction

Closely connected to juridical praxeology is, for obvious reasons, juridical methodology. In the present chapter I shall present, from a methodological viewpoint, some thoughts about statutory interpretation, and in the following chapter some thoughts about the methodology of legislation.

It is commonplace to assert that the interpretation of texts, which are supposed, some way or another, to harbour law, plays a crucial role in juridical thinking. There is, however, far less agreement among legal scholars upon how this interpretative business is to be analysed and explained.

In order to get some kind of perspective, one way to proceed could be to place the juridical interpretative enterprise within a wider framework—that is, to clarify it by the help of some kind of typology over the, indeed immense, variety of interpretative activities going on everywhere in society, and by no means only in academic circles. The following is a humble endeavour in that direction.

Closely connected with the concept "interpretation" is the concept "understanding". The purpose of interpreting some object, we think, is to attain understanding, or an increased understanding of the object itself, or something of which it is a "carrier", or "intermediary". Understanding can take different forms, and perhaps it is possible to classify different kinds of interpretation by relating them to different kinds of understanding, or the other way round.

I take the word "interpretation" in its widest possible sense, including, among other things, the following seven types of activities:

1. Translation from one language to another, e.g., the translation of a novel from English into Swedish, as well as a symphony orchestra's "translation" from musical notation to "tone language".
2. Interpretation of the meaning of linguistic texts: scientific, fictional, legal, etc.
3. Interpretation of the meaning of non-linguistic phenomena: works of art or artefacts on the whole, dancing rituals, etc.

Å. Frändberg, *The Legal Order*, Law and Philosophy Library 123,
https://doi.org/10.1007/978-3-319-78858-6_14

4. A painter's interpretation of the landscape or human being he has as his motive.
5. A physicist's interpretation of (a slice of) reality.
6. A physicist's interpretation of another physicist's theory.
7. An archaeologist's interpretation of what an amphora might have looked like by the help of a few potsherds.

Since, as we all know, the word "interpretation" suffers from a general ambiguity, referring sometimes to some kind of activity (interpreting) and other times to the result of such activities, I use, when needed for the sake of clarity, the term "result of interpretation", or simply "result", for the latter sense of the word.

In Sect. 14.2 I shall try to clarify some different significations of the term "interpretation" in general. Section 14.3 will be devoted to statutory interpretation specifically.

14.2 A General Typology of Interpretation

14.2.1 Introduction

I shall make a distinction between three basic types of interpretation, namely transposing interpretation (Sect. 14.2.2), elucidating interpretation (Sect. 14.2.3), and pragmatic interpretation (Sect. 14.2.4).

14.2.2 Transposing Interpretation

By *transposing interpretation* I mean an interpretation, where the result of the interpretation is intended to depict *the same thing* as the object of interpretation (the *interpretandum*), although the object and the result are not identical. The result is a kind of reproduction of the object, a picture of it. The task of this kind of interpretation is to depict the object exactly as it is—not to explain it, or make theories about its meaning. The result shall have the same degree of clarity, or lack of clarity, as the object. It shall give an unretouched picture of it.

Let us distinguish between three different kinds of transposing interpretation:

1. Translating interpretation
2. Depicting interpretation
3. Realising interpretation.

Translating interpretation is to convey a message from one medium (language) to another in order to make the message *understandable*. Here the receiver of the message is usually not identical with the interpreter, and the interpreter shall see to it that the receiver's understanding of the object is the same as if the receiver himself had known the language in which the message is expressed (the original language)—

but no more! If the object is obscure, then the result must mirror that obscurity. There shall be a semantical identity between object and result. Examples: Simultaneous translation at international conferences or the translation of a novel from Swedish into English.

In order to achieve this, a certain amount of understanding is necessary—the interpreter shall have a mastery of the original as well as the translation languages in both syntactical and semantical respects. Here certain risks lurk. Either the interpreter has an insufficient intentional depth compared to the author; he cannot grasp the author's intention. Or, on the contrary, the interpreter has too great an intentional depth, compared to the author; he reads more into it than the author has intended (or even could have intended)—a phenomenon that has been used to the extreme within the neo-hermeneutical movement. Suppose, e.g., that a historian of logic translates Aristotle's *Categories*. Unlike Aristotle, he is familiar with the long Western tradition of logic, which might influence his translation. Understanding here involves a risk.

There are, in fact, certain kinds of translating interpretation, where the interpreter can be semantically empty, he does not need to understand a thing of the meaning of the object—it might even be an advantage if he does not. An example is the role of the interpreter in Morse signalling. His ability to catch the rapid sequel of symbols (which an experienced radio operator does in forms of wholes, *Gestalten*, rather than as discrete Morse symbols) and to transpose this into letters on a paper is best facilitated if he completely refrains from trying to understand the message. The perfect operator is a sheer translating machine. From my military training as such an operator I have a vivid memory of how much easier it was to receive a coded message than one in plain language.

A general problem confronting a person translating a legal text from one language to another, e.g., from Swedish into French, is that not only the languages are different but also the legal systems involved. What would seem to be a literal translation of words like "murder" (e.g., translating the Swedish word for "murder", "*mord*", by the French word "*assassinat*"), "marriage", or "ownership" is not literal at all, because the factors constituting, e.g., ownership are different in the two systems, and so are the legal consequences of ownership as well.

While translating interpretation tries to attain semantical identity, *depicting interpretation* tries to make the result as faithful a reproduction of the object as possible. Example: The portrait painter whose ambition it is to depict his model as life-like as possible. Instead of semantical identity, we could talk about structural identity. With respect to this kind of interpretation, the object of interpretation more often than not does not have, nor even can have, a meaning in a semantical sense—a face, a tree, or an orange is not a language (the fact that we can use our faces mimically does not make it, any more than the rubber stamp, a language).

When the object is a work of art itself, we talk, as far as the visual arts are concerned, of depicting interpretation as copying (cf. quotation of a piece of music in another piece of music).

How does depicting interpretation relate to the "understanding" of the object of interpretation? What is necessary for the interpreter to understand of it, in order to make his depiction? Well, it might be the case here, as it is with Morse signalling, that the portrait painter is better off if he does not know so much about his model.

Depicting interpretation does not seem to have any noteworthy place in juridical interpretative activities.

Interpretation of literary works, especially poetical ones, is sometimes both of the translating and the depicting kinds. We usually demand of a translation of a poem from one language to another that it shall be both meaning-preserving and structure-preserving. If the original is in blank verse, the translation shall be the same. If the original has the rhyme scheme a-b-b-a, then the translation shall have the same.

Judges might in certain cases be forced not to perform a depicting interpretation but to examine whether a certain phenomenon is a depicting interpretation of another phenomenon or not. This is the case within intellectual property law, e.g., when someone claims that his right to a certain trademark has been violated by way of plagiarism.

A third kind of transposing interpretation is *realising interpretation.* There is a certain category of objects such that they are produced for the very purpose of being objects of transposing interpretation. We might talk about *recipes for interpretation.* Examples: Musical notation and score, an architect's blueprint, recipes in a cook-book. The very point is that these objects shall be transposed into music—tone language—and buildings, and delicious dishes on the table. If the pianist, the conductor, the master-builder, or the *chef* has the ambition slavishly to follow the recipe for interpretation without tricking out or adding something of his own, he is doing a realising interpretation.

The quality of the object as a recipe for interpretation is what separates realising interpretation from translating and depicting. We do not walk around wearing our faces for the task of their being depicted (with a certain reservation, perhaps, for one or another movie star or politician), and a novel is hardly written with the direct purpose of its being translated (even if the author is pleased if it happens). Some objects have a double function in this respect: dramas can both be performed and looked at, and read. In the latter case, the reader becomes his own director and stage designer; he himself creates the cast, the costumes, and the décor. (Less enjoyable for reading are perhaps opera and operetta libretti, which can be surprisingly plain. Figaro (in *The Barber of Seville*) admits as much when intimating that what is too stupid to be said could always be sung.) A sensitive, and in the language in question experienced person, is able to transpose recipes of interpretation in his imagination. In the head of the deaf Beethoven it must have resounded with a symphonic ringing. And what about the story I once read, I do not remember where, of the man on the train. A man entered a railway compartment, sat down and pulled out of his briefcase a stiff sheet of paper which the curious fellow travellers soon found out was a restaurant menu. For several hours the man studied the menu intensely and there was no doubt whatsoever among the other passengers that he was sitting there *eating* his way through the menu. "Dinner" successfully completed, the man folded his hands around his belly and fell into a deep and invigorating sleep.

In a wide sense of the notion "recipe for interpretation" norms as a whole can be regarded as such recipes—they are normally created in order to be realised. Then every statutory provision is a recipe for interpretation. A judge who adheres to the principle of legality—demanding the law-applier strictly to comply with the statutory text—performs a realising interpretation as a component of his application of law. It is even possible to regard all recipes for interpretation as norms.

When, with respect to realising interpretation, is the result adequate in relation to the object of interpretation? As I just suggested, one way to look upon it is to regard the recipe as a norm to be followed in order to achieve a certain goal, and the result might be said to be adequate relative to the object, if the interpreter slavishly follows this norm. Another way of looking upon adequacy with respect both to realising and depicting interpretation is to regard it as a relationship of isomorphy between object and result.

An interpretation can be both realising and depicting. The performance of a musical work, for instance, involves two different structures, on the one hand the recipe of interpretation—the notation (or composition)—and on the other the result—the flow of tones. And the flow of tones is a kind of depiction of the composition.

A sceptic could doubt the possibility of a transporting interpretation altogether. For does not the very change of medium (language) necessarily transcend sheer transposing? Perhaps this is the case when both media are vastly different, as, e.g., a screen version of a novel. But I am not sure that this is always the case.

14.2.3 Elucidating Interpretation

We now pass on to elucidating interpretation, and here the concept of "understanding" is brought even more to the fore. The task of elucidating interpretation is to make the object of interpretation *intelligible*, not only understandable, as is the case with transposing interpretation. In science, interpretations of this kind can be regarded as theories about the object. The connection between interpretation and understanding can be expressed by the word "meaning". The task of elucidating interpretation is to disclose a meaning of the object, or to assign a meaning to it. And to understand the object is to know that meaning.

To understand something can mean a lot of things and to each of these things, one could imagine, corresponds a special variant of elucidating interpretation. Let us regard seven such types of elucidating interpretation.

(1) *Precision-making interpretation.* This kind of interpretation applies to texts and is characterised by the result of interpretation being a precisation of the object.[1] To give a trivial example, the sentence

[1]In the sense of "precisation" used by Naess (1953). In Naess' vocabulary, precisation is not the same as "interpretation". While interpretation, logically speaking, is a symmetric, reflexive, and non-transitive relation, precisation is an asymmetric, irreflexive, and transitive relation. In other words, as for precisation the set of possible meanings of the result formulation is a proper subset of the set of possible meanings of the object formulation.

(s_1) I arrive at 8 o'clock a.m.
is a precisation-making interpretation of the sentence
(s_2) I arrive at 8 o'clock
since the set of possible meanings of s_1 is a proper subset of the set of possible meanings of s_2. There is at least one possible meaning of s_2 that is not a possible meaning of s_1, e.g.,
(s_3) I arrive at 8 o'clock p.m.

Admittedly, this is an "empty" kind of interpretation, which says nothing about reasons but only about a formal relationship between object and result. It focuses on some, among many possible, meanings while neglecting, or even sacrificing, others. With respect to statutory interpretation, however, this kind of interpretation is of importance, due to the fact that interpretation of statutory provisions is an applicative interpretation (see Sect. 14.3, below). The object is a general statutory provision, while the result is a more precise norm exactly covering the case at hand, which is what matters for the judge. Whether or not the provision is applicable to other types of cases is no business of his, unless it is relevant with respect to the case at hand.

(2) *Intentional interpretation.* The aim of this kind of interpretation is to understand some object created by man (a text or a work of art, appearing separate from its creator) by finding out what intentions, ideas, and thoughts its author(s) had in mind when creating the object. With respect to statutory interpretation, the principle of subjective interpretation maintains that statutory provisions shall be interpreted in the light of the legislator's intentions. Within the legal sphere, this kind of interpretation is, for obvious reasons, of particular importance with respect to the interpretation of wills. Another example is the literary historian who is trying to interpret a novel or a poem on the basis of a study of the life and character of its author.
(3) *Motive interpretation.* Like intentional interpretation, the purpose of motive interpretation is to explain something by ascertaining the motives, intentions, or reasons for it. The difference between them is that with motive interpretation the task is not to interpret some "objectified" product, separate from its author, but to interpret some state of affairs—actions, courses of events—in which some human being is involved, by finding out his motives, or reasons. We know, for example, that the Roman emperor Caracalla in the beginning of the third century extended Roman citizenship to all free inhabitants of the empire. Why did he do this? What was his motive? That attempts to achieve equality would animate this brutal beast and fratricide would, indeed, be a highly anachronistic and unpsychological explanation. Then historians tell us that Caracalla intended to enlarge the tax base and facilitate tax collection, and at once we seem to "understand" his action. In law, motive interpretation is of utmost importance when courts of law are dealing with criminal intent.
(4) *Causality interpretation.* To understand some x can also mean to know the causes of x. A train goes off the rails on a hot summer day, and we "understand" this event by the causal explanation that, according to general experience, metals expand when heated, and, in this situation, the heat of the sun caused the rails to

expand. In the law of torts, causality interpretation (examination of the causal relationship between some event or action and some damage) is of great importance.

(5) *Coherence-creating interpretation.* Here the object of interpretation is conceived of as a fragment of a whole (a piece in a jig-saw puzzle), and the interpretation of it consists in putting this piece in its right place in the whole (the puzzle). The object is, or might be regarded as, a part of a whole, and by understanding the whole we understand the object of interpretation better.

To discern ordered, clear, coherent wholes in life and in the world, and to experience, intellectually as well as emotionally, harmoniously ordered forms is, I think, a very deeply felt need among human beings, and in that fact lies perhaps the strongest connections between science, speculative philosophy, art, and religion. All four act on the coherence-selling market. This need also manifests itself in our efforts to incorporate new experience with old into a coherent totality.

To understand something is often taken to mean that we see relations between separate phenomena and, hence, conceive of these as belonging to a connected whole—irrespective of whether this connected whole is a scientific theory, a symphony, a philosophical system, or a mystical experience of God.

An important principle of statutory interpretation is the principle of systemic interpretation. The basic idea behind this principle is that the law-applier in hard cases shall interpret the intriguing statutory rule in the context of a larger portion of the legal system. The legal rules belonging to the system shall, for the sake of clarity—and, as a consequence, for the precious sake of legal certainty—be interpreted in a way that augments the inner coherence of the system. This, indeed, is a coherence-creating kind of interpretation.

A special kind of coherence-creating interpretation could be called *restoring interpretation.* Here the object is a fragment of some whole which once existed but is now gone. The task of the interpreter is to restore that whole. Examples: The philologist trying to fill up some corrupt piece of text by Aristotle, the archaeologist imagining the shape of an amphora by the help of a few potsherds, or the palaeontologist trying by the help of some fossil finding to reconstruct what a tyrannosaurus might have looked like when it strolled about on the earth some 70 million years ago.

(6) *Accentuating and concentrating interpretation.* These two types of interpretation I treat together, since I have found it difficult to formulate a good distinguishing criterion (and perhaps there is none, although, intuitively, they seem, at least partly, to be two separate phenomena).They are most prominent in the arts—i.e., in the artist's interpretation of something, not in our interpretation of the artist's work (interpretation).

Accentuating interpretation lays stress upon, or even exaggerates, certain features of the object of interpretation. Examples are caricatures, parodies, and imitations. (One important component in the aesthetics of humour is, as we all know, exaggeration when it hits on something characteristic of its subject.) But the scope of accentuating interpretation far exceeds the province of humour. A common feature of art is to accentuate some aspect of something in order to lay bare something essential in it. To understand is to experience this essential aspect.

Also concentrating interpretation aims to uncover something essential of its object, but this is achieved, not by enlarging some feature of it but, instead, by reducing it to what is essential—the non-essential dross shall be abstracted away. There is a small painting by Chagall, La Guerre (War, 1943). On the surface, the picture instils a feeling close to serenity. Houses (some of them upside down), a dead man peacefully lying stretched out in the snow, in the sky a mother and her child, a horse with a sledge. And still Chagall's interpretation conveys a picture of the real face of war, which goes straight into our hearts—abstracted away are troop movements, men around green tables, shouting, and roaring of guns. Another example is Giacometti's sculptures. What is it the artist seeks so furiously and with an almost frightening convulsiveness? Is it the pure structure of man as such? Is it the exposure of man in the surrounding eternity? I do not know. All that seems clear is that the artist with manic obsession is busy burning off the dross surrounding us.

(7) *Explicating interpretation.* The purpose of this kind of interpretation is that the result in some respect shall present *a better version* of the object of interpretation. Explication means a constructive development of its object in order to achieve a better understanding of it. But explication is not allowed to be something completely independent of its object. It shall build upon the object while preserving its essential intentions. What is implicit in the object shall be made explicit.

Explicating interpretation is characteristic of legal dogmatics, i.e., the branch of legal science that studies the content of valid law, e.g., constitutional law, civil law, criminal law, procedural law, administrative law, international law, etc.—as opposed to legal sciences such as jurisprudence and philosophy of law, history of law, sociology of law, etc. The task of legal dogmatics is to arrange and elaborate further the, often unsorted, mass of legal rules as they appear in statutes and precedents. That means systematising the rules, performing precision-making interpretations of them, developing a more fruitful system of concepts than that of the official legal material, generalising and synthesising of the material in order to construct a coherent and logically consistent system of rules, formulating recommendations (*de lege ferenda*) for the improvement of the system, and many other things. But all this shall be performed in a spirit of loyalty to the official legal system: it is a matter of explication "in the spirit of the law".

Another example is explication, or rational reconstruction, in analytical philosophy. Such a reconstruction might have as its object concepts like that of "right" in juridical thinking, "time" in modern physics, "democracy" or, why not, the concepts "meaning", "interpretation", and "understanding". According to Carnap,[2] it is not required of an explanation that the *explicandum* (the object of interpretation) should

[2]Carnap (1950), p. 3 ff.

have the same meaning as the *explicatum* (the result of interpretation), although certain criteria of adequacy must be fulfilled: "A concept must fulfil the following requirements in order to be an adequate explicatum for a given explicandum: (1) similarity to the explicandum, (2) exactness, (3) fruitfulness, (4) simplicity".

So much for elucidating interpretation. Before turning to pragmatic interpretation I would like to say a few words about a phenomenon that is common both in science and art, viz., *iterative interpretations.* Someone makes an interpretation of, e.g., an idea in a work of Kant. Then other persons interpret that interpretation, etc. Such sequences are typical of what we call a cultural tradition. Within the neo-hermeneutical movement much attention is paid to this phenomenon, and it is said that the existence of a cultural tradition renders impossible an intentional interpretation of the original object. In juridical thinking, iterative interpretations are common (in an opinion the Supreme Court interprets a statutory provision, a jurist makes an interpretation of that opinion, a district court makes an interpretation of the jurist, etc.). Within the arts many examples can be given.

After the Second World War the Poles wanted to rebuild the Old Town of Warsaw, and they wanted it to look exactly as it did before the destruction. However, they lacked some old plans, necessary for the reconstruction. In that situation they came up with the idea to use paintings by Bellotto (who, as his uncle and teacher had done, took the name Canaletto), from the eighteenth century. So Bellotto interpreted buildings, later destroyed, whereupon similar buildings were built by means of interpretations of Bellotto's paintings—which were facilitated by the fact that these paintings, to a very high degree, were depicting interpretations. There is a kind of circularity in this example of iterative interpretation.

Another striking example can take as its point of departure Modest Musorgsky's piano work *Pictures at an Exhibition* (1874), inspired by an exhibition of drawings and watercolours by his deceased friend Victor Hartmann. Here, as we recall, different pictures are represented, and these representations are bound together by a theme, illustrating the spectators walking from one picture to another ("Promenade"). One of these pictures has the title "The Great Gate of Kiev". Let us proceed from that one. We could, then, think of a series of iterative interpretations on, logically speaking, different levels.

Level 1. I know very little about "The Great Gate of Kiev", but suppose that someone, at some time, made a plan, or sketch, of it.

Level 2. The gate is erected. The gate is a realising interpretation of the plan.[3]

Level 3. V. Hartmann comes running along and depicts the great gate of Kiev. His picture is an interpretation of an interpretation.

Level 4. Musorgsky composes "The Great Gate of Kiev" and his tone painting is an interpretation of an interpretation of an interpretation.

Level 5. But this is not the end of the story. Half a century later (1922), Maurice Ravel makes an orchestration of Musorgsky's composition, thereby

[3]In fact, the gate was never completed.

achieving an interpretation of an interpretation of an interpretation of an interpretation.

Level 6. Let the artistic "Great Gate of Kiev-tradition" switch into a scientific direction. Suppose that a musicologist analyses Ravel's orchestration. His analysis lies, logically, on level 6; it is an interpretation of an interpretation of an interpretation of an interpretation of an interpretation.

Human culture is, indeed, a cake with many layers.

14.2.4 Pragmatic Interpretation

By the expression "pragmatic interpretation" I refer to interpretation made for other purposes than rendering its object understandable or intelligible. The result of interpretation is used for these other purposes, even at the expense of interpretations that give a correct or adequate understanding of the object. The purpose of such "non-intellectual" interpretations often is to influence people's behaviour or attitudes.

A believing layman, for instance, turns to the Bible for solving problems in his personal life. In his ignorance, he makes an interpretation that is all wrong with respect to the author's intentions or to authoritative theological interpretation. All the same, his interpretation might have given him a solution to his problem, which satisfies him, and, if so, his result is correct in a pragmatic sort of way. Or a preacher, not adept at theology, interpreting a text with the purpose to influence the audience in some direction—something that might succeed very well even if his interpretation is absurd. The same applies to the Marxist agitator who has got hold of the wrong end of the stick or intentionally rearranges Marx's thought a bit. In the latter case we can talk about *propaganda interpretation.* A successful propaganda interpretation does not necessarily lead to any understanding of the object. (I do not use the term "propaganda interpretation" in an entirely pejorative sense; it might also refer to totally legitimate methods of influencing people).

For reasons adduced in Sect. 14.3 below, statutory interpretation often takes the form of pragmatic interpretation, irrespective of whether such an interpretation is performed by judges, advocates or academic jurists.

14.3 Statutory Interpretation

14.3.1 The Special Character of Statutory Interpretation: Principles of Statutory Interpretation

The rest of this chapter will be confined to statutory interpretation performed by judges only (although, for the sake of brevity, I retain the expression "statutory interpretation" *simpliciter*), since the judge's interpretation in many respects gives statutory interpretation on the whole its special character. First we shall discern nine circumstances giving statutory interpretation its special character and after that some classic principles governing statutory interpretation are presented. The nine circumstances are the following.

1. Statutory interpretation is a norm-based and norm-creating activity. The object of interpretation is a norm, and so is the result. (With respect to precedents, on the other hand, the result is a norm but not the object.)
2. Statutory interpretation is an applicative interpretation (which, of course, is closely connected to its normative character). The judge is confronted with an alleged state of affairs (the object of application, described in evidence sentences) and he asks himself: Is the statutory provision applicable to this object? Does the object fall under the provision? To obtain money in a bank by threatening with a toy gun, is that robbery? If you buy a horse with inherited restiveness, is that a defect in the goods under the Sale of Goods Act? The existence of an object of application is an important feature of statutory interpretation—as opposed to, e.g., interpretation of poetry. To assert that you apply Goethe's *Über allen Gipfeln* to some state of affairs seems strange. To be sure, you can "apply" a poem in the sense that you find it "expressing", "giving a sense to", or "explaining" some inner experiences of your own—but this is not application in the literal sense of the word, as is the case with statutory interpretation, but rather a metaphorical use of the word.
3. Statutory interpretation has an authoritative nature. The result—the norm of application—gets the same "legal force" as the statutory rule—the object—itself.
4. In some areas of law—especially those where abuse of state power would be particularly disastrous by depriving people of liberty, property, bodily integrity, or even life, such as might be the case within criminal law, social welfare law (deprivation of liberty for the sake of care), or tax law—the principle of legality is of the utmost importance.[4] It forbids interpretation to go beyond a strict literal interpretation of the law, i.e., the interpretation may not result in extensions of the text (*in dubio mitius*), and even less analogies from it. The judge may not by means of interpretation "invent" crimes or punishments (*Nullum crimen, nulla poena sine lege*).
5. Statutory interpretation has a justificatory character. The argumentation developed for the interpretation chosen justifies the very judgment.
6. While, for instance, a historian may end his interpretation of a certain text by asserting that, for the time being, no certain interpretation is possible—some circumstances point in one direction and others in some other direction—this option is not available for the judge. He is under a legal duty to present a solution, even when such a solution is theoretically dubious (the prohibition of *déni de justice* or *non liquet*). In such a situation the judge has to ascribe a certain meaning to the statutory provision. The principles of statutory interpretations

[4]On principles of legality, see Frändberg (2014) Ch. 4.

are nearly incomprehensible if this duty to decide the case is not taken into consideration.

7. The fact that the judge is under a duty to decide does not mean at all that he is free to go his own way in situations where the law is obscure or even silent. He is bound by a certain amount of loyalty towards the existing legal system: he shall interpret the law, or create a new norm, "in the spirit of the law". The judge has to decide, but the law is silent. As he cannot apply some rule directly, he uses the legal system in an indirect, or mediate, way. As a consequence, a statutory provision can have a sphere of influence exceeding its "linguistic sphere of cases" by way of extensions and analogies.[5] (But it also happens that the judge does not apply a certain statutory provision to a case which without any doubt whatsoever falls under the provision—in the juridical vocabulary, he makes a reduction of (the sphere of application) of the rule.) Also this principle of loyalty must be taken into consideration if we want to understand some principles of statutory interpretation.
8. If a judge finds that some action belongs to the set described in a statutory provision (the action complies with the requisites of the provision), he shall pronounce a judgment in accordance with the legal consequence of the provision. By that judgment the scope of what the parties may, may not, or have a duty to do is determined or changed—or someone becomes subject to state compulsion, e.g., imprisonment. That consequences of this kind occur, when an action of the kind that is described in the rule has been performed, can be regarded as the very *raison d'être* of the rule, either because the state of affairs where such consequences are realised is regarded as desirable, or because it is supposed to cause such a desirable state of affairs. Therefore it is not surprising that considerations of such consequences are allowed to influence also the judge's interpretative argumentation. That they *shall* be considered is a main tenet of the teleological (finalistic) currents within the doctrine of statutory interpretation—which have been most influential during the twentieth century.

   Statutory interpretation has, indeed, most obvious social consequences: it can deprive a human being of freedom for the rest of his life, or even life itself, it can take the right to be together with his children away from him, or make him miserably poor. Compared to the judge, the historian or literary historian leads a life rather free of responsibility, when interpreting. The principles of statutory interpretation differ with respect to how far the judge can deviate from the wording of the statute for the sake of immediate social consequences. We find a wide range from strict legalism and literal interpretation, via modifying finalistic considerations, to advanced "free law" attitudes, paying small attention to the wording of the law—and the pragmatic element is the more prominent the more the judge proceeds in the latter direction.
9. The need of preserving stability in the legal system and the need of changing it when the society changes constitute a dilemma that not only legislators but also

[5] See Subsection 7.8 above.

judges are faced with. This dilemma will get a chapter of its own in this book (Chap. 16 below). A deeply rooted idea among judges, reinforced by the democratic ideology, is that the necessary development of law in the practice of the courts shall be very restrictive and, as far as possible, concealed. The judgment shall ideally stand out as something emanating from an already existing legal rule. This idea, of course, has had a strong impact on judges' interpretative argumentation and the principles governing it.

In their interpretative argumentation lawyers are guided by certain time-honoured principles. A significant attempt to systematise the classic *canones* of statutory interpretation was made by Savigny in the nineteenth century.[6]

The main classic principles of statutory interpretation can, roughly, be systematised according to the following schema.

I. Bound interpretation

   A. *Objective interpretation*

      1. Formal interpretation

         a. Literal interpretation
         b. Systemic interpretation

      2. Bound objective teleological interpretation

   B. *Subjective interpretation*

      1. Formal subjective interpretation

         a. Literal subjective interpretation
         b. Systemic subjective interpretation

      2. Subjective teleological interpretation (purposive interpretation proper)

II. Free interpretation

It is important to emphasise that these distinctions do not imply razor-edged dichotomies. On the contrary, the difference between them is a matter of degree. You can adhere more or less to them. Between, for instance, bound and free interpretation in their most radical (optimal, ideal-typical) form there is a scale, with a wide range of intermediate positions.

By "free interpretation" I refer to the idea that judges are free to interpret, re-interpret, or correct statutory provisions by resorting to, e.g., very general social ideals or their own sense of justice, without paying attention to restrictions connected with the particular provision being their object of interpretation. Principles of interpretation are bound, if they restrict the interpretative argumentation by only

[6]von Savigny (1840), pp. 212–216 differentiates between grammatical, logical, historical and systematic elements of statutory interpretation. A most instructive study from a comparative perspective is MacCormick and Summers (1991).

allowing reference to certain specified factors, which vary with respect to the different types of principles (interpretation in the light of . . ., where ". . ." is such a factor).

It might seem strange that a judge adopts a principle of free interpretation—what is the point of legislation, if its appliers can choose to disregard it? However, as I have just said, the whole thing is a matter of degree; some judges may have certain tendencies towards a free style of interpretation. A historical example of this is the *Freirechtsbewegung* in Germany in the beginning of the twentieth century, asserting that the judge should let his sense of justice influence his interpretation.

A common distinction within juridical methodology is the one between objective and subjective interpretation. This distinction does not, strictly speaking, pertain to different principles of interpretation but rather to different kinds of such principles; there are, for instance, several different kinds of objective interpretation. An extreme objectivity means that no attention whatsoever is paid to the intentions of the legislator—the navel-string between the originator and the statute is cut off and the statute appears as an independent, "objectified" product. (Compare the New Criticism in literary analysis during the 1940s and 1950s, where the navel-string between author and work was effectively cut off.) An extreme subjectivity, on the other hand, means that the only relevant aid for the interpreter is subjective factors pertaining to the legislator. (Compare the literary historian trying to understand *Murder in the Cathedral* in the light of T. S. Eliot's life story.) Between these two extremes, more or less objective (subjective) attitudes can be ranged.

The objective principles are confirmed by the constitutional principle of separation of powers in that they accentuate the independence of the courts of law.

Among objective principles we can make a subdivision between formal and teleological principles. According to the latter, an ambiguous or obscure statutory provision shall be interpreted in the light of an evaluation of the social consequences of the application of the provision to the case at hand. A teleological principle is objective when this evaluation is performed with respect to social values dominant in society *just now*, i.e., at the time of the application. (If the judge adopts the evaluations of the legislator at the time of the drafting of the statute, he is using a subjective teleological principle.)

By the way, is there any room for teleological interpretation within the sphere of non-applicative and non-normative interpretation? Well, are we not, all of us, familiar with tendentious interpretations of historical or literary texts for political, religious, or similar purposes—pragmatic interpretation of the kind I referred to (in Sect. 14.2.4 above) as propaganda interpretation?

It goes without saying that the borderline between bound teleological interpretation and free interpretation is diffuse. An interpretative method based upon a bound (objective) teleological principle has been developed by the Swede Per Olof Ekelöf.[7] His method is "bound" in the respect that the social aim of a statutory provision—in the light of which any teleological interpretation must be performed—shall be the

[7]Ekelöf (1958).

aim of the provision when applied to "ordinary cases", i.e., cases to which the provision, literally interpreted, without any doubt is applicable.

With an instrumental view of the legal order the teleological principle presents itself immediately.

In contrast to the teleological approach, there are certain objective principles that can be called "formal"—just because (in their radical form) the judge, in his interpretative argumentation, shall not pay any attention at all to the social consequences of the application of the provision to the case. On the contrary, the social ends that the legislator had in mind are better realised within the administration of the law, if the judge refrains from interfering by means of (objective or subjective) teleological interpretation in the direct contact, established by the statutory text, between the legislator and the public. Most judges probably have a (more or less articulated) teleological, or even subjective teleological, conception of the application of law as a whole. The difference between formally and teleologically disposed judges rather lies in the fact that the former mean that the impact of legislation in society is most effective, if the judge, in his interpretative work, is just a more or less passive intermediary between the legislator and the public, while the latter think that the social function of the application of law is best achieved more actively by way of interpretation on the part of the judge. In legal philosophy, Bentham—strongly utilitarian with respect to legislation—is a prominent advocate of formal interpretation for the sake of the legislator's intention being forcefully realised.

We can distinguish between two principles of formal interpretation: literal (linguistic, logical-grammatical) and systemic. According to the former, the statutory provision shall be interpreted in compliance with ordinary (or, perhaps, established legal) language. A systemic interpretation means that the provision shall be put into the context of a whole system of rules, to which the provision belongs, and that the provision shall be interpreted in the light of that system (concerning coherence-creating interpretation in general, see Sect. 14.2.3 above). Systemic interpretation often consists in using rules of the system in a mediate way. In contrast, literal interpretation is, in a way, "acontextual".[8]

The literal interpretation principle is, no doubt, the most self-evident of interpretative principles, for what sense would it make to legislate, if the law-appliers did not comply with the legislator's own words? The principle is, moreover, an attendant principle to the general principle of legality to the effect that there must not arise any discrepancy between the law and its application—which principle is a guarantor for the protection of the law-state values legal certainty, legal equality, legal accessibility, and legal security.[9]

So, at first sight, the literal principle might seem as the most self-evident of all principles of statutory interpretation. If you are interpreting a written text, of course you shall interpret it in the light of the language of this very text! But what is it in most interpretative situations (although by no means all) that makes the case at hand

[8]The term used in Dworkin (1986), p. 17.

[9]Frändberg (2014), Chs. 5, 6, 7, and 8.

a problematic, hard case? It is, in fact, the language of the text itself, with respect to the case, and problems connected thereto. The language of the text is defective with respect to the case. The means of curing the defect would be the defect itself! So, in hard cases this principle is, in fact, of no use! However, what in fact is intended by the term "literal interpretation" is no doubt an *in dubio principle*, a corollary to the general legality principle: In hard cases, interpret the provision in such a way that the result is restrictive or *e contrario*, not extensive or analogous!

The idea behind the systemic principle is that the application of law shall contribute to preserving that the legal system as a whole is informed by consistency and coherence. Also the systemic principle can, albeit not with the same force as the principle of literal interpretation, be justified as a means to maintain legal certainty.

As the schema above indicates, the principle of subjective interpretation (or, as it is also called, *authentic* interpretation) is not situated at the same level as the literal, systemic, and bound objective teleological principles. On the contrary, we can *mutatis mutandis* construct an identical subdivision under the heading "subjective interpretation" as under the heading "objective interpretation". A subjective literal interpretation would then be an interpretation in the light of the meaning the legislator has attached to statutory terms in the preparatory materials or in other ways outside the statutory text itself. A subjective systemic interpretation would, in a corresponding way, be an interpretation in the light of the legislator's opinions, if he has any, not evident from the statutory text itself, of the structure of law. A subjective teleological interpretation, finally, would of course be an interpretation in the light of the purposes of the legislator with the statutory product (found in the preparatory materials or elsewhere). Subjective interpretation is, obviously, an instance of intentional interpretation (see Sect. 14.2.3 above).

The idea behind the subjective approach is undoubtedly the same as the one behind the principle of literal interpretation, viz., the respect for the legislator, which, in accordance with the democratic ideology, as well as the ideology of the separation of powers, is the instance in society that shall *create*—in contrast to the application of—the law. The principle of literal interpretation starts from the assumption that the legislator has said what he wants to say in the statutory text itself, while subjective interpretation goes a bit further and seeks more evidence for ascertaining the intentions of the legislator. However, while, e.g., an historian can use whatever material he can find in order to shed light on some historical person's thoughts or motives, such as private letters, diaries, interviews, etc., not even the most orthodox subjective interpreter applying the law would proceed in this manner. Here the demand of legal certainty draws the line.

It is important to emphasise that the principles of statutory interpretation presented here are no *methods*, although they are often presented as such. They are far too vague and loose for that. This also becomes apparent in the real use of them in the practice of the courts of law. They are used as principles in the proper sense of that word, viz., as guidelines, indicating factors to be taken into consideration, no more. More often than not we find several of them used in the same opinion (the judge's reasons for his judgment), more or less carefully weighed against each other. We often see them combined. The Court of Justice of the European Union, for instance, has disclosed an inclination for a systemic-teleological interpretative style.

14.3.2 Statutory Interpretation by Means of Mediate Use of Legal Rules

In order to understand the complexity of statutory interpretation within the sphere of the application of law I shall draw our attention to a phenomenon that we can call, somewhat clumsily, "mediate use of a legal rule, r', for deciding the applicability of another rule, r, to a case, c"—where r is a statutory provision. Let us make a distinction between "immediate use" and "mediate use" of a rule.

By an *immediate use of r to c* I simply mean that r is applied to c (be it a pure application, an extension, or a restriction of r).

By a *mediate use of r to c* I mean the following. Suppose that a judge is in a quandary about whether rule r^* is applicable to c. In his argumentation for and against application it sometimes happens that the judge makes use of one or more other statutory provisions—r'; r'_1, ... r'_n—which, themselves, are out of the question to be applied (used immediately) to c. These rules are used exclusively as *interpretative arguments* relative to r^*. More precisely put: (i) There is a rule, r^*, such that it is a candidate for being applied to c but (ii) the applicability is doubtful, and therefore (iii) r' is mobilised as an interpretative argument for or against the application of r^* to c. Mediate use of legal rules can be conceived as a special way of adhering to the systemic principle of interpretation.

Let me give an example of mediate use of legal rules.[10] The circumstances were the following. A prosecutor requested search of premises at an advocate's office in order to seize an original document of relevance in a criminal action. It was suspected that a signature on the document was forged. The prosecutor's request was dismissed by the Supreme Court with reference to an article in the Code of Judicial Procedure (Article 27:2) saying: "Seizure must not be performed on a written document in the possession of a person, if its content is such that this person may not give evidence of it". An advocate is just such a person (Article 36:5).

This case might seem as a clear case falling under the rule. However, what made it in fact a hard case was that the content of the document was already known in the criminal case; a photocopy of it had been referred to by the counsel of the defendant. Moreover, a serious disadvantage of the prohibition of seizure is that it gives criminals a possibility to render evidence innocuous by depositing it in an advocate's office.

The prosecutor referred to an expert opinion written by Professor Ekelöf, who argued that seizure would be permitted. His opinion is a very good example of a

[10]The Swedish Supreme Court case NJA 1977, pp. 403 ff.

mediate use of legal rules—rules that, by themselves, are not applicable at all to the case.

To begin with, Ekelöf investigates rules about seizure outside the Code of Judicial Procedure. In the Tax Assessment Code he finds a rule to the effect that seizure is possible with respect to tax assessment audit, even if the person at whose premises the audit takes place may not give evidence. This speaks in favour of a reduction of the rule in the Code of Judicial Procedure. On the other hand, a rule in another statute about coercive measures in certain criminal actions (concerning some grave offences) speaks, if anything, against seizure. But by referring to the risk that criminals can render evidence innocuous, Ekelöf attaches less value to that provision.

Even older statutory provisions, no longer in force, can be used as arguments in a mediate use of rules. The rule under interpretation can, for example, be illuminated by contrasting it to its predecessors (*interpretation by contrasting*). In the present case Ekelöf makes use of an older provision in a statute from 1933 about coercive measures, being the immediate predecessor of the provision 27:2 in the Code of Judicial Procedure. It would take us too far to reproduce Ekelöf's rather intricate argumentation here, but his point is that older provisions can be helpful when interpreting the one in point.

With this example I wish to show how a mediate use of legal rules can be executed in practice. One reason for a mediate use of rules in statutory interpretation is that it provides the judge with a means to solve the dilemma consisting in, on the one hand, his submission under the prohibition of denial of justice and, on the other, that he, when the law is obscure or silent, shall lay down a rule in the spirit of the law.

14.3.3 Statutory Interpretation and Judicial Roles

The task of the judge is the administration of justice. One way of characterising the role of the judge is by trying to lay down the function of the administration of law. This is no easy task. Administration of justice may well have many different functions, and different opinions about what functions it shall fulfil might compete with one another. Hence, different judicial roles are conceivable.

In moral philosophy we find a distinction between two forms of utilitarianism—rule-utilitarianism and act-utilitarianism. Roughly speaking, a rule-utilitarian is a utilitarian arguing that maximum benefit (or minimum disadvantage) is best achieved by issuing general rules for that purpose, which rules shall be followed in individual situations without any independent examination of beneficial or disadvantageous effects in these situations. An act-utilitarian, on the other hand, argues that independent utilitarian considerations are demanded of moral agents in each individual situation.

If one has a teleological view on legal orders—i.e., if one thinks that they in the last resort are the means of achieving goals outside the legal order itself—but does not want to commit oneself to utilitarianism in a stricter sense, one can generalise this distinction in favour of a distinction between rule-teleology and act-teleology.

Judge A is a rule-teleologist. He thinks that the social goals of the legal order are best realised by means of general rules created by, e.g., a legislative parliament. The ideal situation is that the citizens directly comply with the rules addressed to them, so that the authorities, notably the courts of law, ideally are not confronted with litigations and crimes at all (making the courts in fact superfluous). But when they are, the interference of the courts with the course of events shall be as unnoticeable as possible and they shall only act as the lengthened arm of the legislator. A conceives of his role as a judge to see to it that this is the case. When he takes a stand on individual cases he tries in his decisions to conform as closely as possible to the legal system.

How can a judge such as A be expected to reason in questions of law? Well, no doubt his reasoning will be strongly system-dependent. He is a strict legalist as far as possible, and when the system does not provide him with clear answers, he resorts to a mediate use of it. Such a mediate use can consist in the formulation of formal arguments based on the established systematisation of the content of the legal system, but also on (subjective or objective) teleology. It deserves to be reiterated here that a legalistic view of the administration of justice is well consistent with a teleological view of the legal order, viz., if one is a rule-teleologist. Several philosophers of the Enlightenment offer typical examples (Montesquieu, Beccaria, Bentham). In particular, Bentham argues strongly in favour of codifications based on utilitarian grounds, which shall be followed slavishly by its appliers.

Judge B is an act-teleologist. A judge having such an attitude might seem strange—the task of the judge being just to apply general rules to individual cases. But in our context we can conceive of less extreme forms of act-teleology, adapted to the administration of justice.

B sees—by contrast with A—the application of law as having an, in relation to legislation, independent and partly different social function. But also B is a teleologist. He agrees with A that the administration of justice is a means of attaining social goals outside the legal order itself. But B sees in the first place his role being to bring about socially good solutions in the individual cases—even at the price of deviating from the law in certain situations. The rules of the legal system are to him *all* regarded more or less as guidelines—there are situations where the rules may not be followed. Although the rules themselves do not allow any scope for deviations, this is regarded as an assumption underlying the whole legal system. B's view of his role is in a certain sense more demanding than A's.

How can a judge such as B be expected to reason in questions of law? Well, two features of such reasoning present themselves immediately. First, his argumentation is probably to a higher degree non-juridical in so far as his arguments are of the same kind as those we find outside juridical thinking, and that he to a lesser degree uses source-based arguments for his decisions. Secondly, a certain amount of argumentation for deviations from the rules, when they occur, must be given.

Here a matter of a certain importance must be mentioned. When I talk about how a judge acting in a certain role is supposed to think, what I have in mind is the argumentation I think is typical for the performance of this role *provided that the role in question can be performed freely.* But if some kind of predominant political, religious, or juridical ideology gives the preference to a certain judicial role, or even gives it a monopoly position, the kind of argumentation characteristic of some other role will be in a defensive position or be forced to appear in disguise, i.e., in a cryptic way, or completely unspoken. Perhaps some kinds of juridical argumentation can only be understood properly if we realise that they are argumentation in disguise.

Judges can also differ in their conception of the capacity of the administration of justice to fulfil more extensive social tasks. For some judges the social function of the administration of justice is a more restricted one, which is its proper place.

Judge C conceives, in accordance with this, the administration of justice as a kind of social emergency guard. Its task is not to contribute to the realisation of social goals on a large scale but only to take care of individual cases of emergency—litigations and crimes. The task is to isolate the conflict once people have been subjected to ill fortune and to give an authoritative solution without any intention that this solution shall be a part of a greater social plan.[11] The accomplishment of such plans is the task of other organs in the society. C sees as his role to bring about such societal emergency solutions.

How can a judge such as C be expected to reason in questions of law? Well, as far as he is concerned, the important thing is, in an incisive wording, to give an authoritative solution which, as it were, pacifies the relation between the parties involved without ogling at deeper causal relations and wider social consequences. His argumentation is probably based on rather easily found, "objective" phenomena, in the first place the content of authoritative texts (statutes, preparatory materials to statutes, judgments conceived as authoritative, and the like), and amounts to little more than references to such texts. When they are inadequate, he probably resorts to arguments of a formal character rather than to teleological ones.

Also other functions of the administration of law, and role conceptions determined by them, are conceivable. Judge D, for example, sees his role as being a kind of supervisor of the legislator and the public authorities, while judge E regards as his task to bring about (commutative) justice between the parties of the litigation, without any great consideration of the social goals of the law. We might regard D and E as deontologists (in contrast to the utilitarians A, B and perhaps C), in that they in their argumentation, explicitly or implicitly, refer to certain general principles (moral or, if "positivised", legal), the following of which is regarded as something valuable irrespective of the (utilitarian) usefulness of their following.

For the sake of completeness we must not forget the judge F, who regards the administration of law as a tool for the promotion of some doctrinaire ideology that F believes in—be it Nazism, Marxist-Leninism, Maoism, religious fundamentalism, racism, or the like. F's argumentation is, no doubt, to a high degree dependent on whether the ideology in question is in a dominating position in the society (and hence can openly be referred to) or not (and therefore must be concealed).

---

[11]This aspect is emphasised by Strömholm (1975), p. 596 ff.

Judges A–F are a kind of formalised, typified, representatives of certain different conceptions of the functions of the administration of justice—they all belong to the same ontologically sophisticated family as the honourable *bonus paterfamilias*, *homo oeconomicus*, *homo politicus*, and the like.

References

Carnap R (1950) Logical foundations of probability. University of Chicago Press, Chicago
Dworkin R (1986) Law's empire. Harvard University Press, Cambridge
Ekelöf PO (1958) Teleological construction of statutes, Scandinavian studies in law. Almqvist & Wiksell, Uppsala
Frändberg Å (2014) From Rechtsstaat to universal law-state. Springer, Berlin
MacCormick N, Summers R (1991) Interpreting statutes. A comparative study. Dartmouth Publishing Company, Ltd., London
Naess A (1953) Interpretation and preciseness. University of Oslo Press, Oslo
Strömholm S (1975) Har juridiken en framtid? (Has jurisprudence a future?) Svensk Juristtidning
von Savigny FC (1840) System des heutigen Römischen Rechts

Chapter 15
Operative Goals and Background Goals in Legislative Argumentation

15.1 Introduction

Let us now shift focus from the application of law and statutory interpretation to legislation and pay some attention to the methodology of statutory framing.

In many old Nordic provincial laws we find phrases like "By code shall the land be maintained and not by violent deeds". They reflect a deep conviction among Scandinavians in medieval times that the safest and most efficient way of organising society is by legislative means.

This is an old idea in the Western conception of law. It was highly respected in Ancient Greece, where mythical or real legislators with the status of "Founding Fathers", like Minos, Lycurgus, and Solon, were held in high esteem. In a pregnant way the idea was formulated in two words, *νόμος βασιλέυς*, ("the law is the king"; an early formulation of the general principle of legality)—and "law" here means statutory law. The idea was also revered, albeit to a lesser degree, in Roman civilisation.

Organising society by legislative means has obvious advantages. Evil or improper social states of affairs confronting those in power must be formulated in writing which, at best, might afford the opportunity to reflect upon these states of affairs and how to handle them. The written formulation facilitates the application of normative legal ideas to individual cases by making such cases members of sets of cases, described by the written formulation. The same is the case with respect to the legal consequences, notably sanctions. In the process of formulating them, it is hard to totally avoid reflection upon their efficiency as a means to abolish or prevent evil states of affairs, or achieve good ones. The combination of written requisites for the application of law, and written formulations of the legal consequences to be executed when the requisites are fulfilled, confers legal certainty to those subjected to the law. Legal rules written and presented in legislative standard models are, in quite another way than "tacit" customary rules or rules embedded in precedents, openly exposed to scrutiny and criticism. Finally, a legal system based on legislation is, generally

Å. Frändberg, *The Legal Order*, Law and Philosophy Library 123,
https://doi.org/10.1007/978-3-319-78858-6_15

speaking, easier to change by adding, changing, or abolishing rules than are, e.g., common or customary law. The main reason for this is that legislative normative systems can be—and usually are—equipped with means for changing the system, and those means themselves are formulated legislatively in rules belonging to the system (a quality pertaining to legal systems based on legislation strongly emphasised by Hans Kelsen). In all these respects a legislative organisation of society is superior to a society organised on the basis of custom or precedents given by courts of law, or *ad hoc* decisions on the basis of general values such as peace and order, and, at best, equity (mandarin justice). Precedents are, after all, dependent on the cases which happen to be brought to a court of law.

But organising society legislatively also has its obvious risks—including risks of abuse. Legislation is a very deliberate way of governing and in that fact lie its strongest advantages as well as it greatest risks. In the following I shall describe some such risks. For a legislator who takes the efficiency of his products seriously and, in addition to that, is working in a society informed by the law-state values (the *Rechtsstaat* and the Rule of Law ideas), these risks must be avoided. The aim of avoiding such risks and, of course, of avoiding sheer abuse of legislation, can be articulated in terms of certain legislative goals for a legislator to attain. Apart from the goal of the particular statute in question, every legislative project brings to the fore the general legislative aim of avoiding disadvantages connected with the handling of the very legislative machinery itself, regardless of the present particular legislative project. In fact, this machinery is itself a condition of these disadvantages—if there were no governing of society by legislation, there would be no such disadvantages (but, indeed, others, some of them much worse).

Who is the legislator? Obviously the collective of human beings (or one single human being) having the competence to legislate, e.g., a parliament. But, equally obvious, these people are not the same as those who actually frame the statutes. To help them legislators, in the ordinary sense of the word, have a cadre of officials with the task of drafting the statutes. They are for the most part lawyers working as officials in ministries or in the parliament itself. Let us call this kind of legislators *legislative technicians*. It is in the first place legislative technicians I have in mind in this connection.

Legislation is not an altogether neglected phenomenon in the history of legal science and legal philosophy. Plato and Aristotle have ideas about it and, later, illuminating aspects of it are presented by, e.g., Montesquieu and Bentham.[1] However, a more sustained approach to the subject and attempts in the direction of the establishment of a specific scientific discipline—the theory of legislation—is of a much more recent date. In fact, not until the 1970s does such a thing emerge, and this takes place mainly in German-speaking Europe: Germany, Switzerland, and Austria. As pioneers, can be mentioned the Swiss Peter Noll and the German Jürgen Rödig.[2]

---

[1]de Montesquieu (1748), Ch. 16; Bentham (1838–1843a), p. 297 ff., and Bentham (1838–1843b), p. 231 ff.

[2]Noll (1973); Rödig (1976a and b).

In German the term *Gesetzgebungslehre* is often used for this branch of legal science.

15.2 Operative Goals and Background Goals

Legislation is a complex amalgamation of ideology and technique. This manifests itself on different levels of the legislative enterprise. In respect of legislative goals a distinction can be made between *operative goals* and *background goals,* respectively. *Operative goals* are the goals that the legislator is trying to attain by means of the particular statute at hand—if it is a statute about parents and children, one operative goal is to see to it that children are taken care of and brought up in the best possible way; if it is a statute about forestry, the operative goals are, e.g., to see to it that forestry is done in a proper way from an ecological as well as an economical point of view.

But every legislative project takes place against "a background setting" of a more general, and also more static and inflexible, nature, which ranges the particular project under a wider legislative context. This background setting plays an important role as far as determining the legislative goals is concerned. Its existence brings to the fore some other legislative goals than the operative ones, which goals—*background goals*—in various respects lay restrictions on the means by which the operative goals should be attained. Here four kinds of background goals are discussed.

1. *Systematic goals.* A most powerful background factor is the existing legal system itself, in which the legislative project at hand is intended to interfere. The transition from the old sub-system, which is going to be replaced, to the rules of the new statute must be as smooth as possible. The rules of this new sub-system must be brought into harmony with the rest of the legal system in order to avoid conflicts or tensions between different parts of it. Broadly speaking, the systematic goals consist in preserving consistency and coherence within the legal system when legislating. The systemic goals are investigated further in Sect. 15.3.
2. *Praxeological goals.* The rules of the new statute must be constructed and formulated in such a way that they can be followed without too much difficulty by ordinary citizens as well as the authorities. The praxeological goals consist in making the legal system practicable. The praxeological goals are investigated further in Sect. 15.4.
3. *Legal-ideological goals.* The new rules must be framed in such a way that a reasonable degree of legal certainty, legal equality, legal accessibility, and legal security is guaranteed, i.e. that the demands of the law-state ideology are respected. The legal-ideological goals consist in realising that ideology. The legal-ideological goals will be investigated further in Sect. 15.5.
4. *Economic goals.* The operative goals must be attained by a minimum of costs, and must not exceed a certain reasonable limit. The economic goals consist,

simply, in making the legislative project worthwhile from an economic point of view. The economic goals will be investigated further in Sect. 15.6.

What has been said so far is based upon the simple idea that legislation is a means to obtain certain social goals, i.e., to remedy social states of affairs regarded as unsatisfactory. However, this thought is somewhat over-simplified. The sociology of law has taught us that it is too naïve an opinion to hold that the sole purpose of legislation is to remedy unsatisfactory social states of affairs. Politicians also use the legislative instrument to avoid or gloss over problems, prevent criticism, exhibit initiative, and so on. This must always be borne in mind when legislative activities are studied. This calls for a distinction between genuine legislative goals (where legislation is taken seriously by the legislator) and non-genuine legislative goals (where legislation is used for political-strategic or cosmetic purposes). This chapter deals with the former exclusively.

Let us say a few words about the operative goals before turning to the background ones.

In Sect. 9.3.4 I introduced the concept *legal basis* (in German *Rechtsgrund*). This concept is fundamental in the methodology of legislation. From a teleological point of view, every statutory provision is justified by a legal basis.

The standard form of a legal basis for an obligatory rule, *r*, is this (*f* is an operative fact under *r*, *nf* a normative fact under *r*—the state of affairs that shall be the case according to the legal consequence of *r*—and *s* is the social state of affairs desired by the legislator and which is intended to be achieved by the use of *r*, i.e., *s* is the operative goal of *r*):

(*Sor*) if *f* and, simultaneously or later, *nf*, then probably *s*.

Example: The legal basis for the obligation of the judge to sentence a thief to imprisonment is that, if a theft has being committed and the judge then sentences the thief to imprisonment, it is probable that he will not commit a theft again and others will be deterred from stealing.

The standard form of a legal basis for a prohibitive rule is this:

(*Spr*) if *f* and, simultaneously or later, not *nf*, then probably *s*.

Example: The legal basis of a prohibition to exceed a speed limit is that, if someone is driving his car on a road where a speed limit is imposed and he does not exceed that limit, it is probable that fewer car accidents will occur.

The if. . .then-relation here is, of course, a causal relation. The measure of the efficiency of the rule is the degree of probability of *s* when *f* and (*not*) *nf*.

A given rule, *r*, being a candidate for becoming a statutory provision might be criticised by three different kinds of arguments with respect to the efficiency of *r* as regards attaining its operative goals. In order to test the efficiency of *r* a rational legislator is wise to submit *r* to such a criticism, in the manner of an *advocatus diaboli*. The arguments are:

1. *s* is not a desirable social state of affairs at all.
2. *s* is a desirable state of affairs but complying with *r* also leads to the undesirable state of affairs *t*, and the disadvantage of *t* outweighs the advantage of *s*.
3. *s* is a desirable state of affairs but the fact that the obligation or prohibition expressed by *r* is realised does not lead to *s* with a satisfactory degree of probability. The relation of causality between operative facts and complying with *r*, on the one hand, and the occurrence of *s* on the other, does not hold in a satisfactory manner. In other words, *r* is not well adapted to its purpose.

Objections of these kinds might lead to modifications or rejection of *r*. Modifications can be performed both with respect to the requisites or the theme (the description of the set of normative facts) of a proposed rule.

15.3 Systematic Background Goals

Legislation does not take place in a vacuum. It means intervention in an already established system of rules, where a change in some part of it has repercussions—often most unexpected ones—on other parts. A clumsy interference by an unsuspecting legislator can do much harm to people's welfare, legal certainty and safety, however good his intentions are. Wherever the particular legislative way of organising society is taken seriously, the legislator is in many respects bound by the existing legal system, and surely not only in the well-known sense that the process of legislation is itself governed by constitutional rules belonging to the system. In order to make the system as a whole efficient relative to its purposes, predictable as regards its application and fair in its distribution of legal positions, the sensible legislator has to take great care to prevent logical or practical inconsistencies and, on the whole, tensions of any kind from arising within the system of rules.

Moreover, also the old rules being replaced by the new ones must be taken into consideration for similar reasons. Extant legal relations, created according to older rules, may be affected in various ways by the new rules, or come to exist together with legal relations concerning the same kind of matter and created by the new rules. The legislator ought to pay serious attention to different kinds of transitional problems which may arise (see Chap. 12 above). In addition to that, other legal systems are often also to be considered in order to avoid conflicts in internationally mixed relations.

Considerations of the kind now mentioned may lay restrictions on the free choice between alternative measures aiming at achieving the operative goals of a specific legislative project. A good sculptor adjusts himself to the qualities of his material, and so does a good legislator vis-à-vis the legal system at hand.

Let me mention three danger zones confronting the legislator when making changes in the system, and their corresponding systematic background goals.

1. *Normative collision*. This phenomenon has already been dealt with in Sects. 10.2 and 10.3 above. For logical reasons two colliding rules cannot both be complied

with. Suffice it to say that an important systematic goal is to anticipate such possible conflicts and remove them in order to achieve consistency within the legal system. This presupposes a general view over the immensely comprehensive legal system, something that nowadays can be achieved by means of computers. The technique of remedying inconsistency consists in removing one of the colliding rules, to modify one or both, or to lay down a hierarchy of superiority and inferiority between them by making one of them an explicit or implicit exception from the other (according to principles such as *lex specialis derogat legi generali*, *lex superior derogat legi inferiori*, and *lex posterior derogat legi priori*).

2. *Competition.* Also competition has already been dealt with (Sect. 10.4 above). Here we shall add some commentaries on the legislator's dealing with competition problems.

We recall what competition consists of. Either one and the same case is subsumable under two (or more) legal rules. Or, according to rule r, actions of type A are obligatory in circumstances C and according to another rule, r', actions of type A' are obligatory in C ($A \neq A'$). In the competition situation it is possible to apply two different rules to the same case in a way that (empirically or at least logically) allows compliance. And it is possible (empirically or at least logically) to do both an A-action a and an A'-action a' in C, but doing a & a' in C leads to unwanted states of affairs (collective disadvantages), and for that reason a choice between r and r' might be called for.

A legal system with an abundance of competing rules is no good system.

In the case of competition, the legislator can choose between the following possible solutions, which can be formulated as the following simple strategy.

A. His first choice is (1) whether he shall solve the problem at all or (2) refrain from doing so, leaving the problem to the law-appliers. B. If he chooses to take a stand he has two possibilities: (1) to formulate the statute in such a way that no competition occurs in it, i.e. to prevent competition problems, or (2) permit competition but at the same time provide solutions to it. C. If the legislator chooses alternative B (2) he has three possibilities: (1) to let all competing rules be fully applicable, (2) to let one rule, or some but not all, be fully applicable, or (3) to subject all competing rules to some kind of modification with regard to their range of application. In all three cases, the solution must either be expressed explicitly in the statutory text or be an understood application of an evident principle.

Reasons for the legislator not to take a stand on competition problems could be that the result would be too complicated a regulation, that problems of this kind seldom or never occur, that they are not particularly important, that their solution is self-evident (e.g., with respect to an obvious *lex specialis*-relation), or that there are unwritten principles in the practice of the courts of law to rely upon.

Far from avoiding competition the legislator not seldom creates it. There is, in fact, a legislative technique that consists in formulating rules between which the relation one-case competition of the type specification holds (i.e., the sphere of operative facts of the one rule is a proper subset of the sphere of operative facts of the other). The *lex specialis*-principle is here a silently presupposed operative principle. This technique, which could be called "precisation by means of detachment", consists in constructing a sphere of operative facts covering some typical generic case, out of which is detached a proper subset, to which, in another, separate rule, a matching legal consequence is attached. Technically, this is brought about by adding to the separate rule a further, more precise requisite. This technique is well-known, especially in criminal law.

Let us now say a few words about how the legislator can prevent competition problems.

A first grasp is of the Gordian kind, viz., not to legislate at all in the "substantial" issue and let existing rules do the job. A not unusual situation where there can be reason for the legislator to act preventively is what we can call *dependent many case-competition*. Assuredly, cases that come to the fore in a many case-situation are often totally independent of one another, e.g., a theft and a traffic offence. But the situation that case c belongs to set S and case c' to set S', where S and S' are disjoint, does not mean that c and c' necessarily are independent of each other. For instance, both can be components of the same business transaction or the same criminal scheme, and an action can be a means of performing another action. Such situations are dependent many-case competitions.

Sometimes dependent many-case competition is so common that a legislative measure is called for. A technical device for that purpose is to create a special rule that compensates for, "consumes", the competing rules (e.g., assault + theft = robbery; fraud + forgery = gross fraud). Such a rule is usually a *mixtum compositum* of the competing rules. The technique is, schematically speaking, this (r_1 and r_2 are competing rules, r_3 the competition preventing rule, and $a, \ldots, e$ are requisites):

r_1: ab
r_2: cd
r_3: $abcde$

The requisite e in r_3 ("the coupling requisite") signifies the relevant relation between ab on the one hand and cd on the other. In statutory language e is often expressed by terms like "by means of" or "anyone who, after having committed ..., commits ...", e.g., "Anyone who steals by means of violence to a person ...").

To be sure, it is not always easy to prevent one-case competition in statutes either. A complete avoidance of that means that all rules have disjoint spheres of operative facts—there must be no case that falls under more than one rule. A consequence of this being the case would, not least in criminal law, be extremely casuistic provisions and the extent of the statutory text would be overwhelming. But the legislator can strive at making the overlapping spheres of operative facts as small as possible.

Which legislative solutions in a more proper sense of competition problems are available to the legislator? Let us differentiate between "implicit" and "explicit directions" that they can take. The former is the preference order between competing rules indicated by the very arrangement of the statute in question. The latter decides that order by means of separate (second order) provisions or by special requisites in competing rules.

I formulated above three possibilities for the legislator wanting to solve arising competition problems in a proper sense of "solving": (1) To let all competing rules be fully applicable (cumulation), (2) to let one rule, or some but not all, be fully applicable (selection), or (3) to perform some kind of "rule modification".

(1) *Cumulation.* This solution is of interest mainly with respect to many-case competition. One-case competition is, to be sure, either a system defect (total or partial redundance) or an obvious *lex specialis*-relation.

With respect to cumulation of individualised legal consequences the ultimate borderline would, or so it seems, be what is actually possible (*impossibilium nulla est obligatio*). But this is, as we all know, not always the case; there are, e.g., countries where a person can be sentenced to 175 years imprisonment.

It is not impossible that cumulation leads, not to collective disadvantage, but to the contrary—collective advantage.

(2) *Selection.* Also this technical device is mostly of importance with respect to many case-competition (as for one case-competition (redundance) the legislator can usually fall back on an unwritten *lex specialis*-principle).

The use of selection is an expression of the very sound idea that one should keep to essentials and leave what is less important out of consideration. If the effect of the application of a certain rule is so sweeping that the effect of the application of competing rules is of little consequence, it suffices to apply that rule.

(3) *Modification.* Also with respect to this device many case-competition is in focus. For modification is no confinement of the sphere of application of a rule but only a momentary suspension of the application of a rule (cf. Sect. 10.3 above). Schematically, modification means (i) that the individual normativised facts (see Sect. 7.7 above) are cumulated and (ii) that, after that, a greater or lesser subtraction of "the total sum" is performed. It goes without saying that this can only be achieved if what are handled are commensurable and measurable entities (time, money). How this "discount" shall be determined depends on circumstances peculiar to the branch of law in question.

It is not unusual that the legislator, when making a modification, stipulates a maximum barrier not to be exceeded or a minimum barrier not to be fallen below. For instance, cumulated sanctions in criminal law must not go further than is motivated from the viewpoint of criminal policy, cumulated social benefits must not exceed what is motivated from the viewpoint of social welfare policy and, as for minimum barriers, cumulated sanctions must not have the effect that the culprit gets off lightly and cumulated social benefits must guarantee a minimum protection.

3. *Teleological disintegration of the legal system.* In a diachronic perspective the valid legal system appears as consisting of different layers of rules, created at different times—the bottom layers may be very old—and reflecting different

social or moral values, some of them perhaps highly antiquated. The introduction of new provisions in the system can reinforce such disintegration. For instance, a new statute within the field of labour law, intended to improve equality between the sexes, might conflict in this way with extant family law or tax law—although no collision or competition exists. A systematic goal of great importance is the teleological integration of the system, mainly achieved by changing or repealing statutes no longer corresponding to current values. As is the case with collision and competition this requires a general survey over the whole legal system.

15.4 Praxeological Background Goals

By "praxeological legal concepts" I mean concepts describing legal actions, the most general among them being concepts like "following a rule", "breaking a rule", and "applying a rule". Praxeological background goals are about such actions. (Some fundamental praxeological concepts have been investigated in Chap. 13 above.)

Let us call a statute or a statutory provision *expedient* if its observance leads to its operative goals. For a statute or a statutory provision to be *efficient* two necessary conditions must be fulfilled: (i) that it is expedient and (ii) that it is on the whole observed by its addressees. For however suitable a statute is for its purpose, it is not efficient if it is not on the whole observed; and however much observed it is it is not efficient if it is not suitable for its purpose. Let me mention four typical obstacles to the observance of statutory provisions.

1. They are vague, obscure, ambiguous, complex—or conflicting in ways described in Sect. 15.3 above. What makes them difficult to comply with is the difficulty to ascertain what is contained in the provisions. This obstacle lies in the very formulation of the statutory texts.

It is often argued that statutory texts shall be easily readable. And, no doubt, they shall. But being easily readable is not the same as being easy to apply. These two claims might even conflict. This is something the observant legislator must bear in mind. Let me give two examples.

A provision in the Swedish Liability for Damages Act reads: "For damage caused through fault or negligence by an employee when on duty, he is responsible only if particular reasons with respect to the nature of the action, the position of the employee, the interest of the injured and other circumstances exist".

This provision is fairly easy to understand in the sense that we usually understand a piece of ordinary prose—it contains no strange words and the language is not particularly heavy. But quite different is the situation when reality offers the judge its bewildering constellations of circumstances. Regard the following two cases.[3]

[3] We find both cases in NJA 1980, pp. 302 ff.

I. A sergeant major had left a portable radio station in an unlocked car and went away for 2 h. When he returned the radio station was missing. It was worth about 2.000 kronor.

The Swedish Supreme Court found the provision applicable to this case. As reasons were given that the radio station was expensive and especially liable to be stolen, and that the sergeant major on the occasion served as officer of the guard. These circumstances constituted particular reasons for responsibility.

II. Also in this case action for damages was instituted against a sergeant major (which must not delude us into believing that sergeant majors would be a particularly rash kind of persons). He had left a windcheater (worth 163 kronor) to dry in his office, which he shared with two colleagues. The windcheater disappeared.

In this case the Supreme Court found that the provision was *not* applicable. The court balanced the circumstance that the sergeant major's choice of repository was contrary to existing regulations and the importance of care with respect to supervision of military property on the one hand, and, on the other, the reason put forward by the sergeant major to the effect that the windcheater was dripping wet, that there were no lockers in the regiment's drying room, and that he could not reasonably have had an obligation to dry it at his own place. The Supreme Court concluded that the circumstances viewed together did not constitute particular reasons for tort liability.

What is striking in these two cases is what little help the law-applier can obtain from the statutory text itself and, hence, to what small extent the opinions of the court can be said to be a proper juridical *interpretation* of the provision. Although easy to interpret in the sense of understanding its semantic meaning, it is utterly difficult to understand in the sense of establishing which cases are subsumable under it.

2. It is physically or mentally difficult to comply with them (however clearly they are expressed). They demand too much of their addressees. Suppose, for instance, that citizens are under an obligation to work 18 h a day.
3. People do not want to comply with the rules, since they do not like them, or since the rules conflict with prevailing customs, or moral or religious beliefs.
4. There are legal possibilities to circumvent the rules.

It is a praxeological background goal to prevent obstacles of these kinds, and that might result in making the proposed statute a bit less expedient in order to make it more observable.

As for the first obstacle, dealing with it is a matter of developing techniques for the drafting of statutes. All of them demand of the legislator some knowledge of human nature, of the ways people live in society, a good command of the language and most of all a good portion of common sense. The legislator must sometimes restrain his legislative zeal. A minimum requirement is, of course, that it is possible to follow the proposed rule. With respect to the third obstacle, where do you draw the borderline, the transgression of which on the part of the legislator leads to a widely spread disregard of the statute in question by those affected by it?

The main device used in order to achieve observance is, of course, unpleasant legal consequences, notably sanctions. These are regularly selected from a store of standard means of pressure, the supply of which is usually rather limited, and it is likely that legislators use them in a more or less routine fashion. However, the most important of all praxeological background goals—and the most difficult to attain—is to see to it that the sanctions used actually lead to the observance of the law—with a minimum of negative side effects.

Legislators are also well advised to take into consideration the established juridical technique practised in the courts of law, especially the principles of statutory interpretation, since that technique exerts influence on how the rules will be applied in practice. In this way the principles of statutory interpretation become indirectly a kind of legislative principles as well. Closely connected to this is to predict precedents that can come about as a consequence of the application of proposed statutes.

In order to make a rational choice between different legislative measures a legislator must often try to anticipate the likely behaviour on the part of the citizens and the authorities once they are living with a new regulation. As for the fourth obstacle, not the least important is to *anticipate evasive measures*. In certain fields of law the legislator's anticipating circumvention and private persons, notably big banks, law firms, and firms of accountants, anticipating legislative movements can develop into something like a game of chess. Such "law games" between legislators and professional advisers to the public are not unusual, e.g. in tax law.

15.5 Legal-Ideological Background Goals

Some very important values of a legal-ideological kind lay definite restrictions on the legislative means by which a legislator might obtain the intended operative goals. At least in democracies it is widely held that legislative products must comply with certain standards of quality, articulated in the law-state (*Rechtsstaat*, Rule of Law) ideology (and non-democracies regularly pay lip-service to it). In my book *From* Rechtsstaat *to Universal Law-State* (2014) I have investigated at some length the law-state values legality, legal equality, legal certainty, legal accessibility, and legal security—and how they can be protected and guaranteed by means of legislation. For a more thorough account I refer to that work. For the sake of coherence, however, I shall briefly indicate here what I have in mind when talking about legal-ideological background goals. Let me mention the following ones.

1. Equality in the law. This is taken to mean that law must have a content such that, if the law is loyally and strictly applied to all cases falling under it, no individual is victim of undue discrimination. By undue discrimination I mean a discrimination that violates the life of human dignity for the exposed. As for equality before the law, this is mainly the law-applier's concern. The conditions, however, for the

successful realisation of equality before the law is to no small degree a matter for the legislator to achieve.

2. Legal certainty, or predictability in legal matters. Three basic conditions must be fulfilled in order to guarantee legal certainty. (i) There must be legal rules answering questions of a legal character and these rules must be clear, unambiguous, non-conflicting, uncomplicated, etc., (ii) these rules must be easily available, and (iii) it must be the case that people actually can rely upon the law-applying authorities to loyally and correctly follow the rules. Conditions (i) and (ii) are of special importance from the viewpoint of legislation. As for condition (i) we see that the praxeological and the legal-ideological goals coalesce.
3. Legal safety, meaning that violent measures, restrictions of freedom of movement and activities, and encroachment of premises on the part of the state are permitted only when there are extremely strong humanitarian and social reasons for it, that certain kinds of violence are not permitted at all and, no less important, that the conditions and forms of the exercise of the state's monopoly of violence and coercion are regulated in a precise manner in statutory provisions and, in addition to that, exposed to severe and close examination and control. Of utmost importance are rules imposing liability for damages and criminal sanctions on officials violating the rules regulating the use of violence and coercion.

The legal-ideological background goals consist in safeguarding that these values (and certain others, not mentioned here) are not violated for the sake of accomplishing the operative goals. One way of securing this is to submit the proposed bill to the scrutiny of some independent state organ, whose members are skilled in legal matters (judicial preview).

In spheres of law where the law-state values are of special importance, subordinating the law to statutes is a necessary condition for their maintenance.

15.6 Economic Background Goals

Justice certainly has a price and a rational legislator cannot close his eyes to this brute fact. In many countries all over the world claims have been raised for cost-benefit analyses (CBA) of legislative projects.[4] There are good reasons for regarding it as a legislative background goal to ascertain that the benefits of the legislative project outweigh the costs of it. In a wider sense CBA also involves investigation of alternative measures. Admittedly, this is a matter of economic rather than juridical thinking.

There is always a risk that the costs of a legislative project will outweigh the benefits of it. The costs may lie in the creation of new authorities for the supervision

[4]Boardman (2006); Sen (2000).

of the successful accomplishment of the project (with an increase in taxation as a possible consequence), different kinds of adaption costs for enterprises or individuals, losses in the form of evasive measures (such as some able persons leaving the country), costs for information and education, etc.

An important distinction as far as legislative costs and benefits are concerned is that between direct and indirect costs and benefits. If it is the very purpose of the statute in question to allocate goods in such a way that x bears the cost c for v and y has the benefit b of v' (v and v' being some entities to which a value can be assigned; it is not excluded that $x = y$ and $v = v'$), then c and b are direct costs and benefits. c and b might, or might not, be measurable in monetary units.

Every cost or benefit that is not a direct one is an indirect cost or benefit. Administrative costs are usually of the indirect kind. Indirect costs can be intended or unintended. If they are unintended, they can be known or unknown.

For one thing, the distinction between direct and indirect costs is important since there might be a mental inclination among the proponents of a statute to undervalue its indirect costs, and an inclination among its opponents to overrate them.

A general problem confronting CBA is that some benefits and costs cannot be adequately valued in monetary terms (in fact, however, some economic analysts argue that they can). How many kronor (euros, dollars, pounds) is an insult worth? To be sure, there is a general tendency, when law is concerned, to translate such costs into money, not least within the law of torts (e.g., with respect to "indirect" damages such as defamation). There seems to be no other way out.

References

Bentham J (1838–1843a) Principles of the civil code. In: Bowring J (ed) The works of Jeremy Bentham, vol I. William Tait, Edinburgh

Bentham J (1838–1843b) Nomography. In: Bowring J (ed) The works of Jeremy Bentham, vol III. William Tait, Edinburgh

Boardman NE (2006) Cost-benefit analysis: concepts and practice, 3rd edn. Pearson, London

de Montesquieu C (1748) De l'esprit des lois, Book 29

Noll P (1973) Gesetzgebungslehre, Reinbeck

Rödig J (1976a) Logische Untersuchungen zur Makrostruktur rechtlicher Kodifikate. In: Rödig J (ed) Studien zur eine Theorie der Gesetzgebung. Springer, Berlin

Rödig J (1976b) Zum Begriff des Gesetzes in der Rechtswissenschaft. In: Rödig J (ed) Studien zur eine Theorie der Gesetzgebung. Springer, Berlin

Sen A (2000) The discipline of cost-benefit analysis. J Leg Stud 29:931–952

Chapter 16
Stability and Change: A Study in Juridical Ideology

16.1 Introduction

Roscoe Pound begins his work *Interpretations of Legal History* with the following statement: "Law must be stable and yet it cannot stand still. Hence all thinking about law has struggled to reconcile the conflicting demands of the need for stability and of the need for change".[1] An important component in juridical thinking could be called "continuity thinking".

Pound's observation is the theme of this concluding chapter. More exactly, we shall focus upon, on the one hand, ideas that have promoted stability, and, on the other, ideas in the service of change. I shall touch upon a number of conceptions from different epochs and different connections within Western juridical history of ideas.

First of all, we must be clear about which phenomena we have in mind when talking about "preservation" and "alteration" respectively. What presents itself immediately is the answer "legal systems". However, this answer smooths over a distinction of great importance in this connection, viz., the distinction between maintenance and change of *legal positions* and maintenance and change of *the legal systems* themselves, constituting these positions.

We are all familiar with a common game of dice for children, where the number of pips decides how many steps one is allowed to move a piece along a winding path of fixed points. If the piece lands on such a point the player is in a position which is either to his advantage or disadvantage. Changes of legal positions can be described in an analogous way—by buying and selling, marrying and divorcing, committing crimes, etc., people's mutual relations are continuously changing according to the legal system, i.e., the game itself.

Each legal consequence, as a component of a legal rule, indicates a legal position in which some legal subject is placed in relation to positions held by other legal

[1] Pound (1923), p. 1.

Å. Frändberg, *The Legal Order*, Law and Philosophy Library 123,
https://doi.org/10.1007/978-3-319-78858-6_16

subjects, if certain operative facts occur. If a seller is in a substantive delay of delivering the sold goods, he is in the position that he—potentially or actually—is subject to certain claims of the buyer; and if a person is sentenced for theft to imprisonment she is in the position that she is deprived of certain immunities, in the first place the protection from deprivation of freedom that she had before. Through the delay and through the theft (in combination with other players'—the prosecutor, the judge—actions) the persons in question have "played themselves into" these positions—and the subsequent game must take its point of departure from them.

So, by "changes of law" we can mean two different things: (i) changes of legal positions "within the game" and (ii) changes of the game itself, the legal system.

Hence, a discussion about stability and change can have reference to the position level or the rule level. Changes on the position level can, of course, take place without any changes on the rule level. But changes on the rule level involve greater or lesser changes on the position level. These changes are not brought about by playing the game but by changing the very game over the players' heads. The relation between a landlord and a tenant can be changed by means of a contract between the parties as well as by means of a statutory amendment.

Just as we talk about legal systems as a totality of legal rules we can talk about "the total legal situation" according to some legal system, *S*, at time *t*. *The total legal situation* relative to *S* and *t* is all actually existing legal positions according to *S* at *t*. It goes without saying that, e.g., the Swedish total legal situation undergoes changes every minute.

That legal stability reigns during a given span of time means in its ideal-typical form that no changes at all occur during that period, i.e., that the status quo reigns with respect to rules on the rule level and positions on the position level. The total legal situation remains unchanged during the period.

It is not seldom emphasised that legal orders and juridical thinking are in the service of stability, not change. The idea is that the very point of a legal order would be lost without a considerable amount of stability, in the first place, of course, on the rule level.

Legal stability is a component of social stability in general. If the latter is upset, this usually affects the former. And just like a spider that has got his web tattered and torn frantically spins new thread, so have lawyers in societies tattered by war and revolution by more or less sophisticated means always tried to repair the disturbance of stability. This has, on the level of legal dogmatics and the philosophy of law, been accompanied by the formation of ideas serving as rationalisations of the stability-preserving forces, something that has possibly also initiated, or at least reinforced, such preserving forces.

In these circumstances it is of special interest to investigate such ideas and doctrines that have been mobilised when legal changes come to the fore. The juridical ideology can to some extent be said to put "the burden of proof" on those who aim at change. And even in the most stagnant societies changes must now and then be brought about. The juridical ideology is to a high degree characterised by what Pound lays his finger on in the quotation opening this chapter, namely the efforts to reconcile the claims of stability and change, or, if you like, *the inclination to stabilise the very changes.*

Juridical thinking offers two main devices for tackling conflicts of interest of the type we are discussing. Let us call them "the minimisation device" and "the crypto device".

The minimisation device means *tout court* to see to it that the changes are not more far-reaching than is absolutely necessary given inevitable circumstances.

The crypto device means that the lawyers use the elasticity of the legal system to their utmost in such a way that it appears that the legal system has not changed, although it has. By "elasticity" of a legal system I mean in the first place the unavoidable vagueness and ambiguity of the linguistic formulations of its rules. It could be said that what the crypto device achieves is *crypto stability.*

In the history of juridical ideas we find a rich arsenal of both rationalisations of and techniques for the application of these two devices. In the following some of these shall be presented.

Already in Roman times jurists were confronted with the opposition between stability and change, and how they tackled it has been exemplary, and will be for centuries to come. It is the jurisdictional magistrates, notably the praetors, who can take the credit for a smooth adaption to the changing demands of Roman social life.[2] This aim the praetor achieved by introducing new remedies to (the thereby unchanged) *ius civile*—a skilful use, indeed, of the crypto device. Gradually, a new body of law, the *ius honorarium*, created by the magistrates and more adaptable to changing conditions, evolved alongside the *ius civile.*[3] An important factor contributing to a smooth adaption of the rigid *ius civile* to the needs of society was the development of the *ius gentium*, valid for all inhabitants of the Roman Empire. To a high degree this was built on the edicts of the *praetor peregrinus*, who exercised jurisdiction in disputes between *peregrini* (inhabitants who were not Roman citizens) and between *peregrini* and Roman citizens.

Before illuminating the minimisation and the crypto devices let me make a more general remark. It could be said that the very existence of a legal order in a society has a stabilising, conserving, effect. This lies in the very nature of legal orders. Where an effective valid legal order exists, changes cannot easily be brought about by means of hasty, perhaps irreconcilable, ad hoc decisions. The legislative process gives room to, and time for, reflection and consideration. The judicial process, the judges' adherence to legalism, and a slow and stable development of the law by means of precedents are also factors that guarantee continuity and, as a consequence, stability.

---

[2]Mousourakis (2015), pp. 45–55.

[3]A classical jurist, Marcianus, exclaims: "the *ius honorarium* is of itself the living voice of the *ius civile*". *Ius honorarium* has been compared to the English equity, Mousourakis (2015), p. 49, n. 58. Says Mousourakis: "Such a system [the dualism between *ius civile* and *ius honorarium*] seemed to satisfy the people's desire to believe that things remained the same as long as they were ascribed the same labels. It created the comfortable illusion that nothing really had changed" (Mousourakis 2015, p. 52).

With certain, no small, exaggeration it could perhaps be said that enacted law is in the service of stability and common law in the service of change. If that is argued, however, this assertion must be qualified by several restrictions. For instance, from 1898 to 1966 the British House of Lords was, in theory, strictly bound to follow its own precedents,[4] which, no doubt, led more to stability than change. It could be argued that law creation through precedents is most important in areas of law where the alternative is optional statutes, notably within the law of contracts.

The rest of this chapter is organised thus: First I discuss some ideas concerning stability and change on the position level (Sect. 16.2) and then on the rule level (Sect. 16.3), where, after a short introduction (Sect. 16.3.1), rule creation through administration of justice is treated in Sect. 16.3.2 and rule creation through legislation in Sect. 16.3.3.

16.2 Stability and Change on the Position Level

That agreements entered into are kept, and that one can rely upon this being the case, is a necessary condition for all ordered social life above a very primitive level. A richly differentiated division of labour presupposes, and has as a consequence, a complicated exchange of utilities, and this exchange takes place to a large extent by means of agreements. Therefore it is not astonishing that breach of contract has always been considered as something extremely reprehensible, and rituals and appealing to deities have accompanied entering into contracts.

When reflection over legal phenomena began and evolved gradually through the rise of a scholarly study of them, the claim to fidelity to contracts entered into was given an effective formulation in the sentence *pacta sunt servanda*. This idea has also become a cornerstone in widely differing juridical theories. In Grotius' natural law doctrine it is the *pacta sunt servanda* principle that is the foundation of the total legal system by conferring binding force to the social contract and thereby to positive law—to the internal law of the different states as well as to the agreements of international law entered into by sovereigns. Not least in the theory of international law the *pacta sunt servanda* principle has played an important role also in our times. Kelsen distinguishes, true to his *Stufenbau*-theory, three hierarchically ordered levels of the international law: (1) a lowest level comprising the rules of the international legal organisations, which acquire their validity from the immediately superior level, viz., (2) conventional law, i.e., treaty law, which in turn derives its validity from (3) the customary law of the states, which contains the basic norm of the whole system and to which the *pacta sunt servanda* principle belongs.[5] For Grotius this principle has a natural law character, while for Kelsen it is a rule belonging to the

[4] MacCormick and Summers (1997), p. 326.

[5] Kelsen (1952).

customary law of the states. But for both the principle is a cornerstone in their respective theories.

The *pacta sunt servanda* principle is stability-preserving in the following sense. It is a deeply rooted juridical conception that agreements, entered into by legally competent persons in an honest way, as far as possible shall be maintained, *even if supervening external circumstances obstruct, or even render impossible, a contractual achievement.* If one has entered into a contract, one must in most cases take the risk of changes in the external circumstances, natural or man-made. Only in certain particularly strained situations is one allowed to recede from a contract.

How tenacious the *pacta sunt servanda* conception is becomes the more evident when we pay attention to the fate of its main rival on the level of ideas—the *clausula rebus sic stantibus* principle (things thus standing)—in the juridical literature. The gist of this principle is, as we all know, that an agreement or a treaty in international law is binding only so long as the circumstances are the same as they were at the entering of the agreement. *Clausula rebus sic stantibus* has mainly been discussed in the literature of international law but it is also known in civil law under the term "the doctrine of underlying assumptions of the contract". The *rebus sic stantibus* idea promotes changes on the position level by allowing a party to unilaterally alter a cluster of legal positions constituted by an agreement. The idea is hostile to the status quo. *Clausula rebus sic stantibus* has for juridical thinking been an unfamiliar bird, the menacing wings of which have spread a treacherous shadow over the neat flower beds of ordered legal relationships. To be sure, classics of international law such as Alberico Gentili and Hugo Grotius recognise its validity as a tacit condition (both clearly realising that the analogy between civil law agreements and international law treaties must not be strained), but the tendency to limit its sphere of application is obvious. During the nineteenth century, however, the clause was not uncommon in treaties, especially commercial ones.

Kelsen attacks forcefully the *rebus sic stantibus* idea.[6] He states: "The clause rebus sic stantibus is in opposition to one of the most important purposes of the international legal order, its purpose of stabilizing international relations"; and he argues that it can hardly be proven that the clause belongs to positive international law at all.

If juridical thinking is sceptical to abrupt changes on the position level, it provides us on the other hand with a no small number of intermediary solutions. These are to the effect that, when the circumstances obstruct, make inconvenient, or even render impossible a complete fulfilment of a contractual obligation, a position shall nevertheless be established between the parties *that is as similar to what was originally contracted as the circumstances allow*, i.e., a use of the minimisation device. Let me, as examples, mention three such techniques, worked out already in Roman law.

The first is *perpetuatio obligationis* (the perpetuating of the obligation). The meaning of this is that, if a thing that a person shall deliver to another person is destroyed while the first person is in delay and, hence, it is impossible to deliver the

[6]Kelsen (1952), p. 359.

thing, his obligation has not for that reason expired but is perpetuated by his delay and, therefore, he is under an obligation to compensate for the loss of the creditor. An obligation which is impossible to fulfil is changed into another which, if fulfilled, places the creditor in a position which is intended to be minimally different from the position the creditor would have been in, had the thing been delivered.

The two other examples are also to the effect that a change of contractual obligations comes about, viz., the classical pair *datio in solutum* (assigning for payment) and *datio solvendi causa* (assigning for the purpose of payment). These two mean, roughly, the former that one in a certain situation can fulfil an obligation by performing another thing than the one contracted and the latter that the debtor assigns something, often a claim against a third person, to the creditor, who himself can change it into money as a deduction of the debtor's debt.

These solutions can be regarded as a kind of surrogates for the original obligations. They offer intermediary solutions between the strict fulfilment of the agreement (*pacta sunt servanda*) and the complete rescinding of it (according to *clausula rebus sic stantibus*)—i.e., given the circumstances a minimal divergence from what has been contracted.

16.3 Stability and Change on the Rule Level

16.3.1 Introduction

Let us now investigate some ideas and doctrines to the benefit of, on the one hand, the preserving of stability and, on the other, the promoting of changes in legal systems. Referring to my analogy with the game of dice in the introduction of this chapter, we shall discuss the changes of the game (the handling of the legal system) itself. (By "legal systems" I mean in this section "momentary legal systems".) Such ideas and doctrine are often variations of the minimisation and the crypto devices.

In Sect. 16.3.2 we investigate ideas pertaining to the administration of justice and in Sect. 16.3.3 ideas pertaining to legislation.

16.3.2 Ideas Pertaining to the Administration of Justice

When the law-creating activities of the courts of law are discussed the English doctrine of precedent, the *stare decisis* doctrine, presents itself immediately for consideration. Whether the law-creation of English courts actually is in compliance with this doctrine is of no concern here. We shall focus on the doctrine itself.

Among the components of this doctrine there are some that obviously are suited for promoting stability and some that are obviously suited for promoting change, although with perfect application of the minimisation and crypto devices.

A component of the doctrine which—if taken absolutely seriously—really would curb legal development is the idea that The Supreme Court of the United Kingdom (until 2009 The House of Lords) is bound by its own decisions, although this idea has been undermined in later times (not least after the famous statement of the Lord Chancellor in 1966 to the effect that the House of Lords could digress from its own older decisions if there existed sufficient reasons for it).[7]

But, as we all know, there are well-worn paths to tread for the judge who wants to evade this obstacle and perhaps prepare for a future development of the law in a certain direction. For according to the doctrine it is the *ratio decidendi* of the precedent that is binding, not the *obiter dicta* that may occur. In this way there exists a scope for the judge, who has to take a stand on a precedent (or a series of such) to move away from the field of force of the precedent—for it is he who decides what is the *ratio decidendi* and what is the *obiter dicta.* If the judge performs such a move a change of the law has taken place. But it is a crypto change for, according to the *stare decisis* doctrine no change at all has taken place with respect to the binding force of the precedent. The *stare decisis* doctrine is a perfect example of how judges by means of crypto changes maintain pseudo-stability.

But if the judge wants to evade a precedent without manipulating the opinion expressed in the precedent there is another way out, namely to distinguish the case. This is a permitted device according to the English doctrine of precedent and involves, in brief, a declaration that the present case in some relevant respect differs from the case decided by the precedent.

More interesting in our connection, however, is perhaps the way more and more *general* legal rules can be constructed step by step and in an almost imperceptible way through a long series of precedents. This seems to be a common feature of the development of law in common law countries and it has been called *reasoning by example.*[8] A prime example is the development in the case law of the U. S. concerning the liability for injuries due to tortious qualities in the sold goods. Levi describes a more than a 100 years' development where one precedent is added to another in a long chain.[9] It is striking how anxious the courts are to formulate their opinions in such a way that a more general rule will not so easily be gathered from it viewed in connection to earlier precedents. More than a 100 years after the initial case Dixon v. Bell in 1816 Levi warns us against believing that a "ready" general rule had been established.[10]

So far I have had in mind the "free" law creation of the courts, i.e., law creation not consisting in interpretation of statutes. Now I shall say something about stability- and change-promoting ideas concerning statutory interpretation within the framework of administration of justice.

---

[7]MacCormick and Summers (1997), p. 326.

[8]Levi (1951), p. 1.

[9]Levi (1951), p. 7 ff.

[10]Levi (1951), p. 19.

A basic stability-promoting idea in this connection is, of course, the idea of legalism. Its very point is, to be sure, that the development of the law through statutory interpretation shall be counteracted. Closely related to the idea of legalism—or rather a weaker variant of it—is the idea that statutory interpretation concerning hard cases and law creation when the law is silent shall be performed loyally to the legislator ("in the spirit of the law"). Also this idea, which can be called "the principle of loyalty", aims to counteract radical changes of the law on the level of administration of justice.[11]

The stronger legalism asserts itself, the more strained from a purely intellectual viewpoint the ideology often appears, which is intended to justify—or conceal—changes in judicial practice. Here patterns of thinking in the service of crypto change flourish more or less unrestrained. A prominent example is the Franco-Belgian exegetic school in the nineteenth century that, by building on the fiction of the completeness of the law, was in the service of crypto stability.

Closely connected with the principle of loyalty is juridical analogy thinking to the effect that creation of law on the level of administration of law, where the law is silent, shall be performed by a mediate use of existing rules. Also analogy thinking has a stability-preserving effect and can be seen as a variant of the minimalisation device.

A legal system of the Western type can be compared to a ready-made suit. It is on the whole manufactured by the legislator. Then it is up to the alteration tailor—i.e., the judge—to adapt in detail the suit to the anatomical peculiarities of the wearer: widening the trousers a bit in the waist, lengthening the sleeves a centimetre or so and maybe tactfully putting a patch in the seat. First most carefully so that the suit does not look altered. This is achieved by means of safe analogies and cautious reductions; but the caution can be relaxed more and more the older the statute becomes, just like a pair of trousers. And at last the trousers are perhaps thrown away—obsolescence—and a pair of non-matching trousers is bought instead.

The principles of statutory interpretation are chiselled under the pressure of the demands on the lawyers to maintain legality, constancy and uniformity on the one hand, and adaption to changing social life and ideas on the other. The juridical technique of argumentation is to a high degree an instrument for crypto changes and the maintenance of semblance stability.

This state of things often leads to a common phenomenon, which could be called "glide of law": although the wording of the rule remains unchanged during a certain period of time, the sphere of operative facts might change during this period of time by means of extension, incorporation by means of analogy, restriction, and reduction (or even obsolescence).

[11] Frändberg (2014), pp. 61 ff.

16.3.3 Ideas Pertaining to Legislation

Here two ideas have combated each other in Western juridical thinking since the nineteenth century. Let us call them "the restrictive" and "the expansive ideology of legislation" respectively. The former is in the service of stability, the latter in the service of change.

The restrictive ideology of legislation is represented by the Historical School of Law and stands out clearly in the writing of its standard-bearer Savigny.[12] The basic ideas of this ideology are the conception of the origin of law in the consciousness of the people, the spontaneous development of law, the inability of legislation to express the popular sense of justice in its rich variety of nuances, and the claim, due to all this, of caution with legislation. (It is of some interest to notice that Hegel did not share Savigny's negative attitude to legislation but, on the contrary, disliked it.) A hostile attitude to legislation similar to Savigny's is expressed by the American James Coolidge Carter.[13] Custom is, according to Carter, the basis of every legal system, and violation of customs on the part of the legislator is doomed to ineffectiveness.

A diametrically opposite conception is expressed by *the expansive ideology of* legislation—indeed an important component of the Enlightenment. Its main proponents are Bentham (who, in spite of his hostility to natural law thinking, is a pronounced child of the Age of Enlightenment) and the circle of philosophical radicals surrounding him. In an extreme form this ideology is informed by an almost unlimited confidence in the legislator's ability to achieve far-reaching social changes by producing codifications.

An important corollary of this conception is the idea—expressed clearly by another child of the Enlightenment, Beccaria—that as soon as progressive, clear, and complete statutes have been issued, a high degree of legality can—and shall—be reached and law-making through administration of justice heavily reduced. The expansive ideology is, in the hands of the Enlightenment thinkers, intimately joined with strict claims of legality and loyalty on the part of the law-appliers. Bentham regarded with unconcealed contempt the English administration of justice of his time. This antipathy is shared, although to a lesser degree, by his pupil Austin, who launches heavy criticism against Savigny's hostility to legislation.[14]

It should be clear from Chap. 12 that, as soon as a statute is changed, it is not as simple as that a total breach of the older law has thereby come about—that the legislator has made *tabula rasa* of the old law and then started completely afresh. For extant legal positions established by older law must always be taken into consideration. Such pendency cases lead us to problems concerning legislative interference with existing legal states of affairs.

---

[12]See von Savigny (1814).

[13]Carter (1884).

[14]Austin (1861–63), Lecture 39.

On this battlefield the struggle has been hard between those defending stability and those fighting for change (although with respect to the former it is here merely a question of a detaining defence). The problem is how drastically and quickly the change intended by the legislator shall be accomplished.

The two main solutions from the viewpoint of principle are the infrapendency principle, saying that the older law shall reign with respect to the pendency cases, and the retropendency principle, saying that the new statutory regulation shall reign over such cases. The former has a stability-preserving function, the latter a change-promoting function.

A doctrine that has been formulated in defence of the infrapendency principle—and which is a classic example of juridical formulation of ideas in the service of stability—is *the doctrine of vested rights* (*droits acquis*, (*wohl*)*erworbene Rechte*). This doctrine has played no small role in practice.

The doctrine of vested rights was widespread during the nineteenth and the beginning of the twentieth centuries. Its centre was France, but its impact was great also in other countries, such as Germany and Italy.

The content of the doctrine, more specifically, is not easy to explain due to its extremely nebulous character and, in addition to that, it exists in many variants. The essence of it, however, can be summarised in three points: (1) There are rights that are vested and rights that are not. (2) For the vested rights (and only those) the infrapendency principle is necessarily valid. They shall be protected, immune, against new legislation. (3) The reason for the vested rights being immune to new legislation is that they are vested.

This is, to be sure, not particularly illuminating, especially as the doctrine does not clearly tell us which rights are vested and which are not. As an example of a non-vested right has been mentioned "the right" a beneficiary under a will has against a testator so long as the testator is alive—an expectative right, as it has been called. But when the testator passes away this expectative right is transformed into a vested one.

As has often been emphasised, there is an obvious element of natural-law thinking in this doctrine. And natural law ideas lay, as has often been pointed out, in hibernation in the nineteenth century French positivism.

A perhaps somewhat unexpected representative of this doctrine is Ferdinand Lassalle, otherwise known mainly as one of the fathers of German socialism. In a work from 1861[15] he passionately supports the doctrine by the argument that, if the legislator interferes in existing legal positions established by the free will of the parties, he violates their free will—their freedom to choose—and that is, Lassalle exclaims in the grandiose empty words fashionable in his time, "the absolute non-law".

The criticism against the doctrine of vested rights has been strong. On a conceptual level the question has been posed what a vested right actually is—are not *all* legally correct rights vested?—And also: Why shall just vested rights be immune

[15] Lassalle (1861).

against new legislation—why *all* vested rights and *no* others? On a political level the conservative tendency of the doctrine has been attacked. And, of course, the arguments for the infrapendency principle can be articulated in a much clearer way than is done by this highly abstruse doctrine.

References

Austin J (1861–63) Lectures on jurisprudence; or, the philosophy of positive law, vols I–III. J. Murray, London

Carter JC (1884) The proposed codification of our common law. Evening Post Job Printing Office, New York

Frändberg Å (2014) From Rechtsstaat to universal law-state. Springer, Berlin

Kelsen H (1952) Principles of international law. Rinehart & Company, Inc, New York

Lassalle F (1861) Die Theorie der erworbenen Rechte und der Collision der Gesetze unter besonderer Berücksichtigung des römischen, französischen und preußischen Rechts dargestellt. F.A. Brockhaus

Levi EH (1951) An introduction to legal reasoning. University of Chicago Press, Chicago

MacCormick DN, Summers RS (1997) Interpreting precedents. A comparative study. Dartmouth, Hanover

Mousourakis G (2015) Roman law and the origins of the civil law tradition. Springer, Berlin

Pound R (1923) Interpretations of legal history. The Macmillan Company, Basingstoke

von Savigny FC (1814) Vom Beruf unserer Zeit für Gesetzgebung und Rechtswissenschaft. Mohr und Zimmer, Heidelberg

Chapter 17
Epilogue: Intellectualism as a Cardinal Virtue of the Lawyer

1. The basis of intellectualism—an intellectual attitude to the world we live in—is the concept of *truth*. The basic claim of intellectualism is this. In serious matters: Try to find the facts, stick to them so long as you find your belief in them warranted, i.e., until it is shown that what you believed was a fact wasn't, don't believe in what is asserted about the world without proof—and use the intelligence you have!

For intellectualism, it is the correspondence theory of truth that matters. The proposition "It is raining here and now" is true if and only if it is raining here and now, the proposition "Metals expand when heated" is true if and only if metals expand when heated, and the proposition "Julius Caesar was killed on the 15th of March in 44 BCE" is true if and only if Julius Caesar was killed at that time.

These propositions are true, no matter if pragmatic considerations or the fact that the propositions do not fit into some coherent whole tell otherwise. It is nonsense to say "It is raining here and now but the proposition 'It is raining here and now' is false". Likewise it is nonsense to say "It is raining here and now but the proposition 'It is raining here and now' lacks truth-value".

To have *knowledge* is to have insight into true propositions. Without truth, no knowledge. Abandon adherence to truth and, for instance, it doesn't matter if you sentence a person, guilty or not guilty, to death. Abandon adherence to truth and you are free to manipulate everything at will. Some scatterbrains and scoundrels like that very much, each group for reasons of its own.

As far as I can see, much of the scepticism against the concept of truth lies in the fact that there sometimes is some uncertainty as regards what is supposed to be true or false—let us call it *the truth theme*. In the examples just mentioned the truth themes are:

(i) that it is raining here and now
(ii) that metals expand when heated
(iii) that Julius Caesar was killed on the 15th of March in 44 BCE.

Å. Frändberg, *The Legal Order*, Law and Philosophy Library 123,
https://doi.org/10.1007/978-3-319-78858-6_17

(i)–(iii) are facts. On the other hand, the truth theme (the state of affairs)

(iv) that the planet Earth has two moons

is not a fact. Hence a proposition to this effect is false.

But things become a bit more difficult when we are met with propositions like

(P) The theory of relativity is true.

For, it might be asked, what is the corresponding truth theme to P?

The proper answer to that question must be, I think, that theories such as the theory of relativity do not have one single truth theme. That the theory is true must be taken to mean that, with respect to any specified proposition whatsoever that can be deduced from the theory and with respect to any predictive proposition based on the theory, if their truth themes are facts (and, hence, the propositions true), then the theory as a whole is true.

Statements expressing values and normative ideas do not have truth themes for the simple reason that there is no reality corresponding to them. That does not at all mean that rational argumentation in matters evaluative and normative is impossible.

In serious discussions it is important to keep the truth theme constant.

The value of adherence to truth—to say nothing of the love of truth—cannot be justified by any higher value. For people of the intellectual breed manipulation of truth is something utterly abominable. The only way to justify its value is, by way of contrast, to expose the ugly face of its opposite—the deliberate mendacity or the cowardly fear to face the truth, irrespective of whether it is oneself or others one tries to cheat.

2. Necessarily connected with the concept of truth is the concept of *probability* (in a more general sense). For the statement (s is some state of affairs)

(1) s is probable (with, e.g., probability 0.6 ($0 < 0.6 < 1$))
is equivalent to the statement
(2) s is probably true (with probability 0.6).

Grossly simplified, we could say that some state of affairs is probable to the same degree as one can provide empirical evidence for it. An evaluative argument for or against a state of affairs does not add or diminish anything to the probability that it is a fact.

By means of the probability concept we can formulate what I would like to call *the first golden rule of intellectualism.* It says: *Your belief in the existence of something shall be proportional to its probability.*

This rule is no small thing. If it were from now on universally adhered to by mankind we would face an intellectual and civilising revolution unprecedented in the history of man. A great many of our most cherished doctrines and ideologies would collapse like a house of cards. This, of course, will never happen. Men prefer to believe in what they wish would be true, as Francis Bacon aptly remarks in *Novum Organum* (Book I, 49). (A modest step in an intellectualising direction, though, would be taken, if this golden rule were generally imparted in our schools.)

Moreover, intellectualism also appeals to our intelligence—our adherence to logical thinking. So let us formulate *a second golden rule of intellectualism: Make sure that any set of beliefs you might have does not contain a logical contradiction.* (If it is contradictory in this way, this set of beliefs is, seen as a unity, worthless.) *If it contains a contradiction, reformulate the set by eliminating some part of it until consistency is achieved and, if that is not possible, drop it.* Or, in other words: Use your head! (This too should be trained in our schools!)

3. Intellectualism is essential to how we establish our conception of the world we live in. It amounts to very much the same thing as to state that intellectualism is essential to the way we try to solve serious problems facing us as individuals and members of society. The intellectual approach to problems of this kind is to *intellectualise* them by means of our golden rules. And a first step in the intellectualising of them is to problemise them. By that I mean, roughly, that we shall not take our beliefs in serious matters for given but regard them as problems that we shall try to solve, be it beliefs in the existence of certain states of affairs, or adherence to evaluations or normative ideas. And we shall try to achieve the solutions by means of *rational argumentation.* The arguments, good and bad, we usually find in the general discussion concerning the problem in question.

When is an argumentation rational? First of all, it is of utmost importance to determine *the theme of the argument*, i.e., that which the argumentation is about (a truth theme, an evaluation, or a normative idea). How often does it not happen in the topical debate among politicians and in the media that the participants have more or less different themes of their argumentation although they seem to believe (or pretend) to be talking about the same thing! The theme of argumentation must be kept constant so long as the participants actually intend to discuss the same thing.

There are three necessary conditions for an argumentation to be rational. First, which is self-evident, arguments *pro* as well as arguments *contra* must be taken into consideration. Secondly, the arguments given consideration must be *tenable*. That is taken to mean that, if the theme is a truth theme, (e.g., that the planet Mars has two moons), an argument for it is the more tenable the more it increases the probability that the truth theme is true—and that, if the theme is of an evaluative or normative character, the states of affairs (having truth value as being truth themes) that we refer to in order to underpin such themes are the more tenable the more probable it is that they are true. For instance, the norm "Agreements shall be kept" can be underpinned by the argument that if agreements are kept people's confidence in one another increases, which is an empirical proposition that can be more or less tenable. Thirdly, the argument must be *relevant*. If it is not relevant it is a bad argument however tenable it is. It is difficult to give a more precise signification to the concept "relevance" although we often have a good intuition of what is a relevant argument or not. A relevant argument for "It is raining here and now" is that the barometer is falling, a less relevant one that the swallows are flying low, and a completely irrelevant argument is that the Stock Exchange is falling. With respect to evaluations and normative ideas the relevance usually consists in the accordance to some higher value.[1]

4. In order to work, all this must take place within a certain state of mind, without which rational argumentation is difficult, or even impossible, to accomplish. The best designation I can find for this mental state is *detachment.* When arguing in serious matters we should be detached.

Of course, this does not mean that we shall relieve ourselves of our passions, our anger, or whatever sentiment is accompanying our attitude to some set of beliefs. That would be most inexpedient and, what is more, it is in fact impossible. What I am saying is that, when we set to work at intellectually examining some idea or set of beliefs, we shall try, to the best of our ability, to create a mental distance to them, to regard the examination of them as a purely intellectual problem without any special personal importance for us. Only in such a state of mind can we apprehend the very nature of the doctrine or idea in question, and only in a cool state of mind can we formulate good arguments. (People arguing in an excited frame of mind often go wide of the mark and, in addition to that, often make a slightly ridiculous impression.) We should intellectualise our problems.

But even more important from the viewpoint of intellectualism is that the arguments presented themselves must be based on intellectual grounds, not on emotions, moods, or simple-minded assured faith.

Detachment is a necessary condition for *objectivity.* By "an objective argument" I mean an argument that is based on evidence and logic, not on pure, unquestioned authority or on arguments whose "strength" lies in foul second-order *ad hominem* arguments.

Not least, the importance of detachment stands out when it comes to examining one's own beliefs, attitudes, and inclinations.

Objectivity is of course not the same as neutrality in the sense of not taking sides against or with some of two or more rival opinions.

5. The role of *concepts* and *concept formation* is of a crucial importance in intellectual argumentation.

This is often denied by the "realistically" inclined. The meddling with concepts and the striving for conceptual clarity and precisation, is, according to them, to indulge in a game divorced from reality, in contrast to the endeavours of those down-to-earth and socially-minded people living in real life.

This is sheer nonsense, originating in a confused idea of the function of concepts in serious discussion, notably in scientific discourse. A scientific theory, or "story", or "narrative" (to use two terms popular these days, probably intended to show the user's broad-mindedness but also exposing his lack of confidence in what he is "telling" us), aiming at seriously describing and explaining some slice of empirical reality is, as a matter of fact, unthinkable without its formulation by conceptual

[1]Cf. Naess (1966), p. 108–119, where also several instructive examples are given.

means. Concept formation is an inextricable component of scientific theorising. The same relationship exists between scientific theorising and logic. More generally speaking, concept formation is inevitable in formulating truth themes, argument themes and arguments in all serious discussion.

6. Intellectualism can even be conceived of as a *virtue* in the classical sense of the word.

Let us follow Aristotle in conceiving a virtue in terms of the golden mean, *mesotes*, between two vices (or between what is too much and too little). For instance, bravery is the proper middle between foolhardiness and cowardice, generosity the proper middle between wastefulness and stinginess.

Intellectualism as a virtue could be regarded as the golden mean between the "vices" gullibility (belief in anything) and dogmatic scepticism (belief in nothing). A task of the first golden rule of intellectualism is to vaccinate us against the former. As for dogmatic scepticism, this is a rather extravagant view, in practice cherished only within certain rather small philosophical circles. In our day we find it in postmodern thinking to the effect that "truth" and a reality independent of human beings is no more than a socio-linguistic construction, and knowledge therefore impossible. Rather, "reality", "truth", and "knowledge" are ideas calculated to oppress the lower classes, women, and minority races. This kind of epistemological nihilism is of course also rubbish—there are no reasons whatsoever, worthy of being taken seriously, to believe in it. From stating the fact that our observations of the world must necessarily be conceptualised in scientific theories and that concepts are expressed in language does of course not follow a statement to the effect that the world itself *is* a linguistic construct.[2] On the contrary, conceptualising in science is ultimately based on observation, i.e., the use of our senses. Things and interrelations between them can be *observed* by our senses without conceptualising them, as we often do in our daily, non-scientific life, and as our fellow-animals do. Then it could, of course, be argued that our senses are not reliable. And in certain situations they certainly are not. But by and large there is no reason whatsoever to generally mistrust our senses. To think otherwise would be to assume in a completely groundless way a grand treacherous conspiracy on the part of our sensory organs (which, by the way, would be diametrically contrary to an evolutionistic view on biological life). And since there are facts there are necessarily also truths. Truth as correspondence to reality we can call "natural reality-based truth".

However, we also use the term "truth" as "referring" to "facts" outside the natural physical-empirical world, viz., to facts in the world of artificial reality (see Sects. 3.3 and 6.1 above), in law notably legal rules and legal positions. With respect to such concepts, truth-value is not attached to sentences expressing legal rules and positions but to sentences stating the validity of rules and positions (let us call them "validity

[2] As Hage (2015), p. 7 puts it: "However, facts also depend on the world, because it is the world, not language, which determines the facts that obtain. A language determines which facts can be expressed, the world determines which of the expressible facts actually obtain."

statements")—in the sense of "validity of legal rules" as defined in Sect. 13.4.2 (definitions D1 and D17) and "validity of legal positions" as defined in Sect. 13.4.3. Hence, validity statement r_v ("*r* is valid") is true if and only if the adequately corresponding legal rule *r* is valid, and validity statement p_v ("*p* is a valid legal position") is true if and only if the adequately corresponding position *p* is valid. Here the correspondence is between an idea (e.g., validity) and artificial phenomena being "instances" of that idea (e.g. rule *r* is valid). We can talk about "idea-based truth".[3] *r* is valid if and only if *r* conforms to the idea of legal validity and r_v is true if and only if *r* is valid.

In the case of aesthetic fiction of the type that I called (in Sect. 6.1 above) "describing art" things are totally different. It is reasonable to say that the statement "Sherlock Holmes lived at Baker Street 221 B" is true and the statement "Sherlock Holmes lived in Baker Street 221 A" is false, but in what sense? There is no correspondence to reality here. An answer is that works of describing art can be conceived as special kinds of possible worlds—man-made make-believe worlds—with their own "make-believe ontologies". Correspondence here can be taken to mean correspondence to the content of such a world. In this respect, we can talk about "fiction-based truth". For instance, the sentence "Sherlock Holmes lived at Baker Street 221 B" is true if and only if a component of the make-believe world of Sherlock Holmes is that he lived at Baker Street 221 B.

Within the field of the arts we also meet another concept of truth, much more distant to reality-based truth. "Truth" is sometimes used to designate a kind of aesthetical experience, an experience in the mind of the reader, beholder, or listener caused by his taking part in a work of art. Such an experience is, no doubt, an amalgamation of factual experiences of matters concerning one's own or others' lives, and emotions tied to such experiences. If it is at all meaningful to talk about correspondence here, such correspondence is of a very esoteric kind. The correspondence rather lies in a shared experience of life with the author of the work of art and his audience. Truth here is a subjective truth. In fact, this is something completely different from reality-based truth. John Hospers calls this kind of "truth" "truth-*to* things" as opposed to "truth-*about* things". More precisely, "aesthetical truth" of this kind is to be "true-*to* human nature".[4] An excellent example of an aesthetical truth (for many, I daresay) is this one[5]:

Life's but a walking shadow; a poor player,
That struts and frets his hour upon the stage,
And then is heard no more; it is a tale
Told by an idiot, full of sound and fury,
Signifying nothing.

[3]For this kind of truth Olivecrona (1971), pp. 197 and 259–267, for ontological reasons prefers the term "correctness".

[4]Hospers (1946), pp. 162, 173 and 208–218.

[5]W. Shakespeare, *Macbeth* (Act V, Scene V).

Finally, we have the truths of logic and mathematics, e.g., (1) "It is not the case that Caesar was murdered in 44 BCE and that Caesar was not murdered in 44 BCE" and (2) "2 + 2 = 4". Such truths have been called "necessary truth", "eternal truth", and "logical truth".

In what sense is a sentence of type (1) true? Obviously, it is not a contingent empirical sentence (i.e., not true in some possible world) and, hence, its truth is not a reality-based truth in the same sense as formulated above. Sentences of this kind are true in all possible worlds. Sentence (1) is an instance of the logical law of non-contradiction: *~(p & ~p)*—it is not the case that both *p* and *not p*. That sentences in this logical form are true in all possible worlds entails that their truth in some sense transgresses their truth in one single possible world. This, however, cannot be taken to mean that "necessary truth" is *defined* by being true in all possible worlds. Such a definition would be circular. It can only be defined by stating what it means that a sentence of this kind is true in one, certain possible world (and, then, the definition applies to all other possible worlds).

What kind of correspondence, if any, and between what, would "truth" signify with respect to necessary, logical truth? Let me suggest the following answer. In Sect. 3.3, in connection with a discussion about Popper's three-world ontology, I argued that natural numbers, logical relations, and truth-values (among other things) do not belong to a certain ontological "world" or category but are characteristics of how the universe (the realm of "Everything") happens to be constructed in some of its fundamental respects. This quality of the universe I called *the general state (character) of the universe* (*GSU*). To *GSU* belongs, e.g., the law of non-contradiction. In accordance with this, correspondence with respect to necessary, logical truth could be conceived as a correspondence between, e.g., a sentence of the type "It is not the case that Caesar was murdered in 44 BCE and that Caesar was not murdered in 44 BCE" and *GSU*. The sentence is true if and only if it corresponds to the law of non-contradiction, which belongs to *GSU*. In this perspective, necessary truth could be called "*GSU*-based truth".

From a purely intellectualistic viewpoint reality-based and *GSU*-based truth are for obvious reasons in the forefront.

For the intellectualist also dogmatic scepticism is repudiated by the first golden rule of intellectualism. I have earlier referred to what Bertrand Russell once said, that philosophers, no more than zoologists, can assume the existence of centaurs. Likewise, philosophers cannot, any more than zoologists, deny the existence of horses. The virtue of intellectualism demands of us: Don't believe in everything and don't believe in nothing. Intellectualism is the virtue of vigilance against gullibility on the one hand, and dogmatic scepticism on the other.

7. Intellectualism has its enemies and its abusers: anti-intellectualists and quasi-intellectualists.

Anti-intellectualism we find *par préférence* in Nazism and in more brute, "social-realistic" forms of communism. It was cultivated in Hitler's Germany, Stalin's Soviet Union, and Mao's China. Intellectualism was in these circles an expression of weakness and unworldliness, and the intellectualist was an anti-social figure. The strong, vigorous, honest, and loyal Arian, worker, and farmer stood out diametrically opposed to the intellectualist. We also find anti-intellectualism in different kinds of religious orthodoxy and fundamentalism, a phenomenon disastrously pestering the world in our day.

Quasi-intellectualism is a far more subtle phenomenon. Its highest ambition is to appear intellectualistic. I have just given a striking example, postmodernism. Another good example is the Neo-Marxism that flourished during the 1960s and 1970s. Here we find all the ingredients of quasi-intellectualism. Marxism, with its theoretical basis in abstruse Hegelian philosophy of history, had been successfully undermined already by the end of the nineteenth century, and the predictions built on it turned out to be false. According to intellectualism this would, to say the least, have led to a somewhat reserved attitude towards Marxism. But not so with the Neo-Marxists in the mid-twentieth century. They embraced Marxism with ice-bound dogmatism and tried, indeed, with great zest to outdo each other in staunch fundamentalism—all this in obvious contrast to an intellectualistic attitude to the Marxist doctrine. For them to be intellectual meant to become absorbed in an all-explaining theory, hook, line and sinker. They were not intellectualists; they were believers (and as such sometimes afflicted with a no small amount of self-righteousness and assured faith). Marxism had been raised to a philosophy of life. It is significant of such doctrines, mostly endorsed by the young, lacking in independence, that they become a way of life. The adherents create certain fashions concerning, e.g., how to dress and which musical and literary preferences to share, and take up certain attitudes towards infidels and renegades—in extreme cases their thinking is marred by what could be called ideology poisoning. No harm in itself with much of that—apart from the risk that all these paraphernalia tend to veil the underlying meagre intellectual substance. It can be noted, by the way, that people embracing well-founded theories such as the theory of evolution and the theory of relativity seldom feel an urge to dress up accordingly. A lot of people long for simple, all-embracing explanations of human life and human behaviour, affording them safety and relief. They can find it in doctrines such as Marxism (the productive forces explain everything in human life) or Freudian psychoanalysis (*the libido* explains everything in human life). Others flee into some extremity in a mood of spite and acrimony against something, e.g., against Western liberal democracy.

8. Intellectualism—the virtue of critical intelligence—I regard as one of the two most fundamental virtues of men, lawyers included. The other one is humanism.

In my book "*From* Rechtsstaat *to Universal Law-State*" I argued that humanism is the fundamental value that justifies the law-state (*Rechtsstaat* or Rule of Law) values and that it, hence, can be seen as a virtue to be cultivated by lawyers. The essence of humanism, I argued, is respect for each individual's life of human dignity (that of others as well as one's own).[6] To live a life of human dignity is to live a life in moderation of mind. Violating a person's life of human dignity is degradation of

[6]Frändberg (2014), Subsection 3.4 and pp. 108 ff.

that person's life of human dignity—and one's own. Moderation is a state of mind characterised by the absence of four vicious, or ugly, things: (1) Overestimating oneself in relation to oneself (*hubris*), (2) overestimating oneself in relation to others (depreciation of others), (3) underestimating oneself in relation to oneself (self-depreciation), and (4) underestimating oneself in relation to others (idolisation). The beautiful state of mind that is free from these four extremes could also be called "self-respect". In Aristotelian terms, self-respect is the golden mean between *hubris* and self-depreciation, and between the depreciation of others and idolisation. By having self-respect one also has respect for others, and shows consideration for them. In Kantian terms, respecting other people's life of human dignity is a duty to oneself. The inescapable connection between my own life of human dignity and that of others creates an indissoluble moral bond between human beings.

How, then, is this *virtue of humanism* associated with the *virtue of intellectualism*? No doubt it is possible for a person to be a humanist (in the sense of an adherent to humanism as described here) and not be an intellectualist. And it is possible to be an intellectualist without being a humanist. However, as far as I can see, adherence to humanism, in order to effectively fulfil its ideals, must rely upon a no small amount of intellectualism. Otherwise there is a risk that humanism will become naïve and gullible, and such a humanism can be more dangerous than beneficent.

This struck me in a palpable way some time ago when I watched a German newsreel from the middle of the 1930s on TV. On the screen was shown a crowd of housewives on a pavement enthusiastically shouting and waving little flags adorned with swastikas to a car in the street where Hitler stood upright making his usual Nazi salute. Who were these women? No doubt, most of them were kind and decent persons, loving wives and mothers, loyal to friends, disposed of treating also strangers with respect—generally speaking nice people. And there they were, paying tribute to a person who already at that time had given full rein to the cruel persecution of Jews and other ethnic and disabled groups—all justified by an altogether mendacious doctrine. Did these women not understand that this doctrine was totally groundless? Did they really believe in it? If they did, their "natural humanism" was indeed a poor protector against evil. A small dose of intellectualism could have been a useful vaccination against fatal gullibility. Humanism as such is not enough.

It could even be argued that intellectualism is an integral part of humanism. The reason for that would be that it violates human beings' life of human dignity to let themselves become prey to stern dogmatists, liars, fanatics, swindlers, less scrupulous politicians and preachers, scatterbrains, and the like. That would be a case of underestimating oneself in relation to others (idolisation).

If we combine the virtue of humanism and the virtue of intellectualism into one single virtue, such a virtue could with good reason be called the virtue of wisdom.

9. Can intellectualism be *justified* by reference to some superior value? I think not—unless it would be making it a part of humanism, which, itself, cannot be justified by any higher value. Intellectualism—like humanism—can only be

justified by means of contrast: to expose the dangers, disastrous consequences and ugliness that inform its being violated.

10. Why is intellectualism *a virtue of the lawyer*? Because it is a virtue of everyone, of course. But in which situations that can confront lawyers does this virtue typically come to the fore?

In fact, all problems that a lawyer can encounter in his professional capacity have a relation to truth. That is because in all juridical argumentation reference to facts, one way or another, directly or indirectly, is crucial. This applies to the evaluation of evidence (although some lawyers for muddled reasons have certain difficulties accepting that).[7] It applies to the qualification (interpretation) of statutory provisions and precedents. With regard to this it could be objected that an evaluative standpoint in the final stage is inevitable. And so it is. But the argumentation for the choice of standpoint, if rational, must consist of arguments referring to states of affairs that may occur in the world of reality and then the truth, or probable truth, of statements stating such states of affairs must be proven. It also applies to the choice of individual legal consequence, e.g., imposing a sentence in a criminal case. The state of affairs to be proven here could be, e.g., that the culprit due to mental disturbance had difficulties in controlling his actions or that the crime formed a part of carefully planned criminal activity.

With respect to judges, this applies in full. It also applies, *mutatis mutandis*, to legal scientists. With respect to advocates, however, matters are a bit more complicated. Their position is basically of a subjective kind—theirs is the task to represent their clients and look after their interests. But the difference between the judge and the advocate does not lie in a different attitude to truth; it consists in a different attitude to which arguments to bring forward. Advocates are to a much greater extent free to pick and choose arguments regarded as favourable to their clients. Of course they shall not bring forward arguments to the detriment of their clients. But with respect to the arguments chosen, those referring to states of affairs that may occur in the world of reality must be considered by the advocate himself to be true, or at least highly probable. To use a cliché: Everything the advocate says must be true but he does not have to say everything that is true. But this is subject to a most important modification. What, if, in a criminal case, the advocate is more or less convinced that his client is guilty? How, in such and similar situations, shall the conflict between loyalty to truth and loyalty to the client be solved? The answer is: The advocate is his client's representative. He shall present states of affairs and arguments as his client wants him to, whether he believes in them or not. In such situations the advocate becomes a mere mouthpiece of his client—which is not as bad as it sounds. The client is entitled to his advocate's advocacy; he is not demanding the advocate's judgment. It is the task of the opposite party to falsify the statements of the advocate and criticise his arguments, and it is the task of the judge to make a balanced overall assessment. In this way the trial *in its totality* is in the service of truth. The only

[7] See "Excursus on evidence" in Frändberg (2014), pp. 156–159.

situation where an advocate can refuse to present the defendant's version, according to a commonly held tenet in Western advocate ethics, is when the defendant has confessed his guilt to his advocate but still wants him to plead not guilty.

To conclude. The virtue of intellectualism applies to all lawyers. It includes adherence to the two golden rules of intellectualism—respect of truth and logic—when taking one's stand to the arguments of others as well as when examining the arguments of one's own. In serious argumentation it means balancing and weighing *pro et contra*, and demanding tenable and relevant arguments. It means detachment and objectivity. (This also applies to advocates. Before choosing the arguments speaking in favour of his client, the advocate is well-advised to submit his arguments to critical scrutiny in his own mind in order to avoid his arguments being torn to pieces by the opposite party or the judge.) Finally, the virtue of intellectualism demands from the lawyer conceptual clarity. Ambiguity and vagueness are enemies to sound juridical argumentation. This applies especially to lawyers whose task it is to do concept formation, i.e., legal scientists and draftsmen (statutory technicians).

References

Frändberg Å (2014) From Rechtsstaat to universal law-state. Springer, Berlin

Hage J (2015) The (onto)logical structure of law: a conceptual toolkit for legislators. In: Araszkiewicz M, Pleszka K (eds) Logic in the theory and practice of lawmaking. Springer, Berlin

Hospers J (1946) Meaning and truth in the arts. University of North Carolina Press, Chapel Hill

Naess A (1966) Communication and argument. Elements of applied semantics. Bedminster Press, New Jersey

Olivecrona K (1971) Law as fact. Stevens & Sons, London

FSC
www.fsc.org
MIX
Papier | Fördert
gute Waldnutzung
FSC® C083411

Kolibri 360 GmbH
Ferdinand-Jühlke-Straße 7
99095 Erfurt, Deutschland
produktsicherheit@kolibri360.de